新 教材
N eries
桂杭

U0694073

Marketing

市场营销

主　编 / 邹　莉

副主编 / 张　冰　郑淞月　何嗣锋　马　青　刘艳荣

编　者 / 边洁英　龙　麟　陈林林　杨茜茜　陈　婷

　　　　李　慧　黄芳萍　谭　勇

重庆大学出版社

内 容 提 要

随着经济全球化和企业国际化经营的发展,市场营销对专业人士和从业人员的重要性日益增加。本书力求汇集与营销领域相关的各种主题和案例,以帮助相关专业的学生及市场营销活动的企业从业者熟悉一般的营销原理、国际营销的特点、国内外环境因素的影响、营销策略及其实施等。

图书在版编目(CIP)数据

市场营销／邹莉主编. -- 重庆:重庆大学出版社,
2021.12

新时代商务英语专业本科系列教材

ISBN 978-7-5689-2635-5

Ⅰ.①市… Ⅱ.①邹… Ⅲ.①市场营销—英语—高等
职业教育—教材 Ⅳ.①F713.3

中国版本图书馆 CIP 数据核字(2021)第 128868 号

市场营销
SHICHANG YINGXIAO

主 编 邹 莉

责任编辑:高小平 版式设计:高小平
责任校对:刘志刚 责任印制:赵 晟

*

重庆大学出版社出版发行
出版人:饶帮华
社址:重庆市沙坪坝区大学城西路 21 号
邮编:401331
电话:(023)88617190 88617185(中小学)
传真:(023)88617186 88617166
网址:http://www.cqup.com.cn
邮箱:fxk@ cqup.com.cn(营销中心)
全国新华书店经销
重庆五洲海斯特印务有限公司印刷

*

开本:787mm×1092mm 1/16 印张:21.25 字数:691 千
2021 年 12 月第 1 版 2021 年 12 月第 1 次印刷
ISBN 978-7-5689-2635-5 定价:69.00 元

总　序

随着经济全球化和我国与"一带一路"沿线国家的经济贸易合作,具备英语专业技能、基本国际商务知识和国际商务业务技能的跨文化商务专业人才有了用武之地。

商务英语本科专业自 2012 年获得教育部批准进入我国大学本科教育基本目录,其身份与地位获得了我国官方和外语界的认可。迄今为止,据不完全统计,我国已有 400 多所大学开设了商务英语本科专业;我国的高职高专院校及中职学校大都开设了商务英语专业。我国已经形成了商务英语的本、硕、博的教育层次。此外,各种商务英语学术活动也开始活跃。商务英语专业与英语语言文学专业、翻译专业成为我国英语教学的"三驾马车"。商务英语教学在全国已经形成较大规模,正呈良性发展态势,越来越多的大学正在积极准备申报商务英语本科专业。可以预见,将来在我国,除了研究性大学外的大部分普通本科院校的外语学院都可能开设商务英语本科专业。这是大势所趋,因为随着我国改革开放力度的加大和经济全球化、世界经济一体化进程的加快,各个融入经济一体化的国家和地区急需有扎实英语功底的、熟悉国际商务基本知识的、具备国际商务领域操作技能的跨文化商务交际复合型、应用型商务英语人才。

高校商务英语专业教育首先必须有充足的合格师资;其次,需要有合适的教材。目前市场上各种商务英语教材林林总总、五花八门,但是完整的四年商务英语本科专业系列教材并不多。重庆大学出版社出版的商务英语本科专业系列教材一定程度上能满足当前商务英语本科专业的教学需要。

本套系列教材能基本满足商务英语本科专业 1—4 年级通常开设课程的需要。商务英语专业不是商务专业而是语言专业,所以基础年级的教材仍然是英语语言学习教材。但是,与传统的英语语言文学专业教材不同的是:商务英语专业学生所学习的英语具有显著的国际商务特色。因此,本套系列教材特别注重商务英语本科专业教育的特点,在基础阶段的英语技能教材中融入了更多的国际商务元素,让学生在学习普通英语的同时,接触一些基础的商务英语词汇,通过听、说、读、写、译等技能训练,熟悉并掌握商务英语专业四级和八级考试词汇,熟悉基础的商务英语篇章,了解国际商务常识。

根据教育部《高等学校商务英语本科教学实施方案》(以下简称《方案》),本套系列教材不仅包含一二年级的基础教材,还包含高年级的继续夯实商务英语语言知识的教材,如《高级商务英语》1—3 册等;此外,还包括英语语言文学专业类所没有的突出商务英语本科专业特色的国际商务知识类教材,如《国际商务概论》《国际贸易实务》《国际商法》《市场营销》等。本套系列教材的总主编都是教育部商务英语专业教学协作组成员,是中国国际商务英语研究会的副理事长,参与了该《方案》的起草与制定,熟悉《方案》的要求,为本套系列教材的高质量出版提供了保障。此外,参与编写本套系列教材的教师们都是多年从事商务英语教学与研究的有经验的教师,因而在教材的内容、体例、知识、练习以及辅助教材等方面,编者们都充分考虑到了教材使用者的需求。本套系列教材的编写宗旨是:力求传授实用的商务英语知识和国际商务相关领域的知识,提高学生的商务英语综合素质和跨文化商务交际能力以及思辨创新能力。

本套系列教材在编写过程中也考虑到了全国商务英语本科专业四级和专业八级考试的要求,因此,在教材的选材、练习、词汇等方面都尽可能与商务英语本科专业四级、八级考试范围对接。

本套系列教材特别适合培养复合型、应用型的商务英语人才的商务英语本科专业的教学使用,也可作为商务英语爱好者学习商务英语的教材。本套系列教材中若存在不当和疏漏之处,敬请专家、学者及教材使用者批评指正,以便我们不断修订完善。

翁凤翔

2019 年 10 月

Introduction

Marketing is the pivotal function in business. This textbook introduces related concepts, the marketing strategies and tools that practitioners use to market their products. It carries the dominant themes throughout in order to expose students to marketing in today´s environment.

The book is divided into three parts. The first part focuses on the international marketing environment. This part highlights the impact of different environments on marketing, and gives an overview of business environments composed of economy and finance, society and culture, politics and law, science and technology, culture and demography, and discusses the marketing strategies and policies of enterprises from the perspective of environment and strategy. The second part is about customers and positioning, which focuses on the practices and challenges of marketing research, positioning, consumers' purchasing behavior, international service market, market entry, and market expansion mode selection. The third part illustrates the integrated marketing communication strategy, which mainly includes the contents of brand management, the marketing mix, internet marketing and social media, distribution operation and logistics management, corporate social responsibility and sustainability.

The contents of the book include chapters, charts, cases, tables, glossaries and etc. Key concepts are brought to life with comprehensively updated statistics, recent illustrations, and a variety of real-world examples and case studies. Every industry or company needs strong global awareness. Today´s marketing professionals must understand the world in which they and their companies operate. Therefore, the book presents a wide range of contemporary issues faced by enterprises involved in international business. In particular, it covers some new issues facing the current marketing, including the globalization brought by competition, the urgent demand for new technology and innovation, the importance of consumer satisfaction and services, corporate ethics and social responsibility, the emergence of global communication media and its impact on international business.

This book can be selected by colleges and universities as the teaching or reference material for bilingual course or English course of Marketing for undergraduates, postgraduates and MBAs. It is also suitable for training and self-study of management and marketing personnel, who are engaged in marketing and international business.

编　者

2021 年 11 月

Contents

PART 1
The International Marketing Environment

UNIT 1 Strategic Planning and Global Policy

Learning Objectives

1. Appreciate more fully that a functionalist explanation seeks to adapt an organism's behaviour to environmental change.
2. Recognize the importance of understanding the changes and potential changes in the marketing environment.
3. Have an understanding of the major contemporary environmental trends in marketing.
4. Have a good knowledge of the marketing planning process.
5. Have a good knowledge of the global political environment and corresponding strategies.
6. Have a good knowledge of the global legal environment and corresponding strategies.

1.1 Introduction

A study of international marketing should begin with an understanding of what marketing is and how it operates in an international context. A definition adopted by the AMA (American Marketing Association) is used as a basis for the definition of international marketing given here: "International marketing is the multinational process of planning and executing the conception, pricing, promotion, and distribution of ideas, goods, and services to create exchanges that satisfy individual and organizational objectives." The word "multi-national" implies that marketing activities are undertaken in several countries and that such activities should somehow be coordinated across nations.

One way to understand the concept of international marketing is to examine how international marketing differs from similar concepts. Domestic marketing is concerned with the marketing practices within a researcher's or marketer's home country. From the perspective of domestic marketing, marketing methods used outside the home market are foreign marketing. A study becomes comparative marketing when its purpose is to contrast two or more marketing systems rather than examine a particular country's marketing system for its own sake. Similarities and differences between systems are identified.

Some marketing textbooks differentiate international marketing from global marketing because international marketing in its literal sense signifies marketing between nations. The word "international" may thus imply that a firm is not a corporate citizen of the world but rather operates from a home base. For those authors, global or world marketing is the preferred term, since nothing is foreign or domestic about the world market and global opportunities.

1.2 The Marketing Environment

As is known, one of the key aspects of developing a functionalist explanation is to relate the organism to its environment. In this section environmental trends are examined together with the relationship of organizations and the environment.

1.2.1 General Environmental Trends

Some important aspects of the environment are considered. It is useful to point out that the environment is not simply "seen", it is "perceived". This means what is happening "out there" is seen through the cultural spectacles. It is difficult to see these "cultural spectacles", but if looking at the past and, in particular, at the assumptions about what environmental changes were, it becomes more apparent. For example, during the 1960s people looked forward to the 1970s and 1980s as a time of leisure. Many articles appeared in the popular press to speculate about what people might do with this leisure time. It was only in the 1970s when the grim truth dawned: unemployment was certainly a form of "leisure time" but not the sort that people had expected or found tolerable.

It is noted that, ignoring the bad mistakes, e.g. nuclear energy, hibernation, etc., the authors were close in their predictions. Some of the predictions are so general that they were almost bound to have happened in some shape or form. In hindsight, it seems clear that people's view of the future was influenced by the prevailing social attitude of their time, especially by science fiction. This featured people in individual flying machines, which usually looked like smart sports cars that zoomed across highways in space; helpful robots which cleaned up around the home where almost all energy was provided by means of some form of fission or fusion. So, while the authors managed to get a glimpse of what actually happened, their views were distorted by the context of the times in which they were living. On the other hand, although the seeds of the Internet and bioengineering had been planted at that time, there is no mention of these innovations. That society is condemned to be trapped in a web consisting of the assumptions of the time and place is obvious.

1.2.2　Consumer Society and the Physical Environment

One fragile certainty is that capitalism has triumphed across the world. Nowadays consumer societies are taking root in even the poorest African and South American countries. Just as the East Germans exchanged the "Trabant" for the dream of a "Mercedes" society, so Vietnamese consumers are facing their government with an expectation that they have a right to the same level of prosperity (indexed by access to consumer goods) as everyone else on the globe.

At the same time there is a growing awareness, reflected in the Earth Summit and its successors, that the consumer society has major environmental implications provoking a need to set limits to growth.

1.2.3　Time-space Compression

Time-space compression, perhaps the most pervasive trend in contemporary society, refers to the idea that the logic of capitalism results in a speed-up of time and a reduction in the effects of distance to the extent that they are compressed into a smaller space than ever before. Harvey refers to the constantly accelerating turnover time of capital which is the time of production together with the time of the circulation of exchange. The logic is that the faster the capital launched into circulation can be recuperated the greater the profit will be. Capitalists, spurred on by the threat of competition and the demand to open up new markets and raw material sources, make continuous efforts to shorten turnover times. At the same time the "friction of distance" is condensing. The effects of this speed-up are that goods travel faster, new spaces for distribution and consumption are created (in aviation, rail transport, the World Wide Web). As a result, there is a paradox, with simultaneous trends towards globalization and fragmentation.

1.2.4　Globalization/Fragmentation

It is true that globalization is happening in terms of the proliferation of global brands, these brands are being incorporated in different ways in the various contexts in which they are used. The trend is towards globalization at one level and differentiation at another. There is a growing weight of evidence to suggest that differentiation and, indeed, fragmentation are key aspects of existence in consumer societies.

In the twenty-first century, in the UK all this has been swept away on the tides of change. Employment in "traditional" working-class occupations such as mining, steel, shipbuilding and engineering has been decimated. The proportion of women working has increased substantially. The roles played by men and women are no longer so rigid and while the idea that 'new men' have replaced the traditional male role is a myth, there is no doubt that new roles for men and women have been created. The traditional "cornflake packet" family consisting of two parents and two children is in a minority. The fragmentation of work, class and gender identities has led to the creation of a "mix 'n' match" culture and the creation of new "tribal" identities. The shifting social patterns have made life much more difficult for marketers who use traditional tools for segmenting markets on the basis of family, age, gender and social class.

As social class has become less useful as a means of segmenting markets, so marketers have turned to lifestyle, to the values which people share in common and the sorts of activities they like to engage in as a new basis for segmentation. Advances in technology have enabled marketers to build massive databases containing all sorts of marketing information regarding the purchase behaviour of individuals. Another major force for fragmentation is the coming of the digital age. When people have little in common in terms of their real-life experiences they can share in a discussion of a mythical experience such as what happened in last night's television soap opera, *Neighbours* or *EastEnders*. There is a worry that the massive channel choice which will accompany the digital age will remove even that topic of conversation.

Yet another force for fragmentation is the effect of time/space compression on workers and consumers. Schor (1991) discussed the paradox that while US production doubled between 1948 and 1990, American workers were working longer hours than they were forty years before and so they simply do not have the time to enjoy their hard-won rewards. Schor suggests that:

- Americans spend more time shopping than anyone else.
- Americans spend the highest fraction of what they earn.
- Americans' homes are more luxurious than those elsewhere.
- American average income is 65 times the average of half the world's population.

Schor feels that the consumer society itself and, in particular, the economic assumption that more goods equate with more satisfaction is at the heart of the problem. It is hard to imagine how having more of something might make people worse off. But what if satisfaction depends on relative, as opposed to absolute, consumption? Schor argues that a focus on absolute consumption can lead to an insidious cycle of work-spend-credit-debt. More than anything, the American worker experiences life as a series of packets or episodes filled with time pressure.

1.2.5   Organization and the Marketing Environment

This section returns to the functionalist approach to the role of marketing. It assumes that the firm is an organism whose main goal is to survive by taking advantage of the opportunities and by avoiding the threats that are present in the environment, including responding to competitor actions. The organization is purposive. In order to survive, decision makers seek to attend rationally to environmental problems and opportunities. The problem-solving process involves analysing the current situation, developing goals and strategies to achieve those goals and, finally, providing feedback to gauge whether goals have been successfully achieved. The organizational problem-solving process is analogous to the individual problem-solving process. For example, any individual who wishes to solve any problem must consider where they are, where they want to be and how to get there.

1.3   Levels of Planning: from Corporate to Business Plans

It may be useful to consider firms as organisms for the sake of analysis, but it must be recognized that these are extremely complex organisms. For example, Wal-Mart has a turnover of hundreds of billions of dollars and employs hundreds of thousands of workers. Such complex entities can be organized in different ways, including functional, divisional and matrix forms of organization. A common procedure is that those at the top level of the organization conduct a corporate-level strategic analysis that, in turn, will inform analysis at the business level.

Functional plans, including the marketing plan will be drafted at each level. For example, it can make sense for a vehicle manufacturer to divide its businesses into cars and trucks as it could be argued that these face quite different target markets and challenges. For such a business the top team will devise a corporate plan which will set out the vision and mission of the organization in addition to spelling out the goals for executives in the Strategic Business Units (SBUs) comprising trucks and cars. The executives in each SBU will then work within the constraints established by the corporate plan in setting more precise objectives and in devising strategies of how to achieve these objectives. The corporate marketing plan will be a subset of the main plan focusing on providing the long-term direction of the organization regarding the markets and needs that will be served and will set goals for the SBUs. Managers within each SBU will devise more specific marketing objectives and programmes in the light of this plan. A schematic map of the planning process is shown in Figure 1.1.

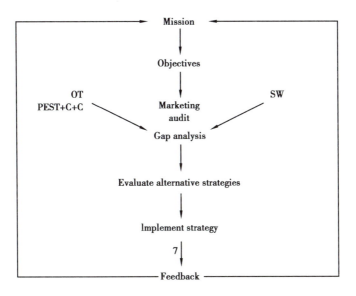

Figure 1.1　The Marketing Planning Process

1.4　Trade Distortions and Marketing Barriers

Free trade makes a great deal of sense theoretically because it increases efficiency and economic welfare for all involved nations, regions and their citizens. South Korea's trade barriers, however, do not represent an isolated case. In practice, free trade is woefully ignored by virtually all countries, and regions. Despite the advantages, nations and regions are inclined to discourage free trade. Restrictive business practices and government regulations designed to protect public health and national security are not considered as trade barriers.

❯ 1.4.1　Protection of Local Industries

While countries generally do not mind exporting, they simply do not like imports. According to a survey of more than 28, 000 people in twenty-three countries, even well-educated workers in poorer countries are against free trade. In addition, workers in the industries that face foreign competition tend to be against free trade. On the other hand, well-educated people in well-educated countries are more likely to favor free trade.

Why do nations impede free trade when the inhibition is irrational? One reason why governments interfere with free marketing is to protect local industries, often at the expense of local consumers as well as consumers worldwide. Regulations are created to keep out or hamper the entry of foreign-made products. Arguments for the protection of local industries usually take one of the following forms: (1) keeping money at home,

(2) reducing unemployment, (3) equalizing cost and price, (4) enhancing national security, and (5) protecting infant industry.

1.4.2   Government：a Contribution to Protectionism

Government can be considered to be the root of all evil—at least as far as international trade is concerned. A government's mere existence, even without tariffs or any attempt to interfere with international marketing, can distort trade both inside and outside of its area. At the international level, different governments have different policies and objectives, resulting in different rates for income and sales taxes.

Taxation is not the only cause of tax and income differences. Some governments allow cartels to operate. A cartel is an international business agreement to fix prices and divide markets, in addition to other kinds of cooperation. Such an arrangement is illegal in the USA, but it is permissible and even encouraged in many countries. Australia and New Zealand, for example, allow livestock firms to cooperate with each other in exporting beef to the USA. Economic cooperation among governments yields economic benefits and problems by significantly affecting internal and external trade patterns.

1.4.3   Marketing Barriers：Tariffs

Tariff, derived from a French word meaning rate, price, or list of charges, is a customs duty or a tax on products that move across borders. Tariffs may be classified in several ways. Tariffs are often imposed on the basis of the direction of product movement; that is, on imports or exports, with the latter being the less common one. When export tariffs are levied, they usually apply to an exporting country's scarce resources or raw materials (rather than finished manufactured products). Tariffs may be classified as protective tariffs and revenue tariffs. The distinction is based on purpose. Protective tariffs may be further classified according to length of time. A tariff surcharge is a temporary action, whereas a countervailing duty is a permanent surcharge. How are tax rates applied? There are generally three kinds of tax rates: specific, ad valorem, and combined. In addition, some taxes are collected at a particular point of distribution or when purchases and consumption occur. These indirect taxes, frequently adjusted at the border, are of four kinds: single-stage, value-added, cascade, and excise.

1.4.4   Marketing Barriers：Nontariff Barriers

Tariffs, though generally undesirable, are at least straightforward and obvious.

Nontariff barriers, in comparison, are more elusive or nontransparent. Tariffs have declined in importance, reaching the lowest level ever of about 4 percent on average after fifty years and eight global rounds of trade negotiation. In the meantime, nontariff barriers have become more prominent. Often disguised, the impact of nontariff barriers can be just as devastating, if not more so, as the impact of tariffs.

There are several hundred types of nontariff barriers. According to the US Trade Representative, countries use a variety of barriers that include non-scientific sanitary standards, customs procedures, and government monopolies. Japan's telecommunications, agriculture, and pharmaceuticals sectors have "structural rigidity, excessive regulation, and market access barriers."

Nontariff barriers may be grouped into four major categories. Each category contains a number of different nontariff barriers.

1. Government Participation in Trade

The degree of government involvement in trade varies from passive to active. The types of participation include administrative guidance, state trading, and subsidies.

2. Customs and Entry Procedures

Customs and entry procedures may be employed as nontariff barriers. These restrictions involve classification, valuation, documentation, license, inspection, and health and safety regulations.

3. Product Requirements

For goods to enter a country, product requirements set by that country must be met. Requirements may apply to product standards and product specifications as well as to packaging, labeling, and marking.

4. Financial Control

Financial regulations can also function to restrict international trade. These restrictive monetary policies are designed to control capital flow so that currencies can be defended or imports controlled.

❯ 1.4.5 Private Barriers

As conventional trade barriers are lowered, governments are shifting their attention to competition policy to address environmental and labor objectives and private barriers. Private barriers are certain business practices or arrangements between or among affiliated firms.

Japan's keiretsu is a good example of private barriers. The keiretsu system deals with cooperative business groups. Such a group includes manufacturers, suppliers, retailers, and customers. Members of the group seek long-term security through inter-locking directorates and through owning shares in each other's companies. Toyota Motor Corp. provided $83 million to help out Tomen Corp., a money-losing trading firm. Both belong to the same keiretsu, and it is a tradition for members of the keiretsu to subsidize each other. Naturally, the companies that belong to the same keiretsu will grant preferential treatment to the other members. Korea's chaebol system also functions in a similar fashion.

1.5 Political Environment

Whether political interests precede or follow economic interests is debatable, but certainly the two are closely interrelated. A country or company may play politics in order to pursue its economic interests, but economic means may also be used to achieve political objectives. The economic interests of Multinational Corporations (MNCs) can differ widely from the economic interests of the countries in which these firms do business. A lack of convergent interests often exists between a company's home country and its various host countries. In the absence of mutual interests, political pressures can lead to political decisions, resulting in laws and proclamations that affect business.

▶ 1.5.1 Multiplicity of Political Environments

The political environment that MNCs face is a complex one because they must cope with the politics of more than one nation. That complexity forces MNCs to consider the three different types of political environment: foreign, domestic, and international. Although political and economic motives are two distinct components, they are often closely intertwined. A country may use economic sanctions to make a political statement. Likewise, a political action may be taken so as to enhance the country's economic prospects. It is also hardly uncommon for governments as well as companies to ignore politics for the purpose of economic interests. Even while the economic sanctions were in place, the USA was actually importing a large amount of oil from Iraq.

Developing countries often view foreign firms and foreign capital investment with distrust and even resentment, owing primarily to a concern over potential foreign exploitation of local natural resources. Nevertheless, developed countries themselves are also concerned about foreign investment. Many Americans have expressed their concern that the increasing foreign ownership of American assets poses a threat to their country's national security, both politically and economically. In some cases, opposition to imported goods and foreign investment is based on moral principle. For example, the citizens of many nations pressured companies in their countries not to invest in South Africa because of that country's policy of apartheid.

Regardless of whether the politics are foreign, domestic, or international, the company should keep in mind that political climate does not remain stationary.

1.5.2 Political Risks

There are a number of political risks with which marketers must contend. Hazards based on a host government's actions include confiscation, expropriation, nationalization, domestication, and creeping expropriation. Such actions are more likely to be levied against foreign investments, though local firms' properties are not totally immune. Charles de Gaulle nationalized France's three largest banks in 1945, and more nationalization occurred in 1982 under the French socialists.

Confiscation is the process of a government's taking ownership of a property without compensation. A recent example involves Occidental Petroleum whose assets were confiscated without compensation by Venezuela.

Expropriation differs somewhat from confiscation in that there is some compensation, though not necessarily just compensation. More often than not, a company whose property is being expropriated agrees to sell its operations—not by choice but rather due to some explicit or implied coercion.

After property has been confiscated or expropriated, it can be either nationalized or domesticated. Nationalization involves government ownership, and it is the government that operates the business being taken over. Burma's foreign trade, for example, is completely nationalized. Generally, this action affects a whole industry rather than only a single company. When Mexico attempted to control its debt problem, then-President Jose Lopez Portillo nationalized the country's banking system. In another case of nationalization, Libya's Colonel Gadhafi's vision of Islamic socialism led him to nationalize all private business in 1981.

In the case of domestication, foreign companies relinquish control and ownership, either completely or partially, to the nationals. The result is that private entities are allowed to operate the confiscated or expropriated property. The French government, after finding out that the state was not sufficiently proficient to run the banking business, developed a plan to sell thirty-six French banks.

Domestication may sometimes be a voluntary act that takes place in the absence of confiscation or nationalization. Usually, the causes of this action are either poor economic performance or social pressures. When situations worsened in South Africa and political pressures mounted at home, Pepsi sold its South African bottling operation to local investors, and Coca-Cola signaled that it would give control to a local company.

Based on this classification, four sets of political risks may be identified: general instability risk, ownership/control risk, operation risk, and transfer risk.

General instability risk is related to the uncertainty about the future viability of a host country's political system. The Iranian revolution that overthrew the Shah is an example of this kind of risk. In contrast, ownership/control risk is related to the possibility that a host government might take action (e.g. expropriation) to restrict an investor's ownership and control of a subsidiary in that host country. Operation risk proceeds from the uncertainty that a host government might constrain the investor's business operations in all areas, including production, marketing, and finance. Finally, transfer risk applies to any future acts by a host government that might constrain the ability of a subsidiary to transfer payments, capital, or profit out of the host country back to the parent firm.

Although the threat of direct confiscation or expropriation has become remote, a new kind of threat has appeared. MNCs have generally been concerned with coups, revolutions, and confiscation, but they now have to pay attention to so-called creeping expropriation. The Overseas Private Investment Corporation (OPIC) defines creeping expropriation as "a set of actions whose cumulative effect is to deprive investors of their fundamental rights in the investment." Laws that affect corporate ownership, control, profit, and reinvestment (e.g. currency inconvertibility or cancellation of import license) can be easily enacted. Because countries can change the rules in the middle of the game, companies must adopt adequate safeguards.

1.6　Legal Environment

Much like the political environment discussed above, there are a multiplicity of legal environments: domestic, foreign, and international. At their worst, laws can prohibit the marketing of a product altogether. To most business people, laws act as an inconvenience. Club Med's policy of rotating its international staff every six months, for example, is hampered by the US immigration law, which makes the process of rotation both time-consuming and costly.

There are many products that cannot be legally imported into most countries. Examples include counterfeit money, illicit drugs, pornographic materials, and espionage equipment. It is usually also illegal to import live animals and fresh fruit unless accompanied by the required certificates. Further-more, many products have to be modified to conform to local laws before these products are allowed across the border. The modification may be quite technical from an engineering standpoint or only cosmetic, as in the case of certain packaging changes.

A company's production strategy can also be affected by the legal environment. The USA bans the importation of the so-called Saturday night specials cheap, short-barreled pistols—because they are often used in violent crime. Curiously, the gun control legislation does not prohibit the sale of such inexpensive weapons; only the import of such weapons is banned. As a result, Beretta, an Italian gun maker, is able to overcome the import ban by setting up a manufacturing operation in the state of Maryland.

There is no international law per se that prescribes acceptable and legal behavior of international business enterprises. There are only national laws—often in conflict with one another, especially when national politics is involved.

1.6.1 Legal Systems

To understand and appreciate the varying legal philosophies among countries, it is useful to distinguish between the two major legal systems: common law and statute law.

There are some twenty-five common law or British law countries. A common law system is a legal system that relies heavily on precedents and conventions. Judges' decisions are guided not so much by statutes as by previous court decisions and interpretations of what certain laws are or should be. As a result, these countries' laws are tradition oriented. Countries with such a system include the USA, Great Britain, Canada, India, and other British colonies.

Countries employing a statute law system, also known as code or civil law, include most continental European countries and Japan. Most countries—over seventy—are guided by a statute law legal system. As the name implies, the main rules of the law are embodied in legislative codes. Every circumstance is clearly spelled out to indicate what is legal and what is not. There is also a strict and literal interpretation of the law under this system.

1.6.2 Jurisdiction and Extraterritoriality

There is no international law per se that deals with business activities of companies in the international arena. There are only national laws that vary from one country to another. The EU area, for example, has high minimum wages, generous unemployment benefits, and employment protection measures. Dismissal restrictions include notice and severance pay requirements, and they can affect labor productivity. Among the advanced economies, Portugal is most restrictive in employment protection, and it has particularly stringent dismissal restrictions.

It is often necessary to file a lawsuit in the defendant's home country. To make certain that the foreign court will have jurisdiction to hear the case, the contract should contain a clause that allows the company to bring a lawsuit in either the home country or the host country.

Whenever possible and practical, companies should consider commercial arbitration in place of judicial trials. Arbitration proceedings provide such advantages as an impartial hearing, a quick result, and a decision made by experts. Both IBM and Fujitsu seemed satisfied with the ruling of their two arbitrators in settling a copyright dispute. Intel, in contrast, did not want arbitration and was frustrated by the pace of its copyright lawsuit against NEC (Nippon Electric Company).

▶ 1.6.3　Legal Form of Organization

Firms doing business in Great Britain have three primary choices for the legal form of organization: British branch, limited company, or partnership. If a limited company is the choice, more decision is needed. A limited company may be either a public limited company (PLC), which can raise capital by selling securities to the public, or a private company (ltd.), which is not allowed to offer shares or debentures to the public. In general, a public company must meet a number of requirements in terms of registration and capital structure, subscription for shares, and profits and assets available for distribution.

In the USA, a business is able to select from among these forms: sole proprietorship, partnership, and corporation. For firms involved in international trade, the most common choice is the corporation due to the limited liability associated with the corporate form, its relatively permanent structure, and its ability to raise money by selling securities. Most large US firms have a Corp. or Inc. nomenclature as part of their trade names.

▶ 1.6.4　Branch vs. Subsidiary

One legal decision that an MNC must make is whether to use branches or subsidiaries to carry out its plans and to manage its operations in a foreign country. A branch is the company's extension or outpost at another location. Although physically detached, it is not legally separated from its parent. A subsidiary, in contrast, is both physically and legally independent. It is considered a separate legal entity in spite of its ownership by another corporation.

A subsidiary may either be wholly owned (i.e. 100 percent owned) or partially owned. GE receives some $1 billion in revenues from its wholly owned and partially owned subsidiaries in Europe. The usual practice of Pillsbury, Coca-Cola, and IBM is to have wholly owned subsidiaries. Although a parent company has total control when its subsidiary is wholly owned, it is difficult to generalize about the superiority of one approach over the other.

As a rule, multinationals prefer subsidiaries to branches. Fiat has 432 subsidiaries and minority interests within 130 companies in sixty countries. The question that must be asked is why Fiat, like other MNCs, would go through the trouble and expense of forming hundreds of foreign companies elsewhere. When compared to the use of branches, the use of subsidiaries adds complexity to the corporate structure. They are also expensive, requiring substantial sales volumes to justify their expense.

1.6.5 Litigation vs. Arbitration

Litigation, no matter where it takes place, is never an easy thing. In certain countries, it can be very complicated. Courts in India have twenty-five million cases pending, and it will take more than 300 years to get through this backlog. To save time, expenses, and relationships, it may be wise to look at litigation as the last resort.

1.6.6 Bribery

At first glance, bribery is both unethical and illegal. A closer look, however, reveals that bribery is not really that straightforward an issue. There are many questions about what bribery is, how it is used, and authorize giving anything of value to influence an act or decision by a foreign government, politician, or political party to assist in obtaining, retaining, or directing business to any person. A bribe is also known as a "payoff" "grease money" "lubricant" "little envelope" "mordida" or "bite" (Mexico), and "under-the-table payment", as well as by other terms. A bribe may take the form of cash, gifts, jobs, and free trips.

1.6.7 Intellectual Property

Intellectual property (IP), as defined by the World Intellectual Property Organization (WIPO), is "creations of the mind: inventions, literary and artistic works, and symbols, names, images, and designs used in commerce." Individuals and firms have the freedom to own and control the rights to intellectual property (i.e. inventions and creative works). The terms patent, trademark, copyright, and trade secret are often used interchangeably. In fact, there are four basic forms of intellectual property, and they hold different meanings.

A **trademark** is a symbol, a word, or an object used to identify a product made or marketed by a particular firm. It becomes a registered trademark when the mark is accepted for registration by the Trademark Office. A **copyright,** which is the responsibility of the Copyright Office, offers protection against unauthorized copying by others to an author or artist for his or her literary, musical, dramatic, and artistic works. A copyright protects the form of expression rather than the subject matter. A **patent** protects an invention of a scientific or technical nature. It is a statutory grant from the government (the Patent Office) to an inventor in exchange for public disclosure giving the patent holder exclusive right to the functional and design inventions patented and excluding others from using those inventions for a certain period of time(twenty years for a functional patent and fourteen years for a design patent). The purpose of ownership rights is to spur inventiveness. The term **trade secret** refers to know-how (e.g. manufacturing methods, formulas, plans, and so on) that is kept secret within a particular business. This know-how, generally unknown in the industry, may offer the firm a competitive advantage. **Infringement** occurs when there is commercial use (i.e. copying or imitating) without the owner's consent, with the intent of confusing or deceiving the public.

1.6.8   Counterfeiting

Counterfeiting is the practice of unauthorized and illegal copying of a product. In essence, it involves an infringement on a patent or trademark or both. According to the US Lanham Act, a counterfeit trademark is a "spurious trademark which is identical with, or substantially indistinguishable from, a registered trademark." A true counterfeit product uses the name and design of the original so as to look exactly like the original. On the other hand, some counterfeiters partially duplicate the original's design and/or trademark in order to mislead or confuse buyers.

Counterfeiting is a serious business problem. In addition to the direct monetary loss, companies face indirect losses as well. Counterfeit goods injure the reputation of companies whose brand names are placed on low-quality products. To make matters worse, the pirates have entered the export business.

Products affected by counterfeiting cover a wide range. At one end of the spectrum are prestigious and highly advertised consumer products, such as Hennessy brandy, Dior and Pierre Cardin fashion, Samsonite luggage, Levi's jeans, and Cartier and Rolex watches. At the other end of the spectrum are industrial products, such as Pfizer animal feed supplement, medical vaccines, heart pacemakers, and helicopter parts. Although fakes are more likely to be premium-priced consumer products, low-unit-value products have not escaped the attention of counterfeiters. Fakes can come from anywhere, including industrialized countries. Italy may even be a bigger counterfeit offender than some Asian countries.

Controlling the counterfeit trade is difficult in part because counterfeiting is a low-risk, high-profit venture. Just as critical, if not more so, is the attitude of law enforcement agencies and consumers. Many consumers understand neither the seriousness of the violation nor the need to respect trademark rights. Law enforcement agencies often believe that the crime does not warrant special effort. It is not sufficient for a company to fight counterfeiting only in its home country. The battle must be carried to the counterfeiters' own country and to other major markets. The cooperation a company receives from foreign governments in reducing the amount of counterfeiting varies greatly. Finally, the company must invest in and establish its own monitoring system. Its best defense is to strike back rather than rely solely on government enforcement.

Key Terms

international marketing 国际营销	International marketing is the multinational process of planning and executing the conception, pricing, promotion, and distribution of ideas, goods, and services to create exchanges that satisfy individual and organizational objectives. 国际营销是一种多国参与的过程，对思想、商品和服务的概念、定价、促销和分销进行规划和执行，以创造交换满足个人和组织的目标。
global economy 全球经济	The system of industry and trade around the world that has developed as the result of globalization (the way in which economies have been developing to operate together as one system). 由于全球化而发展起来的世界范围内的工业和贸易体系（指各经济体发展成一个体系共同运作的方式）。
globalization 全球化	The fact that different cultures and economic systems around the world are becoming connected and similar to each other because of the influence of large multinational companies and of improved communication. 由于大型跨国公司的影响和交流的改善，世界各地不同的文化和经济体系正在变得相互联系和相似。
MNCs 跨国公司	A multinational corporation (MNC) has facilities and other assets in at least one country other than its home country. A multinational company generally has offices and/or factories in different countries and a centralized head office where they coordinate global management. These companies, also known as international, stateless, or transnational corporate organizations tend to have budgets that exceed those of many small countries. 跨国公司（MNC）至少在其母国以外的一个国家拥有设施和其他资产。跨国公司通常在不同的国家有办事处和（或）工厂，并有一个集中的总部，在那里他们协调全球管理。这些公司，也被称为国际、无国籍或跨国公司组织，往往有超过许多小国家的预算。

Continued

strategic business unit 战略业务单位	A strategic business unit, popularly known as SBU, is a fully-functional unit of a business that has its own vision and direction. Typically, a strategic business unit operates as a separate unit, but it is also an important part of the company. It reports to the headquarters about its operational status. 战略业务单位,通常被称为 SBU,是一个拥有自己的愿景和方向的业务功能齐全的单位。通常,战略业务单位作为一个独立的单位运作,但它也是公司的重要组成部分。它向总部报告其运作状况。
trade distortion 贸易扭曲	Used to describe a tax or action that changes the normal characteristics of trade. 用来描述改变正常贸易特征的税收或行为。
trade barrier 贸易壁垒	Something such as an import tax or a limit on the amount of goods that can be imported that makes international trade more difficult or expensive. 使国际贸易更加困难或昂贵的诸如进口税或对进口货物数量的限制等措施。
protectionism 保护主义	The theory or practice of shielding a country's domestic industries from foreign competition by taxing imports. 通过对进口商品征税来保护本国产业免受外国竞争的理论或实践。
tariff 关税	A tax or duty to be paid on a particular class of imports or exports. 对某一特色类别的进口或出口商品征收的税。
nontariff barrier 非关税壁垒	A way to restrict trade using trade barriers in a form other than a tariff. Nontariff barriers include quotas, embargoes, sanctions, and levies, etc. 使用关税以外的贸易壁垒来限制贸易的一种方式。非关税壁垒包括配额、禁运、制裁和征税等。
confiscation 没收	The process of a government's taking ownership of a property without compensation. 政府无偿获得财产所有权的过程。
nationalization 国有化	The transfer of a major branch of industry or commerce from private to state ownership or control. 把工业或商业的一个主要分支从私有转移到国家所有或控制。
domestication 归化	The process of foreign companies relinquishing control and ownership, either completely or partially, to the nationals. 外国公司将全部或部分控制权和所有权交给本国公民的过程。
creeping expropriation 蚕食征用	The continual restriction of private property rights gradually over time by a government. Creeping expropriation involves legislation, regulation, and taxation, which together over time make it difficult for a person or business to own property. Creeping expropriation, where it exists, makes it increasingly difficult to conduct commerce. 政府对私有财产权的不断限制。缓慢的蚕食征用涉及立法、法规和税收,随着时间的推移,这些加在一起使得个人或企业很难拥有财产。在存在这种情况的地方,蚕食性的征用行为使得商业活动越来越困难。

Continued

common law system 英美法系	A legal system that relies heavily on precedents and conventions. Judges' decisions are guided not so much by statutes as by previous court decisions and interpretations of what certain laws are or should be. 严重依赖先例和惯例的法律体系。法官的决定与其说是受法规的指导,不如说是受以前法院的决定以及对某些法律是什么或应该是什么的解释的指导。
statute law system 大陆法系	The main rules of the law are embodied in legislative codes. Every circumstance is clearly spelled out to indicate what is legal and what is not. There is also a strict and literal interpretation of the law under this system. 法律的主要规则体现在立法法典中。每一种情况都清楚地说明了什么是合法的,什么是不合法的。在这个制度下,对法律也有严格的字面解释。
jurisdiction 管辖权	The limits or territory within which authority may be exercised. 行使权力的范围或领域。
extraterritoriality 治外法权	The right of foreign citizens to be tried by the laws of the country they are from, not the laws of the country where they live. 外国公民受其来国法律而非其居住国法律审判的权利。
private company 私人股份有限公司	A firm held under private ownership. Private companies may issue stock and have shareholders, but their shares do not trade on public exchanges and are not issued through an initial public offering (IPO). 私人所有的公司。私人公司可以发行股票并拥有股东,但是他们的股票不会在公开交易所交易,也不会通过首次公开募股(IPO)来发行。
litigation 诉讼	The process of taking legal action. 采取法律行动的过程。
arbitration 仲裁	The submission of a dispute to an unbiased third person designated by the parties to the controversy, who agree in advance to comply with the award—a decision to be issued after a hearing at which both parties have an opportunity to be heard. 将争端提交给争端各方指定的公正的第三人,争端各方都事先同意遵守其裁决——争端各方都有机会在听征会上辩诉后做出的决定。
intellectual property 知识产权	Creations of the mind: inventions, literary and artistic works, and symbols, names, images, and designs used in commerce. 脑力创造:用于商业的发明、文学和艺术作品、符号、名称、形象和设计。
patent 专利	The granting of a property right by a sovereign authority to an inventor. This grant provides the inventor exclusive rights to the patented process, design, or invention for a designated period in exchange for a comprehensive disclosure of the invention. They are a form of incorporeal right. 由主权当局授予发明者的财产权。这项授权给予发明者在指定期间内对专利过程、设计或发明的专有权,以换取该发明的全面披露。它们是一种无形的权利。

Continued

trademark 商标	A trademark is a recognizable insignia, phrase, word, or symbol that denotes a specific product and legally differentiates it from all other products of its kind. A trademark exclusively identifies a product as belonging to a specific company and recognizes the company's ownership of the brand. 一种可识别的标志、短语、词或符号，它表示一种特定的产品，并在法律上区别于其他同类产品。商标专门标识一个产品属于一个特定的公司，并承认该公司对该品牌的所有权。
copyright 版权	A bundle of intangible rights granted by statute to the author or originator of certain literary or artistic productions, whereby, for a limited period, the exclusive privilege is given to that person (or to any party to whom he or she transfers ownership) to make copies of the same for publication and sale. 一些无形权利法规授予某些文学或艺术作品的作者或发起者，即在有限的时间内，给予指定之人(或其转让给任何一方或个人之所有权)对其作品进行复制出版和销售的独家特权。
infringement 侵权	The encroachment, breach, or violation of a right, law, regulation, or contract. 对权利、法律、法规或合同的侵占、违反或妨害。

Review & Critical Thinking Questions

1. Why is environmental scanning consistent with a functionalist approach to marketing?

2. What factors should the marketer take into account in scanning the marketing environment?

3. Name three important trends in today's marketing environment.

4. What factors should the marketer take into account in implementing marketing strategy?

5. Explain：confiscation, expropriation, nationalization, and domestication.

6. Will tariffs play a more significant role than nontariff barriers during the 2020s in affecting world trade?

7. Discuss how you can overcome the financial control imposed by the host country.

8. How should MNCs generally cope with trade barriers?

9. Why do MNCs prefer to use corporate subsidiaries in foreign markets?

10. Distinguish among patent, trademark, copyright, and infringement.

Discussion Questions

1. What is creeping expropriation? What is its economic impact on foreign investors?
2. What measures can be undertaken to minimize political risk?
3. Distinguish between common law and statute law systems.
4. Cite examples of products that cannot be imported legally into China.
5. Why is it so difficult for an MNC to deal with bribery?

Case Study

International Auto Safety and Patents

Mercedes-Benzes has long been an international leader in automobile safety. In 1951, Mercedes-Benz engineer Béla Barényi obtained a patent for the occupant safety cell. In 1953, the crumple zone was premiered with Mercedes-Benzes 180. In 1957, Mercedes installed seatbelts, which were initially installed for aircrafts. In 1959, the Mercedes-220 had a strict combined pleated area for passenger cars and cars. The 1981 Mercedes s-class world debuted with an airbag.

Mercedes undoubtedly has enormous marketing advantages from this corporate image and goodwill; Mercedes-Benzes, however, shows a high degree of moral awareness of its inventiveness. In the early 1950s, Mercedes was a leader in Formula One racing. Mercedes disqualified the team for more than 20 years after a terrible sports car accident at Le Mans. In the accident, a car crashed into the audience, killing many of them.

On 23 January 1951, Daimler-Benz applied for patent No. DB854.157, using unvarnished instructions on motor vehicles, in particular for human transportation. Behind this lie the invention of the ruffles. Over the next few decades, the patent revolutionized the entire car industry and became a determining factor in passive safety. In recent years, it has even been used in the design of railway locomotives and cars.

The genius behind the idea was Béla Barényi for whom the maxim was that safe cars could not be compromised, but that stability was entirely inappropriate. He was the first to discover that kinetic energy must be absorbed through deformation to protect occupants in a collision. He logically divided the car into three separate boxes: a soft front, a hard passenger and a flexible rear. The patent was granted on 28 August 1952.

Patent law allows companies to retain full control of their inventions for seventeen years. Mercedes, however, chose not to patent its creases so that its competitors could adopt the technology. As a result, tens of thousands of lives around the world have been saved.

Questions

1. Did Daimler-Benz enhance its marketing strength by its failure to enforce the crumple zone patent rights?

2. What is the difference between Mercedes-Benz's crumple-zone patent protection actions in the 1950s and the current pharmaceutical industry's pricing policies on AIDS drugs to Africa? What would you recommend?

3. Are there certain "intellectual property rights" (patents and copyright) which are so vital to the health and safety of consumers that they should not be allowed to be patented or copyrighted?

中文概述

国际营销是一种多国参与的过程,对思想、商品和服务的概念、定价、促销和分销进行规划和执行,以创造交换满足个人和组织的目标。消费者环境分析是功能主义营销方法的基石,不能适应不断变化的环境趋势的营销人员将不能确保公司的生存。

国际营销环境包含很多方面,如环境大趋势、消费者社会和物理环境、时空压缩、全球化、碎片化、组织和营销环境的关系等。计划有多层次的特点。

自由贸易在理论上意义重大,因为它提高了所有相关国家及其公民的效率和经济福利。但是在国际市场存在很多贸易扭曲和营销障碍,如地方保护主义对地方产业的保护。此外,还有政府通过征税实行贸易保护主义,一些政府还允许企业垄断联盟的存在。另外,还有关税壁垒和非关税壁垒、政府在贸易中扮演的角色、海关和准入流程、产品(特殊)要求、财政控制、私人障碍等。

国际营销环境还包括政治环境。

国际政治环境具有多重性,跨国公司必须面对多国不同的政治环境,这种复杂性迫使跨国公司考虑三种不同类型的政治环境:国外环境、国内环境和国际环境。

市场营销人员必须应对许多**政治风险**。基于东道国政府行为的危害包括没收、征用、国有化、归化和蚕食征用。由此产生了四组政治风险:一般不稳定风险、所有权/控制风险、经营风险和转移风险。

法律环境是多种多样的:国内的、国外的和国际的。有许多产品不能合法进口到大多数国家,一个公司的生产策略也会受到法律环境的影响。需要注意的是:没有一个适用于全世界的国际法来规定国际商业企业的可接受和合法的行为,不同国家有不同的法律,这些法律往往彼此冲突,特别是涉及国家政治的时候。

世界上存在两大法律体系,英美法系和大陆法系。

跨国公司必须做出的一个法律决定是,是否使用分公司或子公司来执行其计划和管理其在外国的业务。**分公司**是公司在其他地方的延伸或前哨。虽然它在物理上是分离的,但在法律上它并没有与公司分离。相反,**子公司**在物理上和法律上都是独立的。尽管它的所有权属于另一个公司,但它被认为是一个独立的法律实体。

无论发生在哪里,**诉讼**都不是一件容易的事。此外,还有贿赂和知识产权以及伪造的问题。**知识产权**是指精神创造:用于商业的发明、文学和艺术作品、符号、名称、形象和设计。知识产权包括专利、商标、版权和商业秘密。专利保护具有科学技术性质的发明。**商标**是一种符号、文字或物体,用来标识某一特定公司生产或销售的产品。**版权**由版权局负责,保护作者或艺术家的文学、音乐、戏剧和艺术作品免受他人未经授权的复制。**商业秘密**是指在特定企业中保密的专有技术(如制造方法、配方、计划等)。这种行业中通常不为人知的技术可能会给公司带来竞争优势。在商业用途(即复制或模仿)中未经业主同意,意图混淆或欺骗公众,就产生了**侵权**行为。**伪造**是指伪造货币,即为获利而制造的假币,是一种伪造行为,通过复制某物以换取真品而进行欺骗。

UNIT 2 | The Political and Economic Environment

Learning Objectives

1. Understand the elements of a country's political environment that can impact marketing activities.
2. Learn about political risk and its categories.
3. Know sovereignty and seizure of assets.
4. Identify and briefly explain the major changes in the world economy.
5. Study economic system and its types.
6. Understand stages of market development and its marketing implications.

2.1 Political Environment

The political environment in international business consists of a set of political factors and government activities in a foreign market that can either facilitate or hinder a business' ability to conduct business activities in the foreign market. Any company doing business outside its home country should carefully study the political culture in the target country and analyze any issues arising from the political environment. These include the governing party's attitude toward sovereignty, political risk, taxes, the threat of equity dilution, and expropriation.

2.1.1 Nation-States and Sovereignty

Sovereignty can be defined as the supreme, absolute, and uncontrollable power by which an independent state is governed and from which all specific political powers are derived. A sovereignty state is independent and has the right and power of regulating its internal affairs without foreign interference. Thus, sovereignty is the power of a state to do everything necessary to govern itself, such as making, executing, and applying laws; imposing and collecting taxes; and forming treaties or engaging in commerce with foreign nations. Government actions taken in the name of sovereignty occur in the context of two important criteria: a country's stage of development and the political and economic systems in place in the country.

The economies of individual nations may be classified as industrialized, newly industrialized, or developing. Many governments in developing countries exercise control over their nations' economic development by passing protectionist laws and regulations. Their objective is to encourage economic development by protecting emerging or strategic industries. Government leaders can also engage in cronyism and provide favors for family members or "good friends". Finding connections presides over building relationships in those countries.

Conversely, when many countries reach advanced stages of economic development, their governments declare that any practice or policy that restrains free trade is illegal. Antitrust laws and regulations are established to promote fair competition. Laws in these countries often define and preserve a nation's social order; laws may extend to political, cultural, and even intellectual activities and social conduct.

With globalization, some observers believe global economic integration is eroding national economic sovereignty. If the issue is framed in terms of marketing, the concept of exchange comes to the fore: Nations may be willing to give up sovereignty in return for something of value. If countries can increase their share of world trade and increase national income, perhaps they will be willing to cede some sovereignty. In Europe, the individual EU countries gave up the right to have their own currencies, ceded the right to set their own product standards, and have made other sacrifices in exchange for improved market access.

2.1.2   Political Risk

Political risk is the possibility of a change in a country's political environment or government policy that would adversely affect a company's ability to operate effectively and profitably. Political risk can deter a company from marketing or investing abroad. When there is a high level of uncertainty in a country, the country may have difficulty attracting foreign investment. For example, Nike is a globally recognized brand featuring athletic apparel, footwear, sports accessories and equipment. Nike has been very fortunate as the government of the United States has formulated such policies that will foster the growth of business. The company is enjoying stable currency and low-interest rate conditions along with very competitive tax arrangements that help the company in advancing growth. US government has taken initiatives with respect to transparency in the global value chain and Nike has greatly benefited from this. However, Nike is facing hard times in its outsourced manufacturers in other countries like Indonesia, Thailand and Vietnam where there is an increase in political unrest.

Generally, executives often fail to conceptualize political risk because they have not studied political science. Thus, they have not been exposed to the issues that students of politics ask about the activities of global companies. Valuable sources of information regarding political risk include *The Economist*, the *Financial Times*, and other business periodicals. The Economist Intelligence Unit (EIU) and the Political Risk Services (PRS) publish up-to-date political risk reports on individual country markets. Note that these commercial sources vary somewhat in the criteria they consider to constitute political risk. For example, the PRS Group focuses more directly on government actions and economic functions (see the table below).

Table 2.1 Categories of Political Risk

EIU	PRS Group
War	Political turmoil probability
Social unrest	Equity restrictions
Orderly political transfer	Local operations restrictions
Politically motivated violence	Taxation discrimination
International disputes	Repatriation restrictions
Change in government	Exchange controls
Pro-business orientation	
Institutional effectiveness	Tariff barriers
Bureaucracy	Other barriers
Transparency or fairness	Payment delays
Corruption	Fiscal or monetary expansion
Crime	Labor cost
Foreign debt	

Any companies are supposed to conduct risk assessment before they enter a foreign market. In face of any political risk, companies can purchase insurance to offset potential risks arising from the political environment. In many industrialized countries such as Japan, Germany, Britain and the United States, various agencies offer investment insurance to corporations doing business abroad. The Overseas Private Investment Corporation (OPIC) provides various types of political risk insurance to U.S. companies; in Canada, the export development corporation performs a similar function.

2.1.3   Taxes

Governments rely on tax revenues for the funds necessary for social services, the military, and other expenditures. Unfortunately, government taxation policies on the sale of goods and services frequently motivate companies and individuals to profit by not paying taxes. For example, in China, import duties have dropped since the country joined the World Trade Organization (WTO). Even so, many goods are still subject to double-digit duties plus a value-added tax (VAT). High excise and VAT taxes can also encourage legal cross-border shopping as consumers go abroad in search of good values. At present, 67% of global consumers who shop abroad are buying because prices are lower outside of their own country.

High taxes also encourage many enterprises to engage in cash or barter transactions, which are off book and shunned from tax authorities. This, in turn, can create a liquidity squeeze that prevents companies from paying wages to employees, and unpaid workers can contribute to political instability. Meanwhile, global corporations make efforts to minimize their tax liability by shifting the location of income. For example, it has been estimated that tax minimization by foreign companies doing business in the United States costs the U. S. government billions of dollars each year in lost revenue. "Earnings stripping" is a case in point. It is a technique used by multi-national corporations that try to minimize their U.S. tax bills by shifting profits abroad to countries with lower tax rates.

2.1.4   Seizure of Assets

In international marketing, the ultimate threat a company confronts is that the government in a host country seizes its assets. Expropriation is the act of government claiming the property of a company or investor for the public use. Government expropriation is widely found around the world, generally accompanied by agreement that owners should receive appropriate compensation for the property they lose. If no compensation is provided, the action is referred to as confiscation. International law is generally interpreted as prohibiting any act by a government to take foreign property without compensation. Nationalization is one form of seizure of assets. It refers to when a government takes control of a company or industry, which generally occurs without compensation for the loss of the net worth of seized assets and potential income.

In defense of the country's economy and sovereignty, Cuba nationalized U. S. companies in 1960. The nationalized were the businesses and properties of the national telephone and electricity companies; Texaco, Esso and Sinclair oil companies; and the 36 sugar mills owned by U.S. firms in Cuba on August 6, 1960. Castro offered compensation in the form of Cuban government bonds, which was adequate under Cuban law. However, the U. S. State Department viewed this particular act of nationalization as discriminatory and the compensation offered as inadequate. Also on this continent in February 2007, Chavez announced a new law-decree to nationalize the last remaining oil production sites that are under foreign company control, to take effect on 1 May, allowing foreign companies to negotiate the nationalization terms. Under the new regulations, the earlier joint ventures, involving Exxon Mobil, Chevron Texaco, Statoil, Conoco Phillips, and BP, were transformed giving Petróleos de Venezuela, S.A. (PDVSA) a minimum 60 percent stake. When governments expropriate foreign property, a number of impediments can limit actions to reclaim that property. For example, according to the U.S. Act of State Doctrine, if the government of a foreign state is involved in a specific act, the U.S. courts will not get involved. However, representatives of expropriated companies may seek recourse through arbitration at the World Bank Investment Dispute Settlement Center. It is also possible to buy expropriation insurance from either a private company or a government agency such as Overseas Private Investment Corporation(OPIC).

2.2　Economic Environment

2.2.1　World Economic Overview

With the deepening of globalization since 1990s, there has been an increasing interdependence between the economies around the world. According to its proponents, globalization will continue to cause growth and prosperity to spread. Economic integration stood at 10 percent at the beginning of the twentieth century; today, it is approximately 50 percent. Integration is particularly striking in the European Union (EU) and the North American Free Trade Area.

However, the trend was interrupted by the international financial crisis of 2008—2009. The financial crisis resulted in the first downturn in global output since 1946 and made the world economy unpredictable. Even while this textbook is being compiled, Covid-19 is spreading worldwide, dimming the global economic prospect. And the world economic environment becomes increasingly volatile, though dynamic. To achieve success, executives and marketers must identify the global trends that are shaping the world economy:

1. There is an ongoing shift in global economic activity from developed to developing

economies, accompanied by growth in the number of consumers in emerging markets.

2. Technologies are facilitating a relatively free flow of information, goods, and capital around the world.

3. Cooperation among governments is undermined or discontinued.

4. Globalization continues to create tremendous wealth and opportunities.

The first trend is the economic activity shift from the developed to the developing countries. China, leader among the developing countries, is a case in point. According to data from the World Bank, China accounted for 35% of total global GDP growth (in nominal U.S. dollar terms) between 2017 and 2019, doubling America's share of 18%, and more than four times that of the EU's 7.9%. Also known as emerging economies or developing countries, emerging markets, with populations that are young and growing, not only have become the focus of rising consumption and production but also have simultaneously increased the potential size and worth of current major international trade. This will make it imperative for most companies to succeed in emerging markets.

The second trend is the relatively free flow of information, goods and capital thanks to advanced technology. The free global flow of information has already resulted in radical pricing transparency and new networks of engaged consumers. The growth of E-commerce spurs the flow of goods around the world. In 2019, global retail E-commerce rose 20.7%, with its sales amounting to 3.53 trillion US dollars, while it grew 28.0% in 2017 and 22.9% in 2018. At present, China is the world's biggest E-commerce market, led by E-commerce subsidiaries of the Alibaba group, namely Taobao, Alibaba.com, Tmall and others. With an annual growth rate of 35%, China is also one of the fastest-growing E-commerce markets.

The third trend is disrupted cooperation among governments. When Donald Trump came to power in White House, his administration launched trade wars against China, imposing higher tariffs on a wide range of goods or services. The trade war significantly impacted confidence around the world in 2019 and is expected to reduce global GDP by $700 billion in 2020. So far tariffs have resulted in a loss of $15 billion in U.S. exports while reducing Chinese imports by $53 billion. At the same time, Trump has also levied steel and aluminum tariffs on Brazil and Argentina and proposed a new retaliatory tariff on France (in response of a tax on U.S. technology companies). In a word, tariffs, NAFTA reforms and angst about Brexit have thrown foreign trade into a tailspin.

The fourth trend is continued globalization. As U.S. is the leading economy, some Americans contend globalization is a threat to its workers. But it has been shown that to some extent labor demand outpaces supply due to new opportunities created by international expansion. Trade also isn't a zero-sum contest: the benefits of access to emerging markets vastly outweigh overseas competition. Globalization will continue to define economic trends in the next century as developing countries seek to achieve the living standards of developed nations.

2.2.2　Economic Systems

An economic system is a means by which societies or governments organize and distribute available resources, services, and goods across a geographic region or country. Economic systems regulate factors of production, including capital, labor, physical resources, and entrepreneurs. Economists identified four main types of economic systems: market capitalism, centrally planned socialism, centrally planned capitalism, and market socialism. As shown in Figure 2.1, this classification was based on the dominant method of resource allocation and the dominant form of resource ownership. Due to globalization, economic systems are harder to categorize within the confines of a four-cell matrix. The descriptive criteria are as follows:

- **Type of economy**. Is the nation an advanced industrial country, an emerging economy, a transitional economy, or a developing country?
- **Type of government**. Is the nation ruled by a monarchy, a dictatorship, or a tyrant? Is there a one-party system? Is the nation dominated by another country, or is it a democracy with a multiparty system? Is it an unstable or terrorist country?
- **Trade and capital flows**. Is the nation characterized by almost completely free trade or incomplete free trade, or is it a part of a trading bloc? Is there a currency board, or are there exchange controls? Is there no trade, or does the government dominate trade?
- **The commanding heights**. (e.g. the transportation, communications, and energy sectors.) Are these sectors state-owned and operated? Is there a mix of state and private ownership? Are they all private, with or without controlled prices?
- **Services provided by the state and funded through taxes**. Are pensions, health care, and education provided? Pensions and education but not health care? Do privatized systems dominate?
- **Institutions**. Is the nation characterized by transparency, standards, the absence of corruption, and the presence of a free press and strong courts? Or is corruption a fact of life and the press controlled by the government? Are standards ignored and the court system compromised?
- **Markets**. Does the nation have a free market system characterized by high-risk/high-reward entrepreneurial dynamism? Is it a free market that is dominated by monopolies, cartels, and concentrated industries? Is it a socialized market with cooperation among business, government, and labor or is planning, including price and wage controls, dominated by the government?

Market Capitalism

Market capitalism is an economic system in which individuals and firms allocate

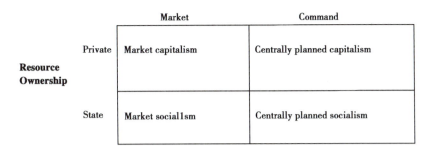

Figure 2.1　Resource Allocation

resources and production resources are privately owned. Consumers decide what goods they desire and firms determine what and how much to produce; the role of the state in market capitalism is to promote competition. Market capitalism is widely practiced around the world, mostly in North America and the EU.

It would be absolute, however, to assume that all market-oriented economies function in an identical manner. American economic system is featured by freedom of enterprises. By contrast, outsiders sometimes refer to Japan as "Japan Inc." the label can be interpreted in different ways, but it basically refers to a tightly run, highly regulated economic system that is also market-oriented.

Centrally Planned Socialism

Centrally planned socialism is an economic system in which the state has broad powers to serve the public interest as it sees fit. State planners make "top-down" decisions about what goods and services are produced and in what quantities; consumers can spend their money on what is available. The government owns industries as well as individual enterprises. Government ownership of every industry as well as individual enterprises is characteristic of centrally planned socialism. As demand typically exceeds supply, the elements of the marketing mix are not used as strategic variables. Product differentiation, advertising, or promotion matters little; even distribution is controlled by the government so as to eliminate "exploitation" by intermediaries. Centrally-planned socialism was found in the former Soviet Union.

Centrally Planned Capitalism

In reality, market capitalism and centrally planned socialism do not exist in "pure" form. In most countries, more or less, command and market resource allocation are practiced simultaneously, as are private and state resource ownership. The role of government in modern market economies varies widely. An economic system in which command resource allocation is utilized extensively in an overall environment of private resource ownership can be called **centrally planned capitalism**. Market socialism is also possible.

Market Socialism

Market socialism is an economic system in which market allocation policies are permitted within an overall environment of state ownership.

In Sweden, for example, although 90% of resources and companies are privately owned, 5% state owned and 5% co-operatives, two-thirds of all expenditures are controlled by the government. And resource allocation is more "voter" oriented than "market" oriented. Thus, Sweden's so-called "welfare state" has a hybrid economic system that incorporates elements of both centrally planned socialism and capitalism. In face of financial crisis and world economic downturn, the Swedish government has been pursuing reforms to sustain its economic stability.

Market reforms and emerging markets are creating opportunities for large-scale investments by global companies. For instance, Coca-Cola returned to India in 1994, two decades after being forced out by the government. A new law allowing 100 percent foreign ownership of enterprises helped pave the way for its return.

Economic freedom, or economic liberty, is the ability of people of a society to take economic actions. One approach to economic freedom comes from the liberal tradition emphasizing free markets, free trade, and private property under free enterprise. An American conservative think tank based in Washington D. C., the Heritage Foundation takes a conventional approach to classifying economies: it compiles a survey of more than 170 countries and regions ranked by degree of freedom. A number of key economic variables are taken into account such as property rights, judicial effectiveness, government integrity, tax burden, fiscal health, government spending. A high correlation exists between the economic freedom and the extent to which a nation's mixed economy is market oriented. However, the criteria for the ranking have been subject to debate. Nevertheless, it offers insights into classification of economic systems around the world.

2.2.3 Stages of Market Development

In any country, market is at different stages of economic development at any given time. The World Bank has developed a four-category classification system that uses per capita gross national income (GNI) as a base. GNI is the total amount of money earned by a nation's people and businesses. It is used to measure and track a nation's wealth from year to year. The number includes the nation's gross domestic product plus the income it receives from overseas sources. The income definition for each stage is derived from the World Bank's lending categories, and countries within a given category generally have a number of characteristics in common. Thus, the stages provide a useful basis for global market segmentation and target marketing. As of July 1st, 2019, the new thresholds for classification by income are:

Table 2.2   Thresholds for Classification by Income

Threshold	2020 GNI/Capita (current US $)
Low-income	< 1, 025
Lower-middle income	1, 026−3, 995
Upper-middle income	4, 038−12, 375
High-income	> 12, 376

As seen in the chart above, many countries' incomes have transcended the income group thresholds over time. Because most parts of the world have experienced considerable economic growth in recent decades, and the classification thresholds are held stable in real terms, there are now fewer low-income countries and more countries have gained middle or high-income status. Just since 2003, the number of low-income countries has nearly halved, declining from 66 to 32 in 2019. The number of high-income countries is currently 80, up from less than 50 in the 1990s. The number of middle-income countries is 107 (60 UMICs and 47 LMICs) and has not changed much as countries have transitioned both in and out of this group.

Low-Income Countries

According to the World Bank, low-income countries are nations that have a per capita gross national income (GNI) of less than $1, 025. Low-income countries are often synonymous with underdeveloped countries, also known as developing countries, emerging markets, or newly industrialized countries. These countries receive development aid, which is financial aid given by governments or agencies to boost and support the economic, political, social, and environmental development in other countries. Bilateral aid is given directly from the donor country to another, and multilateral aid is given to an international organization which then distributes the aid to developing countries. World Bank and United Nations agencies such as United Nations International Children's Emergency Fund (UNICEF) are examples of organizations that are involved in development aid.

Low-income countries face struggles relating to a poor economy. Issues related to poor economic health include below average life expectancy, high infant mortality rates, poor educational outcomes, degrading infrastructure, environmental and climate conditions, and poor health outcomes. These low-income countries suffer high rates of illnesses and infections due to lack of clean water, low levels of sanitation, malnutrition, and lack of access to quality medical care. There are currently 32 countries in the low-income country category. Somalia is at the bottom of the low-income country list, with a GNI per capita of $130.

Nevertheless, some low-income countries are making efforts to develop their economy. Ethiopia is a case in point. Ethiopia GNI per capita is $790.Yet, according to the report by the New York University Stern Center for Business and Human Rights, as one of Africa's fastest-growing economies, Ethiopian government pursues a bold economic experiment by building industrial parks and providing a range of financial incentives to attract garment manufacturers. The government predicts the sector will one day have billions of dollars in sale. And some of the world's best-known brands—among them H&M, Gap, and PVH—employ tens of thousands of Ethiopian workers. Based on Ethiopian country data, in the last 5 to 6 years, the textile, and apparel industry have grown at an average of 51% and more than 65 international textile investment projects have been licensed for foreign investors, during this period. Ethiopia's government embarks on the road to diversifying exports from agricultural product to strategic sectors like textile and garment manufacturing.

Lower-Middle-Income Countries

World Bank has historically broken down countries' economies into three categories: high income, middle income, and low income. Now economies are further specified, with middle economies broken down into two additional groups: lower-middle-income countries and upper-middle-income countries. This is because middle-income economies are diverse in their regions, sizes, populations, and income levels. Lower middle-income nations have a GNI per capita of $1,026 to $3,995. Consumer markets in these countries are expanding rapidly. Countries such as Indonesia and India represent an increasing competitive threat as they mobilize their relatively cheap—and often highly motivated—labor forces to serve target markets in the rest of the world. The developing countries in lower-middle-income category have a major competitive advantage in standardized, labor-intensive light industry sectors such as footwear, textiles, and toys.

With a 2011 GNI per capita of $1,410, India has removed from the low-income category and is now classified as a lower-middle-income country. In 2007, India commemorated the 60th anniversary of its independence from Great Britain. For many decades, economic growth was weak. But in the late eighties and in the beginning of the 1990s, the Indian policy makers realized that state controlled economy was not able to produce desired results in almost 45 years. It was decided to pursue economic policy based on liberalization, privatization and globalization. In this era of liberalization, privatization and globalization, India has witnessed rapid growth in some sectors of economy.Today it has become one of the fastest growing economies in the world with a GDP growth rate of around 6%–7%.

Yashwant Sinha, the country's former finance minister, once declared that the twenty-first century would be "the century of India." His words seem to have come true. India is now home to a number of world-class companies with global reach, including Infosys, Mahindra & Mahindra, Tata, and Wipro. Meanwhile, the list of global companies operating in India is growing longer, which include Apple Inc., Xiaomi, Haier, Intex Technologies, Nokia, Uniqlo, Coca-Cola, Dupont, Unilever, and Walmart. India's huge population base also presents market potential for automakers. Suzuki, Hyundai, General Motors, and Ford are among the global car manufacturers doing business in India.

Upper Middle-Income Countries

Upper middle-income countries, also known as industrializing or developing countries, are those with a GNI per capita of $3,996 to $12,375. In these countries, the process of urbanization is speeding up. Malaysia, Chile, Mexico, Venezuela and many other countries at this stage are rapidly industrializing. They have high literacy rates and strong education systems; wages are rising, but they are still significantly lower than in the advanced countries. Innovative companies can become formidable competitors and help contribute to their nations' rapid, export-driven economic growth.

Brazil ($9,140 GNI per capita in 2018), Russia ($10,230 GNI per capita in 2018), China ($9,460 GNI per capita in 2018) and South Africa ($5,750 GNI per capita in 2018) are the four of the BRICS countries that currently fall into the upper-middle-income category. Russia's economic situation improves and declines as the price of oil fluctuates. In Russia, the level of governmental regulation and red tape accompany business transactions, and thus it is undeniable that the Russian Government exercises strict control over commercial procedure and infrastructure, as well as the economy at large. This makes foreign companies hesitant to expand business there. For example, prominent UK retailer, New Look, withdrew from Russia and Ukraine in late 2014 amid fears over the nations' political stability, and many others have followed suit. Still, the market opportunity is enticing: wages have increased dramatically and consumers are tending to spend rather than save.

Brazil is the largest country in Latin America in terms of its economic size, population and geographic territory. It boasts the richest reserves of natural resources in South hemisphere; China, Brazil's top trading partner, has a great demand for iron ore and other commodities. Government policies aimed at stabilizing Brazil's macro-economy have yielded impressive results: Brazil's GNI grew at an average annual rate of 4 percent between 2005 and 2011. Also during this period, nearly 50 million Brazilians have become the middle class as incomes and living standards have improved. Needless to say, this trend has been a boon to global companies doing business in Brazil such as Exxon Mobil, Chevron, General Motors, Ford and Apple.

China is the third BRICS country in the upper-middle-income category. China represents the largest single destination for foreign investment in the developing world. Attracted by the country's vast area and market potential, companies in Asia, Europe, and North and South America are making China a key country in their global strategies. Shenzhen and other special economic zones have attracted billions of dollars in foreign investment. China joined the World Trade Organization (WTO) in 2001. To ensure that the country's export-led economic transformation is sustained, policy-makers have launched hundreds of infrastructure projects. These include airports, cargo ports, highways, and railroads. Avon, Coca-Cola, Dell, Ford, General Motors, Honda, HSBC, JPMorgan Chase, McDonald's, P&G, Toyota, Volkswagen are among many global companies that have entered China. And the world's top retailers Walmart, Carrefour, Costco and ALDI have opened physical stores in China.

China invited South Africa to join the original group of four BRIC countries in December, 2010.

In 2013, South African President Jacob Zuma welcomed leaders from the other four BRICS countries to a summit in Durban. One important item on the agenda: how to increase trade and investment among the five countries. In addition, President Zuma hopes to attract more direct investment in the African continent as a whole.

Lower-middle- and upper-middle-income countries that achieve the highest steady rates of economic growth are sometimes referred to collectively as **newly industrializing economies (NIEs)**. Overall, NIEs are characterized by greater industrial output than developing economies; heavy manufactures and refined products make up an increasing proportion of their exports. Goldman Sachs, the firm that developed the original BRICS framework more than a decade ago, has identified a new country grouping called Next-11 (N11). Five of the N11 countries are considered NIEs. These include three lower-middle-income countries: Egypt, Indonesia, and the Philippines. Mexico and Turkey are N11 NIEs from the ranks of the upper-middle-income category. Among these five countries, Egypt, Indonesia, and the Philippines have posted positive GDP growth over the past several years.

There are approximately 5 billion people live within MICs. Approximately one-third of global GDP is represented by these nations and over 70% of people in the world live in MICs. There are a total of 109 MICs—53 lower-middle-income countries and 56 upper-middle-income countries. Both lower-middle income and upper-middle income countries face their separate challenges. Lower-middle-income countries typically struggle to provide their citizens with basic services such as clean water. Upper-middle-income countries might face government problems such as corruption.

Marketing Opportunities in Developing Countries

Despite many problems in developing countries, it's possible to nurture long-term market opportunities. Today, Nike produces and sells only a small portion of its output in China, but when the firm refers to China as a "two-billion-foot market," it clearly has the future in mind.

One of marketing roles in developing countries is to focus resources on the task of creating and delivering products that are best suited to local needs and incomes. Appropriate marketing communications techniques can also be applied to accelerate acceptance of these products, marketing can be the link that relates resources to opportunity and facilitates need satisfaction on the consumer's terms.

Consumers in these markets focus more on the scale and reassurance of big brands; projection of status and adherence to tradition that characterize hierarchical societies; and benefits that "do good" rather than "feel good." In the developing world, the watchwords are *protection* and *pragmatism*. That is why Safeguard, Procter & Gamble's germ-killing soap, is especially popular in places like China and the Philippines; in economically developed countries consumers are drawn to hedonistic benefits. These consumer commonalities lead to a number of crucial strategic imperatives. Marketers should:

- Introduce mega-brands (brands with offerings across several related categories) rather than stand-alone brands.
- Adjust their products to maximize perceived value.
- Capitalize on trends driven by the country's stage of economic development.
- Compete across, not within, categories.
- Develop communications that are rational and linked to social context.

Middle-income countries are also essential to global economic growth. Growth in MICs, according to the World Bank, has positive ripple effects on other countries such as international trade, reduction of border conflicts, sustainable energy development, and food and water security.

High Income Countries

The World Bank defines a high-income country as one that has a gross national income per capita exceeding $12, 056. Both developing and developed countries may be classified as high-income countries. In 2019, there are 81 countries and territories classified by the World Bank as high-income countries. Some of these countries, such as the United States, have held this classification consistently since the 1980s. Other nations, like Saudi Arabia, have held the classification, dropped off the list, and have now reappeared. Some countries, such as Russia and Venezuela, have been classified as high-income in the past but no longer hold that distinction.

High-income countries are also known as *advanced*, *developed*, *industrialized*, or *postindustrial countries*. **Postindustrial countries** are marked by a transition from a manufacturing-based economy to a service-based economy, a transition that is also connected with subsequent societal restructuring. Post-industrialization is the next evolutionary step from an industrialized society and is most evident in countries and regions that were among the first to experience the Industrial Revolution, such as the United States, Western Europe, and Japan. American sociologist Daniel Bell first coined the term *postindustrial* in 1973 in his book *The Coming of Post-Industrial Society: A Venture in Social Forecasting*, which describes several features of a postindustrial society. Postindustrial societies are characterized by:

- A transition from the production of goods to the production of services, with many outsourced manufactured goods.
- The replacement of blue-collar manual laborers with technical and professional workers such as computer engineers, doctors, and bankers.
- The replacement of practical knowledge with theoretical knowledge.
- Greater attention being paid to the theoretical and ethical implications of new technologies, which helps society avoid some of the negative features of introducing new technologies, such as environmental accidents and massive widespread power outages.
- The development of newer scientific disciplines—such as those that involve new forms of information technology, cybernetics, or artificial intelligence—to assess the theoretical and ethical implications of new technologies.
- A stronger emphasis on the university and polytechnic institutes, which produce graduates who create and guide the new technologies crucial to a postindustrial society.

Product and market opportunities in a postindustrial society are heavily dependent upon new products and innovations. Ownership levels for basic products are extremely high in most households. Organizations seeking to grow often face a difficult task if they attempt to expand their share of existing markets. Alternatively, they can undertake to create new markets. Today, E-commerce is preferred as it allows companies to conduct business without having physical presence, thus reducing infrastructure, communication and other related overhead costs and speeding up the transactions by eliminating many unnecessary intermediaries. Apart from these economic factors, customer interaction and marketing forces and multimedia convergence fuel E-commerce growth.

To succeed, a company needs to have a strong, reliable and efficient supply chain and connectivity network to ensure timely processing of orders. With products' pricing and features transparency and wider range being easily accessible at best prices, consumers have also been exploring the E-commerce market. According to Statistics MRC, the Global E-commerce market accounted for $3.69 trillion in 2018 and is expected to reach $18.89 trillion by 2027 growing at a CAGR of 19.9% during the forecast period. These disruptive changes in consumer behavior could have great impact on business in the near future. Companies will focus on increased innovation, greater consumer awareness and knowledge, and increased product and service customization.

Seven high-income countries, including the United States, United Kingdom, France, Canada, Italy, Japan and Germany are collectively known as the **Group of Seven (G7)**. It represents the world's largest industrialized economies. The G7's finance ministers and heads of state meet periodically to set international economic policy. Ever since its inception, the group has been vocal about preventing the global economy from entering into a recession, taking lead in ensuring economic prosperity and monetary stability. Established in 1999, **G20** is a global forum for central bank governors and governments to discuss numerous policies affecting the promotion of global financial stability. G20 is composed of Argentina, Australia, Brazil, Canada, China, France, Germany, India, Indonesia, Italy, Japan, Republic of Korea, Mexico, Russia, Saudi Arabia, South Africa, Turkey, the United Kingdom, the United States and the European Union. Its membership is a mixture of the biggest emerging and **advanced economies** on Earth that represents 75% of the world trade, 85% of the planet's gross domestic product and over 66% of the world's population. The forum engages with numerous non-governmental sectors through their multiple engagement groups like youth (Y20), labor (L20), civil society (C20) and business (B20).

Marketing Implications of the Stages of Development

The stages described previously can serve as a guide to marketers in evaluating product **saturation levels**, or the percentage of potential buyers or households that own a particular product. As of February 2019, about 1.58 billion mobile phone subscriptions had been registered in China. While the vehicle population in China has been increasing in the last decades and stood at 240 million as of the end of 2018, but car ownership in China remains relatively low, only 54 cars per 1,000 people.Thus, there is a strong potential for incremental growth in vehicle sales.

Key Terms

sovereignty 主权	The supreme, absolute, and uncontrollable power by which an independent state is governed and from which all specific political powers are derived. 一个独立国家对其管辖区域所拥有的至高无上的、排他性的政治权力。
political risk 政治风险	The possibility of a change in a country's political environment or government policy that would adversely affect a company's ability to operate effectively and profitably. 东道国的政治环境或该国政府政策发生改变而给外国投资企业的经济利益带来的不确定性。
expropriation 没收财产	The act of government claiming the property of a company or investor for the public use. 东道国政府会扣押或没收外国子公司的实物资产和金融资产的行为。
economic system 经济体制	A means by which societies or governments organize and distribute available resources, services, and goods across a geographic region or country. 社会或政府经济组织生产、交换、分配过程中采取的资源配置方式。
market capitalism 市场资本主义	An economic system in which individuals and firms allocate resources and production resources are privately owned. 一种经济制度。在这种制度里,个人和企业分配资源,而且生产要素为私人所有。
centrally planned socialism 中央计划社会主义	An economic system in which the state has broad powers to serve the public interest as it sees fit. 国家掌握主导权来服务于公众利益的一种经济体制。
market socialism 市场社会主义	An economic system in which market allocation policies are permitted within an overall environment of state ownership. 在国有制基础上市场进行资源分配的一种经济体制。
economic freedom 经济自由度	The ability of people of a society to take economic actions. 指人们采取经济行动的能力。
gross national income 国民总收入	The total amount of money earned by a nation's people and businesses. The number includes the nation's gross domestic product plus the income it receives from overseas sources. 全体国民和企业创造的总价值。公式是国内生产总值(GDP)加上来自国外的要素收入,再减去对国外的要素支出。
newly industrializing economies (NIEs) 新兴工业化国家	Lower-middle- and upper-middle-income countries that achieve the highest steady rates of economic growth. 指经济增长率保持稳定高增长的低中等收入和高中等收入国家。

Continued

group of seven（G7） 七国集团	Seven high-income countries, including the United States, United Kingdom, France, Canada, Italy, Japan and Germany are collectively known as G7. 7 个高收入国家,包括美国、英国、法国、加拿大、意大利、日本和德国。
G20 20 国集团	A global forum for central bank governors and governments to discuss numerous policies affecting the promotion of global financial stability. G20 is composed of Argentina, Australia, Brazil, Canada, China, France, Germany, India, Indonesia, Italy, Japan, Republic of Korea, Mexico, Russia, Saudi Arabia, South Africa, Turkey, the United Kingdom, the United States and the European Union. 各国央行行长和政府研讨影响全球金融稳定的诸多政策的国际平台。20 国集团包括:阿根廷、澳大利亚、巴西、加拿大、中国、法国、德国、印度、印度尼西亚、意大利、日本、韩国、墨西哥、俄国、沙特阿拉伯、南非、土耳其、英国、美国和欧盟。
product saturation level 产品饱和度	The percentage of potential buyers or households that own a particular product. 潜在购买者或家庭拥有某个产品的百分比。

Review & Critical Thinking Questions

1. What are political and economic environments?

2. What is sovereignty? And why is it an important factor of political environment?

3. What are forms of seizer of assets?

4. What are the criteria used by the textbook to describe economic systems?

5. What are G7 or G20 respectively?

6. What is GDP or GNI?

7. Why are product saturation levels important to international marketers?

Discussion Questions

1. How does political environment influence international marketing?

2. Research into global market trends for the next 3 or 5 years. And discuss the implications for the industry concerned.

3. Use the criteria in the textbook to analyze one of BRICK countries and its marketing opportunities.

4. Classify countries using World Bank method and give examples of each category.

5. Discuss the marketing strategies at each stage of development.

6. Explore customer behaviors and buying habits in emerging economies.

Case Study

Here's Why China Embraced Costco, but Spurned Amazon and Tesco

Soon after opening the doors to its first location in China, Costco was forced to shut them, as crowds flooded the store eager to snatch up its discount offerings. It's a reaction that few Western companies entering China's retail market have experienced. Giants like Amazon and Tesco have withdrawn from the country after struggling to gain market share. Analysts believe Costco was welcomed with such enthusiasm because it was able to meet China's needs for new concepts, at a time when its market maturity is ideal.

"They're an established brand, they're going into a market that is a well-developed retail market, but that is still hungering for new concepts and new interests," said Greg Portell, a retail consultant at A.T. Kearney. "It would be very different if they went into Germany or the U.K., where the concept is not necessarily as new, and it'd also be different if they went into... some of the more emerging markets, where the retail environment is not as mature. China presents a great opportunity for them because consumers have a financial base that is mature enough, so you can have that kind of demand."

Walmart-owned Sam's Club has operated its wholesale stores in China since 1996, but Portell likened the opening to IKEA's impact in the U.S., where enough markets have heard about the furniture chain and are fascinated with it, but haven't had a chance to shop there yet.

"When those stores open in the U.S., they tend to get very strong reactions, because it's an interesting concept, it's a mature market, and it's a market that's open to those new business concepts."

Portell said that might explain why other Western retailers like Amazon, Tesco and Carrefour have had trouble entering China. French hypermarket chain Carrefour sold its China business in June after a weak response, and Amazon shut down its China e-commerce marketplace in April. Tesco withdrew from China in 2013.

"Just being the third or fourth store with items on the shelf, that's not enough anymore. You have to have reasons for consumers to pick you over other options. To do that in a crowded and sophisticated marketplace, you have to have some sort of newness in the concept," Portell said.

But he also cautioned that consumers being excited on the first day doesn't necessarily mean the company will see sustainable success.

"It's one thing to create strong demand and get consumers excited out of the gate, it's another challenge to run a profitable long-term business in those markets," he said. "When you think about Amazon or Tesco, the infrastructure and logistics network that are needed to be built up are not inconsequential."

Gordon Haskett analyst Chuck Grom added that Costco store openings are always met with frenzy.

"Most times Costco moves into a new country, whether it's been in Australia or Japan, or even France and Spain more recently, the first store openings tend to be wild and successful for Costco," he said.

That's why Costco prudently introduced itself to Chinese consumers five years ago, by selling its signature Kirkland products on a Chinese E-commerce site, according to Raymond James analyst Bobby Griffin.

"They were there ahead of time, they got to learn about the Chinese consumer through their E-commerce website, and the Chinese consumer knew about the brand from their other Asia operations in Korea and Japan," he said. Griffin also said that there's a growing middle class in China that are interested in Western goods and items.

Portell said that Costco's first-day success shouldn't be discounted. "It's a lot easier to start with a lot of demand and maintain momentum than to open your doors and have no one show up. It's the best possible way for them to start off."

Questions

1. What are the reasons for Costco's success in China?
2. Why have Amazon, Tesco and Carrefour withdrawn from China?
3. How does Costco make its first-day opening wild in Shanghai?
4. Why does Costco choose to enter Chinese market?

中文概述

政治环境由一系列政治因素和政治活动所构成,会对一个企业的商业运营起到帮助或阻碍作用。因此,从事国际营销的组织或个人尤其要理解主权对各国政府的重要性。以主权为名义采取的政府行动通常有两个重要衡量标准:一个是国家的发展阶段,另一个是这个国家实行的政治和经济体制。政治风险是指会影响公司有效经营和盈利能力的一个国家的政治环境或政府政策。政治风险会阻止公司对外进行营销和投资。如果一个国家政治环境存在较高的不确定性,那么这个国家很难吸引国外的投资。鉴于各国的政治环境都有差异,所以政治风险评估至关重要。同样重要的是了解特定政府在税收、资产获得以及征用方面采取的行动。资产获取的方式包括征用、没收和国有化三种。

经济环境是一个国际市场潜力和市场机会的主要决定因素,在当今全球经济中,发展中国家经济成为重要部分,随之而来是新兴市场消费群体的增长;尽管金融危机使世界经济举步维艰,全球化趋势将持续。全球的经济活动正不断从发达国家转向发展中国家,同时新兴市场的消费者人数不断攀升。科技促使信息,货物和资本在全球范围内相对自由地流动。尽管各国政府的合作受到削弱或中断,但是全球化持续创造着巨大财富和机会。

基于资源配置和资源所有形式,世界各国的经济体制可分为市场资本主义,中央计划资本主义,中央计划社会主义和市场社会主义四种类型。20世纪后期世界经济体制显现了体制转型的特征,即许多以往由中央计划控制的经济制度转向了市场资本主义,但在经济自由度方面这些国家仍存在巨大的差异。

国家可以按经济发展阶段划分为低收入、中低收入、中高收入和高收入等类型。国内生产总值(GDP)和国民收入总值(GNP)是两个常用于衡量经济发展的指标。低收入国家有时被称为最不发达国家(LDCs)。具有高增长率的中高收入国家时常成为新兴工业化经济体,其中最为瞩目的就是金砖四国,即巴西、俄罗斯、印度和中国。七国集团、二十国集团代表了高收入国家为促进世界经济发展和繁荣,确保金融稳定做出的努力。依据收入水平可以确定产品饱和度,并以此方法评估产品的市场潜力。

UNIT 3 Scientific and Technological Environment

Learning Objectives

1. Understand the components of the scientific and technological environment.
2. Identify the important new trend of science and technology development.
3. Understand the impact of digital technology on marketing management.
4. Recognize the importance of monitoring and forecasting technological change.

3.1   Introduction

Scientific and technological environment refers to the forces that create new technologies and facilitate new product and market opportunities. It is perhaps the most dramatic and dynamic force that continually shapes our lifestyle. For example, with the advent of the digital era, China has been moving closer to a cash-free society. Nowadays, when we go out, all we need to take along is just a smartphone, through which we could pay bills, make investments, purchase groceries, order meals, make reservations, get coupons, use navigations, take transportations, and etc.

Such convenience may thank to thousands of technology-driven companies that provide the innovative and reliable products and services. Among them Alibaba Group is one of the most important players, which was launched in 1999 in Hangzhou by Jack Ma, a former English teacher, along with a group of 17 friends. After it hit success in E-commerce and built enormous customer base, Alibaba gradually expanded to several business areas and built an ecosystem that has rooted in almost all the aspects of Chinese people's daily life, including shopping, paying, working, investing, entertaining, and etc. (see Figure 3.1).

The development path of Alibaba benefits from the devolvement of science and technology. The penetration of the Internet has stimulated the boom of E-commerce, and then the digital technologies including application of big data enabled it to provide more services around precise marketing and smart logistics. However, not all the companies

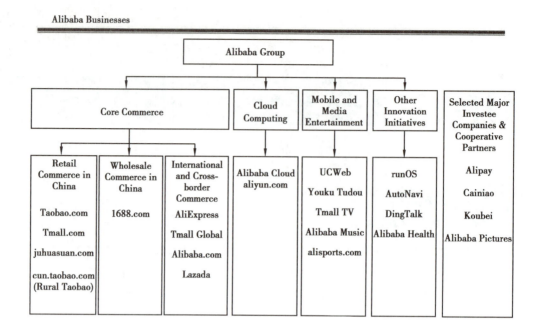

Figure 3.1　Alibaba Group's Ecosystem in 2017

were as excited as Alibaba about opportunities brought by those new technologies. For example, offline department stores used to complain that E-commerce took away their customers and made their businesses decline. Therefore, as the scientific and technological environment changes rapidly, new markets and opportunities, as well as threats may emerge, depending on the firm's capability to adapt to and take advantage of the environment.

In this chapter, we will first look at the components of scientific and technological environment that relate to marketing management, and then outline the important new trends of science and technology development, and later we will discuss their specific impacts on marketing practice in detail. Managers should keep close track of the scientific and technological environment, understand the latest trends and their possible direct or indirect impact on marketing activities. They may also seek to adopt new technologies in new product development, service innovation, and efficiency enhancement, so as to survive and thrive in the fierce market competition.

3.2　The Components of Scientific and Technological Environment

From the standpoint of companies, the scientific and technological environment consists of the external and internal environments. External environment refers to the macro, socio-technical environment, which is an important indicator to measure the general development level of science and technology. The internal environment refers to the micro, company-specific technology strength. Through comparing the internal environment with the external environment, one company could recognize its position in involved industry and predict its prospect in future. If it is in the leading place, it is highly likely to make profits, and possess a powerful social status. It also has the potential to promote the innovation of other enterprises and then facilitate progress of the entire technological environment. Likewise, improvement of external science and technology environment can also promote improvement of internal technology level of companies.

3.2.1 External Environment

The progress of science would in turn stimulate the advances of technology, which may result in inventions and innovations. Technology comprises of both machines (hard technology) and scientific thinking (soft technology) used to solve problems and promote progress. It consists of not only knowledge and methods required to carry on and improve production and distribution of goods and services, but also entrepreneurial expertise and professional knowhow. Therefore, when evaluating external scientific and technological environment, we should focus on the research capacity of a country or region that can generate new knowledge, methods, and expertise. The external environment mainly includes three aspects: scientific and technological policy, infrastructure, and talents environment.

Scientific and technological policy is the sum of various organizations, institutions, and codes of conduct formed by the national or regional governments to administer and direct science and technology undertakings. To be specific, the government can design and promulgate documents related to science and technology, which may guide the development direction of science and technology. And official organizations and institutions can supervise the implementation of those documents, provide support for scientific and technological innovation, promote the transformation of scientific achievements into market applications, and promote the development of relevant enterprises. Governments can be significant catalysts in starting the research process through grants, subsidies and tax allowances, particularly when external security or national competitive advantage is being sought. For example, in order to reduce carbon emissions for sustainable development, the Chinese central government has issued a series of policies to support new energy vehicles (NEV) since 2009. In the following decade, huge amounts of capital, research and development resources were pouring into the sector, and technical difficulties were overcome at a rapid pace. Relevant companies in the value chain of NEV also benefit from the fiscal subsidies, tax reduction and exemption, funding aid and other support. All these efforts facilitated leapfrog development of NEV market. Therefore, managers should be aware of the importance of scientific and technological policy, and strive to take advantage of it.

Science and technology infrastructure is the material basis for scientific exploration and technological innovation. The infrastructure first relates to scientific research laboratories, technical research centers and other sites used for scientific research; it also includes relevant instruments and equipment used for scientific research, such as measuring gears, observation tools, experiment facilities, computer hardware, etc. In addition, the information support platform is another important element of the infrastructure, which includes various databases and technology communication platforms, such as the professional library, website and online community, etc. All these infrastructure components provide a necessary guarantee for all scientific research activities.

The talents environment refers to the macro factors that influence the value creation of scientific and technological human capital. On the one hand, talents environment involves policies and social atmosphere that stimulate working motivation and passion of scientific and technological talents. For example, big cities (e.g. Beijing, Shanghai, Shenzhen) tend to have an overwhelming advantage in attracting top university graduates, not only because there are more jobs available, but also because they often have better talent policies such as housing subsidies and settlement funds. On the other hand, talents environment also involves the number and quality of colleges, universities, higher education institutions, and other types of training schools or institutions in one region. Those institutions are usually the information communication platform and can influence the innovation efficiency of scientific and technological innovation talents. If the talents environment of a country or region is not good enough, it may be difficult to meet many business needs there, such as localization research, or the complex after-sale service.

3.2.2   Internal Environment

The internal scientific and technological environment of a company could be simply equivalent to its technology strength. This relates to the knowledge advantage, research achievement, resource availability, and application ability of the technology team. High level of strength could be the source of competitiveness for the firm in many aspects, such as product quality, operation efficiency, and cost control. From a dynamic perspective, the internal scientific and technological environment also relates to the firm's research and development system. Such system involves the organizational structure, personnel composition, and management system of research and development work. If the system is appropriate for encouraging innovation and improvement, the firm's technology strength will be pushed further, and vice versa.

3.3　Important New Trend of Science and Technology Development

Business is the main conduit by which science and technology influence society. Most development of science and technology is incremental and progressive in nature, but breakthroughs can and do bring sudden and dramatic change. Thus firms need to monitor their scientific and technological environment more closely than others. While it is not possible to present a comprehensive list of technological developments impinging on business, several are indicative of the kinds of advancements that should be watched carefully. Over the past few decades, the development of ICT (information and communication technology) and computer science have profoundly changed the world, and continue to represent the most important forces that will transform business and organizations. In the following, we will discuss the important new trend of those forces.

3.3.1　Artificial Intelligence (AI) and Machine Learning

Artificial intelligence (AI) is a wide-ranging branch of computer science concerned with building smart machines with human attributes—speaking, reading, seeing and even recognizing emotion—completing tasks while also "learning" from repeated interactions. Using algorithms that adapt to location, speech or user-history machines can perform tasks that are dangerous or tedious, more accurately or much faster than humans, who have consciousness and emotions. AI is probably the most important and ground-breaking trend in technology today, and the trend shows no signs of slowing down. It is already known for its superiority in image and speech recognition, navigation apps, ride-sharing apps and so many more. Other than that AI will be used further to analyze interactions to determine underlying connections and insights, to help predict demand for services like hospitals, enabling authorities to make better decisions about resource utilization, and to detect the changing patterns of customer behavior by analyzing data in near real-time, driving revenues and enhancing personalized experiences. Those applications are often referred to as Narrow AI or Weak AI, which operates within a limited context and is a simulation of human intelligence, such as the smartphone personal assistants (e. g. Apple iPhone's Siri).

Much of Narrow AI is powered by breakthroughs in machine learning and deep learning. Simply put, machine learning feeds computer data and uses statistical techniques to help it "learn" how to get progressively better at a task, without having been specifically programmed for that task, eliminating the need for millions of lines of written code. Deep learning is a type of machine learning that runs inputs through a biologically-inspired neural network architecture. The neural networks contain a number of hidden layers through which data is processed, allowing the machine to go "deep" in its learning, making connections and weighting input for the best results.

To sum up, AI is interdisciplinary science with multiple approaches, but advancements in machine learning and deep learning are creating a paradigm shift in virtually every sector of the tech industry. The advent of smart homes, smart cities, and the Internet of Things means that AI will be integrated more and more into our everyday lives. Perhaps in the near future, the Artificial General Intelligence or so-called Strong AI can be developed. Strong AI is a machine with general intelligence and, much like a human being, it can apply that intelligence to solve any problem. In that case, we may witness stuff of science fiction being made into reality.

3.3.2 Cloud and Edge Computing

Cloud computing is the on-demand availability of computer system resources based on Internet, especially data storage (cloud storage) and computing power, without direct active management by the user. This Internet-based technology enables firms to utilize highly sophisticated computer applications without having to have their own hardware, software, office computing space and staff. Instead, by being part of the network, or "cloud," the user can access the computing capabilities needed on demand from a third-party provider via the Internet. Famous providers include Alibaba, Tencent, Huawei and Baidu, which may take 80 percent of the domestic market share in total. The worldwide major providers are Amazon Web Service (AWS), Microsoft Azure, and Google CloudPlatform.

Cloud computing brought many advantages in terms of its inherent cost advantages, the powerful applications provided, and the great flexibility it provides to users. First, as mentioned earlier, the user of cloud computing services can save substantial cost of investment in the information technology needed to support sophisticated applications, including facilities and staff. By participating in the cloud, the client user pays only for the computing services actually used, similar to paying utility bills. Or the user can purchase a fixed charge per time period, similar to the monthly subscription fee. Second, given that the third-party provider offers its services to numerous other clients, the economies of scale and scope provided by such multi-tenancy enables the cloud computing provider to develop powerful applications that would otherwise be feasible only for the largest customers to provide on their own. Therefore, this technology has revolutionized the information technology industry by making the need for individual firms to invest heavily in IT technology unnecessary.

While cloud computing has become mainstream, more and more businesses are migrating to a cloud solution. But the latency caused by cloud computing and getting data to a datacenter for processing may cause problems in some situations. **Edge computing** is designed to help solve some of those problems as a way to bypass such latency, where data is processed on smart devices (like phones). Thus edge computing can be used to process time-sensitive data in remote locations with limited or no connectivity to a centralized location. In those situations, edge computing can act like mini datacenters, and take cloud computing to the next level.

3.3.3 Virtual Reality (VR) and Augmented Reality(AR)

Virtual reality (VR) is an exciting technology that immerses the user in an environment, where you enter a computer-generated world using headsets that blend out the real world. This technology makes it possible for us to experience things such as entertainment and learning in a whole new way. VR has primarily been used in the entertainment industry, with video games and other platforms hopping on the bandwagon thus far. In the future, VR could be used more in training and education, especially when it comes to important work that needs to be done with a pair of hands; practicing something with the use of VR is an excellent way to receive hands-on training without any risk or consequences if mistakes are made. For example, the U.S. Navy used VirtualShip, a simulation software to train ship captains.

In contrast, **Augmented Reality (AR)** is an interactive experience and enhances users' environment by overlaying digital objects onto the real world via smartphone screens or displays. It allows information such as images or texts to be superimposed in a real-world environment. Mobile AR-enabled devices and mobile AR apps are introduced to new users daily as novel ways of shopping and solutions for enterprises that include mixed reality settings to their traditional training methods. AR and VR have enormous potential in training, entertainment, education, marketing, and even rehabilitation after an injury. Either could be used to train doctors to do surgery, offer museum goers deeper experience, enhance theme parks, or even enhance marketing. This trend highlights the move towards creating more immersive digital experiences.

3.3.4 Blockchain

Blockchain could be viewed as a super-secure method of storing, authenticating, and protecting data through distributed ledgers. A blockchain, originally block chain, is a growing list of records, called blocks, that are linked using cryptography. By design, a blockchain is resistant to modification of its data. This is because once recorded, data in any given block cannot be altered retroactively without alteration of all subsequent blocks. In the simplest term, blockchain can be described as data you can only add to, not take away from or change. Hence the term "chain" is because you're making a chain of data. Not being able to change the previous blocks is what makes it so secure. In addition, blockchains are consensus-driven, so no one entity can take control of the data. With blockchain, you don't need a trusted third-party to oversee or validate transactions. Although most people think of blockchain technology in relation to cryptocurrencies such as Bitcoin, this technology actually could revolutionize many aspects of business—particularly when it comes to facilitating trusted transactions. For example, blockchain could be used in detecting counterfeits by associating unique identifiers to products, documents and shipments, and storing records associated with transactions that cannot be forged or altered.

3.3.5　Internet of Things（IoT）

Internet of Things（IoT）refers to the ever-growing number of "smart" devices and objects that are connected to the Internet. Such devices are constantly gathering and transmitting data, further fueling the growth in Big Data and AI, which can be used to improve the product or service. The network that connects everything is the future, but the application of small scale IoT has already benefited our daily life. For example, IoT enabled devices, home appliances, cars and much more to be connected to and exchange data over the Internet. We can lock our doors remotely if we forget to when we leave for work and preheat our rooms on our way home from work. Apart from consumer applications, the IoT can also enable better safety, efficiency and decision making for businesses as data is collected and analyzed. For example, the IoT can connect various manufacturing devices equipped with sensing, identification, processing, communication, actuation, and networking capabilities. So the manufacturing process may be optimized, the response to product demands may be expedited, and the maintenance of facilities can be more accurately predicted. In addition, the IoT technology will have extensive set of applications in medical and health care, transportation, agriculture, etc., and may offer benefits we haven't even imagined yet.

3.3.6　5G

5G is the fifth generation technology standard in telecommunications for broadband cellular networks, which cellular phone companies began deploying worldwide in 2019. Where 3G and 4G technologies have enabled us to browse the Internet, use data driven services, increase bandwidth for streaming on QQ Music or Youku and so much more, 5G services are expected to revolutionize our lives by enabling services that rely on advanced technologies like AR and VR, alongside cloud based gaming services like Google Stadia and much more. Up to 100 times faster than 4G, 5G enables the super-fast and stable Internet access anywhere, and offers drastically reduced latency that makes it possible to share data extremely quickly, erase processing delays and ensure factory systems can react in real time. The increased bandwidth will enable machines, robots, and autonomous vehicles to collect and transfer more data than ever, leading to advances in the area of the Internet of Things (IoT) and smart machinery. Therefore, it is expected to be used in factories, HD cameras that help improve safety and traffic management, smart grid control and smart retail too.

3.3.7　Robotic Process Automation (RPA)

Robotic process automation (RPA) is a form of business process automation technology based on metaphorical software robots (bots) or on AI/digital workers. Robots in manufacturing go back to the 1960s. Now it's the scale and breadth of the transformation that automated systems make possible, as a result of other advances in machine learning and connectivity, for example, that puts automation firmly at the forefront of technology trends. From convenient devices at home to industrial applications on a massive scale, automation will be a key focus of technological change, with potentially far-reaching economic and social consequences. RPA software can be used for automating repetitive tasks such as interpreting applications, processing transactions, dealing with data, handling business data, and even replying to emails, all of which used to be done by some low-level employees and even higher-ranking officials. So, this technology is going to threaten a lot of jobs, but it's also creating new jobs while altering existing jobs. Currently, professional services such as legal and finance industry are being disrupted by automation. According to McKinsey, less than 5 percent of occupations can be totally automated, but about 60 percent can be partially automated. In the future, core technical skills together with management and people skills are more important than ever.

3.3.8　Cybersecurity Mesh

Cybersecurity mesh is a distributed architectural approach to scalable, flexible and reliable cybersecurity control. It might not seem like an emerging technology, given that cybersecurity has been around for a while, but it is evolving just as other technologies are, partly because threats are constantly new. Identifying common IT security weaknesses and developing cybersecurity maturity is central to building truly resilient digital organizations. Many assets now exist outside of the traditional security perimeter. Cybersecurity mesh essentially allows for the security perimeter to be defined around the identity of a person or thing. It enables a more modular, responsive security approach by centralizing policy orchestration and distributing policy enforcement. As perimeter protection becomes less meaningful, the security approach of a "walled city" must evolve to current needs.

3.4　The Impact of Digital Technology on Marketing Management

As mentioned in the previous section, much of the huge transformation that took place over the past few decades was related to ICT (information and communication technology) and computer science. It was often described as the **digital revolution** (also known as the Third Industrial Revolution), which is the shift from mechanical and analogue electronic technology to digital electronics. Such revolution began in the latter half of the 20th century, with the adoption and proliferation of digital computers and digital record-keeping, and continues to the present day. Digital technologies and devices such as smartphones, smart products, the Internet of Things (IoT), AI and deep learning have transformed marketing from traditional to digital era. They have made campaigns more personalized and immersive for people and created ecosystems that are more integrated and targeted for marketers. And new technology in marketing has permeated the infrastructure and systems on which companies are built, delivering value to procurement and adding to the bottom line. Therefore, digital technologies have fundamental impacts on marketing management. They may not only change the way of marketing research and customer management, but also revolutionize almost every aspect of the marketing mix.

▶ 3.4.1　On Marketing Research and Customer Management

Digital technologies today allow companies to understand their customers better and even deal with customers on an individual basis. On the one hand, many traditional marketing research could be conducted online with more convenience. On the other hand, there are various techniques emerged to analyze and gain insights from the richer veins of unsolicited, unstructured, spontaneous customer information already coursing around the Internet. The customer relationship can also be precisely managed through customer information that is continually collected based on database technology and customer relationship management programs. The marketing research and customer relationship management in the digital era will be discussed in more detail in Chapter 6 (International

Marketing Research).

▶ 3.4.2　On Products and Services

The concept of product is undergoing a rapid transformation with the involvement of digital technologies. First, the augmentation of the core product with services is becoming increasingly digital.In the early stage, the digitization of the core product with augmented service was simply shedding the physical form to become entirely digital—books became e-books, music/video distribution changed from CD/DVD to streaming, video games migrated online, and so on. Nowadays, the core value of the product is increased with value derived from digital enhancements (e.g. automobiles with GPS systems, sensor-based self-driving technologies).

In addition, online and mobile technologies have enabled products/services themselves to morph into digital services, especially in the domain of information products such as software, and content such as music, video and text. Therefore, companies now have opportunities to create product lines of various digital and traditional non-digital formats with diversified pricing tactics, which allow new models such as "freemium". For example, the basic version can be offered for free while the enhanced version is offered for a fee (e.g. digital storage and online content). In other words, companies can customize and personalize customer offerings by varying not only the core product/service but also the augmented digital services.

Third, new products and services are possible because of digital technology. Those help to increase revenues and profits of companies. At different times in history, technologies have created new businesses like automobiles, railways, telephones, computers, etc. Currently we are seeing new products and services being developed by digital technologies like mobile connectivity, and also nanotechnology, genetic engineering, etc. For example, the networking of products using digital technologies (e.g. big data and machine learning) is spawning a sharing economy wherein dormant value of owned-products (e.g. housing and automobiles) is released through digital networking for rental options (e.g. Airbnb and Uber).

Finally, another significant impact of the digital technologies on product strategy is the facilitation of **mass customization**, which is the use of flexible computer-aided manufacturing systems to produce custom output. Such systems combine the low unit costs of mass production processes with the flexibility of individual customization. Manufacturers can design the "choice board" (or a menu of choices) of various features and options for configuring specified products and services, and the digital interface makes it easy for customers to choose options and configure the product according to their specifications. For example, the Chinese suit brand RED COLLAR (红领) is a pioneer in offering tailored suits at affordable prices, rather than offering traditional standard-size products.

3.4.3 On Pricing

Digital technologies also have significant impacts on firms' pricing strategy, especially making the pricing process become more dynamic and flexible. The primary reason is that the customers are doing more price comparisons due to lower search costs.With the rapid development of electronic commerce, customers can easily compare the price of the same product on different sites with offline stores, and even some websites provide price tracking services. Thus the price becomes almost transparent and forces firms to adopt a more dynamic and flexible pricing strategy. For example, a few new pricing strategies emerged on the Internet, including the auction model (e.g. eBay), demand aggregation (i.e. group purchase), dynamic posted prices, and others. As for service products such as telephone, mobile data, and car rental, contracts with three-part pricing (base fee, free usage allowance, and perunit charge for usage exceeding the free allowance) have become more common.

Another reason is that changes in the shopping environment are rapid, and retailers can respond to customers' searches more quickly. Especially in the online environment, the retailers can adjust the price quickly according to time and occasions. Retailers are increasingly relying on digital technologies (e.g. Web analytics, big data) to diversify prices for different customers. Additionally, the increasing use of auctions to acquire customers(through search engines, re-targeting, etc.) brings in more selective customers to the retailers' site.

In a general sense, digital technology makes the price reduction possible in the long run. On the one hand, advances in information technology have made it possible to plan truly global supply chains, in which manufacturing and warehousing are distributed throughout the world depending on where these activities can be performed best. On the other hand, advanced technologies like smart manufacturing enable both automation and miniaturization,which bring down product costs. Companies will be able to make better products at lower cost, and will be able to distribute them economically when supply chains become global. As a result, products and services once considered exclusive are now available to mass markets all over the world, such as Tata Nano's $2,000 car in India.

3.4.4 On Marketing Channel

Digital technologies have broadened the depth and breadth of marketing channels, no matter in the geographical or temporal sense. The emergence of E-commerce makes online retailing borderless and timeless. Currently, people can make transactions of products or services with their counterparts from almost any country at any time. Different types of E-commerce include B2B, B2C, C2C, C2B models, etc. Online shopping is increasingly taking larger part of the total retail economy and important role in our daily life. With the advent of mobile Internet, mobile devices provide a new platform for existing digital marketing channels such as email, display advertising (in mobile apps), search, etc.Therefore, when firms configure their distribution channel, they have multiple choices and can combine online channels with offline channels. This would increase their touchpoints with customers and have the potential to better serve customers.

Digital technologies also greatly enhance distribution efficiency and effectiveness, resulting in substantial benefit to all channel members as well as final customers. **Electronic data interchange (EDI)** is one of the important tools, which refers to the linking together of channel member information systems to provide real-time responses to communication between channel members. For example, a retailer's computerized inventory management system is connected to and monitored by the supplier's (manufacturer's or wholesaler's) computers. When the retailer's inventory level of supplier's products falls below the preset minimum points, reorder can then take place automatically.The more sophisticated EDI systems can also forecast demand based on sales history and initiate the order in advance. Another important technology is **radio frequency identification (RFID),** which is a tag attached to a product and enables it to be identified and tracked using radio waves. This technology dramatically enhances the effectiveness and efficiency of inventory control and supply chain, and makes the self-checkout in retail stores become realistic.

With the promotion of the degree of channel digitalization, more and more organizations have realized the opportunities and advantages of integrating multiple channels by adopting an **omnichannel** approach. Omnichannel means seamless and effortless, high-quality customer experiences that occur within and between contact channels. For example, the retailer's websites, email offers, social media messaging and physical stores all show the same messages, offers, and products. Consumers can receive the same quality products or services through in-store, websites, and mobile phones. The order can either be delivered to the address directly, collected at the store, or collected from a retail partner. To ensure such strategies are implemented efficiently, brand owners and retailing firms need to use powerful platform software to centrally manage product information, listings, inventory and orders from vendors, and to integrate different channels.

▶ 3.4.5　On Promotion and Communication

Marketers used to rely on the mass media such as television, radio, newspapers, magazines, and outdoor advertising to deliver commercial messages to large audiences. The increasing penetration of electronic devices such as laptops, tablets, and smartphones is changing the way customers access information and use media. The Internet and mobile media have become the heart of marketing as traditional channels such as broadcast television and cable television become obsolete, and are no longer used by affluent, ambitious, and classes with large purchasing power. Nowadays, smartphone usage has also gained popularity among elders, thus online promotion and communication turn to be extremely important.

First, social media marketing has become necessary. It involves using peer recommendations, building brand personality, and addressing the market as a heterogeneous group of individuals. Marketers usually encourage customers to create their own content and buzz around a product on communication platforms like Weibo, Douyin, Youku or other types of media. In other words, programs usually center on efforts to create content that attracts attention and encourages audiences to share it with their social networks. As people can be hugely influenced by their peers, this way of communication is driven by word-of-mouth, and generates results in earned media rather than paid media.

Also with the increase in smart phone usage, QR (quick response) codes have become much more prevalent in marketing pieces both on and offline. Acting as a visual hyper-link to a page, QR codes make it easy for someone to reach a mobile optimized offer page. As such, they represent a very powerful tool for initiating consumer engagement at a time when the marketing piece is likely to trigger its most emotional response. Their potential for tracking offline sources and delivering the types of analytics previously reserved for online tracking is another powerful reason why marketers are flocking to QR codes in droves.

More importantly, the online promotion and communication not only reaches target consumers more efficiently, but also more effectively. Unlike mass media advertising that sends messages without targeting and has difficulties in assessing performance, the online promotion and communication can be more easily tracked and evaluated. The problems concerning how many consumers received the message, to what extent they got interested, whether information leads to purchase, and so much more could be accurately answered by the digital technologies.

3.5　Forecasting Scientific and Technological Environment

As discussed above, we live in a dynamic world with science and technology evolving quickly. Technological changes, though continual, do not occur evenly or predictably over time. If a rival succeeds in achieving a technological advantage, it is a much more significant competitive edge due to the time, difficulty and resource commitments required to counter it. Therefore, successful managements have always kept a cautious eye on the pace of change in both their own and adjacent industries. Other than such a defensive outlook on the danger of being overtaken by substitute technology, mangers also need to take a proactive intention to achieve technological advantage, which may create new market and new opportunities. A forecast in the scientific and technological environment should be the foundation block of long-term plans, based on effective collaboration between the technologists, designers and marketers. This is necessary to achieve the essential balance between creating and satisfying the needs of the customer.

We may forecast the technological progress in three possible ways. The first one is simple, which only focuses on the current focal technology by identifying and then extrapolating the existing trends. The second way is morphological, which means exploring technological opportunities by systematically defining the basic features of current technology, identifying the known alternatives to each and then looking for feasible alternative combinations. For example, a car can have alternative fuels: petrol, diesel, battery, gas, solar and hydrogen fuel cell. It can have alternative body materials: steel, plastic, aluminum and fiberglass. It can also have alternative braking systems: friction disc, air, cable, and so on. These three components can then be combined in different formulas to produce alternative concept cars (hybrids are also possible, e. g. petrol/battery). This method can be used for brainstorming feasible product alternatives and renewing perspective on customary technologies. The third way involves scenarios, which provide broader views of the future and insight into more diverse developments than the second way. Back to the car example, beyond the road traffic scenario, alternative personal transportation systems such as microlight aircraft systems may emerge in the future. Alternatively, developments in interactive video, teleworking and virtual reality might make many such journeys unnecessary in the future.

Based on the technological forecast, a firm may need to make an extra effort to obtain potential benefits. First, it needs to identify the potential impacts not only for the industry itself but also for channel intermediaries and end-users. Then it can screen feasible technologies to remove improbable options due to cost and environmental safety for instance. Next is to determine a timescale for the remaining technologies and accordingly set against marketing forecasts of what the demand will be. Timing is also critical for the innovative product. If it only has the requisite technical building blocks in place, lacking receptive users with the need, income and strength of preference to demand it in profitable volumes, it will end up with market failure. Finally, unanticipated consequences should also be considered, such as the impacts on current methods as well as complementary effects. After conducting those processes, the firm may realize the advantage of correct technological forecast and early movement.

Key Terms

scientific and technological environment 科技环境	The forces that create new technologies and facilitate new product and market opportunities. 创造新技术、促进新产品和市场机会的环境力量。
scientific and technological policy 科技政策	The sum of various organizations, institutions, and codes of conduct formed by the national or regional government to administer and direct science and technology undertakings. 国家或地区政府为管理和指导科学技术事业而形成的各种组织、事业单位和行为规范的总和。
science and technology infrastructure 科技基础设施	The material basis for scientific exploration and technological innovation. 进行科学探索和技术创新的物质基础。
talents environment 人才环境	The macro factors that influence the value creation of scientific and technological human capital. 影响科技人力资本价值创造的外部环境因素。
artificial intelligence (AI) 人工智能	A wide-ranging branch of computer science concerned with building smart machines with human attributes—speaking, reading, seeing and even recognizing emotion—completing tasks while also "learning" from repeated interactions. 计算机科学的一个广泛分支,涉及构建具有人类属性的智能机器——如说、读、看甚至识别情感,并在完成任务的同时从重复的交互中"学习"。
cloud computing 云计算	The on-demand availability of computer system resources based on Internet, especially data storage (cloud storage) and computing power, without direct active management by the user. 无须用户直接主动管理,基于互联网的按需可用的计算机系统资源,尤其是数据存储(云存储)和计算能力。
virtual reality (VR) 虚拟现实	A technology that immerses the user in an environment, where you enter a computer-generated world using headsets that blend out the real world. 一项让用户通过头戴设备进入计算机生成的世界,并与现实世界融为一体的技术。

Continued

augmented reality（AR） 增强现实	An interactive experience and enhances users' environment by overlaying digital objects onto the real world via smartphone screens or displays. 一种通过智能手机屏幕或显示器将数字对象叠加到现实世界，从而增强用户的环境交互体验的技术。
blockchain 区块链	A super-secure method of storing, authenticating, and protecting data through distributed ledgers. 一种可以通过分布式账本存储、验证和保护数据的超级安全的方法。
internet of Things（IoT） 物联网	The Internet that connects the ever-growing number of "smart" devices and objects. 将越来越多的"智能"设备和物体连接起来的互联网。
5G 第五代移动通信系统	The fifth generation technology standard in telecommunications for broadband cellular networks. 电信宽带蜂窝网络的第五代技术标准。
robotic process automation（RPA） 机器人流程自动化	A form of business process automation technology based on metaphorical software robots（bots）or on AI/digital workers. 一种基于类似软件机器人（bots）或人工智能/数字工人的业务流程自动化技术。
cyber security mesh 网络安全网格	A distributed architectural approach to scalable, flexible and reliable cyber security control. 一种进行可扩展、灵活和可靠的网络安全控制的分布式架构方法。
digital revolution（the third industrial revolution） 数字革命	The shift from mechanical and analogue electronic technology to digital electronics. 从机械和模拟电子技术到数字电子技术的转变。
mass customization 大规模定制	The use of flexible computer-aided manufacturing systems to produce custom output. 使用灵活的计算机辅助制造系统来生产定制的产品。
electronic data interchange（EDI） 电子数据交换	The linking together of channel member information systems to provide real-time responses to communication between channel members. 将渠道成员信息系统联接在一起，保障成员之间的实时沟通响应的技术。
radio frequency identification（RFID） 射频识别	A tag attached to a product and enables it to be identified and tracked using radio waves. 附在产品上的标签，可以通过无线电波对其进行识别和跟踪。
omnichannel 全渠道	Seamless and effortless, high-quality customer experiences that occur within and between contact channels. 在相联系的渠道内部和渠道之间无缝、轻松、高质量的客户体验。

Review & Critical Thinking Questions

1. What are the components of the scientific and technological environment? How could they affect one another?
2. What are the differences between Narrow and Strong Artificial intelligence (AI)?
3. What is the use of cloud computing? How can it help firms? What is edge computing?
4. What are the differences between Virtual Reality (VR) and Augmented Reality (AR)?
5. What are the main features of Blockchain? How could it be applied in the business sector?
6. How could Internet of Things (IoT) affect our daily life? How could this technology be applied in various industries?
7. What is the impact of digital technology on products and services?
8. What is the impact of digital technology on pricing?
9. What is the impact of digital technology on marketing channel?
10. What is the impact of digital technology on promotion and communication?
11. How could we forecast the technology progress?

Discussion Questions

1. Artificial intelligence (AI) has brought many benefits to our lives and AI technology is still evolving. Is the development of AI always good for human beings?
2. Virtual Reality (VR) and Augmented Reality (AR) have primarily been used in the entertainment industry. How could they be applied in higher education to improve the teaching effectiveness?
3. What is the relationship between AI, Internet of Things (IoT) and 5G?
4. What are the threats brought by Robotic Process Automation (RPA) to your major? How could you defend yourself from such threats?
5. Are there any other impacts of digital technology on marketing management in addition to those mentioned in this chapter?

Case Study

YeeCall is a super call app that can be used for audio and video calls in areas with poor network environment such as 2G, which would be one of its technological advantages in the field of communication. This app was developed in 2015 by Lei Zhang, a former Baidu senior manager, and his co-worker Jiajun Xu. When considering the target market, Lei Zhang knew that YeeCall would not be able to rival WeChat from the front, so he casted his eyes on the overseas market. At that time, WhatsApp had not released point-to-point audio call. A temporary time window emerged in the field of communication software, which was very suitable for a niche battle.

The territory of Internet products in the global market can be divided into the following segments: The first segment, which includes the US and Europe, is called by Lei Zhang as the largest single market with strict rules and a high threshold. The second includes the Japanese and Korean markets, which are closed market. Those markets are inherently hostile toward foreign goods, and thus no Internet infrastructure or social media products can penetrate. The third type includes several relatively large regional markets, like Southeast Asia, the Middle East, North Africa, and South America. The last segment type includes the fastest growing single markets such as India. The target markets of YeeCall are the fourth type.

Finally, YeeCall chose to start with "cross-border communication". For those people staying abroad, one of their strong demands was to communicate with their families. The user data also proved this point. The earliest users of YeeCall were overseas students and workers and the product became more popular among these students due to its word of mouth reputation.

In the selection of markets, YeeCall first selected the markets where the rivals were weak like the Middle East and North Africa but avoided mature markets, such as Europe, America, Japan, and Korea. Lei Zhang and his team conducted market research and found that 60% of the population of these countries and regions were migrant workers, reaching around 20 million. They had a strong demand for communication and cross-border video calls with their families back home. At that time, there was no product dedicated to cross-border communication worldwide. The cost was higher, and quality was not good if they used the conventional international circuits. For example, Skype can be used smoothly in countries with high network coverage and good network environment, but it was difficult to use Skype in the Middle East, North Africa, and India, where only 2G networks were available. After surveying the urgent demand of the users, Lei Zhang tried to improve the technology of YeeCall. After identifying the key cue, the YeeCall team concentrated on connectivity, the core of online products, and completed the adaptation of the main functions.

During this period, YeeCall had been strongly combating with the mainstream instant messaging competitors. The 2G audio call market window lasted only a year, and competitors such as WhatsApp quickly conquered the technology for high-quality 2G telecommunication. However, due to the first-mover advantage and barriers to entry,

YeeCall already has around 40 million users worldwide.Since the fourth quarter of 2016, Lei Zhang has attempted to make earnings from advertising. YeeCall has also explored more profit models，such as props and facial expressions.

Questions

1. How does the scientific and technological environment affect YeeCall's marketing strategy?
2. Do you think YeeCall can maintain its market advantage? Why? What other content operations and social functions may it pursue to gain more profits and why?

中文概述

科技环境是指创造新技术、促成新产品和市场机会的环境力量。它可能是不断塑造我们的生活方式的最具戏剧性和活力的力量。随着科技环境的迅速变化,新市场、新机会和新威胁都可能会出现,这取决于企业适应和利用环境的能力。

从企业的角度来看,科技环境包括外部环境和内部环境。外部环境是指宏观的社会技术环境,是衡量科学技术总体发展水平的重要指标。内部环境是指微观的、公司特有的技术实力。通过内外部环境的对比,可以看出公司在所属行业中的地位,并预测公司未来的发展前景。在评价外部科技环境时,我们应该关注一个国家或地区能够产生新知识、新方法和新技能的研究能力。外部环境主要包括三个方面:科技政策、基础设施和人才环境。**科技政策**是国家或地区政府为管理和指导科技事业而形成的各种组织、事业单位和行为规范的总和。**科技基础设施**是进行科学探索和技术创新的物质基础。**人才环境**是指影响科技人力资本价值创造的外部环境因素。一个公司的内部科技环境可以简单地等同于它的技术实力。动态来看,企业内部的科技环境也与企业的研发体系有关,涉及研发工作的组织结构、人员构成和管理制度。

在过去的几十年里,信息通信技术(ICT)以及计算机科学的发展深刻地改变了世界,并将继续代表改变商业和组织的最重要力量。在最新的发展趋势中,有一些是尤为值得注意的。**人工智能**(AI)是计算机科学的一个广泛分支,涉及构建具有人类属性的智能机器——如说、读、看,甚至识别情感,并在完成任务的同时从重复的交互中"学习"。**云计算**是无须用户直接主动管理,基于互联网的按需可用的计算机系统资源,尤其是数据存储(云存储)和计算能力。**虚拟现实**(VR)是一项让用户通过头戴设备进入计算机生成的世界,并与现实世界融为一体的技术。**增强现实**(AR)是一种通过智能手机屏幕或显示器将数字对象叠加到现实世界,从而增强用户的环境交互体验的技术。**区块链**可以被视为一种可以通过分布式账本存储、验证和保护数据的超级安全的方法。这种技术可能会彻底改变商业的许多方面,尤其是在促成可信交易方面。**物联网**(IoT)指将越来越多的"智能"设备和物体连接起来的互联网,这些设备不断地收集和传输数据,进一步推动了大数据和人工智能的发展,并用来改进产品或服务。**5G**是电信宽带蜂窝网络的第五代技术标准,可在任何地方接入超级快速和稳定的互联网。**机器人流程自动化**(RPA)是一种基于类似软件机器人(bots)或人工智能/数字工人的业务流程自动化技术,可用于自动完成重复性任务,如解析应用程序。**网络安全网格**是一种进行可扩展、灵活和可靠的网络安全控制的分布式架构方法。

由信息通信技术(ICT)和计算机科学所带来的巨大变革也经常被描述为**数字革命(或第三次工业革命)**,指的是从机械和模拟电子技术到数字电子技术的转变。数字技术对营销管理有着根本性的影响,不仅改变了市场调查和客户管理的方式,还变革了营销组合的几乎每一个方面。

在产品和服务方面:核心产品与服务的扩展正变得越来越数字化;在线和移动技术使产品/服务本身转变为数字服务,特别是在软件等信息产品领域,以及音乐、视频和文本等内容领域;数字技术使新产品和新服务成为可能,还带来了**大规模定制**,即使用灵活的计算机辅助制造系统来生产定制的产品。这种系统兼顾了大规模生产过程的低单位成本和个人定制的灵活性要求。

在定价方面:数字技术使得定价过程变得更加动态与灵活,同时也使得定价在长期来看处于下降趋势。

在渠道方面:数字技术从地理以及时间意义上拓宽了营销渠道的深度和广度;数字技术也大大提高了分销的效率和有效性,为所有渠道成员和最终客户带来了实实在在的利益。**电子数据交换**(EDI)是其中的重要工具,指的是将渠道成员信息系统连接在一起,保障成员之间的实时沟通响应。另一项重要的技术是**射频识别**(RFID),它是一种附在产品上的标签,可以通过无线电波对产品进行识别和跟踪。该技术极大地提高了库存控制和供应链的有效性和效率,使零售商店的自助结账成为现实。随着渠道数字化程度的提升,越来越多的组织意识到采用**全渠道**方式整合多渠道的机遇和优势。全渠道指的是在相联系的渠道内部和之间无缝、轻松、高质量的客户体验。

在促销与沟通方面:互联网和移动媒体已成为营销的核心,尤其是社交媒体营销已是必然。此外,随着智能手机使用量的增加,QR(二维码)在线上和线下的营销产品中变得越来越普遍。更重要的是,网络推广和传播不仅更高效地触达目标消费者,而且更容易被跟踪和评估绩效。

技术变化虽然持续不断,但在一段时间内并不均匀或可预测地发生。如果一个竞争对手成功地获得了技术优势,由于需要时间、难度和资源来对抗它,这是一个更重要的竞争优势。因此,成功的管理者总是小心翼翼地关注所属及相关行业的变化情况。除了害怕被替代技术超越而进行的防御性展望之外,管理者还需要积极主动寻求技术优势,从而创造新的市场和新的机会。

UNIT 4 — The Cultural and Demographic Environment

Learning Objectives

1. Understand the meaning of culture and cultural environment.
2. Describe elements of culture and provide relative examples.
3. Describe characteristics of culture and provide examples.
4. Understand how cultural environment affects global marketing strategies.
5. Understand the meaning of demographic environment and its main factors.
6. Discuss global demographic trends.

4.1 The Definition of Culture and Cultural Environment

Home Depot is the world's largest home improvement retailer with nearly 400,000 orange associates and more than 2,200 stores in the U.S., Canada, and Mexico. It was set up to serve the DIY (Do-It-Yourself) community such as homeowners and professional customers. In 2006, Home Depot bought Chinese home improvement company Home Way and its twelve stores in the country. With its booming economy and strong real estate market, China seemed to be the perfect market for the America's home improvement giant. But after six-years of struggling, by 2012, Home Depot had to leave Chinese market, closing the last seven of its twelve original stores, and dismissing 850 employees. Data from Euromonitor shows that China accounted for only about 0.3% of Home Depot's annual net sales. Analysts say the key reason for the giant's failure was that it was not aware of the massive cultural differences between American and Chinese consumer attitudes toward home improvement during that period.

However, contrary to Home Depot's failure, its major competitor IKEA, having its own DIY model in China has been growing successfully. There are many articles analyzing IKEA's success in China, however the two distinct differences of operations between the two companies in Chinese market are:

Firstly, apart from providing furniture, IKEA also offers the option of assembling furniture for customers in China. This means Chinese consumers may either do it themselves, or they may ask IKEA staff to assemble it for them with an extra service fee, which is reasonable and greatly satisfies the needs of many Chinese consumers.

Secondly, IKEA carefully decorates showrooms in western style, to teach consumers "how to decorate their homes, and thereby experience western culture." The stores of Horne Depot, on the other hand, are like big, boxy warehouses, which are seen as "boring" to Chinese customers.

From the two different outcomes of the two international giants within Chinese market, we can see and feel the profound cultural influences over any multinational corporation. In fact, it is significant for marketers/analysts to pay close attention to the cultural differences between their native culture and the culture of the target markets, before launching any marketing strategies.

4.1.1　The Definition of Culture

Culture is the sum of the values, rituals, symbols, beliefs and thought processes that are learned and shared by a group of people, then transmitted from generation to generation.

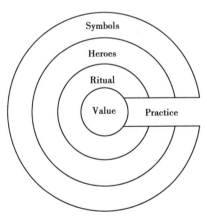

Figure 4.1　Levels of Culture

As to the manifestation of culture, it permeates all aspects of our lives, yet, like an onion with layers, which can generally be divided into four layers: symbols, heroes, rituals and at its core, values (see Figure 4.1)

1. **Symbols:** refer to languages, gestures, pictures or objects that carry a specific meaning which are only recognized and understood by people who live in that culture. For instance, the cross is a typical religious symbol in Christianity, while the lotus flower has been used as a symbol in many teachings of Buddhism. America, for example, takes the bald eagle as its national bird, while the panda is considered to be a well-known symbol of

China. It is worth noting that symbols can carry specific meanings in one culture yet have completely different meanings in another. For example, the gesture "thumb up" means "All things are great!" in America, but it would be very rude and insulting to show that gesture in Iran, since it is equivalent to holding a middle finger up. Therefore, it is necessary to understand specific symbols in different cultures to avoid misunderstandings related to multicultural co-operations.

2. **Heroes:** are persons that represent characteristics highly appreciated within a culture; they may be living, dead, real or fictional, some are even comic strip characters. They serve as role models for many members of a culture. Perhaps the most popular hero in America would be "Captain America", although he is only a fictional superhero in American comic books and Hollywood films, many Americans take him as a role model and the epitome of American values and identity, representing truth, strength, liberty, and justice. There are also numerous heroes and heroines in Chinese legends. For example, Kua Fu, the giant who chased the sun and died on the road due to a lack of water and exhaustion. He turned the wooden cane he carried into a forest of peach trees in his last moment.He represents the undying spirit of fighting for one's dreams, no matter how unreal it sounds. If we think carefully, many Chinese mythical figures show similar qualities such as Jing Wei and Yu Gong, they all displayed the qualities of pursuing one's dreams, fighting against difficulties and being resilient and persistent. And those values run in the blood of the Chinese people. "Heroes run deeper than symbols" in cultural manifestations, since usually only people in these cultures may have a true understanding of the values these heroes and heroines represent.

3. **Rituals:** are conventional patterns that are used in specific situations (e.g. conversation routines, welcome rituals, table manners, religious practices); they are regarded as essential for social interactions.

4. **Values:** in the center of the onion are the values and assumptions that influence all of the other layers. Many values remain unconscious to those who hold them. Therefore, they often cannot be directly observed or discussed. They can just be recognized by deeper analysis and through understanding of each of the layers and their interactions.

4.1.2 The Definition of Cultural Environment

Cultural environment refers to the behaviors, norms, and values that people use to understand and explain their physical and social environment. Cultural environments shape the way that every person develops, influencing ideologies and personalities. It is one of the most crucial factors affecting the global expansion of multinational corporations.

A trend in cultural environment we need to be aware of is the increasing impact of **cultural diversity (the existence of a variety of cultural or ethnic groups within a society)**.

With the deepening of globalization and further international business co-operations, cultural diversity has increasingly caught the world's attention. People from all ethnic groups, different countries, various cultural backgrounds are trading and collaborating in today's business world. In fact, the number of countries experiencing cultural diversity is on the rise. Another concept we need to know is **socio-cultural environment, which refers to the trends and developments of changes in attitudes, behaviors, and values in society**. It is closely related to populations, lifestyles, cultures, tastes, customs, and traditions, factors which are created by the community and often are passed down from one generation to another. This term is important and is commonly used in business, especially for companies conducting market analyses before entering into a foreign market.

4.2　The Elements of Culture

Sociologists believe that the six basic elements of culture are: languages, norms, beliefs, symbols, values, and **cognitive elements (those through which individuals know how to cope with an existing social situation)**. Considering the practicability of international marketing, in this unit, we select a few elements that have great impacts on marketing: material culture, languages, aesthetics, education, religions, cultural values and social organizations. Apart from the material culture, all other elements fall into the category of non-material culture. **Non-material culture refers to a component of culture that consists of the abstract or intangible human creations of society (such as attitudes, beliefs, and values) that influence people's behaviors**. Material and non-material culture make up the overall culture of any society.

❯ 4.2.1　Material Culture

Material culture refers to the totality of physical objects made by people for the satisfaction of their needs, which is represented by attire, food, artifacts, architecture, resources, technology, etc. Technology, in particular, has become a vital aspect of material culture in today's world. It is worth noting that material culture has a significant impact on regions' development. For example, the poor condition of transportation and telecommunication in sub-Saharan African countries is holding their further economic development back, and tremendous efforts are under way to upgrade the infrastructure, to attract more foreign investments. The introduction of material culture into a country may also bring along cultural changes to a certain extent, which could be favorable or otherwise.

4.2.2　Language

Language refers to the principal method of human communication, which consists of words used in a structured and conventional way and conveyed by speech, writing, or gesture. It includes both verbal and non-verbal languages. Languages (including dialects) reflect the nature and values of societies, and many countries have more than one official language. For example, there are three official languages in New Zealand: English, Maori language and New Zealand sign language. It is worth mentioning that even countries that share the same language could have different cultures and values. For instance, people in the U.S. and people in the UK all speak English as their main language, but it would be a huge mistake if marketers/analysts ignore the cultural differences between the two countries.

4.2.3　Aesthetics

Aesthetics refers to the ideas in a culture concerning beauty and refinement as expressed in the arts—music, art, drama and dancing; alongside the particular appreciation of color and form. Aesthetic differences affect enterprises' marketing in many aspects: product design, colors, packaging, brand names and media messages, etc. For instance, traditional western paintings are concerned with details, geometric lines, balance and symmetry, which reflects the western value of being logical, emphasizing external perception and individuality. However, traditional Chinese paintings try to capture the feelings and spirit of beauty, by skillfully leaving space on the paintings, indicating the appreciation of a holistic view and imagination.

4.2.4　Education

Education is how societies pass on knowledge and values to the next generation. One of education's fundamental goals in all societies is to impart culture from generation to generation. Education can also transform cultural ideas into productivity, such as a university may improve local economic performance by supplying high-quality talents.

4.2.5　Religion

Some religious factors may need to be taken into consideration when marketers/ analysts conduct marketing research in a foreign country:

- Religious holidays—e.g. During Ramadan (a holy month for the Islamic faith), over one billion people worldwide forgo food and drink from dawn until dusk each day.

- Consumption patterns—e.g. religious-cultural clothing, entertainment, food...
- Caste systems—e.g. The Hindu caste system.

4.2.6 Social Organization

Social organization refers to the network of relationships in a group and how they interconnect. This network of relationships helps members of a group stay connected to one another in order to maintain a sense of community within the group. The social organization of a group is influenced by many factors, such as kinship, political preference, religion, etc., all of which may affect companies' marketing strategies.

4.2.7 Cultural Values

Cultural values refer to the perceptions, beliefs and standards that people acquire from the society in which they grew up. Probably the most useful information on how cultural values influence various types of businesses and market behaviors is Hofstede's Cultural Dimensions. Studying more than 90,000 people in 66 countries, Professor Geert Hofstede has developed a framework for cross-cultural communication, which describes the effects of a society's culture on the values of its members, and how these values relate to behaviour. He found that the cultures of the nations studied differed along six primary dimensions as follows: the Power Distance Index (PDI), the Individualism (IDV) vs. Collectivism, the Uncertainty Avoidance Index (UAI), Masculinity (MAS) vs. Femininity, Long-term Orientation (LTO) vs. Short-term Orientation, Indulgence vs. Restraint (see Figure 4.2). The theory has been widely applied in several fields as a paradigm for research, particularly in cross-cultural psychology, international management and cross-cultural communication. Hofstede scored each country using a scale of roughly 0 to 100 for each dimension. The higher the score, the more that dimension is exhibited in society.

1. Power Distance Index (PDI). The power distance index considers the extent to which inequality and power are tolerated. In this dimension, inequality and power are viewed from the perspective of the followers (the lower level). High PDI indicates that a culture accepts inequity and power differences, encourages bureaucracy and shows high respect for rank and authority. In high PDI countries, people accept an unequal distribution of power, and understand "their place" in the system. Malaysia, Guatemala, Panama and the Philippines are the top 4 countries ranking high in PDI. Low PDI indicates that power is shared and well dispersed. It also means that societal members view themselves as equals. Countries like Austria, New Zealand and Denmark show low PDI scores.

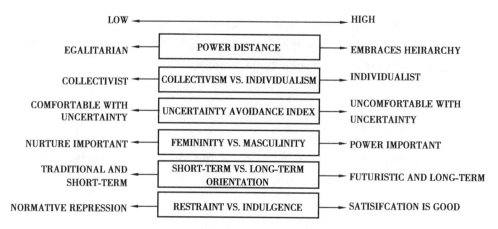

Figure 4.2　Hofstede's Cultural Dimensions

2. Individualism vs. Collectivism (IDV). The Individualism (IDV) vs. Collectivism dimension considers the degree to which societies are integrated into groups and their perceived obligation and dependence on groups. Individualism indicates that there is greater importance on attaining personal goals. In this type of culture, people are seen as independent and autonomous, a high IDV score also shows loose connections in groups. In countries with a high IDV score, there is a lack of interpersonal connections and little sharing of responsibility in groups. Cultures in North America and Western Europe tend to rank high on IDV.

Collectivism indicates that there is a greater importance on the goals and wellbeing of the group. In this type of culture, people emphasize fitting in; they value a sense of belonging, harmony and they care about their relationships within groups, often by treating group members differently than treating strangers or out-group members. A society with a low IDV score would have strong group cohesion, and there would be a large amount of loyalty and respect for members of the group. Asian countries tend to have higher scores on collectivism.

3. Uncertainty avoidance index (UAI). The uncertainty avoidance index considers the extent to which uncertainty and ambiguity are tolerated. This dimension considers how unknown situations and unexpected events are dealt with. High uncertainty avoidance index indicates a low tolerance for uncertainty, ambiguity, and risks. The unknown is minimized through strict rules, regulations, etc. For instance, Germany has a relatively high UAI score compared to that of the USA. Low uncertainty avoidance index indicates a high tolerance for uncertainty, ambiguity, and risk-taking. The unknown is more openly accepted, and there are fewer rules and regulations.

4. Masculinity vs. Femininity (MAS). This refers to how much a society sticks with, and values, traditional male and female roles. Masculinity is seen to be the trait which emphasizes ambition, acquisition of wealth, and differentiated gender roles. Femininity is seen to be the trait which emphasizes caring and nurturing behaviors and equal gender

roles. High MAS scores are found in countries where men are expected to be "tough", to be the provider and to be assertive. If women work outside the home, they tend to have separate professions from men. For instance, Japan ranks the highest in MAS. In a low MAS society, the roles are simply blurred. You may see women and men working together equally across many professions. Sweden shows the lowest MAS score among countries.

5. **Long-term Orientation vs. Short-term Orientation (LTO).** The long-term orientation vs. short-term orientation dimension refers to the connection of the past with current as well as future challenges. Long-term orientation shows focus on the future and involves delaying short-term success or gratification in order to achieve long-term success. Long-term orientation emphasizes persistence, perseverance, and long-term growth. Short-term orientation shows focus on the near future, delivering short-term success or gratification and pays more attention on the present than the future. Some Latin American countries score low in LTO, which may be due to various reasons.

6. **Indulgence vs. Restraint (IVR).** The IND dimension was added to the list of cultural dimensions more recently. There is less extensive research, and fewer countries are represented in the results. This dimension considers the extent and tendency for a society to fulfill its desires. In other words, this dimension revolves around how societies can control their impulses and desires. Indulgence indicates that a society allows relatively free gratification related to enjoying life and having fun. Restraint indicates that a society suppresses gratification of needs and regulates it through social norms. Some African countries are prone to indulgence, while many Asian countries tend to rank towards the restraint side.

There are other aspects of culture, but the above 7 points cover the main elements of culture. In one form or another, they have to be considered by companies when doing business abroad.

4.3　Characteristics of Culture

It is necessary for us to know culture's main characteristics. The following is a simple introduction of the six main characteristics of culture.

4.3.1　Culture Is Learnt

Culture is not inherited biologically, no one is born with a sense of culture. People learn their culture through social experiences. Daily routines such as wearing traditional clothes, cooking food, etc. are passed down from one generation to another. Culture is learnt, understood, adopted and assimilated from the environment.

4.3.2 Culture Is Shared

Every culture is shared by a group of people, usually living in the same geographic region. People of the same community share the same values, beliefs, and traditions. Their history, legends, philosophy tend to also be the same. Culture is shared and depends upon group life for its existence.

4.3.3 Culture Is Transmitted Across Generations

Culture is capable of being transmitted from one generation to the next, not through genes, but by means of symbols and languages. The languages which are a part of culture, are integrated into the educational system. The art, music, and dance forms demonstrating a culture are also transmitted across generations.

4.3.4 Culture Cannot Be Isolated

Studies have shown that no thriving culture can remain in isolation. Almost all cultures are influenced by neighboring cultures to some extent. This is especially true in the process of globalization today.

4.3.5 Culture Is Continuous and Cumulative

Culture exists as a continuous process, and tends to become cumulative in its historical growth. Culture is growing completely which includes in itself the achievements of the past and present while making provision for the future achievements of mankind.

4.3.6 Culture Is Dynamic and Adaptive

Culture is subject to slow but constant change. These changes/growths are latent, therefore, culture is dynamic. And as it is responsive to the changing conditions of the physical world, it is adaptive.

4.4 Cultural Environmental Effects on Global Marketing Strategies

Cultural environment has an immense impact on international marketing, especially in the following areas: language, customs and taboos, values, time and punctuality, business norms, religious beliefs, etc. It is imperative for marketers/analysts to learn and appreciate the cultures in target markets which are different from their own. From the case of Home Depot's failure in China's market, we have gained a clear understanding of the significant role culture plays for those multinational companies when they are entering a foreign market. Capable marketers/analysts who can identify the cultural differences and make proper adaptations are valuable assets for any multinational enterprise. Below are the major factors affecting global **marketing strategies (a general plan or a set of plans dealing with marketing, especially over a long period)**.

4.4.1　Language

Over 7,000 languages are spoken in the world today. Language differences can be the first challenge for marketers designing Integrated Marketing Communication (IMC) campaigns, product labels, product names and brands, tag lines, etc. Finding a single brand name that works universally in terms of pronunciation and meaning is no easy task. For example, Bai Xiang batteries produced by a company in Shanghai are selling well in the Chinese market. However, its sales records abroad have been disappointing. Finally, marketers found out one of the key reasons—the product's English name. The company translated into "White Elephant". But in English speaking countries, "White Elephant" has another meaning: it means something that costs a lot of money but is not useful. As we can imagine, the product's English name left a negative first impression on customers, which explains the poor sales performance in English-speaking markets.

4.4.2　Customs and Taboos

All cultures have their own unique sets of customs and taboos. It is vital for marketers to study these customs and taboos so that they can avoid potential public relation disputes. For example, the number 4 is considered unlucky when buying a new apartment in China, apartments on the fourth floor are usually less expensive than those on other floors.

4.4.3　Values

As the core of culture, values play a vital role in cross-cultural marketing. It may also influence policies of the host countries. Take Germany for example, Germans place great emphasis on Eco-economy and environmental protection. In order to reduce packaging waste as much as possible, on January 1st, 2019, the new German Packaging Law came into force, posing a stricter policy on companies who sell goods in the German market. Companies who fail to abide by this law will face heavy fines.

4.4.4 Time and Punctuality

Sensitivity towards time and punctuality varies from country to country. In some countries, being punctual shows basic respect for customers, while being late is seen as rude. However, in other countries, being slightly late to a meeting is acceptable.

4.4.5 Business Norms

Business norms may be another challenge to foreigners who are new to the host countries. Taking the role of alcohol in business meetings for example: in Middle Eastern cultures, alcohol is forbidden, it may be insulting to serve an alcoholic beverage. But in China, especially in northern China, the word "business drinking" indicates the important role alcohol plays at the dining table when making a deal. Likewise, business norms around greetings and physical contact also vary from country to county. Please seek guidance from trusted local colleagues or friends before business meetings.

4.4.6 Religious Beliefs and Celebrations

Religious beliefs and practices may strongly influence consumer behaviors. Perhaps the most well-known example is that there is no beef-burger at McDonald's in India, because in the Hindu religion, cows are considered sacred. Failing to respect religious beliefs or cultures can seriously destroy the reputation of a brandname or even a company in target markets.

In conclusion, cultural environment has a significant impact on marketing strategies of multinational companies. Only when marketers/analysts identify the cultural differences in different markets and make appropriate adaptations, can companies successfully do businesses abroad.

4.5　Definition of Demographic Environment

Demographics is the study of a population in a specific area over a specific time interval, covering multiple factors like age, race, gender, level of education, income, etc. A Demographic environment refers to the number, distribution, age, and gender structure of the population, which is used to segment the target population for effective marketing. (see Figure 4.3) For instance, "all 16 to 30-year-old females within first-tier cities in China". The analysis of demographic environments is a crucial marketing practice for almost all businesses, and it is an essential requirement before companies launch any marketing campaigns, especially for target customers.

Figure 4.3   Demographic Environment

The following dynamic qualities should be taken into consideration when researching a demographic environment.

4.5.1   The Population Size

Generally speaking, a larger population means a bigger market and more opportunities. Any changes in the population size can have a profound impact on the business. Main changes in the population size are: an overall increase/decrease in the population size; increase/decrease in the population's birth rate; changes in the average family size. Marketers may also need to consider the impact of a fast-growing population on the natural resources/food.

4.5.2 Geographical Distribution of Population

Geographical distribution of population refers to the way that population is distributed over a geographical area and represented on a map. There are a few reasons why companies need to consider geographical distribution of population: one reason being that the economic performance may vary in different parts of host countries, it is important for companies to locate their ideal market carefully. For example, for companies selling top brands and luxury products in China, first-tier cities like Beijing, Shanghai would be better options than third-tier cities. Another reason is that the target consumers may shift from one region to another over the coming years, companies need to track their paths and make adjustments accordingly.

4.5.3 Ethnic Mix

Ethnic mix can affect companies' activities in many aspects, such as identifying potential customers and employing workforce, it is another important factor to consider especially in multi-ethnic countries like Malaysia and Vietnam, etc.

4.5.4 Income Distribution

Income distribution refers to the division of a country's Gross National Product among the multitude of people making up its population. It is essential for any business to understand the income and purchasing power of its target customers for designing products/services. Take America for example, its average household income, both before and after means-tested transfers and federal taxes, grew between 1979 and 2017, however, income inequality also rose in the same period.

4.6 Demographic Segmentation

Demographic segmentation divides the market into smaller categories based on demographic factors, such as age, gender and income. This method is widely applied in business when a company conducts marketing research before entering a new market. Because it can assist companies to focus their resources on their target consumers more efficiently, rather than allocating resources to the whole market. Other benefits demographic segmentation can bring. May include improving product and service quality with more accuracy, promoting customer loyalty, optimizing market strategies and increasing the returns on investments (ROI), etc. Major demographic segmentation variables are as follows.

4.6.1　Age

Age is probably the most basic variable of demographic segmentation, because people's needs and preferences constantly change with age. Marketers/analysts could put customers into several categories: babies, children, adolescents, adults, and seniors. Age segmentation can also be based on generations, such as: baby boomers (persons born between the end of WWII and the mid-1960s), Generation X(persons born between the early 1960s and the 1980s), Generation Y(persons born between the early 1980s and 1990s), etc. Since customers in the same generation usually share similar experience and buying behaviors, their accepted ways of advertising would be quite similar. For example, Generation X are more attracted to advertisements on TV, while Generation Y find online ads. more accessible.

4.6.2　Gender

There is a saying that "the consumption desire and consumption power of women are much stronger than men.", whether it is true or not, it indicates the impact of gender differences in marketing. It is essential for many companies to identify their customers by gender. Cosmetic products are good examples, as most of them are aimed at female customers.

4.6.3　Income and Buying Behaviors

Customers' income and buying behaviors are the other two key factors to consider before making any marketing plans. Customer income helps companies to measure the buying power of customers and set the pricing strategies accordingly. **Buying behavior refers to the decision processes and acts of people involved in buying and using products.** For instance, consulting search engines, reading customer's reviews, asking for friends' recommendations, etc.Through studying the buying behaviors of customers, companies may enhance customer loyalty and attract more new customers.

▶ 4.6.4 Family Structure

Whether being single or having a large family can strongly affect customers' buying habits and decisions. For instance, due to declining marriage and increasing divorce rates, "single person economy" and the pet industry are thriving.

We now have a clear understanding of how demographic environment influences businesses, especially on marketing strategies. A well-designed demographic segmentation can help companies predict industrial trends. But there are a few pitfalls marketers/analysts need to pay attention to: for one thing, in reality, even though marketers/analysts use accurate data to predict the future trend of customers, there is no guarantee the prediction will come true, for much of demographic data is based on assumptions or stereotypes and influenced by culture; for another, populations are never constant, some people are born, some people pass away, some people migrate. This means companies need to collect and analyze demographic data regularly; finally, it would be easy for marketers to get into adequate details when conducting demographic segmentation without keeping an open mind.

4.7 Global Demographic Trends

Demographics are vital to any business, because people's needs are the ultimate reason for businesses to exist, and the driving force of markets. Since demographic environment is constantly changing, it is essential for marketers to keep a close eye to the future trends of demographics, to prepare and adjust marketing strategies accordingly. Some major trends of the world's population are listed below:

▶ 4.7.1 World Population Growth

The world population is growing at an explosive rate. In 1950 there were 2.5 billion people on the planet, this number has grown to 7.6 billion by 2020 and is expected to reach 8.6 billion in 2030. But the growth rates among countries vary drastically. It seems that the highest population growth rates mostly occur in countries where wealth and stability are absent. For instance, the top three countries with the largest increases in population are Syria, Angola and Malawi, mainly in West-Asia and Africa. Although countries with higher growth rates could enjoy the **demographic dividend: the economic growth potential that can result from shifts in a population's age structure, mainly when the share of the working-age population(15—64) is larger than the non-working-age share of the population**

(14 and younger, and 65 and older).

Strong growth rates also bring challenges: it usually means a growing need for food, water, resources, infrastructure and services. All these would be additional expenses for those developing countries in need, especially if the population grows rapidly. On the other hand, most developed and stable countries are experiencing a slowing down population growth. Countries like Japan and Germany have recorded low growth rate consecutively. The explosive yet uneven population growth worldwide has offered companies both opportunities and challenges in the future, which requires managers and marketers to trace and make effective adjustments during marketing process.

⏩ 4.7.2   Changing Age Structures

The changing age structure of world population is another critical factor influencing global marketing. Again, the age structure also varies from country to country. Some countries will have more favorable age structures compared to others. For instance, Indian population is one of the youngest around the globe, and it is predicted that the media age in India will be around 28 years by 2020, compared with almost 48 years in Japan, and 38 years in America. Median age is an important indicator of a country's age distribution in population. Generally speaking, lower-income countries tend to have a lower median age, because of the high **fertility rates (the number of live births in a year per 1,000 women of reproductive age in a population)**. While higher-income countries, across North America, Europe and East Asia tend to have a higher median age due to their low fertility rates and longer life expectancy. Overall, our world is stepping into an aging population.

⏩ 4.7.3   Changing Family Structures

Family structures also have a strong impact on many businesses, especially in the household products industry. Various new family structures start emerging in many countries: **nuclear families (a couple and their dependent children, regarded as a basic social unit)** are gradually replacing larger families; the number of single-parent and single-person households are growing; and in some countries, an increasing number of young people choose to be **DINK families (Dual income, no kids. Couples have made the conscious decision not to have a child)**. All these changes will have far-reaching effects on businesses.

⏩ 4.7.4   Geographic Shifts in Population

Another trend in the process of globalization is migration, both domestically and internationally. By 2050, global migration is expected to double. This will have a profound impact on businesses, for migration not only shows market shift, but also indicates the changes of the needs of consumers. Other important factors are the ethnic diversity and **urbanization** (the process in which there is an increase in the number of people living and working in a city or metropolitan area).

Key Terms

culture 文化	The sum of the values, rituals, symbols, beliefs and thought processes that are learned and shared by a group of people, then transmitted from generation to generation. 世代相传的，人们学习并共享的价值、仪式、符号、信念和思维过程的总和。
cultural environment 文化环境	The behaviors, norms and values that people use to understand and explain their physical and social environment. 人们用来理解和解释客观环境和社会环境的行为、规范和价值观。
cultural diversity 文化多样性	The existence of a variety of cultural or ethnic groups within a society. 社会中各种文化或种族群体并存。
non-material culture 非物质文化	A component of culture that consists of the abstract or intangible human creations of society (such as attitudes, beliefs, and values) that influence people's behavior. 文化的一部分，由影响人们行为的抽象的或无形的人类社会产物（如态度、信念和价值观）组成。
material culture 物质文化	The totality of physical objects made by people for the satisfaction of their needs, which is represented by attire, food, artifacts, architecture, resources, technology, etc. 人们为了满足自己需求而制作的全部物品的总称，以服装、食物、艺术品、建筑、资源、科技等为代表。
social organization 社会组织	The network of relationships in a group and how they interconnect. 组织内的关系网络以及它们之间的互联方式。
cultural values 文化价值观	The perceptions, beliefs and standards which people acquire from the society in which they grow up. 人们从其成长的社会中获得的观念、信仰和准则。
Hofstede's Cultural Dimension 霍夫斯泰德文化维度	A framework for cross-cultural communication, developed by Geert Hofstede. It describes the effects of a society's culture on the values of its members, and how these values relate to behavior. 吉尔特·霍夫斯泰德提出的一个跨文化交际的框架。它描述了一个社会的文化对其成员价值观的影响，以及这些价值观与成员行为的关系。

Continued

marketing strategy 营销策略	It is a process that can allow an organization to concentrate its limited resources on the greatest opportunities to increase sales and achieve a sustainable competitive advantage. 这是一个可以使组织将其有限的资源集中于最大机会的过程,以增加销售并实现可持续的竞争优势。
demographics 人口统计学	Demographics is the study of a population in a specific area over a specific time interval, covering multiple factors like age, race, gender, level of education, income, etc. 人口统计学是对特定时间段内特定区域内的人口的研究,涵盖年龄、种族、性别、教育水平、收入等多个因素。
demographic environment 人口环境	The number, distribution, age and gender structure of the population, which are used to segment the target population for effective marketing. 人口环境是指人口的数量、分布、年龄和性别结构,用于对目标人群进行细分以进行有效的营销。
geographic distribution of population 人口地理分布	The way that population is distributed over a geographical area and can be represented on a map. 以在地图上标示的方式展现的人口在地理区域上的分布。
income distribution 收入分配	The division of a country's gross national product among the multitude of people making up its population. 一个国家的国民生产总值在组成其人口的众多人群中进行划分。
demographic segmentation 人口细分	Demographic segmentation divides the market into smaller categories based on demographic factors, such as age, gender and income. 人口细分是根据年龄、性别和收入等因素将市场划分为较小的类别。
buying behavior 购买行为	It is the sum total of the attitudes, preferences, beliefs and decisions regarding the consumers behavior when purchasing a product or service in a market. 消费者在市场上购买产品或服务时的态度、偏好、信赖和决定的总和。
demographic dividend 人口红利	The demographic dividend is the economic growth potential that can result from shifts in a population's age structure, mainly when the share of the working-age population (15 to 64) is larger than the non-working-age share of the population (14 and younger, and 65 and older). 人口红利是指人口年龄结构变化可能带来的经济增长潜力,主要指在劳动年龄人口的比例(15 岁至 64 岁)大于非劳动年龄人口的比例(14 岁及以下和 65 岁以上)时。
fertility rates 生育率	The number of live births in a year per 1,000 women of reproductive age in a population. 每年出生活婴数与同期平均育龄妇女人数之比,通常用千分数表示。
nuclear family 核心家庭	A couple and their dependent children regarded as a basic social unit. 一对夫妇及其抚养的子女组成的家庭,被视为基本社会单位。

Continued

| DINK family
丁克家庭 | A household in which there are two incomes and no children
丁克家庭一般指不生孩子的家庭。夫妻"双收入、无子女"。 |
| urbanization
城市化 | Process in which there is an increase in the number of people living and working in a city or metropolitan area.
人口向城市集中的过程。 |

Review & Critical Thinking Questions

1. What are the basic elements of culture which affect marketing?

2. Why is material culture considered as an important element of culture?

3. What are Hofstede's Cultural Dimensions? Please list the six dimensions with their meanings.

4. Why should marketers be concerned with the cultural environment of the host country?

5. How does the cultural environment influence global marketing strategies?

6. What are the main characteristics of culture?

7. What are the dynamic qualities that need to be considered when conducting demographic environment research?

8. What is demographic environment and why does it affect companies' marketing strategies?

9. What is demographic segmentation and why is it widely applied in marketing research?

10. What are the major global trends of demographics in the last few years?

11. Please explain the definitions of income distribution, demographic dividend, and urbanization respectively.

12. How does family structure affect global marketing? Please cite examples.

Discussion Questions

1. Why is it said that "Culture is like an iceberg"? Please list your reasons and discuss with your group members.

2. Why is it said that "Culture is pervasive in all marketing activities"? Explain the reasons why this might be.

3. Why should marketers/analysts conduct demographic research regularly?

4. Please discuss the demographic trends in China with your group members.

Case Study

When it comes to international marketing, one of the biggest challenges multinationals face with is to keep a balance between standardization and localization. Product standardization refers to the process of maintaining uniformity and consistency of a particular product or service available within different markets. Localization, however, is the process of adapting a product, service, advertisement, or any other type of content to a specific market. Standardization is widely used by multinationals for a number of reasons: it may reduce the cost of production, promote efficiency, strengthen the brand name, and ensure the standard of product and service quality. However, the drawbacks of standardization are also obvious when being conducted within different markets: it disregards the cultural differences among countries, which may cause confusion to local management while failing to meet the needs of the local customers. As one of the few achievers in international marketing, McDonald's has set a good example of how to achieve balance between standardization and localization for multinationals, the key to its success lies in its principle: "think global, act local".

McDonald's keeps its basic menu structure unified globally; that is, the franchise's burgers, fries and drinks are available among different countries regardless of political statements or religious beliefs, while other products may vary according to different cultural environments. For instance, in India, McDonald's restaurants do not sell beef burgers, but provide Chicken Maharaja Mac instead; in Italy, McDonald's offers espresso and cold pasta; in China, McDonald provides Spicy McWings. All those adaptations are made to satisfy the local consumers' tastes.

As for promotion, McDonald's may still apply universal marketing campaigns worldwide, which are mostly co-operations with other multinational companies (such as Walt Disney). Since Disney has a worldwide influence and disseminates similar values to many countries, there is no need for McDonald's to do the same. Both parties have benefited greatly from this alliance, and in 2018 they decided to cooperate once again.

Apart from the above-mentioned global co-operations, McDonald's marketing approaches also vary among countries. Firstly, its slogan "I'm lovin' it" is printed in the native languages of different countries; in addition, McDonald's makes use of local celebrities as endorser to influence the younger generations in different countries; for instance, in 2020, McDonald's initiated the services of Jackson Yee, making him the endorser within Chinese market. Furthermore, McDonald's advertisements (the content) caters to local consumers' tastes. Example being that Chinese pay more attention to the food quality. In response to this, McDonald's marketing in China utilizes bright colors and clear pictures to showcase its fresh vegetable/organic ingredients in burgers. In France,

McCafé is set up as the coffee/pastries-only subsection of Mc Donald's, offering high-end coffee and pastry with table service, and is extremely popular among young people. Lastly, within the management level, McDonald's absorbs cultural elements of host markets, by employing local managers and providing pragmatic training.

With the skillful combination of standardization and localization, McDonald's has proven that its marketing is an art form, not just a data-driven cog in the metaphorical system that is consumerism.

Questions

1. Please explain the definition of product standardization and localization.
2. What measures has McDonald's taken in global marketing? Please list the cultural elements involved in these measures.
3. Can you think of any failed case of international marketing? Cite one case and explain the reasons for its failure and give some suggestions.

中文概述

文化环境

1. 文化和文化环境

文化是人类世代相传的、学习并共享的价值、仪式、符号、信念和思维过程的总和。由浅入深分为四个层次：符号、英雄、礼仪和价值观。

文化环境是指人们用来理解和解释客观环境和社会环境的行为、规范和价值观。

2. 文化的基本要素

本章节根据国际营销的实用性，选取了对国际营销影响较大的几种要素进行说明。

(1)物质文化。

(2)语言。

(3)美学。

(4)教育。

(5)宗教。

(6)社会组织。

(7)文化价值观。

3. 文化的特征

以下为文化的6个主要特征：

（1）文化是通过学习得来的。

（2）文化是共享的。

（3）文化世代相传。

（4）文化不能孤立。

（5）文化是累积和连续的。

（6）文化是动态的和适应性的。

4. 文化环境如何影响全球营销策略

文化环境对于企业的国际营销活动影响巨大,国外营销人员必须学习和欣赏目标市场的文化。

跨文化营销对跨国公司能否在海外顺利扩张起着重要作用,只有营销人员能够识别文化差异并做出适当的调整,公司才能顺利地制订和执行营销策略。

5. 人口统计学

人口统计学是对特定时间段内特定区域内的人口进行研究,涵盖年龄、种族、性别、教育水平、收入等多个因素。人口环境是指人口的数量、分布、年龄和性别结构,用于对目标人群进行细分以进行有效的营销。

6. 人口细分

根据年龄、性别、收入等人口因素将市场划分为较小的类别。此方法被广泛应用于营销调研中,因为它可以帮助公司更有效地将资源集中于目标客户。

虽然人口细分在营销中非常实用,但营销人员也需要注意避免一些陷阱:首先,在现实生活中,即使营销人员使用准确的数据来预测客户的未来趋势,也无法保证这种预测一定会成为现实,因为大部分人口统计数据基于假设或成见,并受到不同文化的影响;其次,人口永远不会恒定,有些人出生,有些人去世,有些人迁移,这意味着公司需要定期收集、分析人口统计数据;最后,分析者在分析人口统计数据时容易陷入过于细分的陷阱,忽视潜在的客户。

7. 全球人口趋势

我们在这一章总结了世界人口的一些主要趋势:

（1）世界总人口增长。

（2）年龄结构的改变。

（3）家庭结构的改变。

（4）人口分布的地理变化。

UNIT 5 / The Legal Impact on Marketing

Learning Objectives

1. Understand the meaning and classification of the law and the legal environment.
2. Be familiar with the constitution of the law system.
3. Identify the purpose of business law / economic law.
4. Understand the relationship between the law and marketing.
5. Interpret the legal factors that affect marketing.
6. Discuss the legal impacts on marketing from positive and negative viewpoints.

Legal environment has obvious impact on business activities. Any business should know the legal settings in which it operates and adheres to the legal regulation. With the advent of digital economy, many questions concerning marketing have emerged such as the blurred line between data collection and the invasion of privacy, the conflict between attracting consumers and deceptive advertisements, etc. Businesses must be careful not to cross the line between legal and illegal.

5.1 The Definition of Law and Legal Environment

5.1.1 Law

The definition of the law depends on how we look at its purposes or functions. A basic purpose of the law in our society is to maintain order and to manage **disputes**. In this connection we must bear in mind that the law is not simply a set of rules of conduct. It is also the means to impose responsibility and to enforce social **justice**. Law has also been defined as a command from a superior to an inferior. The tax law fits in well with this concept of the law. Law is also a method of social control. The law brings about changes in our society and the society brings about changes in the law. In this sense, law is both an instrument of changes and a result of changes.

Judicial decisions as part of law are a unique characteristic of American laws. This concept of decided cases as a source of law is often referred to as the common law system, which must be contrasted with the civil law system developed in continental Europe. The civil law countries have modified their law so that the main source of law in those countries is to be found in the statutes rather than in the cases. Under the common law system, statutes as well as cases are sources of law. Laws are formulated or recognized by the state and guaranteed by the state's coercive force. Some countries base their laws on their religious laws. No matter what base it is on, the nature of the law being justice is the essence which is permanently unchangeable.

5.1.2　Functions of Law

In a nation, the law can serve to (1) keep the peace, (2) maintain the status quo, (3) preserve individual rights, (4) protect minorities, (5) promote social justice, and (6) provide for orderly social change.

5.1.3　Characteristics of Law

1. Predictability

Law is a kind of codes to regulate people's behaviors. The law realizes the adjustment of social relations by adjusting and integrating human behaviors. A legal norm can be applied repeatedly to anyone under the same condition. In other words, it embodies the normality of the law and its general characteristics.

2. Standardization

Laws are norms made or recognized by the state. And the standardization is also one of the main characteristics that distinguish laws from other social norms.

3. State Compulsion

Laws are norms that the state's coercive force guarantees their implementation. To implement laws is to use legal norms to adjust social relations and maintain social order.

5.1.4　Categories of Law

Laws can be classified into differentiated groups based on various standards. Here we just elaborate the categories on the ground which have close relation to marketing activities.

1. Laws Affecting Market Entities

So far, the law has been largely completed. The forms of enterprises used to be decided by ownership are now decided by the forms of investment, which is a common international practice. The introduction of The *Law on Sole Proprietorship Enterprise*, The *Law on Partnership Enterprise* and The *Law on Foreign Investment* has given market operators a variety of choices.

2. Laws Affecting the Market Freedom

Market freedom can be divided into property freedom, trade freedom and business freedom. At present, The law of market freedom is generally comprehensive, and market freedom is basically protected by law in return. For example, in terms of property freedom, the promulgation of The Property Law stipulates that the state cannot arbitrarily requisition corporate property or private property, thus affirming the basic rights of private property. The *Contract Law* guarantees the right of trade and business freedom.

3. Laws Affecting Business Operation

A business needs to take time to understand any legal obligations since the inception. From employment rights to customer data safety, the legal factors affecting business can be read like a laundry list of law terms. But making sure your business meets legal requirements can avoid expensive mistakes. According to a research carried out by *YouGov for LawBite*, SMEs lose more than £13.6bn each year failing to take care of legal issues, with disputes costing £1.7bn, and employee and contractor issues costing £1.6bn.

5.1.5 The Understanding of the Legal Environment

1. Definition of Legal Environment

Legal environment refers to the regulations, decrees and regulations promulgated by the national or local government. By studying and being familiar with the legal environment, enterprises can not only ensure their operation in strict accordance with the law and use legal means to protect their own rights and interests, but also predict the market demand trend through changes in legal provisions. It mainly includes two levels inside and outside: one is the explicit surface structure, that is, legal norms, legal systems, legal organizations and legal facilities; the other is the internal structure and the legal ideology.

2. Elements of Legal Environment

(1) Legal Norms

In particular, economic laws and regulations are closely related to the operation of enterprises, such as The *Company Law*, The *Law on China-Foreign Joint Ventures (JV)*,

The Contract Law, The Patent Law, The Trademark Law, The Tax Law, The Enterprise Bankruptcy Law, etc.

(2) The State Adjudication and Law Enforcement Organizations

In the United States, there are mainly courts, electorates, public security offices and various administrative law enforcement agencies. The administrative law enforcement organizations closely related to the enterprises include the industrial and commercial administrative offices, tax offices, price offices, etiological control offices, technical and quality control offices, patent offices, environmental protection administrative agencies and government auditing offices. In addition, there are some temporary administrative law enforcement agencies, such as the financial, tax and price inspection organizations of governments at all levels.

(3) The **Legal Awareness** of Enterprises

Enterprise's legal consciousness is enterprise's understanding and evaluation of the legal system. The legal consciousness of enterprises may eventually materialize into legal ACTS of a certain nature and cause certain consequences, thus constituting the legal environment that every enterprise has to face.

(4) The International Legal Environment

For enterprises engaged in international marketing activities, they should not only abide by the domestic legal system but also understand and abide by foreign legal systems and relevant international regulations, practices and norms.

For example, the Japanese government restrained foreign capital by stipulating that any foreign company entering the Japanese market must find a Japanese partner. Only by understanding the relevant trade and business policies of these countries, can companies take effective marketing countermeasures or other initiatives.

5.2   The Purpose of Business/Economic Law

5.2.1   Protect Enterprises from Unfair Competition

Unfair competition is also called "illegal competition", referring to the use of dishonest or other improper means to gain benefits that may infringe rights of others. As stipulated in *Anti-Unfair Competition law*, unfair competition refers to the ACTS of business operators that violate the provisions of this law, damage the legitimate rights and interests of other business operators, and disrupt the social and economic order. In essence, unfair competition is a kind of illegal behavior that violates fair, equal, honest and trustworthy competition rules.

The primary purpose of formulating *The Law against Unfair Competition* is to stop unfair competition. In order to promote healthy development of the socialist market economy, it is necessary to protect the legitimate rights and interests of both operators and consumers, and encourage fair competition. The operators who do not abide by the competition rules in the market competition should be stopped in time and severely punished.

The law guarantees fair competition in the market and encourages honest operators to strive to improve technology, improve product quality and reduce costs which may drive continuous improvement of the whole social productivity.

▶ 5.2.2　Protect Consumers from Business Fraud

Counterfeit and fraud behaviors violate the legal provisions, and cause negative consequences to consumers and market order. They may even disturb the social and economic order with serious social harm for long-term welfare of the society and market.

Business Laws regulate that any business operator shall not, by means of advertising or other means, offer false and misleading message concerning quality, composition, performance, use, producer, term of validity or place of origin of a commodity. An advertisement agency shall not act without knowing the relative law or regulations.

In summary, all marketing activities are subject to a large number of laws and regulations. Each law has its two sides, which, undoubtedly, is a challenge as well as an opportunity for enterprises to develop in a better direction. As a result, managements have to negotiate plans with corporate counsel, public relations, and consumer rights sectors.

5.3　The Relationship Between Law and Marketing

Although the vast majority of business people conduct in a responsible and ethical manner, it's too risky to assume that everyone will do so. To protect consumers and maintain economic stability, the U. S. government periodically institutes laws and regulations to deter harmful marketing behavior. Areas of marketing that are of particular interest to legislators include the following:

- False advertising
- Deceptive pricing practices
- Tobacco advertising

- Children's advertising
- Product safety
- Nutritional labeling
- Consumer privacy
- Fairness in lending practice

The federal government has created several official agencies to protect the interests of consumers and the general public. These agencies are taken very seriously, because business people who violate the agencies' standards can be affected professionally and personally, and face fines or imprisonment. Each of the following regulatory bodies have impacts on policy related to marketing:

Consumer Product Safety Commission (CPSC)—This agency monitors product safety and issues recalls for unsafe products. It also establishes standards for product safety.

Environmental Protection Agency (EPA)—The EPA develops and enforces regulations to protect environment, some of which affect materials and processes companies may use to manufacture products.

Federal Communications Commission (FCC)—Any firm that uses broadcast media (telephone, radio, or television) for marketing is affected by FCC rules.

Federal Trade Commission (FTC)—The FTC enforces laws against deceptive advertising and wrong product labeling.

Food and Drug Administration (FDA)—This agency enforces laws and regulations on foods, drugs, cosmetics and veterinary products. Before introducing new drugs and other products into the market place, manufacturers must first obtain FDA approval.

Interstate Commerce Commission (ICC)—The ICC regulates all interstate bus, truck, rail and water operations. ICC regulations and policies can impact the efficiency of marketing distribution channels.

A regulation is a rule or an order issued by an official government agency that carries the force of law. Marketers must learn to successfully operate within constraints imposed by these requirements. Table 5.1 contains some major federal laws that have fostered regulations on marketing activities.

From a consumer perspective, the most visible areas of government regulation on marketing are advertising, pricing and product safety. The FTC is responsible for ensuring compliance with a wide range of regulations on pricing and promotion. Examples of federal regulations in these areas include the following:

- There must be documented proof of any claims made in an advertisement before the ad runs, letters from satisfied customers are usually not sufficient.
- It is illegal to say that a product has "a retail value of $15.00, your price: $7.50," if $15.00 is not the prevailing price for the product in the retailer's geographic area.
- It is illegal to advertise any product that is not for real sale, but instead switching

customers to another item at a higher price (called a bait—and—switch).

Another organization that issues regulations that affect marketing is the Consumer Product Safety Commission (CPSC), which is a watchdog organization for protecting safety of consumers. It issues regulations on the ingredients and processes of production. It also carries the authority to ban or seize potential harmful products. Marketers who violate the regulations face severe penalties.

Table 5.1   Major Federal Laws and Regulations of United States

Law	Areas of Marketing Regulated by Law
Sherman Antitrust Act (1890)	Distribution (for example, exclusive territories) Pricing (for example, price fixing, predatory pricing)
Food and Drug Act (1906)	Product safety (for example, food and drugs)
Clayton Act (1914)	Distribution (for example, tying contracts and exclusive dealings)
Federal Trade Commission (FTC) Act (1914)	All areas of marketing that result in unfair business practices
Robinson-Patman Act (1936)	Pricing (for example, price discrimination)
Wheeler-Lea Amendment to FTC Act (1938)	Promotion (for example, deceptive and misleading advertising)
Lanham Trademark Act (1946)	Branding (for example, brand names and trademarks)
Fair Packaging and Labeling Act (1966)	Packaging (for example. truth in labeling)
National Traffic and Motor Vehicle Safety Act (1966)	Product safety (for example, automobile and tire safety)
Cigarette Labeling Act (1966)	Product (for example, cigarette package warnings)
Child Protection Act (1966)	Product safety (for example, children's product safety)
Child Protection and Toy Safety Act (1969)	Packaging (for example, child-resistant packages)
Consumer Credit Protection Act (1968)	Promotion (for example, credit terms, loan terms)
Fire Credit Reporting Act (1970)	Information sharing (for example, credit reporting)
Consumer Products Safety Commission Act (1972)	Product safety (for example, safety monitoring, recalls, safety standards)
Magnuson-Moss Consumer Product Warranty Act (1975)	Product (for example, warranties)
Children's Television Act (1990)	Promotion (for example, children's advertising)
Nutrition Labeling and Education Act (1990)	Packaging (for example, food and drug labeling)
National Do Not Call Registry (2003)	Promotion (for example, telemarketing)

For enterprises, the law is the criterion to judge their marketing activities. Only the lawful marketing activities can be effectively protected by national laws. Therefore, to carry out marketing activities, enterprises must understand and abide by the relevant laws and regulations on operation, trade and investment. If engaged in international marketing activities, enterprises should not only abide by the domestic legal system but also understand and adhere to the legal system of host country as well as relevant international regulations, practices and norms.

In short, law and marketing are interrelated. Only by being recognized and accepted by the public can value of law be realized. The public image of the law is very similar to the image of the product in marketing. The public's perception of the law is like a consumer's identification with a product. The consumer's impression of the product has a profound influence on the sale of the product. The image of law on people's minds is also directly related to the influence of law on the public. Law is an important tool for the public to defend their rights.

5.4   Legal Issues of Marketing

5.4.1   Data Collection and the Invasion of Privacy

Data collection is often considered as one of the most significant stages of marketing. Extensive data allows businesses to choose the most optimal marketing techniques. In fact, many outstanding global companies in the field of Internet primarily rely on tracking users' web history to generate returns.

However, while law makers are yet to decide on a legal position, individuals are striving for tougher privacy laws. For example, in a recent survey of 11, 000 people, almost 70% said they would gladly use a "do not track" feature on search engines if available. Companies such as Baikal in China have also received backlash over privacy issues. Thus, businesses need to become more conscious of consumers' privacy when collecting data.

5.4.2   Distribution of Data

Marketing channels such as telemarketing, door to door sales and unsolicited emails are some of the most controversial areas of marketing. The law in some countries allows telemarketing and door to door sales in specified time frames. For instance, a sales person can only approach you between 9 am to 6 pm on weekdays and 9 am to 5 pm on

Saturdays. Further, "do not knock" stickers and a "do not call" register must be obeyed by marketers. While these protections are in place, legal and ethical issues arise because the majority of consumers are either unaware of such protections or not bothered to report petty offences. As a result, marketers often get away with illegal and unethical behaviors.

More specifically in Australia, email Anti-spam laws require that a business has the receiver's consent, identifies the sender and contains an unsubscribed option. The key problem involves the definition of consent. For example, finding a client on a shared directory does not constitute consent. Consent must be explicitly stated or inferred from situations such as an existing business relationship.

5.4.3　Misleading Claims

Misleading claims in advertising may involve claims about the quality of the product, the availability of a service and any exclusions on a product. Many famous companies have all been found liable for misleading claims in the past.

However, problems arise because it is extremely difficult to claim for misleading advertisement. For instance, if a product was "50% off from before", a consumer must have evidence of before and after prices to make a claim.

5.4.4　Doorstep Selling

There are certain rules you must abide by if your sales strategy involves selling to customers in their homes or place of work. One of the most important rules is to allow a "cooling off period" during which a customer is free to back out of any contract without any penalties. There are various exceptions but, in general, you need to inform the customer of this right for any goods sold over £35 in UK.

5.4.5　Various Advertising

Sending your message through the medium of TV and radio can give you a substantial marketing reach. However, broadcast advertising is subject to a wide range of regulations so you should do some research before embarking upon this type of campaign. In particular, take heed of the UK Code of Broadcast Advertising, which is enforced by the Advertising Standards Authority.

Another type of ASA enforced code, the UK Code of Non-broadcast Advertising, Sales Promotion and Direct Marketing, applies to non-broadcast forms of advertising. Similar issues need to be considered, including the potential of an advert to cause harm or offence and the importance of avoiding any exaggerated claims about products which could be deemed as misleading.

5.4.6　Pricing and Promotions

Although you can often increase customer loyalty by making sure your prices are competitive and introducing promotions from time to time, your pricing needs to be clear and unambiguous. Sale items must refer to original prices and product promotions should indicate closing dates.

5.5　The Legal Impact on Marketing

5.5.1　How Does the Law Affect Marketing Strategies?

Many businesses focus on marketing strategies that can be quickly developed and implemented to promote either a new product/service or an existing one. However, businesses must be wary when utilizing these strategies, as there are laws that affect the course of marketing. In fact, government at various levels have implemented rules and regulations specifically regarding marketing tactics that businesses must abide by.

Furthermore, there are laws that protect consumer's rights by prohibiting businesses from creating deceptive advertisements. Business owners are required to use accurate graphics, just comparisons, and proper verbiage in their product/service advertisements to avoid misleading consumers.

In addition, they must also be mindful of all applicable industry regulations. The government constantly revisits and modifies or even changes these business laws, so companies need to stay on top of the latest information. Companies need professionals in their corner to address all their advertising and promotional needs while tracking legal and regulatory changes. An experienced marketing professional will understand the industry and target market trends.

It's imperative for companies to study the regulations that relate to their industry as well as research trends, demographics, and their target users. Never conduct a marketing campaign without first doing some in-depth research. And, if you're too busy to address the campaign yourself, talk to an experienced marketing professional to handle all your marketing needs.

5.5.2 Characteristics of Legal Effects on Marketing

The legal environment is an important component of the business environment faced by companies. The influence of the legal environment on an enterprise's marketing activities has the following characteristics:

1. Directness. The national legal environment directly affects the operation status of enterprises.

2. Unpredictability. For enterprises, it is difficult to predict the changing trend of national political and legal environment.

3. Impressibility. Once the legal environment factors affect the enterprise, the enterprise will be of very rapid and obvious changes, and the changes of the enterprise are unable to control.

5.5.3 Adverse Effects of the Legal Environment on Enterprises

The legal environment may bring some inconvenience to enterprises, here are some examples:

1. In order to meet the legal requirements (such as strict emission standards), the cost of enterprises will increase, thus reducing their competitiveness against overseas competitors.

2. Complex regulatory procedures may create entry barriers for small companies. In the enterprise legislation of various countries, the essential and procedural conditions of enterprise establishment are the main contents. However, their strictness or looseness may vary from country to country.

3. Small companies are more affected by law. Since small firms typically produce a single product or operate in a single market, the impact of regulations on them is more likely to be on the enterprise as a whole, rather than on a subset of its products and markets, as large firms do.

5.5.4 Favorable Effects of the Legal Environment on Enterprises

First of all, sound laws will correct market inefficiencies and ensure fair competition. Legislation to prevent restrictive practices and **monopoly** power can promote competition and help enterprises to grow. What's more, a good legal environment can provide legal guarantee for the operation and development of enterprises, and boost industrial development. In the third place, the practice of market economy for hundreds of years shows that the formation of orderly market competition needs the protection of the legal system, and the anti-unfair competition law and anti-monopoly law are the indispensable legal environmental factors for enterprise operation and regional economic development.

Key Terms

legal environment 法律环境	Various regulations, decrees promulgated by the national or local government. It mainly includes two levels inside and outside, say, legal norms, legal systems, legal organizations and legal facilities. The other is the internal structure, the legal ideology. 法律环境是指国家或地方政府颁布的各项法规、法令、条例等。它主要包含内外有别的两个层次：一个是外显的表层结构，即法律规范、法律制度、法律组织机构及法律设施；另一个是内化的里层结构，即法律意识形态。
civil law system 大陆法系	In western legal works, it is mostly referred to as the *civil law system*, which includes the legal system established by most countries in continental Europe based on *The Roman law* in the early 19th century, represented by *the French Civil Code* in 1804 and *the German Civil Code* in 1896, as well as the legal system established by other countries or regions following this system. It is a law system of long origin and great influence, which is parallel with the common law system in western countries. 在西方法学著作中多称民法法系，指包括欧洲大陆大部分国家从 19 世纪初以《罗马法》为基础建立起来的、以 1804 年《法国民法典》和 1896 年《德国民法典》为代表的法律制度以及其他国家或地区仿效这种制度而建立的法律制度。它是西方国家中与英美法系并列的渊源久远和影响较大的法系。
common law system 英美法系	Also known as "common law", "English law", "case law". A general term for law based on English common law. It refers to a unique legal system formed in Britain from the 11th century mainly based on the common law derived from Germanic common law, and the legal system imitating some other countries and regions in Britain. It was born in The UK and later expanded to many countries and regions that were once colonies and dependencies of the UK, including the US, Canada, India, Pakistan, Bangladesh, Malaysia, Singapore, Australia, New Zealand and individual countries and regions in Africa. It is a law system with a long history and great influence, which is parallel with the civil law system in western countries. It pays attention to the continuity of the code and takes tradition, precedent and custom as the basis for judging cases. 亦称"普通法系""英国法系""判例法系"。以英国普通法为基础发展起来的法律的总称。指英国从 11 世纪起主要以源于日耳曼习惯法的普通法为基础，逐渐形成的一种独特的法律制度以及仿效英国的其他一些国家和地区的法律制度。产生于英国，后扩大到曾经是英国殖民地、附属国的许多国家和地区，包括美国、加拿大、印度、巴基斯坦、孟加拉、马来西亚、新加坡、澳大利亚、新西兰以及非洲的个别国家和地区。是西方国家中与大陆法系并列的历史悠久和影响较大的法系，注重法典的延续性，以传统、判例和习惯为判案依据。

Continued

legal awareness 法律意识	Part of the social consciousness. It is a general term for people's thoughts, opinions, theories and psychology about law. It includes two parts: legal psychology and legal thought system. The former covers people's views on nature and the function of the law, and their requirements and attitudes toward the existing law, which are often formed spontaneously and belong to the primary stage of legal consciousness. The latter refers to people's evaluation and interpretation of the law, the evaluation of the legality of people's behavior and the concept of the legal system, etc. belong to the advanced stage of legal consciousness, which needs to be cultivated and educated to gradually form. 社会意识的组成部分。是人们关于法的思想、观点、理论和心理的统称。包括法律心理和法律思想体系两部分,前者涵盖人们对法的本质和作用的看法,对现行法律的要求和态度,常是自发形成的,属于法律意识的初级阶段;后者指人们对法律的评价和解释,对人们的行为是否合法的评价以及法制观念等,属法律意识的高级阶段,需经培养、教育才能逐步形成。
Economic Law 经济法	The general name of the legal norms that regulate economic relations in economic management and coordinated development of economic activities. 调整国家在经济管理和协调发展经济活动中所发生的经济关系的法律规范的总称。
unfair competition 不正当竞争	Also known as "illegal competition". The act of using dishonest or other improper means to violate the rights of others and seek illegal profits in the field of industry and commerce. 又称"非法竞争"。在工商业领域中采用不诚实或其他不正当的手段侵犯他人权利,牟取非法利益的行为。
monopoly 垄断	In economic terms, generally divided into seller's monopoly and buyer's monopoly. A seller's monopoly refers to a single seller facing competitive consumers in one or more markets through one or more stages; A buyer's monopoly is the opposite. Theory presumes that a monopolist in a market can adjust the price and output according to its own interest needs, but there are no firm cases to date to support this. Monopoly, as an economic phenomenon, is more obvious in the developed stage of capitalist society. Monopoly is the inevitable result of the development of competition, which appears and inhibits competition. 经济学术语,一般分为卖方垄断和买方垄断。卖方垄断指的是唯一的卖者在一个或多个市场,通过一个或多个阶段,面对竞争性的消费者;买者垄断则恰恰相反。理论推断垄断者在市场上,可以根据自己的利益需求,调节价格与产量,但至今为止没有确切案例提供支持。垄断作为一种经济现象,在资本主义社会发展阶段的表现较为明显。垄断是竞争发展的必然结果,其出现又抑制了竞争。

Review & Critical Thinking Questions

1. What is the implication of the law? And what are the characteristics of the law?

2. How is the law classified in this unit? Discuss its theoretical basis.

3. How would you understand the law environment? What elements are involved in the legal environment?

4. What is the main purpose of economic law? Please illustrate the legal function with an example of a business or a marketing activity.

5. How does the Law of Anti-unfair competition protect the proper operation of the economy? It is favorable to discuss this issue with the case around you.

6. How would you understand the relationship between the law or legal environment and marketing?

7. How many legal factors affecting marketing are mentioned in this unit? Could you figure out any other factors which have influence on marketing?

8. Try to analyze the positive and negative impacts of the law on marketing with your partner.

Discussion Questions

1. How would you understand the function of the law? Please discuss it with 1–2 partners.

2. Recently, online purchases are quite popular, but the exposure of privacy is a great snake in the grass. Suppose you are a supervisor of a courier service company, what measures will be taken to protect customers' information and protect you from legal claims?

3. If you are a marketing manager in charge of big data collection from online sales and marketing, what legal problems should you consider to avoid possible lawsuits? How to protect your users' information within the scope of the relative law?

4. Have you ever experienced or heard of unfair competition? What should we do to protect ourselves from unfair competition in marketing or other economic activities?

5. What is fraud, and how does it affect marketing? Do you know what measures have been taken in our country to be against it?

Case Study

In recent years, dumping and anti-dumping have become the buzzwords in the international trade war and international marketing strategies.

Dumping is the practice of exporting goods with less than their normal value in the normal course of trade. It has caused or is likely to cause damages to counterparts in the importing country and is therefore opposed by the importing country.

As a response, the importing country may impose anti-dumping duties and other punitive measures through the competent authorities, after placing an investigation and confirming the conduct of damping which has caused damages to the domestic industries.

When Wen Zhou entered the world market for metal-coated lighters in the mid-to-late 1980s, it rapidly changed the situation of the market, which was dominated by Japan, South Korea and Taiwan. By 2002, Wen Zhou had produced more than 500 million metal-coated lighters annually, accounting for 80% of the global output and 70% of the world market share. When Zhou has become the world's production center of metal-coated lighters, while more than 90% of the original lighter enterprises in Japan and South Korea have stopped production.

In September 2001, the European Union introduced the Child Resistance Act (CR) at the request of European cigarette lighter manufacturers. The bill requires all lighters under 2 euros to be fitted with safety devices. Wen-zhou-made metal-clad lighters, which cost about 1 euro, would be subject to the law. The technical standard will become a technical barrier for China's cigarette lighter exporting to the European market. Before the bill was formally introduced, the Wen Zhou Tobacco Products Association sent a delegation to Europe to lobby with fair trade officials from the Ministry of Foreign Trade and Economic Cooperation, but failed to prevent its passage.

On June 28, 2002, the EU issued a notice to initiate an anti-dumping investigation against Chinese lighters exported to the EU. According to WTO regulation, the exporter involved in anti-dumping must respond to the complaint within 15 days, otherwise it will be regarded as an automatic waiver act, which may lead to Chinese cigarette lighters exported to EU Countries facing high anti-dumping duties.

After urgent Constitution, Wen Zhou cigarillo equipment Association decided to choose 16 lighter enterprises for damage defense, 1 for market economy status defense (that is, lower than the cost price). On September 11, 2002, several officials for the EU anti-dumping Committee visited Wen Zhou twice to conduct field investigations, strictly checking the products, sales, finance and other aspects of the respondent enterprises in Wen Zhou understanding and approving the opinions and facts put forward by the respondent enterprises. On October 8, 2002, Wen Zhou Dong Fang Lighter Factory was granted the market economy status of EU. In February 2003, the EU decided not to proceed with preliminary determination. On July 14, 2003, the European Lighter Manufacturers' Federation withdrew its anti-dumping action against Chinese lighters, and the anti-dumping proceeding was terminated automatically.

Questions

1. Based on the case description, why did this Chinese enterprise succeed in anti-dumpling dispute? Please analyze with relative knowledge.
2. In this case, what legal factors are embodied in handling the dispute?

中文概述

　　法律的基本目的是维护秩序,平息纠纷。法律不仅仅是一套行为规则,它也是强制执行责任与社会正义的手段。

　　法律判例是普通法系的基本特征,与欧洲大陆发展起来的大陆法系形成对比。大陆法系国家已将其法律编纂为成文法,因此这些国家的法律主要来源于成文法而非判例法。在英美法系,成文法和判例都是形成律法的基础。法律由国家制定或承认,并由国家强制力保障。它们反映了由特定社会的物质生活条件所决定的统治阶级的意志。它是以权利义务为内容,以确定、保护和发展有利于统治阶级的社会关系和社会秩序为目的的一种规范或行为体系。

　　就社会规范而言,法律区别于其他社会规范的基本特征是法律具有国家意志性,由国家制定或认可;以权利、义务、权力、职责为主要内容。

　　法律类别包括三种:影响市场主体的法律、影响市场自由的法律、影响市场秩序的法律。

　　市场秩序的法律主要有三个方面的内容:一是商业欺诈,包括产品质量、信用、财务报告等方面的欺诈。二是商业贿赂。三是商业垄断。市场经济是自由竞争,不能垄断。

　　法律环境是指国家或地方政府颁布的各项法规、法令、条例等。法律环境对企业的营销活动具有一定的调节作用,同时对市场消费需求的形成和实现也具有一定的调节作用。企业研究并熟悉法律环境,不仅可以保证自身严格依法经营和运用法律手段保障自身权益,还可通过法律条文的变化对市场需求及其走势进行预测。它主要包含内外有别的两个层次:一个是外显的表层结构,即法律规范、法律制度、法律组织机构及法律设施;另一个是内化的里层结构,即法律意识形态。社会中的人处于各种受法律调整的社会关系中,所以,法律关系也应当是法律环境的重要组成部分。

　　法律要素一般包括四大类。(1)法律规范。(2)国家司法执法机关。(3)企业的法律意识。(4)国际法所规定的国际法律环境和目标国的国内法律环境。

　　经济法的目的主要体现在两个方面:(1)保护企业免受不正当竞争。(2)保护消费者免受商家欺诈。

　　总之,所有的营销活动都要服从大量的法律法规。虽然每一部法律都有自己的立法基础,但它仍然在无意中阻碍了创造力和经济增长,并对营销人员施加了更多的限制。然而,每个联盟都有自己的两面性,这无疑是促进企业向更好的方向发展的巨大挑战。越来越多的企业和商家进入虚拟空间,建立了电子商务伦理的新标准。

市场营销法律范畴包括：(1)**数据收集和侵犯隐私**。(2)**数据分布**。(3)**营销误导**。(4)**上门销售**。(5)**各种广告**。(6)**电话销售和直接邮寄**。(7)**网络营销**。(8)**定价、促销和竞争**中的法律问题。

法律和**法律环境**对企业营销都有重要的影响。

法律环境给企业带来的影响有利有弊。**不利影响**包括为了达到法律的要求（如严格的废气排放标准），企业的成本费用增加，降低了相对于海外竞争对手的竞争力；规章制度的复杂程度可能产生针对小公司的进入壁垒。在各国的企业立法中，企业设立的实质条件和程序条件都是主要内容。

实际上，所有的市场活动都受制于大量的法律和法规的管制，而这些法律法规都有可能是国家之上、国家、本地等不同级别政府的产物，甚至不同级别的法律法规都有可能发生重叠的现象。

有利影响诸如纠正市场运转不灵的情况并保证市场的公平。阻止限制性行为和垄断权力的立法促进竞争机制，有利于企业的发展壮大；良好的法律环境也可以为企业的经营发展提供法律保障，促进业内更加公平、公正，为自身的发展创造良好的环境。企业的生存与发展从来都不是孤立的，它需要依靠市场条件和竞争机制来实现效益。企业的本质取决于经营模式和管理模式，单纯依靠企业的自律来完成有序市场竞争的想法确实不够成熟。数百年的市场经济实践表明，有序市场竞争的形成需要法律体系的保护，完善的反不正当竞争法和反垄断法是企业经营和区域经济发展不可缺少的法律环境因素。

PART 2
Customers and Positioning

UNIT 6 International Marketing Research

Learning Objectives

1. Understand the meaning and classification of marketing research.
2. Describe the methods of marketing research for collecting different types of data.
3. Identify the steps and relevant issues in the marketing research process.
4. Understand the differences of marketing research in the online environment.
5. Explain the relationship between marketing research and MIS.

6.1 The Definition and Classification of Marketing Research

To design and implement successful marketing programs, marketers must have fresh and deep insights into what customers need and want. And such insights come from good marketing information from a wide range of sources.

Marketing research is traditionally defined as systematic gathering, recording, and analyzing of data to provide information useful to marketing decision making related to the identification of opportunities and solution of problems in marketing. For example, marketing research can provide a deeper understanding of customer motivations, purchase behavior and satisfaction, and better assessment of the effectiveness of pricing, product, distribution, and promotion activities.

According to this definition, we can broadly classify marketing research into problem-identification research and problem-solving research, as shown in Figure 6.1.

Problem-identification research is undertaken to help identify problems that are probably not obvious at the moment but may come to the surface in the future. Such kind of research usually involves the assessment of market potential, market share, company or brand image, sales prediction, industry trends, etc. The relevant information helps firms better understand the marketing environment and diagnose possible problems. For example, the market size of instant noodles has begun to decline since 2013. Many companies, even those market leaders such as Uni-President Group（统一集团）and

Figure 6.1   A Classification of Marketing Research

Master Kung（康师傅），faced the difficulties of realizing growth targets. One of the major reasons for the market decline is the fast development of the take-out food industry. People can conveniently order various dishes via online platforms such as Meituan or Eleme, and receive the dishes in a short time. Upon further analysis, the problem was identified as a change in consumer perception. Since the traditional instant noodle was produced by deep frying, it was viewed as unhealthy. With the improvements in living standards, consumers gradually put more emphasis on health and paid more attention to food nutrition, so instant noodles were abandoned. This information helps Uni-President Group and Master Kung adapt their strategies and devote more effort to introducing the high-end instant noodles with better taste and nutritional values. Similarly, the recognition of other cultural change, or economic and social trends, may also link to the potential problems or opportunities.

In contrast, **problem-solving research** is undertaken to look for a solution to the problem or opportunity that has been identified. It is common for most companies to conduct such kind of research and use the relevant findings to make decisions for resolving the specific marketing problems. These problems may be concerned with segmentation, product, pricing, promotion, and distribution. It is noticeable that although it is conceptually and practically useful to distinguish problem-solving research from problem-identification research, these two types of marketing research are usually used together. In other words, a given marketing research project may combine both types of research.

6.2   The Basic Methodology of Marketing Research

To fulfill the marketing research goal, the researchers need to gather secondary data, primary data, or both. **Secondary data** consists of information that already exists somewhere, having been collected for another purpose. **Primary data** consists of information collected for the specific purpose at hand. Researchers usually start by gathering secondary data. If available information cannot meet the manager's information needs, then they may need to take action to gather primary data.

6.2.1 The Methods of Gathering Secondary Data

Company's internal database provides a good starting point. However, the company can also utilize various sorts of external information sources. Companies can buy secondary data from outside suppliers. For example, Nielsen sells shopper insight data from a consumer panel of more than 250,000 households in 25 countries worldwide, with measures of trial and repeat purchasing, brand loyalty, and buyer demographics. Another example is DATAWAY (零点有数), which is a famous Chinese consulting group founded in 1992, and sells insight data concerning various industries such as automobile, finance, tobacco, logistics, etc.

At the same time, there are various commercial online databases, which could be used by marketing researchers to conduct their own searches of secondary data sources. Beyond commercial services offering information for a fee, most industry associations, government agencies, business publications, and news media also offer free information to those who visit their websites or apps. In addition, many relevant secondary information sources may also be identified through Internet search engines. But the searching process could be very inefficient and frustrating due to the need for overloaded information filtering. Still, well-structured, well-designed online searches provide a good start to any marketing research project.

Generally speaking, the time and monetary cost of collecting secondary data is lower than that of collecting primary data. Also, secondary sources can sometimes provide data to an individual company which cannot collect on its own—information that is not accessible or would be too expensive to collect. For example, it is not realistic for a consumer products manufacturer, such as WAHAHA or HERBORIST (佰草集) to conduct an ongoing retail store audit to find out about the market shares, prices, and displays of its own and competitors' brands. But those store sales and audit data may be purchased from marketing research companies.

However, secondary data also has some limitations. Since secondary data is usually not collected for specific reasons, it may not satisfy all the needs of the researchers. For example, the population census could provide useful information for evaluating the purchasing power of residents in different cities, but more details about how they spend their money are not available. In other cases, companies cannot find existing information regarding consumer reactions about new products yet to be launched either. Therefore, secondary information must be carefully evaluated by researchers to ensure it is relevant (fits the research project's needs), accurate (reliably collected and reported), current (up-to-date enough for current decisions), and impartial (objectively collected and reported).

6.2.2 The Methods of Gathering Primary Data

When secondary data is not available or insufficient to satisfy information needs, researchers must collect primary data through original research pertaining to the particular confronted problem.

1. Survey Research

Survey research utilizes questionnaires designed to elicit quantitative data (e.g. "How much would you pay?"), qualitative responses ("Why would you buy?"), or both. It is the most widely used method for primary data collection, and best suited for gathering descriptive information, such as people's knowledge, attitudes, preferences, or buying behavior. When a company wants to know such information, it can often find out by asking them directly. The questionnaires could be distributed through mail, asked over the telephone, and asked in person or online. Thus the use of survey research could be very flexible, and able to gain many different kinds of information in many different situations.

However, this method also has some limitations. The answers drawn from the questionnaire could be inaccurate or even misleading, because sometimes the respondents cannot remember or have never thought about what actions they will take or why they do so. Social desirability bias is another possible issue. It means the respondents may answer survey questions even when they do not know the answer just to appear smarter or more informed, or they may give pleasing answers as an attempt to help the interviewer. In other situations, the respondents may be reluctant to respond to unknown interviewers or about things they consider private, such as their salary number or work content. When people are busy, they may not take time, or even resent the intrusion into their privacy. Therefore, researchers need to be careful to design the questionnaires and use many skills to enhance the response rate and accuracy level, as well as reduce the social desirability. For example, the first question should create interest, and difficult or personal questions should be asked last so that respondents do not become defensive. And all the questions need to be arranged in a logical order.

After the questionnaire was drafted, it is necessary to conduct a pre-test with a subset of the population under study, or at least with knowledgeable experts and/or individuals. The pre-test should also be conducted in the same mode as the final interview. Without this process, the risks of poor research would be great. In other words, the validity and reliability of the questionnaires should be assured.

2. Observational Research

Observational research means one or more well-trained observers (or a mechanical device such as a video camera) watch and record the behavior of actual or prospective buyers. For example, a marketer of kitchen blenders might send researchers to pre-selected households at 6 p.m. to watch families go about their dinner routines. The researcher could also accompany family members to supermarkets to observe their behavior under actual shopping conditions, and record their reactions to in-store promotions linked to an advertising campaign.

Observational research can glean customer insights that cannot be obtained by simply asking customers questions, such as information that people are unwilling or unable to provide. It also provides a window into customers' unconscious actions and unexpressed needs and feelings. Of course, this method has its own limitations as well. First, not all things could be observed, such as attitudes, motives, or private behavior. Long-term or infrequent behavior is also difficult to observe. The second potential problem is reactivity, which means if the research subjects know they are under study, they may tend to behave differently. And companies using observation as a research methodology must be sensitive to concerns about privacy issues. In some cases, recording people's behaviors should get their consent, otherwise they may feel offended when they find out. Finally, observations can be very difficult to interpret. Therefore, observational research is usually used along with other data collection methods to draw more reliable conclusions.

3. Focus Group Research

A focus group involves encouraging an invited small group of participants (usually 6 to 10 people) to share their thoughts, feelings, attitudes, and ideas on certain subjects, such as a product concept, brand's image and personality, an advertisement, a social trend, or another topic. A typical focus group meets at a facility equipped with recording equipment and a two-way mirror behind which representatives of the client company observe the proceedings (see Figure 6.2). And through video-conferencing and Internet technology, off-site marketers can observe, and even participate in the focus group. The group interactions are led by a trained moderator, who encourages free and easy discussion among the group members, and at the same time ensures the discussion does not digress from the topic. The moderator can not only hear consumer ideas and opinions, but also observe facial expressions, body movements, group interplay, and conversational flows. Therefore, focus group research yields qualitative data that is likely to differ from those gathered through more direct questioning. But such data tends to be directional rather than conclusive, and they suggest rather than confirm hypotheses. The focus group method is quite valuable in the exploratory phase of a project, such as generating new concepts for a product, and predicting consumers' behavior and interactions with the new product.

Figure 6.2　A Typical Room for Focus Group Research

Likewise, focus group research faces some challenges. To keep time and costs down, the focus group usually consists of a small number of participants, and thus the generality of the results may be questionable. Moreover, participants in focus groups are not always open and honest about their real feelings, behaviors, and intentions in front of other people. It is important to create a suitable environment and help consumers relax, which may lead to more authentic responses. And the moderator can utilize various approaches such as visualization and role plays to facilitate reactions and responses. To obtain better results, it would be necessary to use focus group research in conjunction with data gathered via observation and other methods.

4. Experiment Research

It means selecting matched groups of subjects, giving them different treatments, controlling unrelated factors, and checking for differences in group responses. Therefore, the experiment research attempts to find out cause-and-effect relationships. This method is commonly adopted in test marketing, in which a product under study is placed on sale in one or more selected locations, and its reception by consumers and the purchases could be recorded and analyzed. For example, when deciding the price of a newly launched burger, KFC might use experiments to test the effects on sales of two different prices it might charge. The new burger may be sold at one price in one city and at another price in another city. If the cities are similar and if all other marketing efforts for the burger are the same, then differences in sales in the two cities may be attributed to the price charged. Performance in the test markets also provides some indication of the performance to be expected when the product goes into the general market.

However, interpreting data obtained from experiment research should be cautious. It is necessary to isolate the effects of other confounding factors. Only when other conditions are held constant or are comparable across the research subjects, the effect difference could be related to the variable of manipulation. But in reality, such controls may not be easily satisfied outside the lab environment. Thus the use of experiment research may be limited.

6.3　The Process of Marketing Research

▶ 6.3.1　Step 1：Defining the Problem and Research Objectives

Defining the problem and research objectives is always the first step in any marketing research project. While the managers as the decision makers best understand which information is needed, the researchers best understand how to obtain information. Therefore, they must work together closely to fulfill the first step, which may be the most difficult but also the most important step. They could have broad discussions, consult with industry experts, and analyze secondary data and qualitative research. These tasks should lead to an understanding of the environmental context of the problem and an evaluation of the certain essential factors, including past information and forecasts about the industry and the firm, objectives of the managers, buyer behavior, resources and constraints of the firm, the legal and economic environment, marketing and technological skills of the firm, and etc. Such analysis will assist in the identification of management decision problem, which should then be translated into a marketing research problem.

Not only the marketing research problem should be carefully defined, the research objectives also need to be clearly set. There are often three types of objectives. First, the objective of **exploratory research** is to gather preliminary information that will help define the problem and suggest hypotheses. Second, the objective of **descriptive research** is to describe things like the market potential for a product, or the demographics of target consumers. Finally, the objective of **causal research** is to test hypotheses about cause-and-effect relationships, such as the possible effects of the package change on the customer preference. Managers and researchers often start with exploratory research and later follow with descriptive or causal research. Whereas observation is best suited for exploratory research and surveys for descriptive research, experimental research is best suited for gathering causal information.

▶ 6.3.2　Step 2：Formulating a Research Design

Once the research problem and objectives have been defined, researchers must formulate a research design, which covers details of the procedures that must be implemented for obtaining required information. Its purpose is to design a study that will test the hypotheses of interest, determine possible answers to the research questions, and provide information needed by managers for making decisions. In addition, the research design also needs to determine the type of research to be conducted, define the variables precisely, and design appropriate scales to measure them. If primary data is required, issue of how data should be obtained from the respondents (for example, by conducting a survey or an experiment) must be addressed. The researcher has to develop a sampling plan that specifies how to select respondents for the study and must prepare a preliminary plan for data analysis. When a survey method is used, it is also necessary to design a questionnaire. The typical research design for primary data collection is illustrated in Figure 6.3. The issues relevant to those aspects will be explained more detailedly in the following.

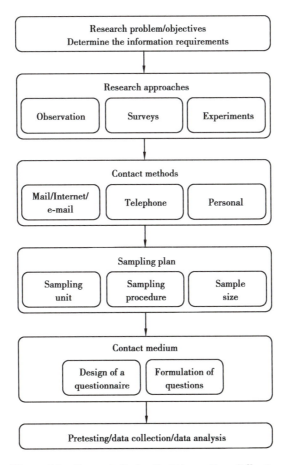

Figure 6.3　Research Design for Primary Data Collection

1. Contact Methods

Information can be collected by mail, by personal (face-to-face) interviews, by telephone, or Internet/E-mail. Each contact method has its own strengths and weaknesses. When choosing the method of contact, researchers have to trade-off among speed, degree of accuracy and cost.

Mail surveys are among the least expensive, but it may take a longer time to receive responses. They allow respondents to answer at a convenient moment, and will make the respondents feel less intrusive as with a phone or personal interview. In contrast, personal (face-to-face) interviews are more flexible and could collect larger amounts of information because trained interviewers can hold a respondent's attention for a long time and can explain difficult questions. However, personal interviews face the problem of high costs, sample number limits, and interviewer bias. Telephone interviews are somewhere between personal and mail surveys. They generally have a higher response rate than mail surveys but lower than personal interviews, while their costs are usually less than with personal interviews, and they allow somewhat flexibility when interviewing. However, the use of visual aids is not possible, and there are limits to the number of questions that can be asked before respondents either terminate the interview or give quick (invalid) answers to speed up the process. Finally, online surveys are both very economical and very fast. And it is possible to attach pictures and sound files. They can be web-based (such as in the form of pop-up survey) or conducted through e-mail. However, the response rate of online surveys may be relatively low.

2. Sampling Plan

Except in very restricted markets, it is usually unrealistic for a researcher to contact all the actual and potential users/customers of a particular product or service. Thus the researcher needs to select a segment of the consumer population as a sample to represent the entire population. Ideally, the sample should be representative, so that reasonable estimates could be made from the small sample to predict the thoughts and behaviors of the larger population. Selecting the sample involves three key decisions: sampling unit, sampling procedure, and sample size .

First, the *sampling unit* refers to the research subject, or who is to be contacted. For example, to study the purchase behavior of household appliances, the questionnaire could be separately designed and distributed to the decision makers, other family members, or the frontline salespeople.

Second, *sampling procedure* refers to how the people in the sample should be chosen. There are two major categories of sampling: *probability and non-probability sampling*. Probability sampling means that each element in the population has a known (not necessarily equal) probability of being included in the sample. Then researchers can calculate confidence limits for sampling error. In contrast, non-probability sampling means the probability for each element of being included in the sample is unknown, and thus the sampling error cannot be computed.

Finally, *sample size* means how many respondents should be chosen. Large samples usually obtain more reliable conclusions than small samples, but also cost more time and money. It's not always necessary to include large samples to generate reliable results. To determine the sample size, the researcher may take into consideration the available budget, the number of subgroups to be analyzed (if applicable), and common practice in particular industry.

3. Contact Medium/Measurement Instrument

In collecting primary data, marketing researchers can utilize two main research instruments: questionnaires and mechanical devices.

A *questionnaire* is probably the most frequently used instrument, and it is the vehicle whereby the research objectives are translated into specific questions. It could be designed in a relatively unstructured form with *open-ended* questions that allow respondents to answer in their own words. For example, to investigate the service quality perception of residents, Atour hotel might directly ask them: "What is your impression of Atour hotel service?" Or it can ask the residents to complete a sentence like "In my opinion, the most important factors of hotel services are..." Such kind of questions are useful in exploratory research that can help to identify the frame of reference of the respondents. Alternatively, the questionnaire could also be designed in a relatively structured form with *closed-ended* questions that include all the possible answers, and respondents make choices among them, such as multiple-choice questions and scale questions. For example, to establish the identity of a respondent, a nominal scale could be used to label male respondents as "1" and female respondents as "2." There is also scaling in some kind of continuum such as the Likert scale, which asks respondents to indicate whether they "strongly agree" with a statement, "strongly disagree," or whether their attitude falls somewhere in the middle. Thus the closed-ended questions provide answers that are easier to interpret and tabulate. In general, the type of information sought, and the type of respondents to be researched, will have an impact on the contact method to be used, and this in turn will influence the form of questionnaire. But no matter the form, the questionnaire should be clear (i.e. simple, direct, and unbiased) wording.

Another important way to obtain market information (e.g. consumer behavior) data is to utilize various *mechanical instruments*. For many years, companies like Nielsen has conducted television audience measurement (TAM) by studying the viewing habits of household panels. Broadcasters use audience share data to set advertising rates, and companies also use the data to choose programs during which to advertise. Meanwhile, retailers traditionally use checkout scanners to record shoppers' purchases.

With the development of neuromarketing, neuro technologies such as EEG (electroencephalo-graph) and MRI (Magnetic Resonance Imaging) are also used to track brain electrical activity to measure consumer involvement and emotional responses second by second. Although such brain responses can be difficult to interpret, used in combination with biometric measures such as heart/respiration rates, facial and eye movements (see Figure 6.4), they can provide useful insights into the direct responses of consumers toward their brands, product designs, advertising, and other marketing efforts. In a word, these mechanical instruments can help researchers understand not only the outcome of (or exposure to) the marketing effort but also the entire process customers go through in arriving at a decision.

Figure 6.4　The Eye Tracker Can Record Consumer's Responses in Real Situations

6.3.3　Step 3: Implementing the Research Plan

After formulating the research design, the next step is to implement the research plan. This involves collecting, processing, and analyzing data.

Data collection could be done by the firm itself or outsourced to third-party providers. The market researcher should establish the parameters under which research is conducted to reduce problems with data collection techniques and technologies, data quality, and timeliness. For example, without clear instructions, the interviews may be conducted in different ways by different interviewers. Therefore, interviewers have to be instructed about the nature of the study, starting and completion time and sampling methodology. For the focus group interview, spot checks on the administration procedures are also vital to ensure reasonable data quality.

Data processing involves adequately preparing data for analysis. Each questionnaire or observation form is inspected or edited and, if necessary, corrected for any errors. In particular, the questionnaires would be coded, which means each response to each question in the questionnaire is represented by number or letter codes. This will result in the dataset being arranged in tabular form. Some data adjustment may be required before further analysis.

Next, data analysis could derive information related to the components of the marketing research problem and thus provide input into management decision making. In qualitative data analysis, researchers usually review recordings of in-depth interviews or focus group sessions, or they may rely on their own notes and recollections from the sessions. Such conditions naturally introduce subjectivity into the process and leave much of the data interpretation and analysis to the skills and experiences of the individual researchers. On the other hand, analyzing quantitative data is much more structured and researchers can use various methods to analyze data. Relatively simple statistical techniques include hypothesis testing and chi-square testing; more advanced data analysis such as analysis of variance (ANOVA), correlation analysis, and regression analysis can also be used.

6.3.4　Step 4: Interpreting and Reporting the Findings

Finally, the market researcher needs to interpret the findings, draw conclusions, finish and submit the report in written form, orally, or electronically via video to management. No matter the form, the report should be clearly related to the problem or opportunity identified in step 1. In particular, discussions between researchers and managers are necessary to lead to the best interpretations of the findings, which in many cases could be interpreted in different ways. They may work together closely and share knowledge, experience, and expertise to better understand the research results, and even share responsibility for the following decisions.

Although we have described the research process as a sequence of steps, in reality these steps may not occur sequentially but are interdependent and iterative. In other words, at each step, the researcher needs to not only look back at the previous steps but also look ahead to the following steps, and adjust their actions in time.

6.4　Online Research in the Era of Big Data

The online survey, focus group, and experiment are like traditional marketing research conducted offline, collecting logical consumer responses to structured and intrusive research questions. However, there are richer veins of unsolicited, unstructured, spontaneous customer information already coursing around the Internet. Thus actively tapping into such information has been an important and promising trend in online marketing research. In the following, we present a few of these techniques.

Web browsing. Using web analytics tools such as Google Analytics, WebTrends, StatCounter, and Woopra, researchers can collect clickstream data that tracks the Internet users' browsing behaviors, including the links they clicked on, the length of time spent on specific pages, etc. These data could be effective indicators to assess the general performance of a website and provide insights for understanding and optimizing web usage. They can also be analyzed in conjunction with online surveys or traditional research to explore questions such as visitors' satisfaction, and the effectiveness of different marketing offers. By observing and analyzing application usage over a certain period of time, it is possible to extract users' behavior patterns—what searches they make, the online and mobile sites they visit, how they shop, and what they buy—such information is enormously valuable to marketers. Based on this online information, they can target ads and offers to specific consumers, the practice of which is called **behavioral targeting**. For example, if you add a Huawei smartphone in your Taobao shopping cart but don't place the order, later on you might see some ads for that smartphone or similar products when you visit another webpage such as the news page, or search page.

Text mining. Except for clickstream data, Internet users also leave footprints in the form of huge amounts of textual data on the company's brand site, on shopping sites (e. g. Tmall, JD.com), and on social media sites (e.g. Weibo, Youku, Douban), blogs, forums and chatrooms. This data is usually called user-generated content, and is extremely unstructured, large in magnitude and not easy to syndicate. Commercial (e.g. Nielsen Online) and academic text-mining tools provide marketers and researchers with an opportunity to "listen" to consumers in the market. They can track what consumers are saying or feeling about a product/brand, what's their attitude toward a social event or an advertisement, etc. By doing so, firms can better understand consumers' opinions and preferences, the market structure and the competitive environment. Getting insights from the text-mining, firms may also respond to customers' needs more quickly and appropriately, providing opportunities for building positive brand experiences and relationships with customers.

Data mining. In addition to text mining, there are also other techniques of data mining that extract patterns from large data sets (e.g. E-commerce transaction data) by combining methods from statistics and machine learning with database management. They include: (1) Association rule learning: one example is market basket analysis, which means using a variety of algorithms to generate and test possible rules, so that a retailer can detect which products are frequently bought together and use this information for effective promotion. (2) Cluster analysis: a statistical method for classifying objects that splits a diverse group into smaller groups of similar objects without knowing their characteristics of similarity in advance. This method could be used for segmenting consumers into self-similar groups for targeted marketing. (3) Classification: a machine learning method for identifying the categories to which new data points belong, based on a training set containing data points that have already been classified. This method could be used for predicting customer behavior in specific segments. (4) Regression: a common statistical method for predicting how the value of the dependent variable (such as sales volume) changes if independent variables are modified.

It is noticeable that nowadays social media has become the fastest growing sources of information flow. Examples of social media include social-networking sites or applications (e.g. Douban, Wechat), voice networking (e.g. Skype), product and service reviews (e.g. Meituan-Dianpin, Koubei), video sharing (e. g. Youku, Douyin), photo sharing (e.g. Instagram), music sharing (e.g. Netease Cloud Music), wikis (e.g. Wikipedia, Baidu Baike), virtual worlds (e. g. Second Life), multiplayer games (e. g. Wangzhe Rongyao), Web-based communities (e.g. Baidu Tieba, Tianya), blogs (e.g. Sina blog), and microblogs (e. g. Weibo). These are Web or mobile applications that facilitate interactive information sharing, user-centered design, and collaboration on the Internet. The exploding popularity of social media platforms has resulted in a wealth of **big data**, which refers to extremely large data sets that can be subjected to computation analysis to reveal patterns and trends.

Many companies have drawn benefits from the big data analytics capabilities. No doubt to say, big data management would become the next frontier for online marketing research.

Meanwhile, research shows that consumers are now relying more on the online word-of-mouth rather than the information obtained from news page or search engine, thus they may shop a lot like their friends and are much more likely to respond to ads from brands their friends use. Here, the "friends" refer to a much wider circle in the context of the ubiquitous use of social media. Gradually the online marketing goes further than behavioral targeting that tracks consumer movements across online sites, and moves toward **social targeting,** which means targeting ads and offers to specific consumers by tracking individual online social connections and conversations from social networking sites. Therefore, you might also see the ad for a specific model of Huawei smartphone because a friend that you're connected to via Weibo just bought the Huawei smartphone from Taobao recently, even though you have not searched online for smartphone information.

6.5 The Role of Marketing Research in MIS and CRM

As defined earlier, marketing research is the process of gathering, recording, and analyzing data to provide information useful for marketing decision making. It usually focuses on a specific problem and aims to solve one defined issue at a time, having a definite start and end point. Such project-based marketing research is not able to satisfy all the information needs of managers. It is necessary for companies to design effective marketing information systems that provide managers with right information in the right form at the right time. A **marketing information system (MIS)** is a formalized set of procedures and methods for the regular, planned collection, analysis, and presentation of information for use in making marketing decisions. In other words, an MIS is intended to collect, interpret, and organize marketing information from a variety of sources on an ongoing basis. Therefore, marketing research could be seen as a part of the broader MIS and integrated with information from other sources to generate more useful insights for decision makers.

The other information sources are mainly internal data and marketing intelligence. The internal data come from a variety of functional departments and even network partners: the marketing department reports customer characteristics, sales transactions, and web and social media site visits; the sales force are clear about reseller reactions and competitor activities; the customer service department possesses information on service problems or customer satisfaction; the accounting department keeps track on sales, costs, and cash flows; the operational departments have records on production, shipments, and inventories; and marketing channel partners provide data on sales transactions. Marketing intelligence involves continuous monitoring, collection, and analysis of publicly available and general information about consumers, competitors, and developments in the marketplace. It ranges from observing consumers directly to quizzing the company's own employees, benchmarking competitors' products, online research, and monitoring social media buzz.

Therefore, a MIS offers the potential of much more information than can be obtained from ad hoc marketing research projects. The MIS could be potentially powerful if it can give managers access to vast amounts of information by combining internal organizational information with external marketing intelligence (perhaps including marketing research) into a centralized data warehouse. With the help of advanced analytics to learn more about the relationships within sets of data, managers may gain customer and market insights that will improve their marketing decisions.

Customer relationship management (CRM) is one of the digital business tools that helps companies leverage the data they collect. It consists of sophisticated software and analysis tools provided by international companies such as Salesforce, Oracle, Microsoft, and domestic companies such as Kingdee and UFIDA. The CRM system integrates and analyzes customer and marketplace information from various sources mentioned above, intending to form a complete picture of the customer and his or her relationship to the company and its products or services. The results may enable managers to understand customers better, identify high-value customers, cross-sell the company's products, and create offers tailored to specific customer requirements. For example, in the hotel industry, CRM can give front desk staff real-time access to customer information. When a repeat customer checks in, the system may immediately pull up data on his or her previous accommodation records and other contacts, helping the front desk staff better serve the customer, such as assigning the preferable room and recommending customized additional services. This may result in greater customer satisfaction and loyalty that increases hotel sales.

Key Terms

marketing research 营销调研	The systematic gathering, recording, and analyzing of data to provide information useful to marketing decision making related to the identification of opportunities and solution of problems in marketing. 为了识别和解决营销中的问题和机会而进行的系统收集、记录和分析数据的行为。
problem-identification research 问题识别研究	The marketing research undertaken to help identify problems that are probably not obvious at the moment but may come to the surface in the future. 用来帮助识别已有或潜在的问题的市场营销调研。
problem-solving research 问题解决研究	The marketing research undertaken to look for a solution to the problem or opportunity that has been identified. 用来寻找已被识别出来的问题或机遇的应对之道的调研方法。
secondary data 二手数据	Information that already exists somewhere and has been collected for another purpose. 已经存在于某处，但可能是出于其他目的而被收集的信息。
primary data 一手数据	Information collected for the specific purpose at hand. 又被称为原始数据，是专门为手头特定目的而收集的信息。
survey research 调查研究法	The marketing research method that directly asks the survey object's attitude, preference, purchase behavior and other descriptive information through telephone, Internet, face-to-face and other ways. 通过电话、网络以及面对面等不同方式来直接询问调研对象的态度、偏好以及购买行为等描述性信息的调研方法。
observational research 观察法	One or more well-trained observers (or a mechanical device such as a video camera) watch and record the behavior of actual or prospective buyers. 是指一个或多个训练有素的观察者（或摄像机之类的机械设备）观察和记录实际或潜在买家的行为。
focus group research 焦点小组	The marketing research that involves encouraging an invited small group of participants (usually 6 to 10 people) to share their thoughts, feelings, attitudes, and ideas on certain subjects. 邀请6到10个参与者形成一个小组，由主持人引导他们分享对某些主题的想法、感受、态度和观点的营销调研方法。

Continued

experiment research 实验研究法	The market research method that finds out cause-and-effect relationships by selecting matched groups of subjects, giving them different treatments, controlling unrelated factors, and checking for differences in group responses. 一种寻找因果关系的研究方法,即把匹配的被试对象分成实验组与对照组,将不相关因素控制起来保持一致,再给实验组与对照组不同的刺激或操纵,并检查组间的反应差异。
exploratory research 探索性研究	The marketing research that is conducted to gather preliminary information that will help define the problem and suggest hypotheses 旨在收集有助于定义问题和提出假设的初步信息的营销调研。
descriptive research 描述性研究	The marketing research that is conducted to describe things like the market potential for a product, or the demographics of target consumers. 旨在清楚描绘某些事物,比如一个产品的市场潜力,或者目标消费者的人口统计数据的营销调研。
causal research 因果性研究	The marketing research that is conducted to test hypotheses about cause-and-effect relationships 旨在验证因果关系假设的营销调研。
sampling plan 抽样方案	The plan that specifies how to select respondents for the study and decide sampling unit, sampling procedure, and sample size. 关于如何选择样本中的调查对象的方案,包括抽样单位、抽样程序和样本量的决定。
contact medium 接触媒介	The means or instrumentality for storing or communicating information in collecting primary data. 在收集原始数据时存储或传递信息的方法或手段。
web browsing 网页浏览追踪	The web analytics tools used to collect the click stream data that track the Internet users' browsing behaviors, including the links they clicked on, the length of time spent on specific pages, etc. 利用网络分析工具收集追踪互联网用户浏览行为的点击流数据,包括他们点击的链接、在特定页面上花费的时间长短等。
behavioral targeting 行为定向	Based on information of consumers' online behavior patterns, marketers target ads and offers to specific consumers. 基于消费者在线行为模式的信息,营销人员针对特定的消费者投放广告和优惠。
text mining 文本挖掘	The techniques that analyze the huge amounts of textual data left by the Internet users on various sites to understand consumers' opinions and preferences, the market structure and the competitive environment. 从互联网用户在各种站点中留下的大量文字数据中整理、分析出消费者的意见和偏好,市场结构和竞争环境等信息的技术。

Continued

data mining 数据挖掘	The techniques that extract patterns from large data sets（e. g. E-commerce transaction data）by combining methods from statistics and machine learning with database management. 通过结合统计、机器学习和数据库管理的方法,从大型数据集(如电子商务交易数据)中发现相应的模式与规律。
big data 大数据	Extremely large data sets that can be subjected to computation analysis to reveal patterns and trends. 可以通过计算分析来揭示模式和趋势的超大数据集。
social targeting 社交定向	Marketers target ads and offers to specific consumers by tracking individual online social connections and conversations from social networking sites. 营销者通过跟踪个人在线社交联系和社交网站上的对话,将广告和服务投放给特定的消费者。
marketing information system（MIS） 营销信息系统	A formalized set of procedures and methods for the regular, planned collection, analysis, and presentation of information for use in making marketing decisions. 一套正式的程序和方法,用于定期、有计划地收集、分析和展示信息,以用于市场营销决策。
customer relationship management（CRM） 客户关系管理	One of the digital business tools that help companies leverage the data they collect, which consists of sophisticated software and analysis tools. 帮助企业利用其收集的数据的数字业务工具之一,包括复杂的软件和分析工具。

Review & Critical Thinking Questions

1. What are the differences between problem-identification research and problem-solving research?

2. How could marketers obtain secondary and primary data? What are the advantages and disadvantages of these two types of data?

3. What are the possible limitations of the survey method? How could they be reduced?

4. Is observational research always superior to survey method? Why?

5. Under what circumstances a focus group is the suitable form of marketing research?

6. What is the uniqueness of experiment research? Why should it be cautiously used?

7. When collecting data via survey, what are the strengths and weaknesses for different contact methods?

8. What are the two different forms of questionnaires? What are their respective benefits and drawbacks?

9. Except for surveys, what are the mechanical instruments researchers could use to

collect primary marketing information data?

10. What techniques could be used to analyze spontaneous customer information already coursing around the Internet, and how do they work?

11. What are the differences between behavioral targeting and social targeting?

12. What is the marketing information system (MIS), and how is it related to marketing research?

Discussion Questions

1. The process of marketing research is featured by several distinct and important steps. In your opinion, which is the most important step? Explain the reasons you say so.

2. A Chinese manufacturer of smartphones intends to figure out the potential market attractiveness of its products in Vietnam. What are the sources and the types of data that the firm will need to obtain a preliminary estimate?

3. If you are a marketing manager whose firm adopts behavioral and social targeting online, when consumers and public advocate that it is a form of stalking consumers, how could you respond to that concern?

4. What are the differences between internal databases and marketing intelligence? What are their advantages and disadvantages respectively?

5. What is big data, and how does it affect marketing research? What opportunities and challenges does it bring to marketers?

Case Study

Brewer A is a successful regional beer brand that is based and has a high level of market share in the Northwest of China. To further enhance market size and competitiveness, Brewer A began to enter the Chongqing market in the recent year. Xiao Li, a senior marketing manager from the headquarters, was appointed to the Chongqing Company, taking charge of setting up and leading the marketing team to open up the market. As an experienced and passionate manager with the spirit of entrepreneurship, Xiao Li designed and initiated a series of regular marketing programs in the beginning. For example, they organized a new product launch event to attract public attention, following with multiple media advertisements including TV, radio, bus body, outdoors, etc. They also adopted several promotion tools, such as lucky draw, buy three get one free, personal promotion in supermarkets and restaurants, and so on. Market acceptance feedback was exciting as the sales performance of Brewer A products was great for the first few months. However, the positive situation did not last long—the sales plummeted after the promotion policy ceased. Marketers of Chongqing Company conducted some investigation and found out that many consumers seemed to stop buying Brewer A products without promotional offers, so that the wholesalers and retailers reduced or even stopped the purchase accordingly. While it is unrealistic to continue providing the promotional offer, which will further increase the marketing costs and lead to greater loss of Chongqing Company, it is urgent for Xiao Li and his team to figure out the reason why consumers stopped buying Brewer A and then look for a solution.

First of all, Xiao Li clearly defined the problem they face as poor sales performance. The potential reasons for this phenomenon may come from consumers, the competitors, the company itself, or the environment. From the consumer perspective, perhaps they are not satisfied with the flavor, distributing channels, or price of Brewer A, or they do not recognize the advertisement appeal and brand value of Brewer A; from the competitor perspective, they may have superior brand image, greater promotion strength, similar targeting market, or more attractive discount policy, etc. From the company's perspective, it may be unclear about the target market, lack the flexibility and diversity of promotional tools, fail to form bilateral communication with consumers or fail to identify the points they care about, etc. From the environmental perspective, the industry regulator may have some restrictions on the promotion means, and there may be subtle differences of freshness taste brought by the delivery, etc.

To identify and fully understand the reasons mentioned above, Xiao Li and his team needed more information to do the analysis. Although some data could be obtained from the intelligence center of the headquarters, they do not obtain the needed data about local consumers and competitors, and secondary data is insufficient to solve the problem either. Thus it is necessary to collect primary data. Due to the limited human resources right now, Xiao Li decided to outsource the marketing research project to an external research firm B. After the discussion within the team, he pinpointed several questions that the research firm needs to answer, mainly related to consumers or competitors: (1) How do local consumers recognize the current available beer brands? Why do local consumers keep their loyalty toward (or repeat purchasing) a specific brand if there is one? How much do the local consumers know about Brewer A? In particular, do they know Brewer A uses high quality water to produce the products? Whether they prefer Brewer A and why? What is their impression of the package of Brewer A? What are the main factors consumers consider when they buy beer? Do they care about the city element? Are they impressed with the pile-up display at the retailing end such as supermarkets? Which media channels do the different target consumers mostly use? (2) What are the marketing tactics adopted by the competitors in Chongqing? Which promotion tools utilized by the competitors for consumers, retailers, and wholesalers are effective? How about the relationships between competitors and their wholesalers and retailers? Is there any special service program that is worth learning? What are the advantageous resources and capabilities that competitors have? What brand/enterprise image do the competitors intend to build in Chongqing market and what actions do they take toward the goal?

Receiving those questions, the research project manager Wang Yi did not instantly design the research plan but spent one more week deeply communicating with Xiao Li and other employees in Chongqing Company. After thoroughly reviewing the internal archives and interacting with staff from various departments, Wang Yi came to realize that, from the operational perspective, neither the quality of beer nor the promotion tactic of Brewer A is problematic. Instead, it seems that Brewer A initiated the new market development program without carefully understanding consumers or analyzing competitors, as the marketing department did not assess consumers' preference or their recognition of Brewer A at all. Without solid knowledge of the target market and consumer needs, Brewer A may hardly determine the correct market position. Based on these judgments, Wang Yi recommends Xiao Li to start with research on the usage and attitude of consumers, in order to understand local consumers' purchase behavior of beer and their attitude toward Brewer A, and then to see if the current market positioning is appropriate.

In specific, Wang Yi proposes to collect the following information: (1) Beer market overview, including number and characteristics of target consumers, market size (quantity and amount), brand awareness and approach, market share distribution (quantity and amount); (2) Consumption and purchase habits of consumers, including the consumption/purchase incentive, frequency, amount, place, often chosen brand and reason, preferred flavor, price sensitivity, and the considering factors of purchase; (3) Consumers' opinion and attitude upon beer, including the knowledge of beer and the comments on different types of beer; (4) Consumers' viewpoint of Brewer A, including the brand awareness and image, the recognition of and comments on Brewer A products; (5) The background of target consumers, including the age, income, occupation, education level, and number of family members.

Questions

1. Based on the case description, do you think the Chongqing Company of Brewer A takes the right action to do marketing research? Why? Should Xiao Li accept Wang Yi's suggestion? What else could he do?
2. Review the basic methods of marketing research introduced in the chapter and think, what methods could Wang Yi adopt to collect required information he suggested? Try to

formulate the detailed research design for each method，and design the questionnaires if necessary.

中文概述

营销调研指的是为了识别和解决营销中的问题和机会而进行的系统收集、记录和分析数据的行为,以提供对营销决策有用的信息。从这个定义出发,可以将营销调研分为两类。第一类是**问题识别研究**,用来帮助识别已有或潜在的问题,比如通过评估市场潜力、市场占有率、公司或品牌形象、销售预期、行业趋势等来更好地理解营销环境,诊断可能存在的问题。第二类是**问题解决研究**,用来寻找已被识别出来的问题或机遇的应对之道,例如确定价格、促销模式、分销渠道等。需要指出的是,这两种类型的营销调研常常是被同时使用的。

营销调研所获得的数据有一手与二手两种来源。**二手数据**指的是已经存在于某处,但可能是出于其他目的而被收集的信息。**一手数据**又被称为原始数据,是专门为手头特定目的而收集的信息。研究人员通常从收集二手数据开始,如果现有的信息不能满足管理者的信息需求,那么他们可能需要采取行动来收集一手数据。

一手数据的收集方法主要包含调查研究法、观察法、焦点小组、实验法等。

调查研究法最为常见,适用于收集描述性信息,例如人们的态度、偏好以及购买行为等,并且可以通过电话、网络以及面对面等不同方式来直接询问调研对象。

观察法是指一个或多个训练有素的观察者(或摄像机之类的机械设备)观察和记录实际或潜在买家的行为,例如在超市环境下观察消费者的实际购物行为,以及在网络环境下观察消费者的言论行为。

焦点小组是指邀请6到10个参与者形成一个小组,由主持人引导他们分享对某些主题的想法、感受、态度和观点,比如产品概念、品牌形象和个性、广告、社会趋势等,而其他研究者或者公司代表可以在单面镜背后,或者通过视频会议技术来观察并记录讨论过程。

实验法是指将匹配的被试对象分成实验组与对照组,将不相关因素控制起来保持一致,再给实验组与对照组不同的刺激或操纵,检查组间的反应差异,从而找到不同因素之间的因果关系。

营销调研过程主要包括以下步骤:定义问题并明确调研目标,制定研究设计,开展实地调查或收集数据,准备和分析数据,准备和提交报告。

(1)第一步,在定义问题时,决策者与研究人员需要紧密配合,以了解信息需求并明确调研目标。调研目标可以分为三种:第一,**探索性研究**的目标是收集有助于定义问题和提出假设的初步信息;第二,**描述性研究**的目标是清楚描绘某些事物,比如一个产品的市场潜力,或者目标消费者的人口统计数据;最后,**因果性研究**的目标是验证关于因果关系的假设,例如包装变化对顾客偏好的可能影响。不同的调研目标可能适用不同的调研方法。

(2)第二步,在定义问题与明确调研目标之后,研究人员必须制定相应的研究设计,其中包括为获得所需信息而必须执行的过程细节,确定要实施的调研类型,准确定义可能的变量,并设计适当的量表来测量它们。

其中,对受访者的联系方法可以是邮件、面谈、电话或互联网/电子邮件,它们各有利弊。而**抽样方案**主要包括抽样单位、抽样程序和样本量三个方面:抽样单位是指研究对象,或者是被联系的对象,例如涉及家用电器购买行为的研究中,调查问卷可以针对决策者、其他家庭成员,或者是一线销售人员分别设计与收集;抽样程序是指如何选择样本中的调查对象,包括概率和非概率抽样两类方法;样本量是指应该选择的调查样本数量,应该综合考虑预算、行业惯例等确定。

其次,营销研究者可利用两种**接触媒介**或者测量工具来收集一手数据:调查问卷与机械手段。调查问卷可以是相对非结构化的形式,带有开放式问题,允许受访者用自己的话回答,用于在探索式研究中识别受访者的参照框架;也可以是相对结构化的形式,带有封闭式问题,包括所有可能的答案,受访者从中选择。可以用来收集一手市场信息(如消费者行为)的机械手段有很多种,例如尼尔森的电视观众监测、传统的超市条形码扫描等。

(3)第三步,在制定好研究计划后,下一步就执行研究计划了,包括数据收集、处理与分析。数据收集可以由公司自己完成,或者外包给第三方。

(4)第四步,研究人员需要对调查结果进行解释、得出结论、完成报告并以书面、口头或视频形式提交给管理层。

在线研究非常适于定量研究,尤其是问卷调查法,因为问卷发放和收集非常便利。定性研究中适于在线进行的主要是在线焦点小组和在线实验。除了将这些传统的线下调研方法转为线上进行之外,互联网上还存留着大量未经请求的、非结构化的、自发的客户信息。因此,积极利用这些信息已经成为网络营销研究的一个重要趋势,并可采用一系列新兴技术。

网页浏览追踪是指利用 Google Analytics, WebTrends, StatCounter, Woopra 等网络分析工具收集追踪互联网用户浏览行为的点击流数据,包括他们点击的链接、在特定页面上花费的时间长短等。基于这些在线信息,他们可以针对特定的消费者投放广告和优惠,这种做法被称为**行为定向**。

文本挖掘是指从互联网用户在公司网站、购物网站(如天猫、京东)、社交媒体网站(如微博、优酷、豆瓣)、博客、论坛和聊天室等站点中留下的大量文字数据中整理、分析出消费者的感受、观点、态度与偏好等。所获取的结论有助于企业更快更好地响应消费者需求,并为建立良好的品牌体验和与客户关系提供机会。

数据挖掘是指通过结合统计、机器学习和数据库管理的方法,从大型数据集(如电子商务交易数据)中发现相应的模式与规律,包括关联规则学习、聚类分析、分类学习、回归分析等。值得注意的是,如今社交媒体已经成为增长最快的信息流来源,产生了大量的**大数据**,即可以通过计算分析来揭示模式和趋势的超大数据集。不少公司受益于大数据分析能力,大数据管理将成为在线营销研究的下一个前沿。由于消费者越来越依赖于在线口碑,而非从新闻网页或搜索引擎所获得的信息,网络营销开始超越行为定位这种仅仅跟踪消费者网络点击行为的方式,逐渐转向**社交定向**,即通过跟踪个人在线社交联系和社交网站上的对话,将广告和服务投放给特定的消费者。

营销信息系统(MIS)是一套正式的程序和方法,用于定期、有计划地收集、分析和展示信息,以用于市场营销决策。

客户关系管理(CRM)是帮助企业利用其收集的数据的数字业务工具之一,包括复杂的软件和分析工具,用来整合并分析各种来源的客户和市场信息,形成客户、公司、产品或服务之间关系的完整图景。其结果可使管理者更好地了解客户,识别高价值客户,交叉销售公司的产品,并为特定的客户需求量身定制产品。

UNIT 7 Positioning

Learning Objectives

1. Understand the concept of positioning and its role in international marketing.
2. Know steps of positioning.
3. Master positioning strategies.
4. Master market positioning statement.
5. Know STP model.
6. Know re-positioning.

7.1 The Definition of Positioning and the Role in International Marketing

Positioning refers to the place that a brand occupies in the minds of the customers and how it is distinguished from the products of the competitors. In order to position products or brands, companies may emphasize the distinguishing features of their brand (what it is, what it does and how, etc.) or they may try to create a suitable image (inexpensive or premium, utilitarian or luxurious, entry-level or high-end, etc.) through the marketing mix. Market positioning is the manipulation of a brand or a family of brands to create a positive perception in the eyes of the public. If a product is well positioned, it will have strong sales, and it may become the go-to brand for people who need that particular product. Poor positioning, on the other hand, can lead to bad sales and a dubious reputation.

When a product is released, the company needs to think beyond what the product is for when it comes to positioning. It also describes the kinds of people who want to buy the product. For example, a luxury car manufacturer might be less interested in promoting reliability, and more interested in promoting drivability, appealing to people who are looking for high-end cars which are enjoyable and exciting to drive. Alternatively, a company making mouthwash might want to go for the bottom end of the market with an appealing low price, claiming that the product contains the same active ingredients as the famous brand has, but with a much lower price.

Market positioning is a tricky process. Companies need to see how consumers perceive their product, and how differences in presentation can influence perception. Periodically, companies may reposition, and try to adjust their perception among the public. For example, a company might redesign product package, start a new advertisement campaign, or engage in new activities to capture more market share.

Companies also engage in **de-positioning,** in which they attempt to alter the perception of other brands. While outright attacks on rival brands are frowned upon and may be illegal unless they are framed very carefully, companies can use language like "compared to the leading brand" or "we're not like those other brands." A television advertisement, for example, might contrast two paper towels: the brand being advertised, and a "generic one" with a package which looks suspiciously similar, but not identical to a popular brand of paper towel.

Developing a market positioning strategy is an important part of the research and development process. The marketing department may provide notes during product development to enhance the product's position, and they also determine the price, where the product should be sold, and how it should be advertised.

7.2　Steps of Positioning

Market positioning follows seven basic steps listed below:

Draft a **positioning statement** —There are four simple questions that will yield a set of basic facts about the identity you have determined for your company. The positioning statement is the result of plugging those facts into a basic, formulaic sentence structure.

Compare and contrast to identify your own uniqueness—Differences between your own messaging strategy and communication channels, and those of your competitors reveal openings in the market that your positioning message should address.

Competitor analysis—Investigating and analyzing the competition helps to determine the strengths and weaknesses of your own business measured against the competition. Understanding the differences between a business and its competitors is central to finding gaps in the market that can be filled.

Determine current position—Determining your existing market position is as vital as any competitor analysis. That's because you have to understand your own market position to be able to properly compete for your share.

Competitor positioning analysis—An accessory to the competitor analysis, competitor positioning analysis identifies the conditions of the market that influence how much power competitors are able to exercise.

Develop a unique positioning idea—With all the analytical data in hand, you should have a better idea of who you are, who you are not, and who your best audience is. It's time to make a statement about those facts.

Test the effectiveness of your brand positioning—Testing methodology will consist of qualitative and quantitative data gathering, mainly determined by the steps prior to this, which include focus groups, surveys, in-depth interviews, ethnography, polls, etc. The results of the testing should then be rated against a set of criteria listed below.

7.3 Positioning Strategies

Positioning strategies can be conceived and developed in a variety of ways. It can be derived from the object attributes, application, the types of consumers involved, or the characteristics of the product class. All these elements represent a different approach in developing positioning strategies, even though all of them have the common objective of projecting a favorable image in the minds of the consumers or audience. There are seven approaches to positioning strategies:

7.3.1 Positioning Strategy Based on Product Characteristics / Customer Benefits

This strategy basically focuses on the characteristics of the product or customer benefits. For example, imported items basically illustrate a variety of product characteristics, such as durability, economy or reliability, etc. For example, Some imported motorbikes emphasize on fuel economy, some on desirability, and others on durability.

You may notice that some product is positioned along two or more product characteristics at the same time. For example, many toothpaste brands insist on "freshness" and "cavity fighting" as the product characteristics. It is always tempting to try and position a product alongside several product characteristics.

7.3.2 Positioning Strategy Based on Pricing

Assume that you have to go and buy a pair of jeans, as soon as you enter the shop, you will find jeans in the showroom of different prices possibly ranging from 350 *yuan* to 2,000 *yuan*. You might, stereotypically, assume that the jeans priced at 350 *yuan* are of inferior quality. This is because most of us perceive that an expensive product has superior quality than that of the cheaper one. If we look at the Price-Quality approach, it is important and largely used in product positioning. In many product categories, there are brands that deliberately attempt to offer more in terms of service, features or performance. They charge more, partly to cover higher costs and partly to let the consumers believe that the product is of higher quality.

7.3.3 Positioning Strategy Based on Use or Application

"Nescafe Coffee" for many years positioned itself as a winter product and advertised mainly in winter but the introduction of cold coffee has resulted in a positioning strategy for the summer months as well.

Basically this type of positioning-by-use represents a second or third position of the brand, which is done deliberately to expand the brand's market. If you are introducing new uses of the product, it will automatically expand the brand's market.

7.3.4 Positioning Strategy Based on Product Users

Another positioning approach is to associate the product with its a class of users. Casual clothing like jeans has introduced "designer labels" to develop a fashion image. In this case the expectation is that the characteristics and image of the models or celebrities as product users will influence the product's image.

"Johnson and Johnson" re-positioned its shampoo a product only used on babies, to one used by all types of people who wash their hair frequently and need mild shampoo. This re-positioning resulted in a larger market share.

7.3.5 Positioning Strategy Based on Product Class

In some product class we have to make critical positioning decisions. For example, freeze dried coffee needed to position itself with respect to regular and instant coffee. Similarly dried milk was positioned as a breakfast substitute, while virtually identical product was positioned as a dietary meal substitute.

7.3.6 Positioning Strategy Based on Cultural Symbols

Air India uses the Maharaja as its logo, by this they are trying to show that they welcome guests and give them royal treatment with a lot of respect and it also highlights Indian tradition. Using and popularizing trademarks generally follows this type of positioning.

7.3.7 Positioning Strategy Based on Competitors

Positioning strategies of this kind, have an implicit or explicit frame of reference for one or more competitors. In some cases, reference competitors can be the benchmark of the focal firm. It may either use the same or similar positioning strategies used by the competitors, or make improvement based on that.

A good example of this would be Colgate and Pepsodent. When Colgate entered into the market, it focused on to family protection. After Pepsodent entered into the market with a focus on 24 hour protection and basically for kids, Colgate adopted a similar focus on kids' teeth protection, which was a positioning strategy adopted because of competition.

7.4 Market Positioning Statement

7.4.1 The Definition of Market Positioning Statement

Market positioning statement is a description of the target market and is a situation which determines how the company wants the market to perceive its offerings. Positioning statement is an internal tool for marketers. Every marketing and product related decision needs to align with the positioning statement. A good positioning statement maintains focus on the brand as well as its value proposition, which lays foundation for marketing strategy and tactics.

7.4.2 Importance of Positioning Statement in Marketing

Effective market positioning statement imposes a positive impact on the capability of a business. It allows an organization to understand the benefits of its offerings to target customers. Additionally, a unique positioning statement clarifies how the offering is different from other competitors in the market.

7.4.3 How to Write Positioning Statement Properly

The major purpose of writing a positioning statement is to assure that all marketing activities for target customers are clear and consistent. In order to write a positioning statement, it is important to follow some simple steps:

- Selecting the target group upon which the company needs to focus on.
- Developing a list, writing down the customer needs that the company intends to serve.

• Listing all the benefits of products and services which uniquely fulfill the needs and wants of the customer group.

• Evaluating the positioning statement of the company and ensuring that it is clear, simple and consistent.

• Spreading the word out by consistently conveying the positioning message in every aspect that the business is doing for the customer group.

There is a template for writing a positioning statement in a proper manner as follows:

For (*Mention Your Target Market*), (*Product X*) *is the* (*Point of Differentiation*) *among the* (*Competitive Market*) *because* (*reasons to believe*).

Target Market is the detail of the segments you are targeting

Product X is the name of your product or brand name

PoD is your offerings that solve the problems of target customers better than the competitors do.

FoR is the marketplace you are competing in.

Reason to Believe is the evidence and proof of what you are providing is fulfilling customer's needs better than competitors

❯ 7.4.4 Market Positioning Statement Examples

Zipcar. com. To urban-dwelling, educated techno-savvy consumers, when using Zipcar car-sharing service instead of owning a car, you save money while reducing your carbon footprint.

Volvo. For upscale American families, Volvo is the family automobile that offers maximum safety.

Volvo was historically popular for safety with its Safety First poisitioning. However, in 2011 the company lost this marketing edge because of different campaigns like "All-New Naughty Volvo S60". This campaign did not attract the attention of the public to the innovation and safety features of the new model, which was based on luxury and performance. This led to a decline in sales as safety was a relevant and unique position for Volvo. Concentrating on safety provided the brand with a differentiating and consistent theme for communication, building a reputation and making the brand memorable.

7.5   The Segmentation, Targeting and Positioning Model

Today, Segmentation, Targeting and Positioning (STP) is a familiar strategic approach in modem marketing. It is one of the most commonly applied marketing models in practice.

The STP model is useful when creating marketing communications plans since it helps marketers prioritize propositions and then develop and deliver personalized and relevant messages to different audiences.

7.5.1　Components of the STP Model

STP refers to three activities: segmentation, targeting, and positioning. Marketers segment markets and identify attractive segments to target, before developing suitable positioning strategies and allocating resources to prioritize marketing activities.

1. Segmentation

The STP model starts with dividing up the market, which is called **market segmentation**. Market segmentation refers to the division of a mass market into identifiable and distinct groups (segments). Each of these segments has common characteristics and needs, and displays similar responses to marketing actions. Various segmentation criteria can be used to divide up the market, including demographic, geographic, psychographic and behavioral variables.

Demographic—By personal attributes such as age, marital status, gender, ethnicity, sexuality, education, and occupation.

Geographic—By country, region, state, city, or neighborhood.

Psychographic—By personality, risk aversion, values, or lifestyle.

Behavioral—By how people use the product, how loyal they are, or the benefits that they are looking for.

Example:

The Adventure Travel Company is an online travel agency that organizes worldwide adventure vacations. It divides overseas travel market into three segments.

Segment A is made up of young married couples, who are primarily interested in affordable, eco-friendly vacations in exotic locations. Segment B consists of middle-class families, who want safe, family-friendly vacation packages that make it easy and fun to travel with children. Segment C comprises upscale retirees, who are looking for stylish and luxurious vacations in well-known locations such as Paris and Rome.

According to the popular "DAMP" approach to targeting, as defined by Philip Kotler (1984), for market segmentation to be effective, all segments must be:

Distinct: each segment must clearly differ from other segments, which makes different **marketing mixes** necessary.

Accessible: buyers must be able to be reached through appropriate promotional activities and distribution channels.

Measurable: the segment must be easy to identify and measure.

Profitable: the segment must be sufficiently large to provide a stream of constant future revenues and profits.

2. Targeting

The second part of the STP model is targeting. This refers to determining which, if any, of the segments should be targeted and served with a comprehensive marketing programme.

There are several factors to consider here. First, look at the profitability of each segment. Which customer groups contribute most to your bottom line? Next, analyze the size and potential growth of each customer group. Is it large enough? Is steady growth possible? And how is it compared with the other segments? Lastly, think carefully about how well your organization can serve this segment.

Example:

The Adventure Travel Company analyzes the profits, revenue and market size of each of its segments. Segment A has profits of $8, 220, 000, Segment B has profits of $4, 360, 000, and Segment C has profits of $3, 430, 000. So, it decides to focus on Segment A, after confirming that the segment size is big enough (it's estimated to be worth $220,000,000/ year.)

3. Positioning

The last part of the STP model is positioning, which means to ensure that a brand occupies the right spot in the mind of target consumers. Positioning is the means by which goods and services can be differentiated from one another and thereby give consumers a reason to buy. It encompasses two key elements.

First, consider why customers should purchase your product rather than those of your competitors. Do this by identifying your **unique selling proposition,** and draw a **positioning map** to understand how each segment perceives your product, brand or service. This will help you determine how to best position your offering.

Next, look at the wants and needs of each segment, or the problem that your product solves for these people. Create a **value proposition** that clearly explains how your offering will meet this requirement better than any of your competitors' products, and then develop a marketing campaign that presents this value proposition in a way that your audience will appreciate.

Example:

The Adventure Travel Company markets itself as the "best eco-vacation service for young married couples" (Segment A).

It initiates a competition on social media to reach its target market, because these are the channels that these people favor. It asks customers to share interesting pictures of past eco-vacations, and the best one wins an all-inclusive trip.

The campaign goes viral and thousands of people send in their photos, which helps build the Adventure Travel Company mailing list. The company then creates a monthly enewsletter full of eco-vacation destination profiles.

7.5.2　Benefits of Using the STP Model

The key benefits of using the STP model include:

- enhancing a company's competitive position.
- providing direction and focus for marketing strategies (including targeted advertising, new product development, and brand differentiation) by allocating resources to target segments.
- identifying market growth opportunities through identification of new customers or product uses.
- effective and efficient matching of company resources to target market segments which promise the greatest **return on marketing investment** (ROMI).

Companies should thus always use the STP model as a starting point instead of simply developing a product and then finding the right customers to sell it to. By following the process of segmentation, targeting and positioning, a clear picture of the needs and wants of the customers is obtained, which serves as a foundation for developing suitable solutions to unique customer problems.

7.6　Re-positioning

7.6.1　The Definition of Re-positioning

Re-positioning refers to the major change in positioning for the brand/product. To successfully re-position a product, the firm has to change the target market's understanding of the product. This is sometimes a challenge, particularly for well-established or strongly branded products. Many firms choose to launch a new product (or brand) instead of re-positioning because of the efforts and costs required to successfully implement the change.

Re-positioning can be achieved by advertising or by research & development. Although consumers' perceptions are linked to the brand's physical characteristics, they can be slightly influenced by communication. But the re-positioning effect is limited; this is especially true when the brand awareness level is high, because a brand with which consumers are extremely familiar is more difficult to re-position. Beyond a certain level, brand re-positioning can no longer be done by advertising alone. At this point one must complete an R&D project with physical characteristics matching consumers' needs, and then to upgrade the brand. R&D projects will take time to complete, while re-positioning through advertising has an immediate effect.

7.6.2　The Reasons for re-positioning

Generally brand/products are re-positioned due to a concerning market situation, such as:

- Decline stage of the **product life-cycle** (PLC).
- Declining sales or profit margin due to being positioned to close to a major competitor.
- The introduction of a superior product by the company itself.
- Supporting an overall strategic change by the firm.
- Assisting in entering new marketplaces or pursuing new segments.
- The brand/product has been classified as a dog in the **BCG matrix**.

7.6.3　Strategies for Re-positioning

If your product doesn't sell well, then it might be time to re-position it. That's what the Kansas City Wizards of Major League Soccer did in 2010. It wasn't their first re-branding effort, as they'd changed their name from the "Wiz" to the "Wizards" before, but transitioning to "Sporting Kansas City" made sense. They had a new stadium and had drafted local talent and went from a team that had to beg for attendance to a team that regularly sells out games. It culminated in a 2013 championship for the club.

Not every re-positioning effort will be as successful as Sporting Kansas City's, but nothing will work if you don't make the effort to change in the first place.

1. Understand Your Status

In order to fully re-position your brand and be able to market it effectively, you've got to know what your current status happens to be. There will always be variables, such as current events or challenges from competitors, that must be proactively countered, but you've also got to know why your brand is considered weak in the first place. Is it because of poor initial promotions? Low perceived value? Low actual value? When you've got a clear picture of where you stand, it's easy to choose where your next steps should be when you move forward.

2. Always Review

You must take time to review the history of your brand because it doesn't make sense to stop what has worked. If your product has underestimated value, you just need to find a way to better communicate this value to the market that has evolved since you first introduced your ideas.

3. Ask Questions

The re-positioning is actually starting the marketing process from the very beginning once again. It is another chance to examine how your product differentiates from the competitors' offerings. If you've got customer equity within the market, you have an advantage in many ways. Figure out what makes you different and better and use that as the foundation of your marketing strategies.

4. Profile Your Segments

You've got to specifically tailor your marketing message to each segment you're targeting in order for your re-positioning efforts to be successful. If you send the wrong message to a market segment, then you're going to create chaos within your brand. Make sure your message is consistent and coherent and you'll be able to improve your lines of communication.

5. What Are the Usage Patterns

If your marketplace has evolved, then there is a good chance that your market segments have evolved along with it. You can discover how to properly communicate with your segments by seeing what the usage patterns are for products or services like yours that already exist. Take your strengths, build up the strengths that you see in each segment, and you'll be in a place where you can begin re-positioning your marketing.

6. Be the Niche Expert

One of the most common reasons for a brand to fail is that it loses its reputation as a niche industry expert. With information available at the fingertips of the average consumer thanks to the Internet, it's really easy to verify claims, research the competition, and determine if your goods or services have any actual value. As a niche expert, you automatically have value because you can prove this value through your marketing efforts. Lose this status and you'll lose the business.

7. What Do You Represent?

Your brand must stand for something. If it doesn't stand for something specific, then you haven't really positioned yourself in the market yet and need to complete your initial marketing strategy. What many don't realize, however, is that public perception of what your brand stands for is actually more important than what the company itself believes.

8. Define the Objective

You need to find out just how far you can re-positioning your brand without alienating your existing customer base. It makes no sense to lose a majority of an existing customer base, small as it may be, on the idea that more customers "might" be found once the re-positioning marketing efforts have been completed.

9. Never Assume

The classic mistake in re-positioning is to assume the customer needs. Your re-positioning should be based on segment surveys, sales data, and other unique segment factors so that you can attract new users and turn them into brand ambassadors through your new marketing efforts.

10. Promote the Mission

People want to know how you're going to act or react to the insights that you receive from the marketplace. This is where the mission becomes extremely important. You need to grow customers, develop the brand, and make sure your business is successful. This must be beyond the reach of your competition. How is achieved? By being clear and concise about your purpose and then communicating this in a consistent way to your target market. Only then will you be able to re-position yourself and allow your brand to grow.

Key Terms

positioning 定位	Positioning refers to the place that a brand occupies in the minds of the customers and how it is distinguished from the products of the competitors. 定位是指一个品牌在顾客心目中所占据的位置，以及如何与竞争对手的产品区分开来。
positioning statement 定位陈述	A positioning statement is an expression of how a given product, service or brand fills a particular consumer need in a way that its competitors don't. 定位陈述是一个给定的产品、服务或品牌如何以竞争对手不具备的方式满足特定消费者需求的表达。
target market 目标市场	It is a group of customers within a business's serviceable available market at which a business aims its marketing efforts and resources. 它是企业可服务的可用市场中的一组客户，企业将营销工作和资源瞄准这些客户。
market segmentation 市场细分	Market segmentation is the activity of dividing a broad consumer or business market, normally consisting of existing and potential customers, into sub-groups of consumers (known as segments) based on some type of shared characteristics. 市场细分是指根据某种类型的共享特征，将一个通常由现有和潜在客户组成的广泛的消费者或企业市场划分为细分市场的活动。
targeting 目标市场选择	It is the act of attempting to appeal to a person or group or to influence them in some way. 是指试图吸引某人或群体或以某种方式影响他们的行为。

Continued

marketing mix 营销组合	A marketing mix includes multiple areas of focus as part of a comprehensive marketing plan. The term often refers to a common classification that began as the four Ps: product, price, place, and promotion. Every Gmpany has the option of adding, subtracting or modifying in order to create a desired marketing strategy. 作为综合营销计划的一部分,营销组合包括多个重点领域。这个术语通常指的是一个通用的分类,包括:产品、价格、位置和促销。每个公司都可以根据自身的实际情况进行一定的增成和调整以制定理想的营销战略。
unique selling proposition 独特销售卖点	In marketing, the unique selling proposition (USP), also called the unique selling point, or the unique value proposition (UVP), is the marketing strategy of informing customers about how one's own brand or product is superior to its competitors (in addition to its other values). 在市场营销中,独特的销售主张(USP),也称为独特的卖点,或独特的价值主张(UVP),是告知客户自己的品牌或产品如何优于竞争对手(以及其他价值)的营销策略。
positioning map 产品定位图分析法	Positioning map is an effective analysis tool for enterprises to understand the comparison between their own product lines and competitors' product lines, and comprehensively measure the market position of each product and competitive product. 产品定位图分析法是适用于分析企业了解自己的产品线与竞争对手产品线的对比情况,全面衡量各产品与竞争产品的市场地位的一种有效的分析工具。
value proposition 价值主张	Value proposition refers to what is meaningful to customers, that is, an in-depth description of the real needs of customers. Listing all the advantages, publicizing the interest margin and highlighting the resonance points are the three methods commonly used by suppliers to formulate "value proposition". 价值主张是指对客户来说什么是有意义的,即对客户真实需求的深入描述。罗列全部优点、宣传利差、突出共鸣点是供应商制订"价值主张"通常所用的三种方法。
return on marketing investment (ROMI) 营销投资回报率	It is a metric used to measure the overall effectiveness of a marketing campaign to help marketers make better decisions about allocating future investments. 这是一个用来衡量营销活动整体有效性的指标,以帮助营销人员更好地决定未来投资的分配。
product life cycle 产品生命周期	It refers to the whole movement process of products from the time when they are ready for entering the market to the time when they are eliminated from the market. It is determined by the production cycle of demand and technology. Generally, it can be divided into four stages: introduction stage, growth stage, maturity stage and recession stage. 是指产品从准备进入市场开始到被淘汰退出市场为止的全部运动过程,是由需求与技术的生产周期所决定。一般分为导入期、成长期、成熟期、衰退期四个阶段。

Review & Critical Thinking Questions

1. What is marketing positioning?
2. What are the steps of positioning?
3. What does de-positioning mean?
4. What is a positioning statement?
5. How many positioning strategies are discussed? What are they?
6. How can you write a proper positioning statement?
7. What does segmentation mean in marketing?
8. What does targeting mean in marketing?
9. What are the reasons for re-positioning?
10. What are the strategies for re-positioning?

Discussion Questions

1. Assume you are working in the Coca-Cola company, write a positioning statement for the company.
2. The process of marketing positioning is composed by several steps. In your opinion, which is the most important step? Why?
3. If you are going to launch a new kind of drink, then try to do the STP analysis for your product.
4. What are the differences between positioning and re-positioning?
5. Is there any difference between positioning and targeting? If yes, what are they?

Case Study

When asked, "Who invented the car?" To this question, many people will answer: "Henry Ford!" This common misconception is a compliment to Henry Ford—a dream that has enabled millions of people to own cars. Although it was widely acknowledged that the idea of automobile was first invented in Europe, many American and European experimenters worked hard to test it at the end of the nineteenth Century. But Henry Ford can have all the honors because he made the idea become a realization. His guiding principle is: "I want to produce a car that is good for the public, one that's affordable and accessible to everyone." It was Henry Ford's vision and passion that contributed to the birth of the Ford motor company.

Ford invented a cheap T-model car, opened the new auto market and made a contribution to the rapid emergence of the automobile age in the United States. To this end, in the poll of top 20 events of the 200th anniversary of independence, Henry and his Ford car company ranked tenth, along with the astronauts on the moon and the atomic bomb.

1. Positioning the Mass Market

In early 1908, Henry Ford developed an epoch-making decision, announcing that he was committed to manufacturing standardized, simple, and cheap models. In fact, the plan has been brewing in Henry's Ford for months, even years. This production policy has set a precedent for profitability. The company's production from 1906 to 1907 undoubtedly proved that the lower the price of the product, the greater the profit. Therefore, instead of production variety, the low price and uniform specifications can be accepted by the public.

Henry Ford's dream car is the T-model, which is not decorative or flashy, only focusing on the practicality of the car. Its bodywork is light and firm without attractive outward appearance, but is specially refined in the performance, and ordinary people can easily afford it. The T-model removed all the accessories and was sold for only $850 a piece. The specifications were the same.

T-model cars were widely welcomed soon after production. Ford jumped to the top of vehicle brands at that time, because farmers needed this kind of car, and the average man could afford it. Its driving method is very simple, and any patient layman will soon master it.

All the vehicles, including the T-model, confronted the difficulty of conquering the road left by the carriage age. The average car could not stand the test of dangerous paths and complex roads on the plains, and every part of the T-model car was designed for that. Compared with other types of cars at that time, T-model cars had the advantages of durability, exquisite construction and lightness and convenience. The chassis is higher, has excellent performance when driving through sand, soil and mud rot.

Ford's profitability during this period also proved Ford's decision to make cheap cars. The T-model jumped to the top of the best-selling car list in just one year and became the No. 1 profitable car, with a sales record of 1.1 million that year. Popular product strategy for Ford Motor Co. has won huge market development opportunities, in fact, it can be said that Henry Ford created the U.S. car market.

To meet the surge in demand for cars, talented Henry Ford concentrated on the production process and developed a product line. Relying on good product market and efficient assembly line operations, in January 5, 1914, Henry Ford announced the Ford automobile company's minimum daily wage of $5, almost twice the minimum daily wage at the time, which shocked the world. Since it is possible to produce cheap cars in large quantities, Henry Ford said, they can sell more cars if people can afford them. He believed an eight-hour working day's $5 reward is his best move to cut costs. He said: "We can find ways to create high wages. If you lower workers' salary, you reduce the number of customers."

2. Adapting to the Market

With the maturity of the American auto market, the improvement of the consumption level of the residents and the specialty of consumer demand, Ford Motor Co. timely adjusted the product mix. Consumers at the time needed more luxurious, more powerful cars. Ford's next product, the first V-8 engine launched in March 31, 1932, met these two requirements. Ford, for the first time, successfully built V-8 cylinder blocks, much earlier than its competitors. The powerful engine made ford become an American favorite for automotive performance.

During World War II, the Ford Motor Co. served for the needs of war, produced aircraft engines and other products, as part of a huge war plan launched by Edsel Ford. In less than 3 years, Ford produced a total of 8,600 aircraft engines for B-24 liberator bombers, 57,000 aircraft engines and more than 250,000 tanks and other war machines. In World War II, the outstanding performance of Ford Motor Co. earned it a good reputation corporate image.

After the Second World War, the civil car market expanded rapidly. In order to adapt to the new market demand, Ford Motor Co. launched new models. In June 8, 1948, 1949 Ford models were launched in New York. The Ford 1949 car had independent front suspension and the new rear corner window; fusion body and wing is a kind of innovation, set the standards for automobile design day after. Ford's 1949 model gave Ford motors a powerful drive to regain the runner up position in the highly competitive US auto industry. In 1949, Ford Motor Co. sold about 807,000 cars, and profits rose from $94 million in the previous year to $177 million. It's the highest car sales record since 1929.

With a good first mover advantage, Ford Motor Co. was committed to large-scale production, reduced costs, and thus achieved a sharp price advantage.

In the end, 44 manufacturing plants, 18 assembly plants, 32 parts warehouses, 2 large test sites and 13 process development and research institutions were set up in the United States.

Questions

1. Based on the case description, how does the Ford Company position itself in the mass market?

2. With the maturity of the American auto market, the improvement of the consumption level of the residents and the specialty of consumer demand, how does Ford Motor Co adapt to the market?

中文概述

　　市场定位,也称作"营销定位",是市场营销工作者用以在目标市场(此处目标市场指该市场上的客户和潜在客户)的心目中塑造产品、品牌或组织的形象或个性的营销技术。企业根据竞争者现有产品在市场上所处的位置,针对消费者或用户对该产品某种特征或属性的重视程度,强有力地塑造出此企业产品与众不同的、给人印象鲜明的个性或形象,并把这种形象生动地传递给顾客,从而使该产品在市场上确定适当的位置。

　　市场定位的关键是企业要设法在自己的产品上找出比竞争者更具有竞争优势的特性。竞争优势一般有两种基本类型:一是价格竞争优势,就是在同样的条件下比竞争者定出更低的价格。这就要求企业采取一切努力来降低单位成本。二是偏好竞争优势,即能提供确定的特色来满足顾客的特定偏好。这就要求企业采取一切努力在产品特色上下功夫。因此,**企业市场定位的全过程**可以通过以下三大步骤来完成:1)识别潜在竞争优势,这一步骤的中心任务是要回答以下三个问题:一是竞争对手产品定位如何? 二是目标市场上顾客欲望满足程度如何以及确实还需要什么? 三是针对竞争者的市场定位和潜在顾客的真正需要的利益要求企业应该及能够做什么? 要回答这三个问题,企业市场营销人员必须通过一切调研手段,系统地设计、搜索、分析并报告有关上述问题的资料和研究结果。通过回答上述三个问题,企业就可以从中把握和确定自己的潜在竞争优势在哪里。2)核心竞争优势定位。竞争优势表明企业能够胜过竞争对手的能力。这种能力既可以是现有的,也可以是潜在的。选择竞争优势实际上就是一个企业与竞争者各方面实力相比较的过程。比较的指标应是一个完整体系,只有这样,才能准确地选择相对竞争优势。通常的方法是分析、比较企业与竞争者在经营管理、技术开发、采购、生产、市场营销、财务和产品等七个方面究竟哪些是强项,哪些是弱项。借此选出最适合此企业的优势项目,以初步确定企业在目标市场上所处的位置。3)战略制定这一步骤的主要任务是企业要通过一系列的宣传促销活动,将其独特的竞争优势准确传播给潜在顾客,并在顾客心目中留下深刻印象。首先应使目标顾客了解、知道、熟悉、认同、喜欢和偏爱此企业的市场定位,在顾客心目中建立与该定位相一致的形象。其次,企业通过各种努力强化目标顾客形象,保持对目标顾客的了解,稳定目标顾客的态度和加深目标顾客的感情来巩固与市场相一致的形象。

　　定位陈述是一个给定的产品、服务或品牌如何以竞争对手不具备的方式满足特定消费者需求的表达。定位陈述主要用于描述产品或服务如何满足目标市场或用户的需求,同样这也是你做任何定位战略的必备条件,并且可以为品牌定位创建清晰的愿景。

　　STP 战略中的 S、T、P 三个字母分别是 Segmenting, Targeting, Positioning 三个英文单词的缩写,即市场细分、目标市场和市场定位的意思。STP 营销是现代市场营销战略的核心。此战略可以分为三步:第一步,市场细分(Segmenting),根据购买者对产品或营销组合的不同需要,将市场分为若干不同的顾客群体,并勾勒出细分市场的轮廓。第二步,确定目标市场(Targeting),选择要进入的一个或多个细分市场。第三步,定位(Positioning),在目标市场顾客群中形成一个印象,这个印象即为定位。市场定位就是能否为自己的产品树立特定的形象,使之与众不同,在消费者的心目中为公司的品牌选择一个占据这重要位置的过程,其过程需要结合自身的实力合理地确定经营目标、顺应国际市场的变化、提供综合化服务。确定产品市场大小、发展潜力及空间,然后再根据目标市场、公司的实际情况来定位,已经是很明了的。

　　最后,企业应注意目标顾客对其市场定位理解出现的偏差或由企业市场定位宣传上的失误而造成的目标顾客模糊、混乱和误会,及时纠正与市场定位不一致的形象。企业的产品在市场上定位即使很恰当,但在下列情况下,还应考虑**重新定位**:(1)竞争者推出的新产品定位于此企业产品附近,侵占了此企业产品的部分市场,使此企业产品的市场占有率下降。(2)消费者的需求或偏好发生了变化,使此企业产品销售量骤减。重新定位是指企业为已在某市场销售的产品重新确定某种形象,以改变消费者原有的认识,争取有利的市场地位的活动。如某日化厂生产婴儿洗发剂,以强调该洗发剂不刺激眼睛来吸引有婴儿的家庭。但随着出生率的下降,销售量减少。为了增加销售,该企业将产品重新定位,强调使用该洗发剂能使头发松软有光泽,以吸引更多、更广泛的购买者。重新定位对于企业适应市场环境、调整市场营销战略是必不可少的,可以视为企业的战略转移。重新定位可能导致产品的名称、价格、包装和品牌的更改,也可能导致产品用途和功能上的变动,企业必须考虑定位转移的成本和新定位的收益问题。

UNIT 8 Consumers' Purchasing Behavior

Learning Objectives

1. Understand the meaning and classification of consumers.
2. Grasp the characteristics of consumers' purchasing behavior.
3. Identify the factors influencing consumers' purchasing behavior.
4. Understand the types of consumers' purchasing behavior.
5. Explain the process of consumers' purchasing decision.
6. Understand the classification of organizational market.
7. Identify the characteristics of organizational market purchasing behavior.
8. Explain the decision-making process of organizational market purchasing behavior.

8.1 The Meaning and Classification of Consumers

Since marketing is from the perspective of an enterprise, the market is customers with consumer demand. Under market conditions, all marketing activities of an enterprise must be centered on meeting consumer demand. Logically, according to the purpose of consumption, the market can be divided into two categories according to different customers: individual consumer market and organizational market.

In the whole market structure, the consumer market occupies an important position. Consumer market is also called final consumer market or consumer goods market. It refers to the market where individuals or families buy or rent goods to meet their living needs. The consumer market is the basis of the market system and plays a decisive role.

Organizational market refers to the market formed by industrial and commercial enterprises engaged in production, sales and other business activities, as well as government departments and non-profit organizations to fulfill their duties by purchasing products and services. Organizational market is an important market for enterprises. The organizational market corresponds to the consumer market, which is the individual market, while the organizational market is the market of legal representatives.

According to the consumption status of a certain product or service, consumers can be divided into real consumers and potential consumers.

Real consumers are people who have actual needs for some goods or services, and the consumer produces actual consumption behavior.

Potential consumers are people who do not currently buy or use a product, but at some point in the future, are likely to become real consumers.

For example, most college students lack practical needs for household appliances, but they will have practical needs for them when they have a family in the future. Therefore, at the present stage, college students are potential consumers of household appliances. Usually, the state of consumer demand is caused by the lack of certain necessary conditions of consumption, such as unclear awareness of demand, insufficient purchasing power, etc. Once the required conditions are met, potential consumers may be converted into real consumers at any time. With the intensification of market competition, some enterprises not only focus on competing for the current consumers, but also devote themselves to cultivating future consumers, because potential consumers are an important factor for enterprises to explore new markets, maintain and increase market share in competition.

The study of consumers' buying behavior is essential for effective marketing activities.

8.2　The Characteristics of Consumer Market Purchasing Behavior

Consumer market has a lot of buyers who have frequent transactions, but the number of transactions is small. Therefore, most of the goods are sold through intermediaries to consumers. In order to meet the needs of market consumption, enterprises must analyze the characteristics of consumers, pay close attention to market dynamics, and provide marketable products.

1. Inducibility

Consumers are often restricted by production characteristics and influenced by national policies and plans, and they have spontaneity and impulsiveness. Their choice of products is greatly influenced by advertising and publicity, and consumers' buying behavior is to a large extent inducible.

2. Non-profit

Consumers buy goods for a certain use value and their own or family consumption needs, rather than for profit.

3. Non-professional

Consumers generally lack specialized commodity knowledge and market knowledge. When consumers buy goods, they are easily affected by advertising, promotion, packaging and service attitude.

4. Hierarchy

Due to the different income levels and social classes of consumers, consumers' demands will show certain levels. Generally speaking, consumers always first meet the most basic survival needs and safety needs to buy life necessities, and then gradually meet the needs of a higher level.

5. Alternative

Most of the consumer goods can be replaced or used interchangeably, except for a few commodities that are not replaceable. Therefore, the goods in the consumer market are substitutable.

6. Universality

In consumer market, buyers are not only numerous, but also widely distributed. Consumer markets are everywhere, from cities to countries, from home to abroad.

7. Variability

Consumer market is extensive, and demand is diversiform. Consumer demand is affected not only by internal factors of consumers, but also by external factors such as environment, fashion and values. Different times and consumer demand will also be different, so consumer market goods have a certain variability.

8. Locality

Consumers in different regions have different living habits, consumption habits, consumption levels, etc., so they have great differences when they buy goods.

8.3   The Factors Influencing Consumer Market Purchasing Behavior

Essentially, consumer market buying behavior depends on their needs and desires, which are affected by many factors. To sum up, the factors that influence consumer market buying behavior include social and cultural factors, economic factors, psychological factors and personal factors.

8.3.1   Social and Cultural Factors

Every consumer grows and lives in a certain social and cultural environment, which influences and restricts people's consumption concept, demand and desire, purchasing behavior and lifestyle.

1. Culture

As an important macro-environmental factor, culture has certain influences on consumer behavior. Cultural influences, like air, are everywhere. Culture is the most fundamental determinant of human desire and behavior.

Coca-Cola, for example, is sold in red and white packages in other parts of the world, but in the Arab world, it is sold in a green package, because green means life and oasis for people there. Therefore, the influence of culture on consumers cannot be ignored.

2. Subculture

Culture is a whole concept, but in a large cultural background, it can be divided into several different subculture groups. A subculture refers to a culture that is specific to a small group of people in a society. In terms of race, nationality, religion, region, values and language, there are mainly the following four kinds:

(1) Ethnic subculture

Almost every country has different ethnic groups. In the process of long-term survival and reproduction, each ethnic group has gradually formed its own unique and stable subculture. For example, there are 56 ethnic groups in China. Due to the differences in natural environment and society, each ethnic group has its unique customs and cultural traditions, thus forming its unique consumption behavior.

(2) Religious subculture

Many countries in the world have different religions. Different religious beliefs will lead to differences in values, lifestyles and consumption habits of consumers, thus forming consumer groups of religious subcultures.

(3) Racial subculture

A race is a group of people with different skin colors, such as white, yellow, black, etc. They all have their unique cultural traditions, cultural styles and consumption habits. Even if you live in the same country, you will have your own unique needs and hobbies.

(4) Regional subculture

Different regions have different natural conditions, different levels of economic development and different living habits, which naturally lead to different consumption characteristics. For example, in terms of diet, people in the north of China mainly eat pasta, while people in the south eat rice.

3. Social Class

Social class refers to the classification of social members according to certain social standards, such as income, education, occupation, social status, etc. The behaviors of consumers of different social classes have obvious differences in values, lifestyles and interests. For example, consumers from different social classes show very different shopping environment preferences. White-collar consumers often have full confidence in their purchasing power, and they prefer to shop alone and tend to choose shopping in malls with elegant environments and considerate service, while blue-collar shoppers like to shop at new stores, and tend to be price-sensitive and prefer shopping with partners. Enterprises can choose their target markets by market segmentation based on social class.

4. Reference Group

Everyone lives in a group. The reference group is a group that has direct or indirect influences on a person's habits, hobbies, thought and behavior standards. It is mainly divided into the following three groups:

(1) Member Group

It is a group that has a close relationship with consumers and directly influences them, such as the family, classmates, colleagues and friends.

(2) Admirer Group

It is the object that consumers adore, such as singers, movie stars.

(3) Dissociative Group

It is a group of people that consumers don't like.

The influence of the reference group on consumer market buying behavior is mainly manifested in three aspects: First, the reference group provides consumers with new consumption ideas, consumption behaviors and lifestyles. Second, the reference group prompts consumers to imitate. When a movie star wears a pair of fashionable shoes, many of his fans will follow him to buy the shoes. This is also why many brands use celebrities as their spokesmen Third, reference groups tend to make consumers' behaviors "consistent", thus influencing consumers' choice of certain products and brands. For example, an employee found that many colleagues in his office had bought Huawei mobile phones, so he thought the performance and quality of them were better and decided to buy a Huawei phone.

5. Opinion Leaders

Opinion leaders are usually limited to specific buying situations. Opinion leaders have a strong interest and rich knowledge of certain products. Other consumers turn to him for advice when buying such products. For example, barbers can act as opinion leaders for hair care products.

8.3.2 Economic Factors

Economic factors are the second most important factor affecting consumers. The main factor is the economic condition of consumers, i. e. the level of disposable income of consumers. Economic factors play a decisive role in the purchasing power of consumers. They mainly include consumer income, commodity price and commodity utility.

1. Consumer Income

What kind of products and services consumers buy first depends on their purchasing power. And the ability to buy depends largely on the level of income. Generally speaking, the higher the income level is, the stronger purchasing power consumers have. On the contrary, the lower the income level is, the weaker purchasing power consumers have and the more sensitive they are to commodity prices.

2. The Price of Goods

In any case, price is an important and direct reference factor for consumers to make purchases. The price of a commodity is not only the price of the product itself, but also the price that consumers expect and the price of other comparable products.

3. Commodity Utility

The utility of goods is the degree of satisfaction that a consumer obtains from consuming those goods. Western economists use "the principle of maxmization of marginal utility" to explain the influence of economic factors on consumers' buying behavior. They believe that consumers' buying behavior is relatively rational, and consumers always make the most reasonable buying decisions within their income, so as to meet their own needs to the maximum extent. The utility is the greatest when consumers are most satisfied.

8.3.3   Psychological Factors

Consumers' purchasing behavior is also influenced by certain psychological processes. As the personality of consumers is different, the psychological factors that affect consumers are also very different. Generally speaking, consumers' purchasing behavior is mainly affected by psychological factors such as need, motivation, sense and perception, learning, belief and attitude.

1. Need

Where there is a demand, there is a market. The purchasing behavior of consumer market is the behavior of consumers to solve their needs. Different people have different needs, so people's physical and spiritual needs also have universality and diversity. Each person's specific situation is different, and the order of importance and emergency to solve need problems is naturally different, so there is a hierarchy of needs. The urgent need to be met will stimulate a strong purchase motivation; once the need is met, it will lose the incentive effect on behavior, that is, there will be no motivation to trigger behavior.

Maslow's theory divides needs into five levels: physiological needs, safety needs, social needs, esteem needs and self-actualization needs, which are arranged from the lower level to the higher level. When a certain level of need is relatively satisfied, it will develop to a higher level, and the pursuit of a higher level of need becomes the driving force of behavior. Accordingly, the need for basic satisfaction is no longer a motivating force.

The theory of need hierarchy has two basic starting points. First, everyone has needs.

Figure 8.1 Maslow's Hierarchy of Needs

After one need level is satisfied, another need level appears. Second, urgent needs should be met before various needs are met. After the need is met, the latter need shows its stimulating effect.

2. Motivation

Purchasing motivation refers to the desire or intention of people to purchase in order to meet certain needs. In real life, consumers' purchase behavior is triggered by their purchase motivation, which is generated by human needs. When people are hungry, they will eat; when they are thirsty, they want to drink water. This manifests that needs generate motivation and motivation triggers behavior. The purchasing motivation of consumers is the internal power to promote the purchasing activities of consumers. Thus, it can be seen that people's purchasing motivation is closely related to people's needs, which is the driving force of consumers' purchasing behavior. The urgent need to be met will stimulate a strong purchase motivation; once the need is met, it will lose the incentive effect on behavior, that is, there will be no motivation to cause behavior.

Consumers' purchasing motivation is complex and changeable. The same purchase may be intricately interwoven with multiple motives. However, enterprises should analyze and study the purchase motivation, because the purchase motivation has a profound impact on enterprise marketing activities.

3. Sense and Perception

Perception is the process of perceiving and understanding the world as a whole in order to create a meaningful image of the individual world. Perception depends not only on the characteristics of the stimulus but also on the relationship of the stimulus with the surrounding environment and the individual's situation where he is.

The consumer cannot feed all external stimuli into the brain and respond. Perception is a process of choice. It mainly includes three steps: selective attention, selective understanding and selective memory.

Figure 8.2　The Selection Process of Perception

(1) Selective attention: Consumers receive a lot of information every day, but only a small amount of information will attract their attention and form awareness, and most of the information will be ignored by consumers. Generally speaking, the following situations are easy to attract the attention from consumers: the current needs of consumers; the expected to occur; a stimulant of great intensity.

(2) Selective understanding: Although some stimuli are noticed by consumers, they often make explanations according to their own experiences, preferences, emotions at that time, situations and other factors. This explanation may be consistent with the intentions of the business, or it may vary widely.

(3) Selective memory: Consumers tend to forget most of the information, but they can remember the information consistent with their attitudes and beliefs. Whether the information of goods can be retained in customers' memory has a great influence on their purchase decision.

4. Learning

Most human behavior comes from learning. Buying behavior is not instinctive. It is gained through learning according to the stimulus-response theory. This theory includes five factors: driving force, stimulus, cue, response and reinforcement. These five elements interact to help consumers complete the learning process.

5. Belief and Attitude

Beliefs and attitudes are fixed opinions and attitudes that people form through learning or personal experience, that is, consumers' opinions and tendencies toward certain goods. Once attitudes are formed, they are hard to change. Attitudes affect people's future buying behavior. It can make consumers habitually buy certain goods.

8.3.4　Personal Factors

Consumer market purchasing behaviors are firstly affected by consumers' own factors, which mainly include age, gender, occupation, status, lifestyle, personality and self-image.

1. Age and Gender

Consumers of different ages have different requirements for the interest, variety and style of shopping. Different types of goods are required at different stages of the life cycle. For example, during infancy, people need baby food, toys, etc.; and in old age, people need health care products more. The consumer market purchasing behavior of different genders also varies greatly. China's female consumers are not only large in number, but also play an important role in purchasing activities. They consume more actively. Compared with women, male consumers pay more attention to rational consumption. Most tobacco and alcohol products are purchased by male consumers, while female consumers prefer to buy fashion, jewelry and cosmetics.

2. Occupation and Status

Consumers of different occupations often have different needs and hobbies for goods. A business person, when buying clothes, will generally buy more business types, but for students, sportswear and casual wear are more necessary. Consumers' status also affects their purchasing behavior. High-status consumers will buy higher-level goods to show their status.

3. Lifestyle

Lifestyle is the arrangement mode of life formed by people under certain social conditions and the influence of values. Different lifestyles lead to different shopping interests, shopping habits and shopping evaluations. Some consumers pay more attention to the sense of life ceremony, so they pay attention to the style and appearance of goods when shopping. When making marketing strategies, every enterprise should explore the lifestyle of target consumers and formulate corresponding strategies so as to attract consumers' attention and purchase.

4. Personality and Self-concept

Personality is a personal characteristic. It is because of the differences in personality that the psychological characteristics and behavioral patterns of consumers vary, and at the same time, it shows the unique personal style and characteristics of each consumer. Some scholars classify buyers into six types according to their personalities: habitual, rational, impulsive, economical, emotional and casual types. Regardless of the types, every consumer will choose products and brands that match their self-concept when shopping.

8.4　Types of Consumer Market Purchasing Behavior

Because the products and brands are different, consumer market buying behavior is very different. It can be divided into four categories according to the degree of participation of consumers' purchasing behaviors and the difference of product brands.

Table 8.1　Types of Consumer Purchasing Behavior

		Degree of Participation	
		High	Low
Brand Differences	Large	Complex Purchasing Behavior	Variety-seeking Purchasing Behavior
	Small	Harmonious Purchasing Behavior	Habitual Purchasing Behavior

1. Complex Purchasing Behavior

Complex purchasing behavior refers to the purchase behavior of consumers when consumers buy products with high prices, large brand differences and complex functions. Due to the lack of necessary product knowledge, consumers need to make careful choices and comparisons in order to reduce risks. For example, this behavior occurs when buying cars and houses.

2. Habitual Purchasing Behavior

Because the product price is low, the brand difference is small and they often buy it. Consumers usually buy the goods according to their past usage habits and hobbies, or always go to familiar places to buy goods. They are generally loyal to the commodities, trademarks and distributors they are familiar with. The transaction speed is faster. Buying things like salt, oil is an example of habitual purchasing behavior.

3. Harmonious Purchasing Behavior

For some products, the differences between brands are not large, and the price is high. Consumers have a high degree of participation and invest a lot of energy to make comparisons, but they find that they can only make comparisons and choices in price and place of purchase. The time between the motivation to buy and the decision to buy is short. Therefore, this kind of purchasing behavior is easy to produce a sense of disharmony after purchase. When buying a bed, for instance, people need to look at its design, but generally, there isn't much of a difference between brands, so they buy it if there is an appropriate one. But when they buy it, they find they don't like it.

In order to change such psychology and pursue psychological balance, consumers extensively collect all kinds of favorable information about purchased products to prove the correctness of their purchase decisions. The marketer should provide perfect aftersales service and the product information beneficial to the enterprise through various ways, so as to make customers believe that their purchase decision is correct.

4. Variety-seeking Purchasing Behavior

There are obvious differences among products, but if the price is not high, consumers do not want to spend too much time making choices. Sometimes consumers change the brands they buy randomly and frequently. For example, consumers are free to switch brands when they buy cookies.

8.5 The Decision-making Process of Consumer Market Purchasing Behavior

The process of consumer purchasing decision is the process in which consumers make purchasing decisions. Different purchase types reflect the difference or particularity of consumers' purchase process. In the relatively complex purchasing process, consumers' purchasing decision includes five steps: recognizing the needs, collecting information, evaluating alternative plans, purchasing decision and post-purchase behavior.

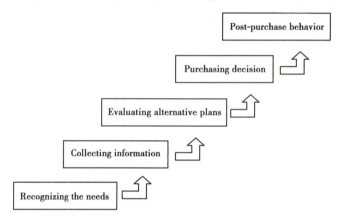

Figure 8.3　Five Steps of Decision-making Process of Consumer Purchasing Behavior

1. Recognizing the Needs

Consumers are aware of the difference between their current reality and their expectations, which leads to decisions. This is the first step in the purchase decision. This need may be caused by internal stimulation or by some kind of external stimulation. For example, getting an advertisement for a new perfume or seeing someone else wearing a fashionable dress makes you want to buy it. Therefore, marketers should lose no time in taking appropriate marketing measures to arouse and strengthen the needs of consumers.

2. Collecting Information

When the aroused demand motivation is very strong, consumers will collect relevant information in multiple ways starting from a rational perspective. There are four main sources of information:

(1) Personal sources, such as families, relatives, friends, neighbors, colleagues, etc.;

(2) Commercial sources, such as advertising, personal marketing, trade fairs, etc.;

(3) Public sources, such as television, the Internet, newspapers and other mass media, consumer organizations, etc.;

(4) Personal experience sources, such as the experience of operation, experiment

and using the product.

3. Evaluating Alternative Plans

Comparison is the key to discrimination. The information consumers receive may be repetitive or even contradictory. Therefore, analysis, evaluation and selection are the decisive steps in the decision-making process. In the process of consumers' evaluation and selection, different consumers pay different attention to various properties of products or have different evaluation standards. Most consumers' selection process is to compare the actual products with their ideal products.

4. Making Decision for Purchasing

After the comparison and selection of commodity information, consumers generally choose their favorite products. However, from the purchase intention to the purchase decision, there are still two factors to be affected:

(1) The attitude of others. If someone disagrees, the possibility of modifying the purchase intention is very high. For example, if a consumer is ready to buy a certain brand of mobile phones, but his sister strongly opposes him, then he will give up the intention to buy it.

(2) Unexpected circumstances. If something unexpected happens, such as job loss, urgent need, price increase, etc., it is likely to change the purchase intention.

5. Post-purchase Behavior

After using the product, consumers will form their own evaluation of the product, that is, the degree of satisfaction after purchase and the activities after purchase.

The degree of consumer satisfaction after purchase depends on the comparison between the expected performance of the product and the actual performance of the product in use. The degree of satisfaction after purchase determines consumers' post-purchase activities and attitudes towards the brand, and also affects other consumers, forming a chain effect. If the use of the product is better than consumers' expectation, consumers will be satisfied and are actively promote the product. But if the use of the product is worse than consumers' expectation, consumers will be unhappy, then they will not buy it again and will grumble and complain.

Marketers should actively contact consumers, understand the use of products timely, and do a good job in after-sales service, so that customers feel satisfied and are convinced of the correctness of their purchase decisions. Enterprises should also improve their products and services timely according to customers' feedback.

8.6　Classification of Organizational Market

An organizational market is a market made up of purchasers of certain organizations.

The organizational market is an important market for enterprises, which can be divided into producers' market, intermediaries' market and non-profit organization market according to the nature of the consumers.

(1) Producers' market, also called industrial market or enterprise market, refers to companies and individuals who buy products or services for the manufacture of other products or services and then sell or lease them to others for profit. Producer markets include agriculture, forestry, manufacturing, banking, insurance and service industries.

(2) The intermediaries' market is also known as the resellers' market. Individuals and companies, including wholesalers and retailers, purchase goods and services for the purpose of reselling or leasing them to others for profit. Wholesalers buy goods and services and resell them to retailers and other merchants, but they do not sell large quantities of goods to final consumers; a retailer's main business is to sell goods or services directly to consumers.

(3) Non-profit organization market refers to a market composed of all kinds of non-profit organizations that purchase products or services in order to maintain normal operation and perform functions. Non-profit organization market is not-for-profit and does not engage in for-profit activities. In China, non-profit organizations are usually called "government organizations and institutions". Government market refers to the governments at all levels and their subordinate departments that buy or rent products for the purpose of performing government functions. It is the main component of non-profit organization market.

8.7 Characteristics of Organizational Market Purchasing Behavior

Compared with consumer market, organizational market purchasing behavior has many significant characteristics.

1. Fewer Buyers

The number of buyers in an organizational market is much smaller than that in a consumer market. If wood is sold to a furniture factory, there may be only a few buyers, but if it is sold to an individual consumer, then everyone may become a buyer.

2. Large Purchase Quantity

Organizational market buys large quantities each time. Sometimes a customer can buy all the products of the enterprise, and the amount of an order can reach tens of millions of RMB.

3. Derived Requirements

Organizations buy products to meet the needs of their customers, that is to say, organizations' demand for products is ultimately derived from consumers' demand for goods. Clearly, winemakers buy grapes because consumers buy wine.

4. Professional Purchase

Many enterprises have special purchasing departments. Most of the purchasing personnel in the organizational market are professionally trained, and have rich professional knowledge and clear understanding of the product performance, quality and specifications. Suppliers provide them with detailed technical information explaining the advantages of their products and services from a technical perspective.

5. Many People Influencing Purchasing

The participants in the purchasing decision process are often not just one person, but many people. Even purchasing managers rarely make independent decisions. Important purchasing decisions are often made by technical experts and senior managers.

6. A Close Relationship Between the Supply and Demand Parties

Since there are few buyers in the organizational market, each customer is very important to the enterprise. If any customer is lost, the sales volume of the enterprise will be seriously affected. Enterprises should try to establish close and long-term relationships with customers, and sometimes they have a marketing team dedicated to serving big customers, so as to obtain and maintain continuous orders.

7. Relatively Concentrated Geographical Location

Buyers in the organizational market tend to concentrate in a certain region, so that the purchase volume of products in these regions accounts for a large proportion of the national market. This kind of geographical concentration is an inevitable trend in the development of the commodity economy, which helps to reduce operating costs.

8. Direct Procurement

Buyers in the organizational market often purchase directly from suppliers without middlemen, which can minimize costs.

9. Reciprocal Purchase

Buyers and sellers often switch roles, acting as buyers and sellers. Towel manufacturers buy in bulk cotton threads for towel production from textile companies, while textile companies buy towels in bulk from towel manufacturers to reward employees.

10. Lease

The organizational market often obtains the desired product through leasing. Many enterprises can't afford some expensive products, so renting can save money.

8.8　The Decision-making Process of Organizational Market Purchasing Behavior

The characteristics of the organizational market are quite different from those of the consumer market, and the organizational market is affected and restricted by different factors. In this way, the process of organizational market purchasing behavior is different from that of consumer purchasing behavior.

Generally speaking, the process of decision-making organizational market is divided into eight stages, which are putting forward the demand, confirming the overall need, confirming product specifications, seeking suppliers, collecting supply information, selecting suppliers, placing formal orders and evaluating the application.

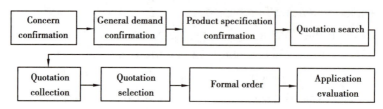

Figure 8.4　Eight Stages of Decision-making Process of Organizational Market Purchasing Behavior

1. Concern Confirmation

The purchasing process begins when someone in the company offers to buy a product to solve a problem or need. It means that concern confirmation is the first step in the purchase decision.

2. General Demand Confirmation

After putting forward the demand, purchasers begin to determine the characteristics and quantity of the desired product. If it is a simple purchasing task, purchasers can make the decision directly. But for complex tasks, the purchasing department makes decisions together with other departments.

3. Product Specification Confirmation

After the general demand confirmation, specifications and characteristics of the products should be specified in detail, which will be the basis for the purchase of goods.

4. Quotation Search

Purchasers start to find the best suppliers by searching online, consulting commercial organizations, attending exhibitions and other ways.

5. Quotation Collection

Purchasers will invite qualified suppliers to submit applications. Of course, if the product is complex and expensive, purchasers will ask suppliers to provide detailed applications.

6. Quotation Selection

Purchasers begin to compare and analyze suppliers after receiving relevant data from them. Enterprise reputation, financial status, price, product quality and delivery time are the main factors that purchasers will consider.

7. Formal Order

After selecting the supplier, purchasers will issue a formal order or a contract will be signed. The supplier will supply the goods according to the order or the contract.

8. Application Evaluation

When the product arrives, the purchasing department will contact the user to find out how the product is being used. After evaluation, the purchaser will decide to continue, modify or discontinue purchasing from the supplier.

Organizational market purchasing behavior is a series of processes. Of course, these eight stages are not necessarily to be carried out, depending on the type of purchase.

Key Terms

consumer market 消费者市场	It refers to the market where individuals or families buy or rent goods to meet their living needs. 它是指个人或家庭购买或租用商品以满足其生活需要的市场。
organizational market 组织市场	It refers to the market formed by industrial and commercial enterprises engaged in production, sales and other business activities, as well as government departments and non-profit organizations to fulfill their duties by purchasing products and services. 它是指从事生产、销售及其他业务活动的工商企业以及政府部门和非营利组织通过购买产品和服务履行其职责所形成的市场。
social class 社会阶层	Social class refers to the classification of social members according to certain social standards. 社会阶级是指按照一定的社会标准对社会成员进行的分类。
reference group 参照群体	It is a group that has a direct or indirect influence on a person's habits, hobbies, thought and behavior standards. 参照群体是指直接或间接影响一个人的习惯、爱好、思想和行为标准的群体。
opinion leaders 意见领袖	They are the minority who have an important source of information and influence in a team and can influence the attitude of the majority. 意见领袖是在团队中构成信息和影响的重要来源，并能影响多数人态度倾向的少数人。
marginal utility 边际效用	The process of value formation is explained by utility, and it is pointed out that the value of goods is people's perception and evaluation of the utility of goods. Utility decreases with the increasing consumption of a commodity. 边际效用是以效用解释价值形成的过程，指出商品的价值是人对物品效用的感觉和评价。效用随着商品消费的增加而减少。

Continued

Maslow's hierarchy of needs 马斯洛的需求层次理论	Maslow puts forward the hierarchy of needs theory. The theory divides needs into five levels: physiological needs, safety needs, social needs, esteem needs and self-actualization needs, which are arranged from the lower level to the higher level. When a certain level of need is relatively satisfied, it will develop to a higher level, and the pursuit of a higher level of need becomes the driving force of behavior. 马斯洛提出需求层次理论。该理论将需求分为五个层次:生理需求、安全需求、社会需求、尊重需求和自我实现需求,依次由较低层次到较高层次排列。当某一层次的需要得到相对满足时,它就会向更高层次发展,对更高层次的需要的追求成为行为的驱动力。
complex purchasing behavior 复杂型购买行为	It refers to the purchase behavior of consumers when consumers buy products with high prices, large brand differences and complex functions. Due to the lack of necessary product knowledge, consumers need to make careful choices and comparisons in order to reduce risks. 复杂购买行为是指消费者购买价格高、品牌差异大、功能复杂的产品时的购买行为。由于缺乏必要的产品知识,消费者需要仔细选择、仔细比较,以降低风险。
habitual purchasing behavior 习惯型购买行为	Because the product price is low, and the brand difference is small and consumers often buy, consumers usually buy the goods according to their past usage habits and hobbies, or always go to familiar places to buy goods. They are generally loyal to the commodities, trademarks and distributors they are familiar with. The transaction speed is faster. 因为产品价格低、品牌差异小并且消费者经常购买,消费者通常根据自己过去的使用习惯和爱好购买商品,或总是到自己熟悉的地点去购买商品。他们一般比较忠于自己熟悉的商品、商标和经销商,成交速度较快。
harmonious purchasing behavior 和谐型购买行为	For some products, the difference between brands is not large, and the price is high. Consumers have a high degree of participation and invest a lot of energy to make comparisons, but they find that they can only make comparisons and choices in price and place of purchase. The time between the motivation to buy and the decision to buy is short. Therefore, this kind of purchasing behavior is easy to produce a sense of disharmony after purchase. In order to change such psychology and pursue psychological balance, consumers extensively collect all kinds of favorable information about purchased products to prove the correctness of their purchase decisions. The marketer should provide perfect aftersales service and the product information beneficial to the enterprise through various ways, so as to make customers believe that their purchase decision is correct. 有些产品,品牌差异不大,价格昂贵,消费者参与程度高,投入了大量的精力进行比较,但他们发现自己只能在价格和购买地点上进行比较和选择。购买动机和决定之间的时间很短。因此,这种购买行为在购买后很容易产生不和谐感。为了改变这样的心理,追求心理的平衡,消费者广泛地收集各种对已购产品的有利信息,以证明自己购买决定的正确性。营销者要提供完善的售后服务,并通过各种途径提供有利于本企业的产品的信息,使顾客相信自己的购买决定是正确的。

Continued

variety-seeking purchasing behavior 多变型购买行为	There are obvious differences between the products, but the price is not high. Consumers do not want to spend too much time making choices, but to change the brands they buy randomly and frequently. 产品之间有明显的差异,但是价格并不昂贵,消费者不想花太多时间做选择,而是随意地、经常地更换他们购买的品牌。

Review & Critical Thinking Questions

1. What is the meaning of consumer market?

2. What is the meaning of organizational market?

3. What is the difference between real consumers and potential consumers?

4. What is the classification of organizational market?

5. What are the characteristics of consumer market purchasing behavior?

6. What are the characteristics of organizational market purchasing behavior?

7. What are the factors influencing consumer market purchasing behavior?

8. What are the aspects of subculture?

9. Describe the influence of social class on consumer market buying behavior.

10. What is the classification of reference group?

11. What are the aspects of economic factors?

12. What aspects do psychological factors include?

13. What is Maslow's Hierarchy of Needs?

14. What are steps of perception process in consumer buying behavior?

15. What are the aspects of personal factors?

16. What are the types of consumer purchasing behavior?

17. What is the decision-making process of consumer purchasing behavior?

18. What is the decision-making process of organizational market purchasing behavior?

Discussion Questions

1. Reference group has a strong influence on consumer market buying behavior. Please illustrate the above-mentioned point with your own purchases.

2. What is your personality? Give an example to show how your personality affects you in shopping.

3. Generally speaking, consumers buy things in order to solve their needs. Different people have different needs. Explain your recent needs and purchasing behavior according to Maslow's hierarchy of needs theory.

4. If you want to buy a computer, what is your decision-making process?

5. Sometimes consumers feel regret after using the product. Do you have this kind of experience? How do you solve the problem like this?

Case Study

There was a copier manufacturing company on Fifth Avenue in New York. They needed a good salesman. The boss selected three applicants for the job, including Anne, a young woman from Philadelphia.

The boss gave them a day to show off their abilities. What was the best way to show the ability? After walking out of the company, three applicants started to discuss their situation. One said, "Sell to people who don't need it! That is the best demonstration. I decided to visit a farmer and sell him a copy machine!"

"That's a great idea! I'll go to a fisherman and sell him my copier!" said another candidate. Before they left, they asked Anne to go with them. Anne thought for a moment and said, "I think those things are too difficult. I'll choose the easy one."

The next morning, the boss called all three into the office again and asked, "What have you done to demonstrate your abilities?"

"It took me all day to finally sell the copier to a farmer!" The first applicant said proudly, "You know, the farmer didn't need a copier, but I made him buy one!"

The boss nodded and said nothing.

"It took me two hours to get to the Hudson River in the suburbs, another hour to find a fisherman, and another four hours of hard talk to convince him to buy a copier!" The second candidate responded with satisfaction, "Actually, he didn't need the copier at all, but he bought it!"

The boss nodded again, then turned to Anne. "What about you?"

"No! I sold my product to three electrical appliance operators!" Anne took some documents out of her bag and handed them to her boss. "I visited three dealers in half a day and got three orders for 600 copiers."

The boss was overjoyed. Then he announced that Anne was hired. At this moment, two other applicants protested. They thought it was common to sell copiers to electrical appliance operators, because they needed the products in the first place.

"I think you have a misconception about abilities. Ability is not about using time to do the most incredible thing, but using the shortest time to do the easiest thing.

The boss went on in a solemn tone, "By asking farmers and fishermen to buy the copier, I suspect you are exaggerating the functions of the copier. I must remind you that this is one of the biggest sales taboos!"

Anne was accepted by the company. In her future work, Anne has always been guided by a principle: use all your energy to do the easiest thing. Years later, Anne set a world record for the annual sales of two million copiers, which no one has ever broken!

In 2001, Anne was not only named by FORTUNE magazine as "one of the world's 100 greatest salesmen of the 20th century (and the only woman among them)," she was also elected CEO of the company for the next 10 years.

Her name is Anne Mulcahy, the recently retired president of Xerox which is the world's biggest copier maker.

Questions

According to this chapter, what do you learn from this case?

中文概述

按照消费的目的,营销学将市场分为两大类:个人消费者市场和组织市场。

消费者市场又称最终消费者市场、消费品市场或生活资料市场,是指个人或家庭为满足生活需求而购买或租用商品的市场。消费者市场是市场体系的基础,是起决定作用的市场。

组织市场指从事生产、销售及其他业务活动的工商企业以及政府部门和非营利组织通过购买产品和服务履行其职责所形成的市场。组织市场和消费者市场相对应,消费者市场是个人市场,组织市场是法人市场。

根据对某种产品或服务的消费状态,可将消费者分为现实消费者和潜在消费者。

消费者市场的特征为:可诱导性、非盈利性、非专业性、层次性、替代性、广泛性、多变性和地域性。企业一定要分析消费者的特征,密切关注市场动态,提供适销对路的产品。

影响消费者购买行为的因素包括:社会文化因素、经济因素、心理因素和个人因素。

社会文化因素包括:文化、亚文化、社会阶层、参照群体和意见领袖。**经济因素**主要指消费者的经济状况,即:消费者的可支配收入水平。主要包括消费者的收入、商品的价格和商品效用等。

消费者的购买行为主要受到需要、动机、感觉和知觉、学习、信念与态度等**心理因素**的影响。

马斯洛提出**需求层次理论**。该理论将需求分为五个层次:生理需求、安全需求、社会需求、尊重需求和自我实现需求,依次由较低层次到较高层次排列。马斯洛认为,当某一层次的需要得到相对满足时，它就会向更高层次发展，对更高层次的需要的追求成为行为的驱动力。

购买动机是指为了满足一定需要而引起人们购买行为的欲望或意念。消费者的购买动机是推动消费者进行购买活动的内部动力。

知觉是外界刺激感官时，人对外界的整体的看法和理解，从而创造出个人世界有意义的形象的过程。知觉是一个选择过程。它主要包括选择性注意、选择性理解和选择性记忆三个过程。

购买行为也是通过学习得来的，而不是本能，即**"刺激-反应"理论**。这一理论包括五个因素：驱动力、刺激物、提示物、反应和强化。这五个要素相互影响，帮助消费者完成学习过程。

消费者购买行为首先受其**个人因素**的影响，这些因素主要包括年龄、性别、职业、地位、生活方式、个性和自我形象。

根据消费者购买行为的参与度及产品品牌的差异，**消费者购买行为的类型**可分为：复杂型购买行为、习惯型购买行为、和谐型购买行为和多变型购买行为。

在较为复杂的购买过程中，消费者**购买决策的步骤**包括五个：认识需求、收集信息、评价可选方案、购买决策、购买后行为。

按照购买对象的不同性质，**组织市场的分类**为：生产者市场、中间商市场和非盈利组织市场。

组织市场购买行为的特点主要包括：买者少、购买数量大、派生需求、专业化购买、影响购买的人多、供需双方关系密切、地理位置相对集中、直接采购、互惠购买、租赁等。

UNIT 9 / International Service Marketing

9

Learning Objectives

1. Describe four unique elements of services.
2. Recognize how services differ and how they can be classified.
3. Explain how consumers purchase and evaluate services.
4. Develop a customer contact audit to identify service advantage.
5. Explain the role of the eight Ps in the international service Marketing Mix.
6. Discuss the important roles of internal marketing and customer experience management in service organizations.

Services play a pivotal role in marketing. It is mainly focused that international services have changed drastically over a period of time. With the advent of electronic media and communications, services marketing at international level has gained much momentum. International service marketing enables businesses to acknowledge cultural differences when advertising in foreign countries. A marketer has to focus on how the services have to be done at international level with varied cultural and regional differences.

Why is International Services Marketing important?

The international business environment has changed drastically thanks to globalization and market liberalization. The widespread use of electronic channels in marketing and product distribution has intensified competition in global markets.

1. International Audience. Services are intangible products generally delivered through interactive channels. They are offered either as primary products or as supplementary components, according to the Management Study Guide.

2. Cultural Expectations. International service marketing enables businesses to acknowledge cultural differences when advertising in foreign countries.

3. International Networks. Service businesses that build and maintain international networks build close relationships with customers. This allows them to raise sales while expanding their market presence abroad. Taking advantage of Internet-based promotional and networking platforms, such as social media, service business can reap maximum benefits in market penetration strategies. Digital platforms are particularly useful for small and medium-sized service companies engaging in international promotion because they are fairly affordable and easily accessible.

4. Promoting Differentiation. International service marketing is an important platform for brand differentiation among service companies offering similar and related products in foreign markets. Indeed, brand recognition enables service companies to stand out and remain competitive. That makes promotional campaigns that engage the audience while establishing brand awareness as critical as the investment required to operate on an international basis.

9.1   The Uniqueness of Services

Services are intangible activities or benefits (such as airline trips, financial advice, or automobile repair) that an organization provides to satisfy consumers' needs in exchange for money or something else of value.

Services have become a significant component of the global economy and one of the most important components of the U.S. economy. The World Trade Organization (WTO) estimates that all countries exported merchandise valued at $13.5 trillion and commercial services valued at $3.2 trillion. In the USA, more than 42% of the gross domestic product (GDP) now comes from services. As shown in Figure 9.1, the value of services in the economy has increased more than 70% since 1990.

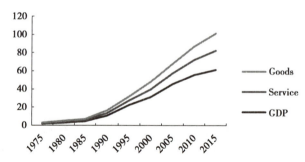

Figure 9.1   Services Are Now a Larger Part of a Certain Country's GDP Than Goods

The growth of this sector is the result of increasing demand for services that have been available in the past and the increasing interest in new services. Concierge services, for example, have been popular in hotels such as the Breakers in Palm Beach, Florida, which has staff of 11 concierges, and the Ritz-Carlton, which offers concierges who specialize in technology support, shopping, and medical issues. Outside the hotel industry, Famous Friends Concierge service offers clients opportunities to fly on private jets with celebrities, private check-in at resorts, hard-to-get restaurants and nightclub reservations, and special event tickets. Concierge services are even available for daily lifestyle needs. Ace concierge, for instance, will schedule car maintenance, pick up and deliver dry cleaning, walk your dog, or even shop for groceries and gifts. Other new services include: The Luggage Club, which offers door-to-door luggage delivery to and from 220 countries; Virgin Galactic, which offers private space travel; and—*friendorfollow. com*, which helps you determine if the people you are following on Twitter are also following you. These firms and many others like them are examples of imaginative services that will play a role in our economy in the future.

The Four I's of Services

There are four unique elements to services—intangibility, inconsistency, inseparability and inventory-referred to as the four I's of services.

Intangibility. Services are intangible; that is, they can't be held, touched or seen before the purchase decision. In contrast, before purchasing a traditional product, a consumer can touch a box of laundry detergent, kick the tire of an automobile, or sample a new breakfast cereal. Because services tend to be a performance rather than an object, they are much more difficult for consumers to evaluate. To help consumers assess and compare services, marketers try to make them tangible or show the benefits of using the service.

Inconsistency. Developing, pricing, promoting and delivering services are challenging because the quality of a service is often inconsistent. Because services depend on the people who provide them, their quality varies with each person's capabilities and day-to-day job performance. Inconsistency is much more of a problem in services than it is with tangible goods. Tangible products can be good or bad in terms of quality, but with modern production lines quality will be at least consistent.

Inseparability. A third difference between services and goods, and related to problems of consistency, is inseparability. In most cases, the consumer cannot (and does not) separate the delivery of the service from the service itself. For example, to receive an education, a person may attend a university. The quality of the education may be high, but if the student has difficulty in interacting with instructors, he or she would find counseling services poor, or does not receive adequate library or computer assistance and he or she may not be satisfied with educational experience. Students' evaluations of their education will be influenced primarily by their perceptions of instructors, counselors, librarians, and other people at the university. Allstate's reminder that "You're in good hands" emphasizes the importance of its agents.

The amount of interaction between the consumer and the service provider depends on the extent to which the consumers must be physically present to receive the service. Some services such as haircuts, golf lessons, medical diagnoses, and food service require the customer to participate in the delivery of the services. Other services such as car repair, dry cleaning, and waste disposal process tangible objects with less involvement from the customer. Finally, services such as banking, consulting, and insurance can now be delivered electronically, often requiring no face-to-face customer interaction. While this approach can create value for consumers, a disadvantage of some self-service technologies such as ATMs, grocery store scanning stations and self-service gas station pumps is that they are perceived as being less personal.

Inventory. Inventory of services is different from that of goods. Inventory problems exist with goods because many items are perishable and because there are costs associated with handling inventory. With services, inventory carrying costs are more subjective and are related to **idle production capacity**, which is when the service provider is available but there is no demand. The inventory cost of a service is the cost of paying the person used to provide the service along with any needed equipment. If a physician is paid to see patients but no one schedules an appointment, the fixed cost of the idle physician's salary is a high inventory carrying cost. In some service businesses, however, the provider of the service is on commission (a Merrill Lynch stockbroker) or is a part-time employee (a clerk at Macy's). In these businesses, inventory carrying costs can be significantly lower or nonexistent because the idle production capacity can be cut back by reducing hours or having no salary to pay because of the commission compensation system. Figure 9.2 shows a scale of inventory carrying costs represented on the low end by real estate agencies and hair salons and on the high end by airlines and hospitals. The inventory carrying costs of airlines is high because of high-salaried pilots and very expensive equipment. In contrast, real estate agencies and hair salons have employees who work on commission and need little expensive equipment to conduct business. One reason that service providers must maintain production capacity is because of the importance of time to today's customers.

Figure 9.2   Inventory Carrying Costs of Services Depend on the Cost of Employees and Equipment

9.2   The Service Difference and Classification

9.2.1   The Service Continuum

The four I's differentiate services from goods in most cases, but many companies are not clearly service-based or good-based organizations. Is Hewlett-Packard a computer company or a service business? Although Hewlett-Packard manufactures computers, printers and other goods, many of the company's employees work in its services division providing systems integration, networking, consulting, education and product support. What companies bring to the market ranges from the tangible to the intangible or good-dominant to service-dominant offerings referred to as the **service continuum** (shown as Figure 9.3).

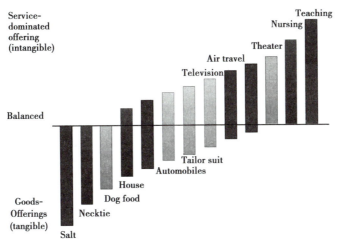

Figure 9.3   The Service Continuum Shows How Offerings Can Vary in Their Balance of Goods and Services

Teaching, nursing and the theater are intangible, service-dominant activities. Intangibility, inconsistency, inseparability and inventory are major concerns in their marketing. Salt, neckties, and dog food are tangible goods, and the problems represented by the four I's are not relevant in their marketing. However, some businesses are a mix of intangible service and tangible good factors. A clothing tailor provides a service but also a good, the finished suit. How pleasant, courteous and attentive the tailor is to the customer is an important component of the service and how well the clothes fit is an important part of the product. As shown in Figure 9-3, a fast-food restaurant is about half tangible goods (the food) and half intangible services (courtesy, cleanliness, speed and convenience).

For many businesses today it is useful to distinguish between their core product-either a good or a service—and supplementary services. A core service offering such as a bank account, also has supplementary services such as deposit assistance, parking or driven-through availability, ATMs and monthly statements. Supplementary services often allow service providers to differentiate their offerings from competitors, and they may add value for consumers. While there are many potential supplementary services, key categories of supplementary services include consultation, finance, order taking, billing and upgrade.

9.2.2 Classifying Services

Through this chapter, marketing organizations, techniques and concepts are classified to show the differences and similarities in an organized framework. Services can also be classified in several ways.

1. Delivery by People or Equipment

As seen in Figure 9.4, many companies offer services. Professional services include management consulting firms such as Booz, Allen & Hamilton or Accenture. Skilled labor is required to offer services such as Sears appliance repair of Sheraton catering service. Unskilled labor such as that used by Brinks store-security forces is also a service provided by people.

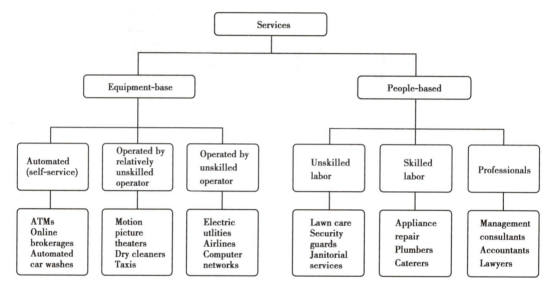

Figure 9.4   Services Can Be Classified As Equipment-based or People-based

Equipment-based services do not have the marketing concerns of inconsistency because people are removed from the provision of the service. Electric utilities, for instance, can provide service without frequent personal contact with customers. Motion picture theaters have projector operators that consumers never see. A growing number of customers use self-service technologies such as Home Depot's self checkout, Southwest Airlines' self check-in and Schwab's online stock trading without interacting with any service employees.

2. Profit or Nonprofit Organizations

Many Organizations involved in services also distinguish themselves by their tax status as profit or nonprofit organizations. In contrast to profit organizations, nonprofit organizations' excesses in revenue exists, money goes back into the organization's treasury to allow continuation of the service. Based on the corporate structure of the nonprofit organization, it may pay tax on revenue-generating holdings not directly related to its core mission. Nonprofit organizations in the United States now have expenditures of \$1.9 trillion and employ 10% of the work force.

Historically, misconceptions have limited the use of marketing practices by such organizations. In recent years, however, nonprofit organizations have turned to marketing to help achieve their goals. The American Red Cross is a good example. To increase the organization's blood donor base, it recently hired an advertising agency to develop a campaign that includes advertising, direct marketing, PR and customer relationship management.

3. Government Sponsored

A third way to classify services is based on whether they are government sponsored. Although there is no direct ownership and they are nonprofit organizations, governments at the federal, state, and local levels provide a broad range of services. The United States Postal Service, for example, has adopted many marketing activities. First-class postage revenue has declined as postal service customers have increased their use of the Internet to send e-mail, pay bills, and file taxes. Instead of fighting the trend, however, the Postal Service is embracing the Internet. Its website, allows consumers to buy stamps, arrange deliveries and manage mailing lists online. In addition, new post office boxes are designed in a shoebox size to better meet the needs of consumers who shop for clothing and shoes online. Businesses can even buy stamps with their company brand and logo on them.

9.3   How Consumers Purchase Services

9.3.1   The Purchase Process

Many aspects of services affect the consumer's evaluation of the purchase. Because services cannot be displayed, demonstrated, or illustrated, consumers cannot make a pre-purchase evaluation of all the characteristics of services. Similarly, because service providers may vary in their delivery of a service, an evaluation of a service may change with each purchase. Tangible goods such as clothing, jewelry and furniture have *search properties* , such as color, size and style, which can be determined before purchase. Services such as restaurants and child care have *experience properties* , which can be discerned only after purchases or during consumption. Finally, services provided by specialized professionals such as medical diagnoses and legal services have *credence properties* , or characteristics that the consumer may find impossible to evaluate even after purchase and consumption. To reduce the uncertainty created by these properties, service consumers turn to personal sources of information such as early adopters, opinion leaders and reference group members during the purchase decision process. The Mayo Clinic uses an organized, explicit approach called "evidence management" to present customers with concrete and convincing evidence of its strengths.

9.3.2 Assessing Service Quality

Once a consumer tries a service. How is it evaluated? Primarily by comparing expectations about a service offering to the actual experience a consumer has with the service. Differences between the consumer's expectations and experience are identified through **gap analysis**. This type of analysis asks consumers to assess their expectations and experiences on dimensions of service quality such as those described in Figure 9.5. Expectations are influenced by word-of-mouth communications, personal needs, past experiences and promotional activities, while actual experiences are determined by the way an organization delivers its service. The relative importance of the various dimensions of service quality varies by the type of service. What if someone is dissatisfied and complains? Recent studies suggest that customers who experience a "service failure" will increase their satisfaction if the service makes a satisfactory service recovery effort, although they may not increase their intent to repurchase.

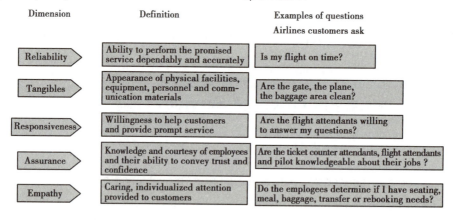

Figure 9.5   Five Dimensions of Service Quality

9.3.3 Customer Contact and Relationship Marketing

Consumers judge services on the entire sequence of steps that make up the service process. To focus on these steps, or "service encounters", a firm can develop a **customer contact audit**—a flowchart of the points of interaction between consumer and service provider. This is particularly important in high-contact services such as hotels, educational institutions and automobile rental agencies. Figure 9.6 is a consumer contact audit for renting a car from Hertz. The interactions identified in a customer contact audit often serve as the basis for developing relationships with customers. Recent research suggests that authenticity and sincerity of the interactions affect the success of the relationships.

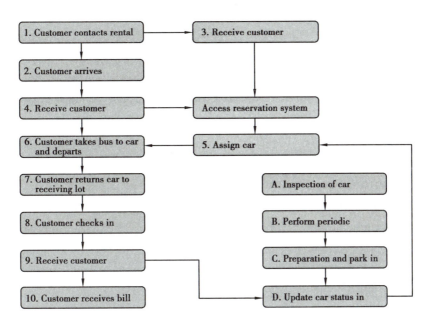

Figure 9.6   Customer Contact Audit for a Car Rental

9.3.4   Relationship Marketing

The contact between a service provider and a customer represents a service encounter that is likely to influence the customer's assessment of the purchase. The number of encounters in a service experience may vary. A travelling agency, for instance, estimates that a park visitor will have 74 encounters with its employees in a single visit. These encounters represent opportunities to develop social bonds, or relationships, with customers. The relationship may also be developed through loyalty incentives such as airline frequent flyer programs. Relationship marketing provides several benefits for service customers including the continuity of a single provider, customized service delivery, reduced stress due to a repetitive purchase process, and an absence of switching costs. Recent surveys of consumers have indicated that while customers of many services are interested in being "relationship customers," they require that there is a higher expectation of future use of the service. Understanding the service characteristics that lead to repeat purchases can help services managers allocate their resources to appropriate relationship marketing activities.

9.4   Managing the Marketing of Services

The concept of an expanded marketing mix for services has been adopted by many servicE-marketing organizations. In addition to the four 4Ps, the service marketing mix includes people, physical environment, process and productivity, or the **8Ps of service marketing.**

9.4.1 Product（Service）

Managers of goods and services must design the product concept with the features and benefits desired by customers. An important aspect of the product concept is branding. Because services are intangible, and more difficult to describe, the brand name or identifying logo of the service organization is particularly important when a consumer makes a purchase decision. Therefore, service organizations, such as banks, hotels, rental car companies and restaurants, rely on branding strategies to distinguish themselves in the minds of the consumers. Strong brand names and symbols are important for service marketers, not only as a means of differentiation, but also to convey an image of quality. A service firm with a well-established brand reputation will also find it easier to introduce new services than firms without a brand reputation.

Many services have undertaken creative branding activities. Hotels, for example, have begun to extend their branding efforts to consumers' homes through services such as Hotels at Home, which offers Westin's "Heavenly Bed", Hilton's bathrobes, and even artwork from Sheraton hotel rooms for consumers to buy and use at home. Look at the logos below to determine how successful some companies have been in branding their service with a name and symbol.

9.4.2 Price

Price reflects the value of unit good or service, and the level of which is determined by the supply and demand in market. In service businesses, price is referred to in many ways in various fields. Hospitals refer to charges; consultants, lawyers, physicians and accountants to fees; airlines to fares; hotels to rates; colleges and universities to tuition. Because of the intangible nature of services, price is often perceived by consumers as a possible indicator of the quality of the service. Do you expect higher quality from an expensive restaurant? Would you wonder about the quality of a $100 surgery? In many cases there may be few other available cues for the customer to judge, so price becomes very important as a quality indicator.

Pricing of services also goes beyond the traditional tasks of setting the selling price. When customers buy a service, they also consider non-monetary costs, such as the mental and physical efforts required to consume the service. Service marketers must also try to minimize the effort required to purchase and use the service. Pricing also plays a role in balancing consumer demand for service. Many service businesses use **off-peak pricing**, which consists of charging different prices during different times of the day or during different days of the week to reflect variations in demand for the service. Airlines, for example, offer discounts for weekend travel while movie theaters offer matinee prices.

9.4.3 Place

Place or distribution is a major factor in developing a service marketing strategy because of the inseparability of services from the producer. Rarely are intermediaries involved in the distribution of a service; the distribution site and the service deliverer are the tangible components of the service. Until recently customers generally had to go to the service provider's physical location to purchase the service. Increased competition, however, has forced many service firms to consider the value of convenient distribution and to find new ways of distributing services to customers. Technology is also being used to deliver services beyond the provider's physical locations. In banking industry, for example, customers of participating banks using the Cirrus system can access any one of thousands of ATMs throughout the United States. The availability of electronic distribution through the Internet also allows for global reach and coverage for a variety of services, including travel, education, entertainment and insurance.

9.4.4 Promotion

The value of promotion, especially advertising, for many services is to show consumers the benefits of purchasing the service. It is valuable to stress availability, location, consistent quality and efficient, courteous service and to provide a physical representation of the service or a service encounter.

Another form of promotion, *publicity*, has played a major role in the promotional strategy of many service organizations. Nonprofit organizations such as public schools religious organizations and hospitals, often use publicity to disseminate their messages. For many of these organizations, the most common form of publicity is the public service announcement (PSA) because it is free. Using PSAs as the foundation of a promotion program is unlikely to be effective because the timing and location of the PSA are under the control of the media, not the organization.

Personal selling, sales promotion and direct marketing can also play an important role in services marketing. Service firm representatives, such as hotel employees handling check-in or wait-staff in restaurants, are often responsible for selling their services. Similarly, sales promotions such as coupons, free trials and contests are often effective tools for service firms. Finally, direct marketing activities are often used to reach specific audiences with interest in specific types of services. Increasingly, service firms are adopting an integrated marketing communications approach, similar to the approach used by many consumer packaged goods firms, to ensure that the many forms of promotion are providing a consistent message and contributing to a common objective.

9.4.5　People

Many services depend on people for the creation and delivery of customer service experience. The nature of the interaction between employees and customers strongly influences the customer's perceptions of service experience. Customers will often judge the quality of the service experience based on the performance of the people providing the service. This aspect of services marketing has led to a concept called internal marketing.

Internal marketing is based on the notion that a service organization must focus on its employees or internal market, before successful programs can be directed at customers. Service firms need to ensure that employees have the attitude, skills and commitment needed to meet customer expectations and to sustain customer loyalty. This idea suggests that employee development through recruitment, training, communication, coaching, management and leadership are critical to the success of service organizations. Finally, many service organizations, such as educational institutions and athletic teams, must recognize that individual customer behavior may also influence the service outcome for other customers. These interactions suggest that the people elements in services include employees and all customers.

Once internal marketing programs have prepared employees for their interactions with customers, organizations can better manage the services they provide. **Customer experience management (CEM)** is the process of managing the entire customer experience with the company. CEM experts suggest that the process should be intentional, planned and consistent so that every experience is similar, differentiated from other service offerings, and relevant and valuable to the target market. Companies such as Disney, Southwest Airlines, the Ritz-Carlton and Starbucks all manage the experience they offer customers. They integrate their activities to connect with customers at each contact point to move beyond customer relationships to customer loyalty.

9.4.6　Physical Environment

The appearance of the environment in which the service is delivered and where the firm and customer interact can influence the customer's perception of the service. The physical evidence of the service includes all the tangibles surrounding the service: the building, landscaping, vehicles, furnishings, signage, brochures and equipment. Service firms need to manage physical evidence carefully and systematically to convey the proper impression of the service to the customer. This is sometimes referred to as impression management, or evidence management. For many services, the physical environment provides an opportunity for the firm to send consistent and strong messages about the nature of the service to be delivered.

9.4.7　Process

Process refers to the actual procedures, mechanisms and flow of activities by which the service is created and delivered. The actual creation and delivery steps that the customer experiences provide customers with evidence on which to judge the service. These steps involve not only "what" gets created but also "how" it is created. The customer contact audit is relevant to understanding the service process discussed here. The customer contact audit can serve as a basis for ensuring better service creation and delivery processes.

9.4.8　Productivity

Most services have a limited capacity due to the inseparability of the service from the service provider and the perishable nature of the service. For example, to "buy" an appendectomy, a patient must be in the hospital at the same time as the surgeon and only one patient can be helped at that time. Similarly, no additional surgery can be conducted tomorrow because of an unused operating room or an available surgeon today-the service capacity is lost if it is not used. So the service components of the marketing mix must be integrated with efforts to influence consumer demand. This is referred to as **capacity management**.

Service organizations must manage the availability of the offering so that (1) demand matches capacity over the duration of the demand cycle (for example, one day, week, month or year), and (2) the organization's assets are used in ways that will maximize the return on investment(ROI). Figure 9.7 shows how a hotel tries to manage its capacity during the high and low seasons. Differing price structures are assigned to each segment of consumers to help moderate or adjust demand for the service. Airline contracts fill a fixed number of rooms throughout the year. In the low season, when more rooms are available, tour packages at appealing prices are used to attract groups or conventions, such as an offer for seven nights in Orlando at a reduced price. Weekend packages are also offered to vacationers. In the high-demand season, groups are less desirable because guests who will pay high prices travel to Florida on their own.

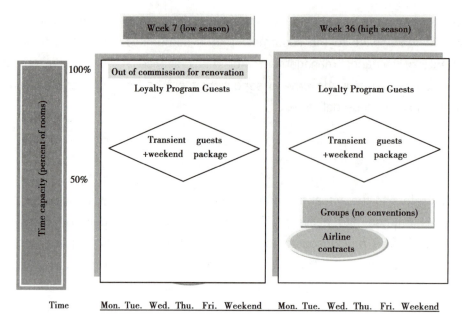

Figure 9.7   Different Prices and Packages Help Match Hotel Demand to Capacity

---

9.5   Services in the Future

What can we expect from the services industry in the future? New and better services, of course, and an unprecedented variety of choices. Many of the changes will be the result of two factors: technological development and an expanding scope in the global economy.

Technological advances are rapidly changing the service industry. In fact, many of the likely changes in the United States have already been occurring in Europe and Asia where new generations of technology have leapfrogged North America. The key elements of future services include mobility, convergence, personalization and collaboration. Mobility will be provided by new generations of networks that will allow TV, GPS, high-speed data transfer and audio programming on portable digital devices. Many high-end electric products are indications of the coming convergence of voice, video and data in a single product. Personalization can also take other forms, such as analyzing past transaction data to let customers know about customized services. Technology-mediated personalization can increase the customers' perceptions of value; however, excessive attempts at personalization can also trigger privacy concerns. Finally, collaboration services that allow Web-conferencing, dating and matchmaking, and even remote involvement of friends when someone is shopping are coming.

An expanding scope of influence in the global economy is also changing service industry. While the past decade has seen services grow to become the dominant part of the economy in the United States, the future is likely to see more emphasis on the global marketing of services and increasing attention to cross-cultural implications for services. Recent studies indicate that consumers in different countries place varying emphasis on service quality and underscore the need to "think global and act local." Finally, some experts predict that the dominant view of economic exchange will shift from its current focus on goods and tangible resources to services and intangible attributes. Countries that expect to complete globally will need to invest in service industry growth and service innovation. In fact, recent research suggests that services marketing strategies create a competitive advantage and are very profitable.

Key Terms

services 服务	Intangible activities or benefits (such as airline trips, financial advice, or automobile repair) that an organization provides to satisfy consumers' needs in exchange for money or something else of value. 某一机构提供的无形活动或好处,比如航空旅行、金融咨询、汽车修理等,能够满足消费者的需求已换取一定的有价值的东西。
four I's of services 服务的 4I 要素	Referring to four unique elements to services: intangibility, inconsistency, inseparability and inventory. 指的是服务的四个独特要素:无形性、差异性、不可分离性和存贮性。
service continuum 服务连续体	Referring to the offerings brought by companies to the market ranging from the tangible to the intangible or goods-dominant to service-dominant. 指企业向市场提供的各种从有形的商品到无形的服务不同产品类别。
customer contact audit 客户触点审查	Research made by the marketers by various means in order to keep relations with customers. 指的是营销人员,为了保持与客户的关系,通过各种方法对客户信息和客户满意度等的调查。
relationship marketing 关系营销	Establish, maintain and stabilize a long-term relationship between the enterprise and its customers and other stakeholders so as to realize the exchange of information and other values, finally win customers' preference and loyalty by satisfying their ideas and needs. 在企业与客户和其他利益相关者之间建立、保持并稳固一种长远的关系,进而实现信息及其他价值的相互交换,最终通过满足客户的想法和需求进而赢得客户的偏爱和忠诚。

Continued

eight Ps of services marketing 服务营销的8Ps	It is the marketing mix of service marketing, including price, product (service), place, promotion, people, process, physical environment and productivity. 它是服务营销的营销组合，包括价格、产品(服务)、地点、促销、人员、过程、实物环境和生产力。
off-peak pricing 非高峰定价	It is a kind of differential pricing method, referring to different ticket prices for different periods of time. 针对不同的时段制定不同的票价，属于差别定价法。
internal marketing 内部营销	All about the relationship an employer forms with its employees. It is said that staff should be seen as internal customers and their needs should be met. 指的是雇主与雇员之间的关系。员工应该被视为内部客户，他们的需求应该被满足。
customer experience management (CEM) 客户体验管理	A new customer management method and technology emerged recently, that is to strategically manage the customer's overall experience of the product or company. 战略性地管理客户对产品或公司全面体验的过程，是近年兴起的一种崭新客户管理方法和技术。
capacity management 产能管理	The action of ensuring a business maximizes its potential activities and production output—at all times, under all conditions. The capacity of a business measures how much companies can achieve, produce, or sell within a given time period. 确保企业在任何情况下潜在活动和产能最大化的行为。企业产能是衡量企业在给定时间内的所获、所产或者所售多少的标准。

Review & Critical Thinking Questions

1. What are the four I's of services?

2. How are services classified?

3. In order to eliminate service inconsistencies, what do companies rely on?

4. Would inventory carrying costs for an accounting firm with certified public accountants be (a) high, (b) low, or (c) nonexistent?

5. How did Hertz create its differential advantages?

6. How does a movie theater use off-peak pricing?

7. Why does service marketing mix different from common marketing mix?

8. How would you understand "productivity" in the service marketing mix?

9. What factors will influence future changes in services?

10. What is the focus of service management?

Discussion Questions

1. Have you recently heard someone use *fake*, *phony*, even *counterfeit* words? It's a common concern of many consumers today and part of a growing tendency that will change most services. In your opinion, how does *fake* or *counterfeit* affect consumers' buying experience?

2. How would you understand the 4 I's of services? Please illustrate their implied relations with an actual kind of service.

3. Suppose a customer would like to buy a smart phone, please describe the purchase process using relative knowledge in this chapter.

4. Snow beer will set up an outlet in your community. If you were the supervisor of this program, how would you launch the marketing with the 8Ps theory?

5. Since the beginning of 2020, there has been a global pandemic which substantially influenced our lives and the product-service providing. In your opinion, how could a drugstore make innovation in the future service offering and management? Please explain why you say so.

Case Study

Management Comes to Dentistry

"I just hope the quality differences are visible to our patients," mused Dr. Barbro Beckett as she surveyed the office that housed her well-established dental practice. She had recently moved to her current location from an office she felt was too cramped to allow her staff to work efficiently—a factor that was becoming increasingly important as the costs of providing dental care continued to rise. While Dr. Beckett realized that productivity gains were necessary, she did not want to compromise the quality of service her patients received.

The classes Dr. Beckett took in dental school taught her a lot about the technical side of dentistry but nothing about the business side. She received no formal training in the mechanics of running a business or understanding customer needs. In fact, professional guidelines discouraged marketing or advertising of any kind. That had not been a major problem 22 years earlier, when Dr. Beckett started her practice, since profit margins had been good then. But the dental care industry had changed dramatically. Costs rose as a result of labor laws, malpractice insurance, and the constant need to invest in updating equipment and staff training as new technologies were introduced. Dr. Beckett's overhead was now between 70 and 80 percent of revenues before accounting for her wages or office rental costs.

At the same time, provider overhead was rising, there was a movement in the United States to reduce health care costs to insurance companies, employers, and patients by offering "managed health care" through large health maintenance organizations (HMOS). The HMOS set the prices for various services by putting an upper limit on the amount that their doctors and dentists could charge for various procedures. The advantage to patients was that their health insurance covered virtually all costs. But the price limitations meant that HMO doctors and dentists would not be able to offer certain services that might provide better quality care but were too expensive. Dr. Beckett had decided not to become an HMO provider because the reimbursement rates were only 80-85 percent of what she normally charged for treatment. She felt that she could not provide high-quality care to patients at these rates.

These changes presented some significant challenges to Dr. Beckett, who wanted to offer the highest level of dental care rather than being a low-cost provider. With the help of a consultant, she decided her top priority was differentiating practice on the basis of quality. She and her staff developed an internal mission statement that reflected this goal.

The mission statement (prominently displayed in the back office) read, in part: *It is our goal to provide superior dentistry in an efficient, profitable manner within the confines of a caring, quality environment.*

Since higher quality care was more costly, Dr. Beckett's patients often had to pay fees for costs not covered by their insurance policies. If the quality differences weren't substantial, these patients might decide to switch to an HMO dentist or another lower-cost provider.

Redesigning the Service Delivery System

The move to a new office gave Dr. Beckett a unique opportunity to rethink almost every aspect of her service. She wanted the work environment to reflect her own personality and values as well as provide a pleasant place for her staff to work.

Facilities and Equipment

Dr. Beckett first looked into the office spaces available in the Northern California town where she practiced. She didn't find anything she liked, so she hired an architect from San Francisco to design a contemporary office building with lots of light and space. This increased the building costs by $100,000, but Dr. Beckett felt it would be a critical factor in differentiating her service.

Dr. Beckett's new office was Scandinavian in design (reflecting her Swedish heritage and attention to detail). The waiting room and reception area were filled with modern furniture in muted shades of brown, gray, green, and purple. Live plants and flowers were abundant, and the walls were covered with art. Classical music played softly in the background. Patients could enjoy a cup of coffee or tea and browse through the large selection of current magazines and newspapers while they waited for their appointments.

The treatment areas were both functional and appealing. There was a small conference room with toys for children and a DVD player that was used to show patients educational films about different dental procedures. Literature was available to explain what patients needed to do to maximize the benefits of their treatment outcomes.

The chairs in the examining rooms were covered in leather and were very comfortable. Each room had a large window that allowed patients to watch birds eating at the feeders that were filled each day. There were also attractive mobiles hanging from the ceiling to distract patients from the unfamiliar sounds and sensations they might be experiencing. Headphones were available with a wide selection of music.

The entire "back office" staff (including Dr. Beckett) wore uniforms in cheerful shades of pink, purple, and blue that matched the office color. All the technical equipment looked very modern and was spotlessly clean. State-of-the-art computerized machinery was used for some procedures. Dr. Beckett's dental degrees were prominently displayed in her office, along with certificates from various programs that she and her staff had attended to update their technical skills.

Service Personnel

There were eight employees in dental practice, including Dr. Beckett (who was the only dentist). The seven staff members were separated by job functions into "front office" and "back office" workers. Front office duties (covered by two employees) included receptionist and secretarial tasks and financial / budgeting work. The back office was divided into hygienists and chairside assistants.

The three chairside assistants helped the hygienists and Dr. Beckett with treatment procedures. They had specialized training for their jobs but did not need a college degree. The two hygienists handled routine exams and teeth cleaning plus some treatment procedures. In many dental offices, hygienists had a tendency to act like "Prim Donna" because of their education (a bachelor's degree plus specialized training) and experience. According to Dr. Beckett, such an attitude could destroy any possibility of teamwork among office staff. She felt very fortunate that her hygienists viewed themselves as part of a larger team that worked together to provide quality care to patients.

Dr. Beckett valued her friendships with staff members and understood that they were a vital part of the service delivery. "90 percent of patients' perceptions of quality come from their interactions with the front desk and the other employees—not from staff's technical skills," she stated. When Dr. Beckett began to redesign her practice, she discussed her goals with the staff and involved them in the decision-making process. The changes meant new expectations and routines for most employees, and some were not willing to adapt. There was some staff turnover (mostly voluntary) as the new office procedures were implemented. The current group worked very well as a team.

Dr. Beckett and her staff met briefly each morning to discuss the day's schedule and patients. They also had longer meetings every other week to discuss more strategic issues and resolve any problems that might have developed. During these meetings, employees made suggestions about how to improve patient care. Some of the most successful staff suggestions include: "thank you" cards to patients who referred other patients; follow-up calls to patients after major procedures; a "gift" bag to patients after they've had their teeth cleaned that contains a toothbrush, toothpaste, mouthwash and floss; buckwheat pillows and blankets for patient comfort during long procedures; coffee and tea in the waiting area; and a photo album in the waiting area with pictures of staff and their families.

The expectations for staff performance (in terms of both technical competence and patient interactions) were very high. But Dr. Beckett provided her employees with many opportunities to update their skills by attending classes and workshops. She also rewarded their hard work by giving them monthly bonuses if business had been good. Since she shared financial data with her staff, they could see the difference in revenues if the schedule was slow or patients were dissatisfied. This provided an extra incentive to improve service delivery. The entire office also went on trips together once a year (paid for by Dr. Beckett); spouses were welcome to participate but had to cover their own trip expenses. Past destinations for these excursions included Hawaii and Washington, D.C.

Procedures and Patients

With the help of a consultant, all the office systems (including billing, ordering, lab work, and patient treatment) were redesigned. One of the main goals was to standardize some of the routine procedures so that errors were reduced and all patients would receive the same level of care. Specific times were allotted for each procedure and the staff worked very hard to see that these times were met. Office policy specified that patients should be kept waiting no longer than 20 minutes without being given the option to reschedule, and employees often called patients in advance if they knew there would be a delay. They also attempted to fill in cancellation to make sure office capacity was maximized. Staff members substituted for each other when necessary or helped with tasks not specifically in their job descriptions, in order to make things run more smoothly.

Dr. Beckett's practice included about 2,000 "active" patients (and many more who came infrequently). They were mostly white-collar workers with professional jobs (university employees, health care workers, and managers and owners of local establishments). She did no advertising; all of her new business came from positive word of mouth by current patients. Dr. Beckett's practice was so busy that patients often had to wait 3-4 months for a routine cleaning and exam (if they didn't have their appointments automatically scheduled every 6 months), but they didn't seem to mind the delay.

The dentist believed that referral was a real advantage because new patients didn't come in "cold." She did not have to sell herself because they had already been told about her service by friends or family. All new patients were required to have an initial exam so that Dr. Beckett could do a needs assessment and educate them about her service. She believed this was the first indication to patients that her practice was different from others they had experienced.

The Biggest Challenge

"Redesigning business was the easy part," Dr. Beckett sighed. "Demonstrating the high level of quality to patients is a hard job." She said this task was especially difficult since most people disliked going to the dentist or felt that it was an inconvenience and came in with a negative attitude. Dr. Beckett tried to reinforce the idea that quality dental care depended on a positive long-term relationship between patients and the dental team. This philosophy was reflected in a section of the patient mission statement hanging in the waiting area: *We are a caring, professional dental team serving motivated, quality-oriented patients interested in keeping healthy smiles for a lifetime. Our goal is to offer a progressive and educational environment. Your concerns are our focus.*

Although Dr. Beckett enjoyed her work, she admitted it could be difficult to maintain a positive attitude. The job required precision and attention to detail, and the procedures were often painful for patients. She often felt as though she were "walking on eggshells" because she knew patients were anxious and uncomfortable, which made them more critical of her service delivery. It was not uncommon for patients to say negative things to Dr. Beckett even before treatment began (such as, "I really hate going to the dentist—it's not you, but I just don't want to be here!"). When this happened, she reminded herself that she was providing quality service whether patients appreciated it or not. "The person will usually have to have dental work done anyway," she remarked, "so I just do the best job I can and make them as comfortable as possible". Even though patients seldom expressed appreciation for her services, she hoped that she made a positive difference in their health or appearance that would benefit them in the long run.

Questions

1. Which of the seven elements of the Service Marketing Mix are addressed in this case?

Give examples of each "P" you identify.

2. Why do people dislike going to the dentist? Do you feel Dr. Beckett has addrssed this problem effectively?

3. Contrast your own dental care experiences with those offered by Dr. Beckett's practice. What differences do you see? Based on your review of this case, what advice would you give (a) to your current or former dentist, and (b) to Dr. Beckett?

中文概述

服务在市场营销中起着关键作用。随着电子媒体和通信服务的出现,国际服务营销发生了巨大的变化,营销人员在提供服务时必须关注文化差异和地区差异。

国际服务营销重要的原因主要有以下四点:受众对象国际化、网络国际化、文化差异化和促销手段差异化。

服务是一种组织向客户提供的满足某种需求的一种无形的活动或者好处,以换取金钱或其他有价值的东西。服务业已经成为全球各国经济的重要组成部分。

服务有四个独特的要素:无形性、差异性、一致性和库存性。**无形性**是相对于有形的商品而言的;**差异性**说明服务质量的好坏取决于提供服务的人,随着每个人的能力和工作表现而变化;**一致性**,也叫不可分离性。在大多数情况下,消费者不能(也不会)把服务的交付者和服务本身分开。**库存性**说明服务的存货不同于商品的存货。服务的库存成本是支付给提供服务的人员以及所需设备的成本。如果病人拿着钱去看医生,但是没有人安排预约,那么空闲医生的工资的固定成本就是一个很高的库存持有成本。

在大多数情况下,四个I可以把服务区分于商品,但是许多公司或者组织并没有明确地区分自身到底是以服务为主导还是以商品供应为主导,许多公司向市场提供的产品范围从有形到无形,从商品到服务,一应俱全,这种情况被称为**服务连续性**。

服务可以通过以下几种方式进行分类:(1)服务是由人提供还是由设备提供,(2)服务是盈利的还是非盈利的,(3)是否由政府赞助的服务。

由于服务无法显示、演示或说明,消费者无法对服务的所有特征进行购买前评估。同样的,服务提供者在交付服务时可能会有所不同,对服务的评估可能会随着每次购买而改变。为了减少这些属性所带来的不确定性,服务消费者在购买决策过程中会转向个人信息来源,如早期采用者的意见、具有代表性的观点或者参考群体成员的意见来做出服务购买的决策。这就是服务的**购买过程**。

一旦使用者尝试服务,会如何**评价服务质量**的呢?主要是通过差距分析,识别出消费者的期望和体验之间的差异。

消费者根据组成服务流程的整个步骤序列来判断服务。要专注于这些步骤,或"服务接触",公司可以开发一个**顾客接触审查**——消费者和服务提供者之间的交互点的流程图。

关系营销为服务客户提供了几个好处,包括单一供应商的连续性、定制化的服务交付、减少重复购买过程带来的压力以及减少转换成本。了解导致重复购买的服务特征可以帮助服务经理将他们的资源分配到适当的关系营销活动中。

扩展服务营销组合的概念已经被许多服务营销组织所采用。除了 4P 之外，服务营销组合还包括**人、实物环境、过程和生产力**，这就是**服务营销的 8P 组合**。

产品是一个广义的概念，是使用价值的载体，顾客通过使用产品而获得需求的满足，企业通过产品向固体提供使用价值。产品概念的一个重要方面是品牌。因为服务是无形的，而且更难以描述，所以当消费者做出购买决定时，服务组织的品牌名称或标志就显得尤为重要。

在服务业中，价格指单位货物或服务的价值，其水平由市场供需关系决定，不同的行业体现方式也略有不同。由于服务是无形的，价格常常被消费者视为服务质量的可能指标。

服务定价也超越了设定销售价格的传统任务。当顾客购买一项服务时，他们还会考虑非货币成本，例如消费该服务所需的脑力和体力劳动。价格在平衡消费者对服务的需求方面也发挥了作用。许多服务企业使用**非高峰价格**，即在一天的不同时段或一周的不同天数收取不同价格，以反映服务需求的变化。

地点或分销是制定服务营销策略的主要因素，因为服务与生产者是不可分离的。很少有中间商参与服务的分发；分发站点和服务交付者是服务的有形组成部分。日益激烈的竞争迫使许多服务公司考虑方便分销的价值，并寻找向客户分销服务的新方法。技术也被用于提供超出供应商物理位置的服务。

促销的价值，尤其是**广告**，对于许多服务来说，就是向消费者展示购买服务的好处。强调可用性、位置、一致的质量和高效、礼貌的服务，并提供服务或服务遭遇的实际表现是有价值的。另一种促销形式——**宣传**，在许多服务机构的促销策略中发挥了重要作用。非营利组织，如公立学校、宗教组织和医院，经常使用宣传来传播他们的信息。**个人销售、销售促进**和**直接营销**在服务营销中也可以发挥重要作用。服务公司的代表，如办理入住手续的酒店员工或餐厅的服务人员，通常负责销售他们的服务。同样的，对服务公司来说，优惠券、免费试用和竞赛等促销活动也是有效的手段。最后，直接营销活动通常用于接触对特定服务类型感兴趣的特定受众。服务公司越来越多地采用一种整合营销传播方法，类似于许多消费品包装公司使用的方法，以确保多种形式的促销提供一致的信息，并有助于实现共同的目标。

员工与顾客互动的性质强烈影响顾客对服务体验的认知。顾客通常会根据提供服务的人的表现来判断服务体验的质量。

内部营销基于这样一种理念，即服务机构必须把重点放在员工或内部市场上，然后才能将成功的项目导向顾客。服务公司需要确保员工拥有满足客户期望和维持客户忠诚度所需的态度、技能和承诺。最后，许多服务组织，必须认识到顾客的个人行为也可能影响对其他顾客的服务结果。这些交互表明服务中的人员元素包括员工和所有客户。一旦内部营销计划为员工与客户的互动做好了准备，组织就能更好地管理他们所提供的服务。客户体验管理（CEM）是全公司一起管理整个客户体验的过程。

提供**服务的环境**以及企业与顾客之间的互动会影响顾客对服务的感知。服务的实物证据包括服务周围的所有有形物品：建筑、景观、车辆、家具、标牌、宣传册和设备。服务公司需要仔细和系统地管理物品，以便向客户传达正确的服务印象。

（服务）流程是指创建和交付服务所依据的实际过程、机制和活动流。实际的创建和交付步骤，客户体验为客户提供了判断服务的证据。顾客接触审查可以作为一个基础，以确保更好的服务创建和交付过程。

　　由于服务与服务提供者的不可分离性以及服务的易逝性，大多数服务的能力有限。营销组合中的服务部分必须与影响消费者需求的努力相结合。这称为**容量管理**。服务组织必须管理产品的可用性，以便(1)在需求周期期间(例如，一天、一周、一个月或一年)需求匹配能力，以及(2)组织的资产以将投资回报(ROI)最大化的方式使用。

　　未来会有新的更好的服务，以及前所未有的各种选择。以下两个因素将带来许多变化：**技术发展**和**全球经济范围的扩大**。

UNIT 10 / Market Entry and Expansion

1. Understand the modes of market entry and expansion.
2. Learn the pros and cons of each market entry and expansion modes.
3. Understand the benefits of (foreign) market entry and expansion.
4. Understand the reasons why companies expand their business into international markets.
5. Identify some important strategies for companies to enter a new foreign market.
6. Understand the challenges of market entry and expansion.

10.1 The 5 Basic Modes of Market Entry and Expansion

Some of the modes of entry into international business you can opt for include direct export, licensing, international agents and distributors, joint ventures, strategic alliances, strategic acquisition, and foreign direct investment.

Each of these entry strategies for international markets are different in terms of the costs involved, level of risk, level of ease of execution, and the level of reward. These modes of entry into international business are shown below and the trade-offs in each of these entry strategies for international markets demonstrated at the same time.

What does each of these entail for an offline product as well as for an online product based company? While the crux remains the same for both types of businesses, how you carry out the strategy could have slight differences.

Let's understand in detail what each of these modes of entry entails.

1. Direct Exporting

Direct exporting involves you directly exporting your goods and products to another overseas market. For some businesses, it is the fastest mode of entry into international business.

Direct exporting, in this case, could also be understood as direct sales. This means you as a product owner in India go out, to say, Middle East with your own sales force to reach out to the customers.

In case you foresee a potential demand for your goods and products in an overseas market, you can opt to supply your goods to an importer instead of establishing your own retail presence in the overseas market.

Then you can market your brand and products directly or indirectly through your sales representatives or importing distributors.

And if you are in an online product based company, there is no importer in your value chain.

2. Licensing and Franchising

Companies which want to establish a retail presence in an overseas market with minimal risks, the licensing and franchising strategy allows another person or business to assume the risk on behalf of the company.

In licensing agreements and franchises, overseas-based businesses will pay you a royalty or commission to use your brand name, manufacturing process, products, trademarks and other intellectual properties.

The licensee or the franchisee assumes the risks and bears all losses, and shares a proportion of its revenues and profits with you.

3. Joint Ventures

A joint venture is one of the preferred modes of entry into international business for businesses who do not mind sharing their brand, knowledge, and expertise.

Companies wishing to expand into overseas markets can form joint ventures with local businesses in the overseas location, wherein both joint venture partners share the rewards and risks associated with the business.

Both business entities share the investment, costs, profits and losses at the predetermined proportion.

This mode of entry into international business is suitable in countries wherein the governments do not allow one hundred percent foreign ownership in certain industries.

For instance, foreign companies which cannot have a hundred percent stake in broadcast content services, print media, multi-brand retailing, insurance, and power exchange sectors are required to opt for a joint-venture route to enter the Indian market.

Here is the difference between a licensing/franchisee kind of a setup and a joint venture.

The subtle nuance was that a franchise setup would work well when you as a franchiser are a bigger brand in that particular product.

You could be big in your own country and not necessarily in the franchisee's country.

In case of a joint venture, both the brands have a similar level of brand strength for that particular product. And therefore, they wish to explore that product in that international market together.

4. Foreign Direct Investment

Foreign direct investment involves a company entering an overseas market by making a substantial investment in the country. Some of the modes of entry into international business use the foreign direct investment strategy including mergers and acquisitions, joint ventures and Greenfield investments.

This strategy is viable when the demand or the size of the market, or the growth potential of the market is substantially large to justify the investment.

Some of the reasons why companies opt for foreign direct investment strategy as a mode of entry into international business can include:

- Restrictions or import limits on certain goods and products.
- Manufacturing locally can avoid import duties.
- Companies can take advantage of low-cost labour, and cheaper material.

5. Strategic Acquisitions

Strategic acquisition implies that your company acquires a controlling interest in an existing company in the overseas market.

This acquired company can be directly or indirectly involved in offering similar products or services in the overseas market.

You can retain the existing management of the newly acquired company to benefit from their expertise, knowledge and experience while having your team members positioned in the board of the company as well.

10.2   Advantages and Disadvantages of Each Market Entry and Expansion Mode

▶ 10.2.1   Advantages and Disadvantages of Direct Exporting

Advantages:

1. You can select your foreign representatives in the overseas market.

2. You can utilize the direct exporting strategy to test your products in international markets before making a bigger investment in the overseas market.

3. This strategy helps you protect your patents, goodwill, trademarks and other intangible assets.

Disadvantages：

1. For offline products, this strategy will turn out to be cost heavy. Everything has to be setup by your company from scratch.

2. While for online products this is probably the fastest expansion strategy, in the case of offline products, there is a good amount of lead time that goes into market research, scoping and hiring of the representatives in that country.

10.2.2　Advantages and Disadvantages of Licensing and Franchising

Advantages：

1. Low cost of entry into an international market.

2. Licensing or franchising partner has knowledge about the local market.

3. It offers you a passive source of income.

4. It reduces political risk as in most cases, the licensing or franchising partner is a local business entity.

5. It allows expansion in multiple regions with minimal investment.

Disadvantages：

1. In some cases, you might not be able to exercise complete control on licensing and franchising partners in the overseas market.

2. Licensees and franchisees can leverage the acquired knowledge and pose as a future competitor for your business.

3. Your business risks tarnishing its brand image and reputation in the overseas and other markets due to the incompetence of their licensing and franchising partners.

10.2.3　Advantages and Disadvantages of Joint Venture

Advantages：

1. Both partners can leverage their respective expertise to grow and expand within a chosen market.

2. The political risks involved in a joint-venture is lower due to the presence of the local partner, having knowledge of the local market and its business environment.

3. It enables transfer of technology, intellectual properties and assets, knowledge of the overseas market etc. between the partnering firms.

Disadvantages：

1. Joint ventures can face the possibility of cultural clashes within the organization due

to the differences in organization culture in both partnering firms.

2. In the event of a dispute, dissolution of a joint venture is subject to lengthy and complicated legal process.

10.2.4   Advantages and Disadvantages of Strategic Acquisitions

Advantages:

1. Your business does not need to start from scratch as you can use the existing infrastructure, manufacturing facilities, distribution channels and an existing market share and a consumer base.

2. Your business can benefit from the expertise, knowledge and experience of the existing management and key personnel by retaining them.

3. It is one of the fastest modes of entry into international business on a large scale.

Disadvantages:

1. Just like joint ventures, in acquisitions as well, there is a possibility of cultural clashes within the organization due to the difference in the organization culture.

2. Apart from that, there mostly are problems with seamless integration of systems and process. Technological process difference is one of the most common issues in strategic acquisitions.

10.2.5   Advantages and Disadvantages of Foreign Direct Investment

Advantages:

1. You can retain control over the operations and other aspects of your business.

2. It leverages low-cost labour, cheaper materials etc. to reduce manufacturing cost toward obtaining a competitive advantage over competitors.

3. Many foreign companies can avail subsidies, tax breaks and other concessions from the local governments for making an investment in their country.

Disadvantages:

1. The business is exposed to high levels of political risk, especially in case the government decides to adopt protectionist policies to protect and support local business against foreign companies.

2. This strategy involves substantial investment to be made for entering an international market.

10.3 Top 5 Benefits of an International Expansion

Globalization is not simply a trend: it's now a necessity for companies to remain competitive in their space. For companies that want to pursue international expansion, there are many opportunities to take advantage of. These include gaining access to new markets, growing teams, and increasing revenue.

Companies of all sizes should be aware of the business benefits of globalization. And here are the top five reasons companies should be thinking about going global:

1. Establishing New Revenue Streams

According to a recent report, 45% of middle market companies make more than half of their revenue overseas. If your business is doing well domestically, you're already a step ahead to succeed globally. With a new customer base, you can identify and create unique opportunities in local markets for your business to fill in the gaps. Just be sure to consider the cultural factors before expanding into a new market.

2. Gaining a Competitive Advantage

Thinking globally is becoming less of an option and more of a requirement when it comes to outpacing the competition. In fact, 56% of middle market companies include international expansion into their growth strategies. Taking your business international presents growth opportunities by expanding options for talent, customers, and creating cost-savings for imports and manufacturing.

3. Accessing a Global Talent Pool

Whether you run a startup or a 50-year-old enterprise, finding skilled workers who can help drive your company is crucial. Expanding globally gives your company the opportunity to access high-quality talent from around the world. Hiring global employees can provide unique insights into local cultural norms. Additionally, many workers from emerging markets may be less expensive than workers from Western countries.

4. Finding New Global Customers

When you have been in a local market for a while, it can be tough to find new customers. They are used to your product and your competitors, and new sales can be a battle hard-fought.

An international expansion opens new doors and gives you access to a whole new set of customers who have never seen your product or service before. But sourcing global talent can be an overwhelming task, even for seasoned internal recruiters. A global talent acquisition partner can help alleviate some of these challenges.

5. Utilizing Government Incentives

Many countries around the world offer incentives for companies looking to expand their operations internationally, as it brings new business to their countries. One common incentive is lowered taxes after deductions. Because of this, many U.S. businesses take the opportunity to expand overseas in order to lower their overall income tax rates.

10.4　Why Companies Expand Into International Markets

1. Commercial Traction

The most common goal of companies going international is to acquire more customers, boost their sales, and increase their revenues.

By entering a new country, your company gets access to customers who were not on your radar yet. Therefore, you can increase your client base and reach revenues that you would not be able to reach, focusing on your market only.

It is also nice to keep in mind that increasing the number of potential customers is not the only interesting aspect for companies looking for commercial traction. Very often, businesses that sell internationally can charge higher prices for the same services in different countries. This way, you can increase your margins without making your customer support team go crazy.

2. Decreasing Operating Costs

It is also common to see companies going international with the goal of reducing their general costs. In the tech scene, this is very often related to finding cheaper talent and suppliers. In this way, companies can achieve more results while expending fewer resources.

The local tax system also plays an essential role in companies chasing this goal. Countries such as Ireland, the Netherlands and Panama attract a lot of companies by offering better conditions than other countries.

3. Boosting Competitiveness

Accessing new markets can provide much more than just "tangible" results such as more customers and cheaper suppliers. By accessing new markets, you will automatically have to face new competitors and adapt your proposition to different local needs. As a result, your company is forced to innovate and find new solutions to stand out in the market.

Being in a new country can also give you access to several great opportunities: new talents, R&D incentives, strategical partnerships, and many other benefits to increase your (national and global) competitiveness, just to name a few.

More than that: your authority grows exponentially when you start selling abroad. As a consequence, you can also get many more clients and/or charge higher prices in your own country.

4. Diversifying Risks

Last but not least, risk diversification is another essential reason why companies expand into international markets. Companies very often chase this goal when they are based in countries with high political and economic instability.

As there are a lot of uncertainties related to their market, it is safer to enter other countries and minimize the impact in case something goes wrong. This strategy allows companies to be more stable and therefore afford risks that were not possible before.

10.5　Strategies to Enter a New Foreign Market

Breaking into a foreign market—especially one with strict rules and regulations—can be a very daunting task. Often, business owners have the ambition to go international... they're just not quite sure where to start.

Here are the eight strategies that you can use to establish a foothold in a new country. Take a look at the list below and see which one is most suited to your business：

10.5.1　Franchising Your Brand

Understanding the processes behind franchising：

1. You create a successful brand (e.g. a restaurant).

2. You allow business owners to open their own branches of your restaurant, aka franchises.

3. The franchisees pay you a certain fee and sometimes a cut of the profits per year, then they keep the rest.

The advantage of franchising is that it's one of the easier ways to break into new markets. All you have to do is to take your existing, successful business model, find a franchisee in your target market, start the construction, and open your doors.

The disadvantage of franchising is that there is almost always a compromise.

You can scout locations as much as you like, but if you don't have firm brand recognition in the country you're trying to break into, you'll be just another business on the side of the street. That's not the end of the world-many individual businesses are still popular-but it's important to realize that franchising can only be used for certain businesses, and it has a sizeable amount of risk behind it as you're putting your brand in someone's hands.

10.5.2   Direct Exporting

Direct exporting is the most common of the eight strategies on this list. It's pretty simple-you sell directly to the market that you're trying to break into. For example, if you want to sell to Japan, you get your product into the appropriate Japanese stores and see how it does.

Your allies in direct exporting are your agents and distributors. These people are the branches between you and the stores. Trying to get a foothold with a major Japanese store as a foreigner is a difficult venture, but with a reliable agent/distributor (and translation services company) on your side, it can make the process a lot less painstaking. Most of the time, your agent/distributor usually have the contacts needed for you to succeed in a difficult market. Of course, you'll have to work out shipping logistics and everything else of that nature-but on the surface, direct exporting is very similar to selling products in your domestic market.

10.5.3   Partnering Up

Partnering is a relatively vague term—you can get a partner in a foreign country to simply help with marketing (and receive a cut of profits) or, you can get a partner in a foreign country who is just as invested in all facets of your business as you are.

Partnering has always been encouraged. Of course, you have to vet your potential partners thoroughly and make sure that you're doing business with someone who will actually help you—not hinder your progress. But if you can get a good partner, you'll be able to get a grip on your new market much more easily—they will have valuable knowledge about the market that you might not have.

In some areas of the world, a partnership is a borderline necessity. For example, in many Asian countries, you simply will not be able to break ground if you're a foreigner— you need a partner in each particular country to help you get by regulations and such.

10.5.4   Joint Venture

A JV (joint venture) is a partnership between two companies or people. They link up and become invested in some sort of business project—the investment is almost always an equal 50/50, and profits are split accordingly.

Usually, the two companies stay separate from each other, but work together on one particular venture to try and succeed.

❯ 10.5.5　Just Buying a Company

Buying a company in a foreign land is by far the easiest way to enter a new market.

1. You immediately claim market share.

2. You have an existing customer base and a brand image.

3. Even if the government has regulations on the industry for newcomers, you can bypass them with relative ease (and these rules and regulations will actually *help* you by keeping competition low).

4. Governments will still treat you as a local firm in most cases in regards to licensing and such.

Of course, there are downsides:

1. You're no longer one company, and your foreign operations in that particular market will be somewhat separate from the rest of your brand's image.

2. It's very expensive, especially if the business you want to buy is thriving.

3. Due diligence on a foreign company-especially one in a more obscure country-is much harder than on a domestic company.

❯ 10.5.6　Turnkey Solutions or Products

If your business is in construction or engineering, it's worth trying to find turnkey projects in foreign countries to bid on.

"Turnkey" is a pretty apt name—a "turnkey product" is where you build something from the ground up, and whoever you turn the product over to just has to "turn the key" before he or she is ready to go.

These are some of the best contracts to get because they almost always come from governments. On the flip side, everyone knows that these are some of the best contracts to get, and you'll often be competing with other foreign and domestic firms for the contract.

❯ 10.5.7　Piggyback

In order to piggyback, you need to already be selling products to other domestic companies.

If those domestic companies have international presences, all you have to do is to give them a ring and ask the following:

"Hi, can you take my products to your international agencies too?"

Of course, phrase it a bit better than that—but you get the point. You're jumping on the back of your existing business relationship and trying to make it into international markets that way.

10.5.8　Licensing

Licensing is somewhat similar to piggybacking, except that instead of talking to domestic firms and asking them to carry the product, you talk to foreign firms and ask them to temporarily *own* the product.

So, for example, if you have a great widget that you feel fits in perfectly with a company's inventory in your new market, all you'd have to do is to contact that company and ask.

We consider licensing to be one of the easiest ways to get started, but it's not necessarily an "easy process" overall. You first have to convince the firm that your product is right for them. Then, you need to convince them that it will sell. Then, you need to deal with governments and lawyers to iron out all of the legal aspects of the "sale" of the license.

You don't lose control of your product—it's not the same as selling the rights to your product. You're merely licensing the rights to your product to a foreign company for a limited amount of time.

10.6　What Every Small Business Needs to Know Before a Market Expansion

10.6.1　Expand Your Industry Vertically, or Introduce New Products

A market expansion can be a make-or-break moment for your small business. Once you've achieved consistent momentum with your current customers, there's a natural tendency to look at where else you can take your brand, and what products or services you might add to your offerings.

But expansions can fail without proper planning, so don't rush into this decision. The following steps will help you lay a strong foundation from which you can grow your business regionally, nationally and even globally.

10.6.2　Start with Feedback from Your Current Customers

Before you can take advantage of new markets—before you can identify opportunities in those markets—you need to understand your strengths. Your idea of why your company is succeeding might be different from your customers' perceptions, so find out why they keep coming back (or not). Obtaining their feedback may reveal strengths and potential product lines you hadn't considered, allowing you to refine and strengthen your expansion strategy.

One way to gain customer feedback is through short, direct surveys. Your instinct might be to incentivize participation through promotions, gift cards or money. But, Trevor Wolfe, founder and CEO of feedback management company BigTeam, recommended leveling with people instead.

"I think one of the mistakes is just to generically send a link and say, 'Hey, I'd like your feedback,'" Wolfe said. "But if they actually explain, 'Hey, I'm looking for my next phase of growth, I'm looking to expand, I'm looking into other territories to launch the business, I value your patronage and I'd really like your feedback'... if they explain the request for feedback is sincere and that they're going to actually use the feedback, that is often enough of an incentive."

You can also offer early access to new products as a thank-you for people's time. But the key is to treat your customers with respect and emphasize that element of the relationship, rather than making the survey request purely transactional.

▶ 10.6.3 Identify Your New Market

There are four different types of market expansion approaches from which you can choose, said Brian Cairns, CEO of ProStrategix Consulting:

1. Vertical markets, in which you're already established within an industry (for instance, selling paper supplies to schools puts you in an education vertical)

2. Geographic markets

3. New products and services

4. Adjacent markets, in which you can leverage your company's current capabilities into success in a new industry

"The first question you have to ask is, 'If I'm going to expand, what makes the most logical sense for me from a cost standpoint, and from a profit standpoint and a revenue standpoint, as well?'" Cairns said.

The expansion should build on what's already working in the business. Cairns gave the example of a restaurant owner looking to expand or open his or her next eatery. "For that restaurant, it's probably not going to be able to go from Italian to Chinese." The owner might have the business side down, but not the competencies to brand and produce Chinese food. Instead, the owner might look at the make-up of the current restaurant's loyal clientele, look for other geographic areas with similar demographics and establish a new business there.

10.6.4   Research the Legalities

Before you commit to an expansion, make sure you understand all of the legalities surrounding your industry and your tax obligations in the new market. To continue with the restaurant example, Cairns noted that a restauranteur looking to expand from New York to New Jersey would need to research the latter's licensing requirements and other laws surrounding food service. They may vary from those in New York, and non-compliance could cause the new business to shut down before it's gotten off the ground.

Regardless of industry or expansion type, you must also ensure that you're prepared to follow all labor and tax laws. Importantly, you want to understand the legal and tax landscape before the expansion, so you can hire the appropriate experts and consultants.

This is equally true with international expansion. You really need to be clear on the laws in the foreign country in which you plan to do business, including tax laws and regulations around trade and business relationships.

10.6.5   Prepare Your Finances

If you need to apply for a small business loan for the expansion, be thorough in preparing your presentation, especially if you're a young startup with limited financial history. Newer businesses must be able to show a strong business plan and make the case for why the expansion will be financially viable, said Allen Lin, a vice president and SBA loan officer at East West Bank.

There are several types of financing available for small businesses, including those for import and export strategies, such as letters of credit and short-term financing for the purchase of foreign goods. But lenders want to see that you understand your market and that there's a good chance you can fulfill the strategy you've outlined for them.

Say you want to sell your product in China. Ideally, you or your joint venture partner will also have a history of doing business in that market. According to Lin, banks look for an established relationship to protect their own investment, but to protect borrowers, as well:

"If the borrower doesn't have any previous experience or a relationship with the foreign buyer... they have high risk, because when they ship out the product, they don't know whether the foreign buyer will pay them or not, so they create a risk (for themselves) and the bank."

A long-standing relationship with buyers and a track record of doing business in the target market reassures the bank that you're likely to get paid and are therefore likely able to repay your loan.

▶ 10.6.6　Customize Your Marketing Content

To reach—and, more importantly, convert—clients and customers in new markets, you must speak to their particular circumstances. Content is a great way to do this. Fortunately, it's possible to leverage existing content into your target expansion areas.

If you've written, say, an e-book that's done well with current clients, build on that to create a version for your expansion market. Update the insights and include references based on the context of who the new customers are, taking into account regional trends and cultural preferences.

"You want to customize and tailor (your content) as much as feasibly possible," said Bryan Hanley, head of client strategy at Digital Mark 360, a digital marketing and business optimization firm. He offered the example of a moving company that wants to expand into neighboring states to grow its geographic footprint.

"The product is the same everywhere, right? However, each of those states probably has different nuances, different interstate transportation laws. Maybe one state has more apartment buildings, maybe one has more rural areas," Hanley said. "You want to customize it for each state because that's going to make the customer feel like you can handle what's going on."

The same mentality applies no matter what type of expansion you're initiating. You are pursuing new clients, and you need to gain their trust. Demonstrating that you understand where they're coming from and emphasizing their pain points is the key to achieving that.

▶ 10.6.7　Don't Spread the Company—or Yourself—Too Thin

Cairns cautioned against investing so many resources in the expansion that there's nothing left over for the existing market.

"It's important to keep enough (financial) reserve and (to understand) the full and entire cost of that expansion," Cairns said. But you also need enough personnel to maintain the current operation while you focus on the expansion strategy. Cairns said business owners often make the mistake of assuming they can manage it all on their own and not putting someone in place to ensure continuity with what's already working.

"Most of your attention is going to be on the new location, so who's going to be picking up the slack in the old location because you're not going to have time to be there?" he said. "It's just a lack of awareness that you're going to need to backfill yourself."

Expanding to a new market could take your small business to new heights, but it won't happen overnight. Take time to study the opportunity, and prepare the company to take advantage of it. When it comes to growth, you want to think long-term so your organization can prosper for decades to come.

10.7　The Challenges of Market Entry and Expansion

No major business decision is without its hurdles, but global expansion comes with its own unique set of obstacles. Here are some challenges you should prepare for before expanding internationally.

1. Language and Cultural Differences

Taki Skouras, co-founder and CEO of international wireless accessories retailer Cellairis, suggests hiring bilingual staff members who can translate for your company.

"If you don't have the budget for full-time translators, outsource tasks like overseas customer service," he said.

Josh Robinson, vice president of franchising and development for Pearle Vision—an optical franchise that has 500 locations throughout North America, including about 60 in Canada-said it is important to understand that there may be cultural and language differences within a country.

"Just as you expect differences in residents of California, the Midwest, and New York, you need to understand the nuances between Vancouver and Calgary (for example)," Robinson said. "You probably expect differences in laws and languages, so you would hire a lawyer and translator from the country you are moving into. But you also might need a local person's perspective to understand how the culture and even taste could affect the market for some consumer goods and services outside the U.S."

2. International Compliance and Regulatory Issues

Learning the different tax codes, business regulations and packaging standards in different countries can be challenging. Trevor Cox, chief financial officer for DataCloud International Inc.—which has offices in the U.S., Canada and Australia-said compliance was the biggest challenge DataCloud faced when expanding overseas.

"In Australia, compliance was a major headache," he said. "It took months to complete the necessary paperwork for compliance and setting up a corporation."

Foreign banks may also be hesitant to deal with the administrative burden of a U.S.-based account, so you may have to set up a separate foreign business entity and bank account to make handling transactions worthwhile for the banks.

"It took just as long to set up a local bank account, with many banks declining to work with us because we were too small," Cox said. "We had to switch to an international bank, which had offices in Australia."

3. Packaging

Stanley Chao, president of AllIn Consulting and author of *Selling to China: A Guide for Small and Medium-Sized Businesses*, said products have to be localized. This means different packaging, foreign language instructions, different voltages, etc.

"The issue here is that you need a local person familiar with your product to suggest these changes," Chao said. "Don't think you can just resell your U.S.-targeted product in a foreign country."

Paris said packaging standards are different from country to country. In the U.S., companies only need to include directions in English and maybe Spanish. "But in Europe, your instructions, even for the simplest product, will be in multiple languages, sometimes up to 24 languages. If your product is sold more regionally, you will have to consider the increase in packaging cost associated with labeling."

4. Slower Pace

In America, the business world moves quickly. This is not necessarily the case in other countries.

"Overseas, doing business is as much a personal event as it is professional," said Bill Bardosh, CEO of green materials and chemicals company TerraVerdae BioWorks. "Things will always take longer to be resolved overseas, but that isn't necessarily a sign of a lack of momentum. You have to be patient and prepared for multiple interactions to build trust."

5. Local Competition

It's not easy to persuade a foreign customer to trust your brand when a similar product is made in their home country. While some big-name U.S. chains have clout overseas, small and midsize companies need to work harder to convince the international market that their brands are trustworthy and better than the competition.

"Why would (customers) buy from you over the local champion?" Paris said. "Can you penetrate the market? If you do, can you be profitable under the circumstances?"

10.8　Advice and Best Practices for Market Entry and Expansion

If you feel you're ready to tackle the challenges of international business, follow this advice from business leaders who have been in your shoes:

1. Find the Right Partners and Team

If you plan on expanding globally, you'll want a great team or partner. Even if your "partner" takes the form of a mentor, you'll want someone you trust and who can vouch for you.

Caicedo said it's crucial to establish a local office and team that understands the market and language to comply with local regulations:

"Having a local country manager can go a long way in not only ensuring that the company is compliant in each new market, but that it is handling its expenses efficiently as well," he said. "Working with a local partner can also help communicate your company's unique selling point in a way that is meaningful to the local market."

The people you hire to deal with your overseas business partners and customers must be immersed in the local environment, but they should also be looking out for your interests.

"The foreign companies that you may deal with probably have more experience doing business in the U.S. than you have in their country," Bardosh said. "Without a core team on your side with the necessary cultural, language and local business contacts, you'll be competitively disadvantaged."

Biolife LLC, developer of bio urn and planting system, the Living Urn, launched in the U.S. in 2014 and has since expanded to 17 countries worldwide. Biolife President Mark Brewer said those expanding internationally shouldn't rush the process of finding trusted and reliable strategic alliances:

"While the potential partner may seem like a great choice today, a better option may be available tomorrow," he said.

When you're looking specifically for a distributor, Brewer said, don't assume the largest one is automatically the best:

"Some of our best and most successful distributors are entrepreneurs like us who are focused on the product and driven to make it successful in their market," he said. "Larger distributors, having many products, may not devote the same amount of time and attention to our product in the market."

2. Have the Right Infrastructure

Morris said it is vital to make sure that when you do expand, you have the right infrastructure in place to ensure a smooth launch.

These are some questions she said you should have answered beforehand:

- Do you have a management team that can deliver your strategy from a satellite office?
- Have you decided which business decisions can be made on a local level and which need to be made centrally?
- Do you have the capabilities to set up IT and telephone systems?
- How will employees share data securely, and does the data you're capturing follow the law and best practices?

3. Consider the Impact of Any New Ideas

Instead of only thinking about how your own country's customers might receive your new ideas, you'll need to think about how foreign customers will receive your ideas.

"As you spitball new ideas, someone definitely needs to think about scalability to your international territories—usually you," said Mike Zani, CEO of business consulting firm Predictive Index. "Time zones, language and cultural appropriateness all need to be considered when you branch out internationally. If you don't do this ahead of time, you run the risk of offending your international partners by appearing to be more concerned about yourself (than) them."

4. Always Do Your Due Diligence

Before making major business decisions, you should think through all possible scenarios—especially during global expansion. Chao advises those expanding their business internationally to spend time in the country they want to break into. An information-gathering trip can be a focal point to develop a plan for moving forward.

"Visit potential customers, distributors, OEM partners, and even competitors who are making either complementary or competing products," Chao said. "After a visit, you'll find out all the hard facts on whether your product can sell, who the competitors are, what price to sell at, and how to sell (directly, distributor, etc.)."

5. Rely on Experts

It is important for businesses looking for international growth to understand that they will need help. Chao said this can be particularly tough for smaller businesses, because they have likely been doing everything on their own up to this point.

"Realize you can't do everything, and rely on some experts to at least guide you through the beginning phases," he said. "You don't have to reinvent the wheel. Rely on experts."

6. Be Willing to Change Direction

Once you do expand, be prepared for some bumps in the road. That may mean changing how you operate in some way. Adrian Fisher, founder and CEO of Property Simple—a real estate technology company with locations in the U.S., Argentina and Chile—said you cant be afraid to pivot.

"With each new country comes new challenges, and businesses must adapt their product," Fisher said. "It's OK if the product shifts; it's more important to meet consumer demand."

7. Alter your Customer Support

Once you launch overseas, you will have a whole new customer base to support. Roger Sholanki, CEO and founder of Book4Time, a provider of next-generation wellness management software that operates in 70 countries, said your current system of customer support will need significant changes when you expand internationally.

"The immediate challenge is servicing customers in different time zones, which could mean a 12-hour time difference," he said. "Your customers will want immediate support and access."

10.9　Six Steps to Create a Winning Market Entry Strategy

Set clear goals and study your competition before entering a new market share.

You have your eye on a new market. You're certain your products or services are a perfect fit. But to get there, you'll first need to develop a strategy.

A market entry strategy is a key tool for clarifying what you aim to achieve and how you're going to achieve it when entering a new market. While an export plan tends to focus on just a few products or services, your market entry strategy will provide you with a roadmap for your whole business.

A typical market entry strategy can take 6 to 18 months to implement. It's well worth the effort because it will ensure you have the best distribution channels in place, launch the right product and align your goals with those of your stakeholders.

Here are six steps you can follow to build a winning market entry strategy and start exporting into previously unknown territory:

1. Set Clear Goals

Be specific about what you want to achieve in your new market, including the level of sales you can expect to reach. Do not lose sight of your goals as you flesh out your strategy to help you stay on track and confirm that your opportunity, products/services and overall business goals are aligned.

2. Research Your Market

Use every means at your disposal to get to know your new market including:

- Doing online research.
- Going there in person.
- Attending trade shows as a participant or exhibitor.
- Learning about the competition.
- Making business contacts in the area.

When getting to know your market, it's important that you also learn about the social, cultural and political climate. If you're entering a region with a different language or cultural norms than Canada, think about how you'll communicate with key contacts.

Explore all of the rules that could affect your product and how you produce and deliver it. You'll also need to understand your labelling requirements to ensure your packaging complies with local regulations. Learn about different distribution channels, too. At this stage, it's advisable to seek information and counsel from embassies, consulates and industry associations.

3. Study the Competition

A detailed competitive analysis based on your research and visits to the target market will help you make key decisions—for example, if you need to modify your product or service to customize it for that market.

Most businesses underestimate the degree of competition existing in new markets. Getting expert advice can help clarify the challenges.

4. Choose Your Mode of Entry

There are many ways to enter a new market. You can use the services of a distributor or agent located there. You might become a franchisee or acquire an existing business. You can even construct an entirely new brick-and-mortar facility.

A lot of companies start by going into the U.S. first—and most choose to partner with an existing distributor. If you choose that path, make sure your strategy includes a unique value proposition for the distributor. Your partner will want to understand what's in it for them, and how your product or service is different enough to stand out in the marketplace, but not so different that buyers won't understand what it is.

5. Figure out Your Financing Needs

Find out if you'll need to get any financing to support your export venture. You may also want to get insurance that protects your company against losses when a customer cannot pay. EDC offers credit insurance that can help you avoid cash flow issues when an international customer fails to pay.

6. Develop the Strategy Document

Once you've worked out the details of your strategy, you'll be ready to write it out. Once created, this document will be your blueprint going forward, detailing your goals, research findings, contacts, budgets, major action items and timelines, and how you'll monitor and evaluate your success on an ongoing basis.

It's important to follow your plan so that you aren't overwhelmed in a new market.

Have your accountant, lawyer and an external specialist review your strategy. You want to ensure you haven't missed anything that will prevent you from entering the market, or require you to pull back after you get there.

Key Terms

market entry and expansion 市场进入和扩张	Also, foreign market entry and expansion, it entails a number of important marketing strategy decisions including selection of specific target countries, structuring of foreign subsidiary units, and management of foreign operations. 又叫做国外市场进入和扩张，它是包含了诸如选择特定目标国家、设置国外分支机构以及管理国外业务等一系列重要的营销决策。

Continued

licensing 授权经营	It is a business arrangement in which one company gives another company permission to manufacture its product for a specified payment. Usually includes brand licensing, patent licensing, etc. 授权经营是一家公司允许另一家公司生产自己的产品并收取特定费用的商业安排。通常包括品牌授权、专利授权等。
acquisition 收购	It is when one company purchases most or all of another company's shares to gain control of that company. Purchasing more than 50% of a target firm's stock and other assets allows the acquirer to make decisions about the newly acquired assets without the approval of the company's shareholders. 收购是指一家公司购买另一家公司的大部分或全部股份,以获得对该公司的控制权。收购方购买目标公司 50% 以上的股票和其他资产,可以在未经公司股东批准的情况下就新收购的资产做出决策。
piggyback 猪驮式出口	It is a form of distribution in foreign markets in which a SME company (the "rider"), deals with a larger company (the "carrier") which already operates in certain foreign markets and is willing to act on behalf of the rider that wishes to export to those markets. 猪驮式出口,又称"附带式出口",国外市场的一种分销策略,是指的是这样一种出口情况:一个是中小企业(称"乘坐者"),另一个是规模更大的产企业(称"负重者")。"负重者"利用自己已经建立起来的海外分销渠道,将"乘坐者"和自己的产品一起进行销售。
turnkey solution 交钥匙解决方案	It is a type of system built end-to-end for a customer that can be easily implemented into a current business process. It is immediately ready to use upon implementation and is designed to fulfill a certain process such as manufacturing (in part or whole), billing, website design, training, or content management. 交钥匙解决方案是为客户端到端构建的一种系统,可以轻松地将其实施到当前的业务流程中。一经实施便可以立即使用,并且旨在完成某些过程,例如制造(部分或全部)、计费、网站设计、培训或内容管理。
(trade) credit insurance (贸易)信用保险	It is also called business credit insurance, export credit insurance, or credit insurance is an insurance policy and a risk management product offered by private insurance companies and governmental export credit agencies to business entities wishing to protect their accounts receivable from loss due to credit risks such as protracted default, insolvency or bankruptcy. 又称商业信用保险、出口信用保险,是私营保险公司和政府出口信贷机构向希望保护其应收账款免受长期违约、资不抵债或破产等信用风险损失的企业实体提供的保险单和风险管理产品。

Review & Critical Thinking Questions

1. What is the meaning of market entry?
2. What is the meaning of market expansion?
3. What is licensing?
4. What is franchising?
5. What are the differences between licensing and franchising?
6. What is an acquisition?
7. What are the differences between acquisition and joint venture?
8. When is the strategy of foreign direct investment viable?
9. What is the most common goal of companies going into the international markets?
10. How do you understand the strategy of partnering up?
11. How to meet the challenge of language and cultural differences?
12. Before going international, what kind of questions should you have answered?
13. Why should your customer support system be altered when you expand internationally?
14. Find out the one way of financing help mentioned in the text?

Discussion Questions

1. There are five basic entry and expansion modes mentioned. In your opinion, which one is the most commonly applied? And why?
2. There are five benefits of market entry and expansion mentioned, which one will the most majority companies seek?
3. Suppose you are running an SME, and now you want to expand your business into Singapore? What are the first three things you have to consider?
4. How do you understand the right partner in a foreign market is vitally important?
5. Is the most commonly applied mode of market entry and expansion suitable for every company? Why or why not?

Case Study

Didi Chuxing's Merger with Uber China

Didi Chuxing confirmed on Monday that it will merge with Uber China's business, putting an end to the two companies' cash-burning fight over the dominance of China's ride-hailing market.

Didi said in a statement that it has agreed to acquire Uber's operation in China in a deal that gives Uber a 5.89 percent stake in Didi. Didi will also gain a small stake in Uber's global business, valued at $68 billion.

"The two sides will operate cross shareholding and become minority shareholders for each other," the statement from Didi said.

According to the statement, Uber Globe's 5.89 percent of Didi's shares will equal 17.7 percent of the economic rights. The other Chinese shareholders in Uber China will achieve 2.4 percent of the economic rights.

Didi Chuxing has become the only enterprise in the country that received investments from China's three major Internet companies—Baidu Inc., Tencent Holdings Ltd. and Alibaba Group Holding Ltd, known as BAT.

"Cheng Wei, founder and president of Didi Chuxing and Travis Kalanick, chief executive officer of Uber, will simultaneously join their counterpart company's board of directors," the statement said.

Western media reported that investors behind the two companies have been pushing them to end the fight in China as both of them have spent a lot to gain loyalty from users.

"Uber and Didi Chuxing are investing billions of dollars in China and both companies have yet to turn a profit there," Travis Kalanick, chief executive officer of Uber, wrote in a blog post obtained by China Daily today.

"Getting to profitability is the only way to build a sustainable business that can best serve Chinese riders, drivers and cities over the long term," he said in the post to announce the company's intention to merge Uber China with Didi.

Last week, a long-awaited regulation giving legal status to online car-hailing services in China was approved and released by the nation's State Council.

Aimed at regulating the taxi market and car-hailing services in China, the regulation requires car-hailing platforms, such as Didi Chuxing and Uber Technologies, to review the qualifications of drivers and their cars to guarantee safe rides.

Last February, Didi Chuxing and Kuaidi Dache, the precursors of the Didi Chuxing, jointly announced their strategic merger, becoming one of the largest vendors in the market.

Questions

1. Did Uber's merger with Didi Chuxing announce its failure in China Market?
2. How do you understand the cross shareholding between Didi Chuxing and Uber? Did it mean to some extent the two companies would no longer be rivals to each other?
3. Can you identify some market expansion strategies in this transaction?

中文概述

通常情况下,企业进入国际市场和进行市场扩张有五种基本的模式,分别是**直接出口、授权和特许经营、设立合资企业、战略性并购以及外国直接投资**。这五种模式各有优劣。

企业进行市场扩张和进入国际市场有很多益处,综合而言,最主要的五大益处分别是**建立新的收入来源、获得竞争优势、获得全球性的人才、获取新的全球顾客以及利用政府激励措施**。这些益处可以为企业赢得新的发展。

关于企业扩张进入国际性市场的原因,主要有以下四个:巨大的**商业吸引力**、可以**降低企业运营成本、提高企业竞争力以及分散企业风险**。

企业进入新的国际市场主要有 8 大策略,分别是(1)**特许经营品牌**。特许经营的优势在于它是一种更容易进入新市场的方式。你所要做的就是利用你现有的、成功的商业模式,在你的目标市场找到一个加盟商,开始建设,然后打开你的大门。其劣势在于你需要不断妥协。(2)**直接出口**。这是企业进入新的国际市场最常见的一种方式,你需要国外的代理商或者分销商伙伴。(3)**开展国际合作**。听起来比较模糊,任何一种可以帮助你进入到新的国际市场的方式都是可行的,比如在很多亚洲国家,你需要其国内伙伴帮你处理与政府的沟通等事宜。(4)**设立合资企业**。两家公司共同成立一家新公司,在其中一方的国内从事研发、生产和经营活动,双方按照投资比例享有相关经营管理权。(5)**收购一家企业**。收购他国境内的一家企业,是目前为止最简单的进入国际市场的方式。(6)**交钥匙解决方案**。这是**一个形象的说法**,跨国公司为东道国建造工厂或其他工程项目,一旦设计与建造工程完成,包括设备安装、试车及初步操作顺利运转后,即将该工厂或项目所有权和管理权的"钥匙"依合同完整地"交"给对方,由对方开始经营。(7)**猪驮式出口**。又称"附带式出口",是指的是这样一种出口情况:一个生产企业叫"乘坐者",另一个生产企业叫"负重者"。"负重者"利用自己已经建立起来的海外分销渠道,将"乘坐者"和自己的产品一起进行销售。(8)**许可证贸易(授权经营)**。许可证贸易是指许可方和许可证接受方签订许可证协议,允许对方使用本企业某项新工艺、新技术、专利权或商标进行生产,并向对方收取一定费用的贸易方式。企业可以根据自身情况,选择合适的策略向国际市场进行扩张。

每一家小型企业要进入国际市场之前,都要注意以下几个问题:(1)垂直扩张,还是引进新产品。(2)重视现有顾客的反馈。(3)确定你的新市场。(4)研究新市场的合规性问题和税收问题。(5)做好资金上的准备。(6)定制针对新市场的营销内容。(7)不要把绝大多数资源投入到新市场开发,从而使现有市场只有很少的资源。

同时,企业进行国际市场进入和扩张,也面临一些挑战,主要有以下几个方面:**语言和文化差异、国际合规和监管问题、包装**(即包装的本地化)、**慢节奏**(并不是所有的市场都必须是快节奏的)以及来自**当地的竞争**。所以,企业必须要应对好这些挑战才能取得成功。

关于企业国际市场进入和扩张,亦有一些好的建议和实践,比如:**寻求正确的合作伙伴和团队、拥有合适的基础设施、充分考虑任何新想法带来的影响、永远都要尽职尽责、依靠专家、**

愿意改变方向、改变你原来的客户支持体系。

　　成功的国际市场进入通常需要遵循六个步骤。第一步:设定清晰的目标;第二步:开展市场调研;第三步:研究竞争状况;第四步:选择合适的进入模式;第五步:清楚你的财务需要;第六步:制定战略文件。

PART 3
Integrated Marketing Communication Strategy

UNIT 11 / Brand Management

Learning Objectives

1. Describe the advantages that are ascribed to branding.
2. Understand the historical development of branding.
3. Familiarize relevant terminology such as brand equity, brand congruity.
4. Understand mainstream of branding and brand loyalty.
5. Explain relations between brand congruity and brand personality.
6. Study the mainstream explanation of how to build a brand.

11.1　Introduction

　　Branding has been associated with property in its widest sense. However, in modern times the concept of branding has taken on a more positive inflection with the development of commodity brands in the early twentieth century that offer to protect and heal the self. Individuals now mark themselves with brands as a means of self-affirmation rather than negation. In Western culture the discourse about brands has travelled beyond the marketing of traditional products and services to swamp every aspect of life. It can be recalled that this was what Kotler called for (or did he?) back in 1972, when he asked that the marketing concept be applied to all institutions. Someone must have been listening because from birth the infant is wrapped in a branded cocoon of "absorbent" diapers, "trustworthy" bottle-feeds and medications, "cute" clothes, and, of course, the ubiquitous branded pram. From about that age the infant begins to learn the language of brands from the mass media and by observation of the actions of those around IT.

　　In this chapter, the traditional world of goods and services is considered. It starts by outlining the conventional wisdom that argues why branding is important. Then themes are discussed under what is loosely referred to as the conventional wisdom about branding, i.e. brand congruity, personality, subculture and community. Consideration is given to discuss a way by which brands gain their meanings and by which they may recirculate this back to consumers as symbolic resources for the construction of identity. Then branding is assessed from a radical behaviourist point of view and different accounts of brand loyalty are explained.

11.2　Brief Modern History of Branding

The work of the behaviourist J.B. Watson was examined as being one of the first who used the fear-sex-emulation model in advertising during the 1920s. The strategy appeared to be simple. Basically, the advertisement had to first identify the problem, deficit or lack in the consumer. This was achieved by inducing feelings of anxiousness or lack of confidence, e.g. with respect to the fear of underarm sweat. Early brand advertising clearly identified the deficit and the benefit in the shape of the product that could cure it. Familiar brands started life as patent medicines, e. g. Coca-Cola and Heinz Ketchup; as part of a controlled "healthy" diet, e.g. Kellogg's Cornflakes; as an aid to the creation of a more "hygienic" domestic environment through banishing "invisible" germs and dirt, e.g. Sunlight soap; or in focusing on the development of "personal hygiene", e.g. Zambuk, Lifebuoy carbolic soap and Odorono. The brand is offered as the means to resolve the anxiety, redress the deficit and fill the lack. This meets with Levitt's advice to marketers when seeking to define consumers' needs; that it is better to start with the deficit. For example, the market for "six-inch holes" rather than the benefit of the market for drills; a hospital may produce surgery; customers seek "relief of pain"; and purchasers of perfume may be purchasing "dreams", those of cosmetics "confidence".

Authors cite a plethora of benefits that arise from branding. Most of these are from the producers' perspective:

- **Protection.** The brand mark and other aspects of the brand constitute a legal sign. Anyone who uses "Coca-Cola" in the particular font prescribed without permission is likely to end up in court. Brands are protected by copyright, trademarks and patents that are underpinned by the notion of intellectual property rights, as written into WTO standards. Such devices have been used to attack brand piracy, where, for instance, Napster featured as a high-profile case. Klein notes that there are two sides to this. Protection of the brand mark has reached the extent that authors such as ourselves, in writing this book, can be accused of "stealing" the brand mark. Klein argues this has become a powerful new form of censorship as global brands dominate huge swathes of social and cultural space.

- **Property.** The brand mark is a shorthand device in that it readily identifies what belongs to one person, what that person has a right to which is different from what belongs to other people. The brand mark needs to be distinctive and easily recognizable if it is to fulfill its function.

- **Differentiation.** The idea of differentiation with a capital D features in most populist books on the subject. The provenance of this idea tracks back to the days of the Unique Selling Proposition (USP) developed in the US in the 1940s. The brand should offer a proposition that is unique and which signifies a benefit that will pull the customer to the brand. Put in behaviourist terms, the various stimuli associated with the brand, e.g. the brand logo and packaging, should act as a discriminative stimulus that prompts the person to associate this with some unique aspect that has provided reinforcement. In cognitive terms the idea is to create a favourable attitude about the brand based on a key set of attributes. Levitt supports this idea in arguing that the core brand should reflect the specific quality which makes the brand different from others. This is known as the " brand property". Once this aspect of the "core" brand has been identified, the marketer has a basis to define the need and the plenitude or wholeness that consumption of the brand will bring. The brand itself is a positive creation which offers the promise of negating the evil of the need.

● **Added value**. The argument for differentiation would make little sense if this did not lead to the creation of added value. The idea is that if the marketer can make an addict of the consumer, by inducing them to rely upon the brand and to consistently demand it, the brand may command a price premium over that which claim to service the same core need. One way of creating added value is by ensuring that the brand consistently delivers a quality offering. One source of information about the relative performance of brands can be found in the Profit Impact of Market Strategies (PIMS) database. This contains financial and strategic information collected by the Strategic Planning Institute on 2,600 SBUs that form part of 450 institutions in the US. Subsequent analyses of this database have revealed the six "PIMS principles". The first and most important principle relates to perceived quality, that in the long run the most important single factor affecting an SBU's performance is the quality of its products and services relative to competitors. By building in higher perceived quality, it is argued, units can charge a higher price and reflect this on the bottom line or on R&D and NPD. There is a strong positive relationship between perceived quality and profitability, which occurs as the result of customer loyalty, more repeat purchases and less vulnerability to price wars.

● **Brand equity**. In some instances the value of a brand (not to be confused with brand values, which are discussed later) has been listed on a company's balance sheet, which is a controversial move. This is understandable given that Nestlé paid £ 2.5bn (US $4.5bn) for Rowntree, which was six times the value of net assets.

● **Market share**. When a company buys a brand, it is buying market share. Although the data is dated, "PIMS" data suggests that there is a strong positive relationship between high market share and profitability. More important, brands promise the purchaser consistent profitability. PIMS findings indicate that on average brands with a market share of 40 percent generate three times the Return on Investment (ROI)—a performance measure used to evaluate the efficiency or profitability of an investment or compare the efficiency of a number of different investments—of those with a market share of 10%. In support of this view, Doyle argues that strong brands generate exceptional levels of profit through a triple leverage effect. The most obvious effect is through the higher volume which provides "experience curve" effects, involving higher asset utilization and scale economies. The second source of advantage is through the higher price that the brand commands. Sometimes this price premium holds at the final consumer level, although it is usually at the retailer or distributor level that it is most apparent. Successful brands build such loyalty that they are able to generate superior earnings. A premium brand can earn 20% higher returns than discounted products. Brand leaders also have lower unit costs as they can take advantage of experience curve effects which may occur in development, production or marketing, depending on the industry's value chain. The larger the brand the more is spent on the total marketing effort, and the larger the brand the less is spent in unit cost terms on marketing. The end result is that the brand leader's market share advantage is magnified substantially at the profit level. Here a brand advantage of 3:1 results through leverage in a profit contribution of nearly 6:1.

● **Functional device**. Although this is the shortest section, it is also probably the most important. Brands enable consumers to identify high-quality products and services and save on search costs.

11.3　Brand Decisions

Companies must make a number of decisions with respect to their brand strategy.

11.3.1　Choice of Presentation Format

The presentation format to be used is important. The following constitutes a simple menu:

● **Company brand**. In this case the company uses the corporate name as the focus for all external communications, through advertising, products and letterheads, e.g. companies such as Coca-Cola, Heinz and ICI.

● Individual brand. Here the company behind the brand maintains a low corporate profile with respect to customers and focuses on the creation of strong brand identities. A prime example in the market for detergents is where P&G and Unilever dominate the UK market, although this is disguised by the focus on competing brands.

● **Mixed format**. Sometimes referred to as an endorsed brand. This is where the brand identity is displayed prominently but the corporate identity also features, e. g.

Kellogg's with Kellogg's Cornflakes, Kellogg's Rice Krispies, etc.

The presentation formats mentioned above could be made more complex by including other elements. Through the cowboy, Philip Morris uses a brand user strategy to promote Marlboro. Another format is the product class or brand family, e.g. Matsushita, family brands under separate range names. For example, Matsushita markets its electronic products under four brand families: National, Panasonic, Technics and Star.

Companies have made use of nationality in building corporate and brand identity. For example, it is of the opinion that 'Sony' was developed as a name not because of what it meant (it did not mean anything), but because it was thought to be a name that might be appealing in the West. Using the same logic in a reverse direction, the British chain of electronics retailers, Currys, chose the Matsui brand name, as it was felt that British consumers would identify it as being of Japanese origin (it was not).

11.3.2 Eight Steps to Building a Brand

The following describes an idealized notion of what ought to be done in building a brand. Later, you will be asked to compare what Midland Bank planners did with this.

- **Identify the brand position**. What are the brand's values? Where does it stand in the mind of the customer? What differentiates it from others?

- **Gap analysis**. Following a SWOT analysis—are there opportunities for brand extensions, i.e. by adding in additional products under the brand umbrella, or might these act to dilute the brand?

- **Develop the brand property**. The brand property is the element that is "unique, memorable and indissolubly linked to that brand and no other". The brand property does not lie in the intrinsic nature of the product, e.g. a sweet fizzy drink, a sweet fizzy drink made with apples, a mint-flavoured chocolate or a medium-alcohol aperitif. Rather it is found in the rich tapestry of available referent systems which the advertisers plunder in their search for the creation of the new, the dazzling, the exclusive, and the necessity. Through such a process the fizzy drink becomes "the real thing", Coke; Babycham turns girls into Cinderella; After Eights are "exclusive", while the "Martini generation" live idyllic lives in tropical bliss.

- **Test alternative propositions**. Once developed, brand propositions may be tested with small groups of customers from the target segment, their reactions noted and changes suggested and implemented.

- **Make the "go/no-go" decision**.

- **Construct the implementation plan**. This involves a consideration of the 4Ps in relation to the brand. All these decisions will defer to the notion of "brand property" and the target market segment which has been identified for the brand.

- Implement the plan.
- **Monitor the plan.** Go back to the beginning—identify the brand position.

In the next section recent ideas about brands are discussed, including brand congruity, personality and community. This view is compared with a behaviourist explanation of brands and brand loyalty.

11.4　Mainstream Explanation of Branding

▶ 11.4.1　Brand Personality

The idea of brand personality is related to brand congruity in that it refers to "the set of human personality characteristics associated with a brand". This argues that, while brands may be functionally similar in fulfilling similar needs, a brand personality allows consumers to select that brand that best expresses their own individuality. Consequently, even allowing that brands may be similar, those which express clear and effective personalities should result in higher preferences and increased market share.

Fournier pushes the idea of brand "personality" to its limits by arguing that a brand can be seen to be an "active contributing partner in the dyadic relationship that exists between the person and the brand". In this view, all marketing mix activities and brand management activities, e. g. advertising and direct marketing campaigns, are construed as being "behaviours" which are enacted on behalf of the brand "personality". These behaviours then trigger attitudinal and other responses on the part of the customer. According to Fournier, this allows the audience to elevate the status of the brand from that of a passive object to that of being a "relationship partner". Following in this line of thought, Govers and Schoormans found that consumers described variants of screwdriver and coffee maker in different ways.

Figure 11.1 shows three coffee makers and three food mixers. According to Govers and Schoormans, respondents used words such as "introvert", "outspoken", "sociable", "kind", "warm", "friendly" and "dependable" to describe the coffee makers in their study. Taking these as cues, how then might you describe the coffee makers in Figure 11.1? In your view do the different variants of coffee maker have different personalities? Now look at the food mixers. Do these have different personalities? What words or signifiers would you use to describe them?

Figure 11.1　Differences in Brand Personality

On the other hand, Cornelissen and Harris make the point that, as brands are not people, the use of terms such as "identity" and "personality" leads to the creation of the false belief that there is some essence of corporate personality or some form of real organizational self. This point is so obvious that it is often missed; brands are not people but rather like puppets that dance to the puppet master's tune. The question is, who are the puppet masters? Arguably brand managers can do little to infuse a brand with life. Brand mascots like the Pillsbury doughboy, Churchill the bulldog (the face and tail of an insurance company) and the Andrex puppy may be lovable but do we form relationships with them? The way in which a brand acquires a "personality" is mysterious and can have an end that was unanticipated by its original designers. For example, the story of how Nazi Germany's "people's car", the Volkswagen Beetle, became transformed into Herbie (beloved emblem of 1960s "flower power" for US and European students) had much more to it than the movie. Returning to consideration of brand personality, some authors do not go to the extreme lengths of Fournier. Allen and Olson, define brand personality more impersonally as: "the set of meanings constructed by an observer to describe the 'inner' characteristics of another person".

11.4.2　Brands, Meaning and Identity

The discussion about brand personality raises the question of how brands attain their meaning and how this in turn is transferred to consumers. Allen and Olsen discussed above, suggest that consumers attribute meaning as well as action and purpose to brands. But what are the mechanics of how this works? In marketing the focus on meaning can be traced to Levy, who argued that people do not buy products for what they do but for what they mean. While these are inseparable in practice, it makes sense analytically to divide the discussion about brand meaning and identity into two sections, one dealing with the role played by brands in our lives, the other which focuses on how brand meaning is mediated through advertising.

In this respect, brands are symbols whose meaning is used to create and define a consumer's self-concept. The Freudian view was discussed showing that possessions can come to be regarded as being part of the extended self. Elliott and Wattanasuwan follow this line of thinking, arguing that consumers invest psychic energy into people and objects. In this view the self-concept is complex as energy may be invested in a number of people and things. Consequently, a person possesses a multiplicity of identities. This account highlights the role played by narratives or stories in the formation of identity. Much of the knowledge that is gained about ourselves and our culture comes to us from the commercial process of story-telling called branding. In building up these stories meaning is constructed from two sources: our lived experience and the mass media.

11.4.3   Lived Experience of Brands

Freudian theory suggests that at a certain point in our life course the issue of identity becomes important to us. In this respect, Erikson argues that identity confusion is experienced by most adolescents. This is because by that stage of development, the individual feels independent of the family and ventures beyond the safe confines of the family to sample other social contexts. New social contexts can be frightening and challenging to the adolescent's sense of self, particularly if they have not previously mastered the ability to take different roles. Consequently, a person may react to this sense of confusion by clinging to the security provided by their peer group and may over-identify with the heroes of that group to the extent that they seem to lose their individuality. Where the adolescent fails in positively responding to the identity crisis they may attempt to create a negative identity by seeking to become everything that they have learned ought to be avoided. From the above, it is important to consider the context in which interaction takes place with products in order to gain meaning from them. As children we consume many food and beverage brands in the familiar and often secure context of the family home. This is why such brands attain such a nostalgic appeal later in life. Life in the school context brings us into contact with others, and here brands may become implicated in the struggle for esteem and status, signifying who is "in" and who is "out" of the group. Most children who must negotiate the changed balance between home, school and a widening circle of social contexts feel confused and some will be disaffected. This latter group is the targets for a host of branded identities, many of which are to be found on MTV or something similar, from Marilyn Manson to Pete Doherty of Babyshambles or, more extremely, the "stars" of Death Metal. Given Erikson's comments, as children grow into adolescence a range of brands targeted at the "anti-hero" image should become salient. Identity is lucrative for marketers; like spots it does not seem to go away. Some claim that the identity crisis is occurring at younger ages than ever and have coined the neologism "tweenie" to describe it.

The idea of a reference group plays a key role in the construction of identity as one moves from the family context to the school and the ever widening social context. This divides the "in group" that we feel comfortable with, from "out groups", those we tend to avoid and in turn the aspirational group to which we seek to belong. In consumer societies brands can play a key role in differentiating "in" groups from "out" groups. For example, in the UK, the luxury Burberry brand has been identified with "chav" culture.

11.4.4   Mediated Experience of Brands

While lived experience is in the here and now, the consumption of media products involves the ability to experience events that are spatially and temporally distant from the practical context of everyday life. Elliott and Watanasuwan argue that individuals draw from mediated experience and interlace this with lived experience in constructing the self. In this view brand advertising is a major source of symbolic meaning. Mediated experience consists of what we learn from the mass media and in particular from our consumption of television, radio and films or movies. We do not simply soak up meaning from advertising but actively recreate this in group situations. We are likely to watch the same television programmes and advertisements as our "in group" does and to swap stories about them. But how exactly is advertising meaning created? This is explained below in more detail.

1. Advertising and Referent Systems

The concept of referent systems discussed here should be distinguished from that of reference groups which were outlined above. A simple but crude way of differentiating them is to say that reference groups tend to exist in the real lived world whereas referent systems exist in the mediated world. When products are new, they have no intrinsic meaning but most draw this from the general cultural context. One way of doing so is to associate the brand with a well-known personality. For example, the perfume Chanel No. 5 was originally associated with its founder, Coco Chanel, who was well known as being a role model for other women, being perceived to be chic, sophisticated and glamorous. Coco was so influential that she is credited with bringing to an end the idea, prevalent in Europe at the time, that having a pale complexion was attractive for women, by staying out in the sun and gaining a "tan" while on holiday in the south of France.

2. Brand as Generator of Meaning

Once the correlation becomes fused with the product so that it appears that the link between them is natural, the product begins to generate meaning in its own right. In this case, if we were to see a person with the product, the transfer might be from the product on to the person. For example, the owner of a Mercedes car becomes recognized as being sophisticated, because the signified "sophistication" has transferred from the car to the person. In this case the person is seen to become sophisticated as a result of her consumption of the car. Here the product purports to become the actual referent (the real thing) for the sign (sophistication). For example, advertisements tell us that they can create the feelings which they represent (if we buy the Mercedes we will be sophisticated).

3. Brand as Stabilizer of Meaning

Not only do brands generate meaning, but it is also argued that they stabilize meaning for people at a time when other cherished institutions are under threat. In modern times, it sometimes seems that the only things that are familiar and unchanging are the brands we have consumed since childhood. Marketers play on such anxieties and just as in the old days of branding they offer the solution, "If only everything in life was as reliable as a Volkswagen". Elliott and Wattanasuwan argue that nostalgia can play a key role here in that adults tend to buy brands that remind them of sensitive periods such as childhood and adolescence. In particular, they contend that adults will use brands that they have had olfactory experiences within childhood as a means of restoring a sense of security. Brands that we have lived experience with acquire a depth of meaning during sensitive periods that are unattainable by brands at a later point in our lives. They discuss Hovis bread, Yorkshire Tea and Levi's.

11.4.5　Brand Groupings: Subcultures, Communities and Tribes

1. Brand Subcultures

The notion of a "subculture" of consumption moves beyond cognitive psychology and into the realms of social psychology and sociology. On this view, while the brand is central, it comprises one aspect of an entire subculture of consumption. The "sub-culture" is marked off from the mainstream through key elements in style, or the way in which a person comports himself. Dick Hebdige describes the emergence of "Mod" and "Rocker" subcultures in England in the 1950s and 1960s. Each group differentiated itself from the other primarily in terms of the bike they rode: Rockers straddled heavy British Triumph or BSA motor bikes; Mods sleek streamlined Italian Vespa scooters. The groups also differentiated themselves from each other in terms of the clothing they wore, where they liked to hang out and their choice of music and recreational drugs.

Hebdige also noticed that within each group a pecking order emerged according to how well one could handle the machine, distinguishing oneself from "inauthentic" riders. A more recent study by Schouten and McAlexander which focuses on the Harley—Davidson user illustrates how the organization of this subculture is layered like an onion, with the "Easy Rider" or "Electra-glide on Blue" leather-clad, tattooed aesthetic forming the centre and day trippers acting as outriders to the culture. The brand positively plays a role in establishing and maintaining a sense of separation, cohesiveness and solidarity necessary for the formation of the subculture, in addition to providing resources for the identity work of members.

2. Brand Community

McAlexander and Schouten have since revised their terms, arguing that the term "community" is more appropriate than that of "subculture". Their subsequent research indicated that, in particular, the notion of subculture overplayed the role of the leather-clad white male biker and underplayed the role by others such as women and minorities who also owned and rode Harleys. Muniz and O'Guinn define community in terms of the following:

- Consciousness of kind, refers to a shared consciousness.
- Shared rituals and traditions.
- Sense of moral responsibility or duty to the community as a whole.

Consciousness of kind means that, although brand users feel a strong attachment to the brand, they feel an even stronger attachment to each other. They refer to a sense of community, whereby owners of Saabs or Apple Macs refer to themselves as "Saabers" or "Mac" people. Muniz and O'Guinn found that each community formed a kind of hierarchy based on the extent to which the brand was used authentically and legitimately. For example, many Saab owners disparaged "yuppies" who bought Saabs because they were rich but who were not really committed to them. A sense of community was sustained through oppositional brand loyalty; Saab owners defined themselves as not-Volvo owners (which they associated with tractors); Mac users were definitely not PC users. The authors found evidence of the exercise of rituals and traditions in the groups which they studied, including Saab drivers flashing their lights and waving at other Saab drivers. While these rituals may at first glance seem to be insignificant, they functioned to create consciousness of kind. It was considered important to know the history of the brand, which often distinguished the "true believer" from the acolyte, and to circulate stories or myths. Finally, these groups were infused with a sense of moral responsibility to the community as a whole. The obverse of this was indicated, e.g. when a Mac user who switched to using PCs was regarded as being "morally reprehensible", a "Mac turncoat". Owners helped each other by providing assistance and advice on how to use the brand. The notion of community enables one to think of a brand as being the common property of those who work for the company and those who form the "community".

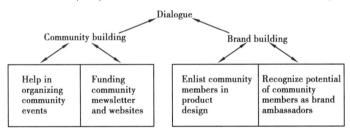

Figure 11.2　Marketing and the Brand Community

As Figure 11.2 shows, the idea of brand community goes beyond that of brand congruence. A person may buy a brand that is congruent with their self-concept. They may also buy brands that fit in with the values of their "in group". However, the notion of community is more active, suggesting management is not simply responsive to the needs of users but maintains a continual dialogue with them so as to ensure that the needs of the community and of the brand that sustains it are met. Academics and researchers such as

Schouten and McAlexander can become part of that dialogue. For example, the latter recounts being recruited to advise Jeep on how to build a community around the brand. Jeep 101 was the first in the Camp Jeep series that flowed from this venture.

The idea of brand community may convey a sense of warmth but also carries the whiff of saccharin to some. For example, one blogger asked, in noting Schouten's "handsome sum" from Harley for his work on brand community, and how film maker Adam Berman had won an award for his film "Biker Dreams", what did the bikers get out of it? She answered her own question: "they are robbed of their bad-boy/tough-chick/Hell's-Angel image by a homogeneous, warm-and-fuzzy portrayal". In any event some might take the ascription of the word "community" in relation to brands to be a step too far. The traditional word "community" can be taken to represent something much deeper by referring to those who share not only their daily food but also their ritual food in common (communion).

3. Brand Tribes

The idea of a brand tribe is looser and has a more dangerous feel to it than that of the brand community described above; there is something here that is beyond the influence of brand managers. A tribe does not necessarily refer to a bounded group. For example, a large enough proportion of the Coca-Cola "tribe" were outraged when managers changed the Coke formula some years back, before telling them that they had done so, that they forced the company to retract. The entire story is interesting. As described by Maffesoli, the neo-tribes consist of configurations of members who are connected by loose bonds of "common effect". The idea of a tribe enables us to think beyond the idea of those who support the brand to those who actively identify against it. There is the possibility that, for every brand community out there, there is also likely to be an anti-community, an anti-McDonald's, anti-Nike, anti-Harley, group. The idea of tribal identities accords with the romantic vision which many anti-consumers have of themselves, as guerrillas who hollow out "temporary autonomous zones" or crevices in the monolithic space of commodity consumption, which become the sites of a never-ending guerrilla war. George McKay's work provides an excellent summary. One might argue that it makes more sense to view those excluded from consumption as constituting a number of different marginalized groupings: the aged poor, immigrants and vagrants.

11.5 Brand Loyalty

Definitions of brand loyalty differ according to whether one shares a cognitive or a behaviourist outlook. Sheth provides a definition that is consistent with a behaviourist understanding, which is stochastic, focusing on relative frequency of purchase. On the other hand, Reynolds et al. are in line with a cognitive, or deterministic, explanation, which defines brand loyalty as the tendency for a person to continue over time to exhibit similar attitudes in situations similar to those he/she has previously encountered.

A strong attitude and commitment are important in the deterministic explanation. This describes the core member of the brand subculture who will refuse to buy an alternative if their favourite brand is not in stock. It links very much into the adoption process which we discuss in more detail in the chapter on communications. On the face of it the findings of stochastic research pose some problems for a deterministic understanding. For example, Ehrenberg's findings suggest that:

- Mainstream accounts emphasize the persuasive role of advertising via the ideas of the USP and AIDA in making people desire the brand before they have bought it. This has led to the idea that the consumer will be influenced by the last advertisement seen or the weight of past advertising. In turn this has led to the use of advertising awareness and recall measures in pre-testing and monitoring advertisements. However, Ehrenberg argues that there is little evidence that advertising for established brands works like this. In its persuasive role advertising is thought to create desire or conviction or at least to add value to the brand. For this reason those advertisements which seek to create a brand image, selling a USP, or informing consumers that they need a special product to meet a particular need, e.g. special shampoo for oily hair. But there is no empirical evidence that advertising succeeds in this aim when there are no differences to sell.

- Comparatively few purchasers of a product are totally brand-loyal to a particular brand over a period of time. Ehrenberg and Uncles explored a range of FMCG categories provided by Nielsen and concluded that on average 11% of customers were 100% loyal. Foxall found that while multi-brand purchasing was found for all products, the proportion of sole buyers ranged from 59% for butter to 14% for cereals and cheese, noting that such findings are entirely consistent with ratio schedules of reinforcement. He also noticed that some consumers switch each week, based on what the cheapest brand is.

- Most consumers are not loyal to one brand but purchase a number of brands from a small repertoire of available brands.

- Most brands within a product category are substitutable in that they are similar in terms of their formulation and functionality. Given that their benefits are directly substitutable, he suggests that it is not surprising that consumers switch brands. Foxall found that all the nine product categories analysed were close substitutes.

- Repeat purchase loyalty tends to be similar for brands that have similar market shares. Smaller brands not only attract fewer buyers but those buyers buy less of the brand, or buy it less frequently.

- The finding of "near instant" brand loyalty.

- There are no real differences in attitudes between users of different brands.

Key Terms

branding 品牌化	The use of techniques by which a company, organization or product distinguishes itself from others. 使公司、组织或产品区别于其他公司、组织或产品的方法。
brand awareness 品牌意识	The buyer's ability to identify (recognize or recall) the brand within the category in sufficient detail to make a purchase. 在一类具有足够信息的产品中购买者能确认出(回想起)某种品牌的产品并购买它。
brand equity 品牌价值	The values of a brand to an organization, including customer loyalty toward the brand, the brand's name awareness, perceived quality, and brand associations. 品牌对组织的价值,包括消费者对品牌的忠诚,品牌名称的知名度,消费者对品牌的质量评价以及品牌联想等。
brand image 品牌形象	Generally speaking, this expresses the total personality of a company or product. It is this, rather than any trivial technical differences, which determines a product's position in the market. Brand identity is concerned with how a company presents the brand to its market. Brand image is how that market perceives the brand identity. 一般来说,这表达了一个公司或产品的全部个性。正是这一点,而不是任何微不足道的技术差异,决定了产品的市场定位。品牌身份与公司在市场中展示其品牌相关。品牌形象是反映市场对品牌身份的认知方式。
differentiation 差异化	A unique feature or characteristic that sets a firm or product apart from others and can be used to gain competitive advantages. 一种把企业或产品与其他企业或产品区分开来的特有的特征或特性,可以形成竞争优势。
added value 附加价值	On the basis of the original value of the product, the new value created through effective labor in the production process, that is, the new value added on the original value of the product. The realization of the added value lies in the connection through effective marketing means. 是在产品的原有价值的基础上,通过生产过程中的有效劳动新创造的价值,即附加在产品原有价值上的新价值,附加值的实现在于通过有效的营销手段进行联接。
market share 市场份额	This refers to the proportion of the sales volume (or sales volume) of a certain product (or category) in the market of similar products (or category). 指某企业某一产品(或品类)的销售量(或销售额)在市场同类产品(或品类)中所占比重。
brand strategy 品牌战略	An enterprise management strategy that the company regards the brand as the core competitive power in order to obtain the differential profit and value 公司将品牌作为核心竞争力,以获取差别利润与价值的企业经营战略。

Continued

parent brand 母品牌	A commercial structure that unifies all divisions, products or services at a company under a parent brand to establish its distinctive personality as a value added. 将一个公司的所有部门、产品或服务统一在一个母公司品牌下的商业结构，以建立其独特的个性作为一种增值方式。
company brand 公司品牌	The company uses the corporate name as the focus for all external communications, through advertising, products and letterheads. 公司通过在广告、产品和信笺中使用公司名称作为所有外部交流的焦点。
individual brand 个人品牌	The company behind the brand maintains a low corporate profile with respect to customers and focuses on the creation of strong brand identities. 品牌背后的公司对客户保持着低调的企业形象，专注于创建强大的品牌形象。
brand positioning 品牌定位	The creation, maintenance and development of the concept of a brand, in the minds of its customers, vis-à-vis that of its competitors. Some motor vehicle brands, for example, may be perceived as good value for money. Others may be seen as expensive, have never been anything else, and are never likely to be. Individual brands of margarine, virtually identical in composition, can be perceived by positioning in different ways: slimming, health-promoting, ideal for baking, convenient because easy to spread, indistinguishable from butter, and so on. 创造、维护和发展一个品牌的理念，在消费者心中与它的竞争对手相比。例如一些机动车品牌，可能被认为物有所值。其他的可能被视为昂贵，从来没有，也永远不可能被认为是物有所值。不同的独立品牌的人造黄油，有着几乎相同的成分，可以被不同定位：减肥、健康、适合烘焙、方便是因为容易涂抹，与黄油难以区分等。
brand property 品牌属性	Images, sounds, slogans, colours and other physical elements designed to carry a brand's imagery over from one advertising medium to another, one campaign to the next. The IBM logo is always blue, whatever the visual medium; hence the company has acquired the nickname Big Blue. Duracell batteries are copper-coloured, and the visuals are accompanied in television commercials by a distinctive sound effect. In its radio advertising, the sound effect is used so that it represents, and is linked to, the visual imagery of the television commercials and full-colour press advertisements. Music from the opera *Lakmé* is closely linked to British Airways, and may be considered its brand property. 从一种广告媒介到另一种广告媒介，从一项活动到另一项活动中使用的图像、声音、口号、颜色和其他物理元素的设计承载品牌的形象。无论视觉媒体是什么，IBM 的标识都是蓝色的；因此，公司获得了"蓝色巨人"的绰号。金霸王电池是铜色的，而在电视广告中，这些视觉效果还伴随着电视广告独特的音响效果。在它的广播广告中，音响效果是用来使它表示并连接到电视广告和广告的视觉形象全色媒体广告。歌剧《拉克美》中的音乐与英国航空公司有着密切的联系，并可能被认为是其品牌属性。
brand personality 品牌个性	Specific "personality-type" traits or characteristics ascribed by consumers to different brands. 消费者归属给不同品牌的具体个性特征或特性。

Continued

brand subculture 品牌亚文化	A strong attitude and commitment in the deterministic explanation, which describes the core member of the brand subculture who will refuse to buy an alternative if their favourite brand is not in stock. 在确定性解释中的一种强烈的态度和承诺,它描述了当他们最喜欢的品牌没有存货时,品牌亚文化的核心成员会拒绝购买替代品。
brand community 品牌社区	A brand community is a community formed on the basis of attachment to a brand or marque. 品牌社区是基于对品牌或品牌的依赖而形成的社区。
brand tribe 品牌部落	A brand tribe could be regarded as a group of people who collectively identify themselves with the product and share similar views and notions about the brand. They are not just consumers of the product, but play a major role in its promotion. 品牌部落可以被看作是一群人,他们共同认同某一产品,并对品牌有相似的看法和观念。他们不仅是产品的消费者,而且在产品的推广中起着重要的作用。
brand loyalty 品牌忠诚度	The consumer's conscious or unconscious decision-expressed through intention or behavior—to repurchase a brand continually. This occurs because the consumer perceives that the brand has the right product features, image, quality, or relationship at the right price. 消费者有意识或无意识重复购买某种品牌。品牌忠诚度源于消费者认为这种产品具有合适的产品特性、形象、质量或合适的价格。

Review & Critical Thinking Questions

1. Summarize the key differences in the explanation of branding from a cognitive point of view.

2. What are the relations between brand communities, brand subcultures and brand tribes?

3. What are the differences between reference groups and referent systems?

4. Can anything be branded?

5. How should a brand like Apple seek to work with the cult?

6. To what extent can a brand rely solely on advertising to boost its fortunes?

7. Compare the different presentations of format.

8. Give an example of a brand subculture and analyze its features.

9. What can a company do to maintain its customer loyalty?

Discussion Questions

1. What are the basic elements of a brand?
2. Mike Meldrum, a British marketing expert claims that a brand is the result of the blending of sensory, rational and perceptual elements, to what extent do you agree or disagree?
3. What is the relation between a product brand and a company brand?
4. Why is it believed that the success of a branded product is not equal to that of the brand in the market?
5. Is the brand subculture always a good thing? Why or why not?

Case Study

Brand Cult: Who Needs Enemies?

The idea of a cult has connotations of religion and even fanaticism. The creation of a fanatical band of loyal customers might seem to be the dream of every marketing executive. But there is another side to the story. First there is the bizarre. For example, Wells describes a ceremony where a priest "marries" a group of devoted Mazda Miata owners to their cars. She follows through by suggesting: "If a person can come to believe that they are genuinely in love with a product, then what happens when the 'love' is not reciprocated?"

Brady et al. describe the case of a self-professed Apple junkie called Niestat who was building his film career using Apple computers and software. When he and his brother discovered that the original iPod's batteries were irreplaceable, they made a film called "iPod's Dirty Secret" and launched a protest website that received 1.4m hits. They argued that they made the film because they believed in the brand so much. Brady makes the point that such loyalty flies in the face of conventional marketing wisdom. Customers demand love rather than simple reliability and want their brands to be a form of self-expression. The senior vice-president of strategic marketing at Samsung is quoted in the article as saying "Consumers are empowered in a way that is almost frightening."

Always there have been cult brands that have a set of 'true' believers. Even in the relatively homespun UK brands such as Guinness, Heinz and HP sauce have raised their heads above the pack. Brady and her colleagues argue that, alongside the iPod, such a band of believers helped Apple to rise almost 24 per cent to $6.9bn (£3.8bn). One problem with this band is that they are not necessarily easy to control. Brand fanaticism can be dangerous, as the Niesdat case described above illustrates. No doubt Steve Jobs of Apple has the occasional sleepless night when he recalls the good old days of the early 1980s when Apple announced the original MacIntosh with the most stunning advertisement ever made. Just one year later, the stock price of Apple fell to ＄14 (from ＄63 in 1983). The cult status of the brand perhaps led Jobs to believe that he could control everything from the design of the hardware to the software. In contrast IBM allowed anyone to clone their system and consequently IBM, and its Windows platform that had been developed by a fledgling company called Microsoft, rapidly took the lead over Apple. Since Jobs's return to Apple in 1997 he has been helped by the same loyal band of Apple devotees—over 85,000 annually attend the MacWorld Expo in San Fransisco. While welcoming the innovative launches of the iMac, G5, iPod and iTunes, devotees were not so welcoming of Apple's deal with Intel in 2005.

Questions

1. What are the characteristics of a brand cult?
2. Is there a brand cult of any Chinese brand? If so, please cite an example to illustrate.

中文概述

在最广泛的意义上,**品牌**已经与财产联系在一起。但是,在现代,品牌的概念已经有了一个更加积极的变化,商品品牌的发展在 20 世纪早期提供保护并治愈自我的作用。

品牌化可以为企业或个人带来很多收益,具体有:(1)保护,品牌的标志及品牌的其他方面构成了法律意义,受到法律保护。(2)财产,商标是一种速记的手段,因为用它可以很容易识别一个东西属于什么人,以及这个人独有的权利。(3)差异化,品牌应该提供一个独特的主张,这意味着把客户拉到品牌面前可能带来的收益。(4)增值,对于品牌上瘾的消费者,如果营销人员可以通过诱导他或她依赖这个品牌,并不断地要求获得这个品牌,那么这个品牌就可能会比那些声称服务于相同核心需求的品牌要求更高的价格。(5)品牌价值,即品牌对组织的价值,包括消费者对品牌的忠诚、品牌名称的知名度、消费者对品牌的质量评价以及品牌联想等。(6)市场份额,当一家公司购买一个品牌的时候,它实际上是购买这个品牌的市场份额。

公司必须要根据自身的品牌战略做出大量的决策。品牌采用的形式简单来说有以下三类:(1)**公司品牌**,即公司通过在广告、产品和信笺中使用公司名称作为所有外部交流的焦点;(2)**个人品牌**,即品牌背后的公司对客户保持着低调的企业形象,专注于创建强大的品牌形象;(3)混合式,也称为**背书品牌**,即背书人的品牌架构是由个别和独特的产品品牌组成,这些品牌由背书的母品牌连接在一起。背书的母品牌起着支撑和链接的作用,背书人的品牌架构在很多方面都可以看作是子品牌架构的倒置。

建立品牌包含8个步骤:(1)品牌定位,品牌的价值是什么? 它在顾客心中的地位是什么? 它和其他的有什么不同?(2)差距分析,根据 SWOT 分析,是否有机会进行品牌扩展,例如在品牌保护伞下增加额外的产品,或者这些行为可能会稀释品牌?(3)开发品牌属性,品牌属性是一种"独特的、令人难忘的、与该品牌密不可分的元素"。从一种广告媒介到另一种广告媒介,从一项活动到另一项活动中使用的图像、声音、口号、颜色和其他物理元素的设计承载品牌的形象。(4)品牌主张测试,一旦制定出来,品牌主张可能会在目标细分市场的一小群客户中进行测试,记录他们的反应,提出建议并实施变更。(5)做决定是否实施行动。(6)制定实施计划,这涉及对与品牌相关的4Ps 的考虑。所有这些决定将遵从"品牌属性"的概念和已确定的品牌目标市场细分。(7)实施计划。(8)监督计划的实施,回到最初,确定品牌定位。

品牌化的主流观点

品牌一致,品牌一致和认知信息处理系统(CIP)相关,即人们在对待人和事的态度上寻求平衡或一致性。消费者倾向于使用某一特定品牌,因为他们认为自己与被认为使用该品牌的人相似。

品牌个性,指消费者归属给不同品牌的具体个性特征或特性。虽然品牌在满足相似需求方面可能在功能上是相似的,但品牌个性使消费者能够选择最能表达自己个性的品牌。因此,即使品牌可能是相似的,那些表达清楚和有效的个性的品牌应该导致更高的偏好和增加市场份额。

品牌生活体验,弗洛伊德的理论认为,在人生的某个阶段,身份问题对我们来说变得很重要。在一个人从家庭环境走向学校和不断扩大的社会环境时,参照群体的概念对身份的构建起着关键作用。这就把我们感到舒服的"内群体"和我们想要避免的"外群体",以及我们想要归属的"外群体"区分开来。在消费社会中,品牌可以在区分"内部"群体和"外部"群体方面发挥关键作用。

媒介化品牌体验,虽然生活经验是在此时此地,但媒体产品的消费包括体验那些在空间和时间上远离日常生活实际背景的事件的能力。个人从中介经验中吸取经验,并将其与生活经验交织在一起构建自我。

品牌分类:品牌亚文化、品牌社区和品牌部落。

品牌亚文化指的是在确定性解释中的一种强烈的态度和承诺,它描述了当他们最喜欢的品牌没有存货时,品牌亚文化的核心成员会拒绝购买替代品。

品牌社区,指的是共同喜爱某品牌消费品或服务的消费群体。一个品牌社区具有以下三大特征:(1)共同的种类意识;(2)共同的仪式和传统;(3)对整个社区的道德责任感或义务感。

品牌部落,品牌部落可以被看作是一群人,他们共同认同某一产品,并对品牌有相似的看法和观念。他们不仅是产品的消费者,而且在产品的推广中起着重要的作用。

品牌忠诚度,即消费者有意识或无意识重复购买某种品牌。品牌忠诚度源于消费者认为这种产品具有合适的产品特性、形象、质量或合适的价格。关于品牌忠诚度的研究发现品牌忠诚度具有以下特点:(1)主流观点强调广告的说服作用,通过 USP 和 AIDA 的办法让人们在购买之前就渴望这个品牌;(2)相对而言,很少有购买者在一段时间内完全忠于某个品牌;(3)大多数消费者并不忠实于一个品牌,而是从为数不多的可用品牌中购买多个品牌;(4)一个产品类别中的大多数品牌都是可替代的,因为它们在配方和功能方面是相似的;(5)对于拥有相似市场份额的品牌来说,重复购买忠诚度往往是相似的;(6)存在"瞬时"品牌忠诚度;(7)不同品牌的用户在态度上没有真正的差异。

UNIT 12 / The Marketing Mix

Learning Objectives

1. Understand the classifications of products.
2. Know the classifications of products.
3. Discuss the ways in which firms set prices for the first time.
4. Distinguish between different contact techniques, such as advertising, direct marketing. personal selling, sales promotions, publicity and sponsorship.
5. Learn the developments taking place within the channels of distribution-VMS & HMS.
6. Study the factors related to the channel intermediaries such as sales agents, distributors, wholesalers and retailers.

12.1　Introduction

Managing the marketing mix is the central task of marketing professionals. The marketing mix is the set of marketing tools—often summarized as the "four Ps": the product, price, promotion and place—that the firm uses to achieve its objectives in its target market.

The central assumption is that if marketing professionals make and implement the right decisions about the features of the product, its price, and how it will be promoted and distributed, then the business will be successful.

In line with the new concept of value-based management, we define the objective of marketing as the development and implementation of a marketing mix that maximizes shareholder value. This definition has two advantages. First, it aligns marketing decision-making to the goals of the board and top management. The board is not interested in sales or market share per se, but rather with marketing strategies that will enhance the company's value. Corporate value is determined by the discounted sum of all future free cash flows. Second, the shareholder value provides rational and unambiguous criteria for determining the marketing mix. The "right" marketing mix is the one that maximizes shareholder value.

12.2 Product

12.2.1 What Is a Product?

- The product is at the heart of the marketing exchange.

If the product fails to deliver to customer expectations then all has been in vain. A product is a complex entity consisting of a number of overlapping layers. The basic anatomy of a product may be represented as a series of four bands representing the core product, the tangible product, the augmented product and the potential product.

- The core product represents the central meaning of the product and conveys its essence.

This is centrally related to the key benefits expected by customers. For example, in considering a holiday some people like to "get away from it all" to relax; others want to "have a ball". Each of these benefits could become core products for a holiday company.

- The tangible product is related to the core product to the extent that it places flesh on the bones of the former. For the holiday described above, this would involve the way in which the holiday was designed to suit customer requirements; including the activities, accommodation, transport arrangements and the brochure.

- The augmented product includes those add-on extras which are not an intrinsic part of the product but which may be used to enhance the product benefits. For the holiday company such extras might include the placement of a bottle of champagne and roses in the hotel room for those who seek to get away from it all.

- While the first three layers describe how the product is now, the potential product constitutes a vision of what it could be in the future. By considering the potential product the marketer is trying to ensure that continuous improvement is at the heart of the process. This is embodied in the question "How can we improve this, how can we do it even better?"

12.2.2 Classifications of Products

Products can be sorted into a number of classifications.

In the past, the threefold classification convenience, shopping and specialty products was used. The idea is that consumers behave in different ways when purchasing convenience products (relatively inexpensive and frequently purchased goods) compared with shopping products (durables such as stereos, bicycles and furniture). Specialty products possess a single unique characteristic on which buyers are willing to expend a considerable amount of effort to obtain, e.g. a Cartier watch.

1. Convenience Products

Convenience products correspond with the routine response buying situation; the buyer puts little effort into the purchasing situation and convenience takes precedence over brand loyalty. The marketing implications for convenience products are similar to those for low-involvement products.

2. Shopping Products

By contrast to convenience products, shopping products represent something of a risk to the purchaser and so the consumer is likely to be more active in searching out information and evaluating them. Specialist sources and friends are likely to be consulted. The classification of a product into this category depends on the individual consumer's perception of the importance and complexity of the purchase; one person's convenience good could be another person's shopping good or specialty good. The implications for marketers are that they should focus on all items of the marketing mix and not just on the product. The mass distribution strategies of the convenience marketer may no longer be appropriate. So, for example, in buying a camera it is likely that the consumer will visit specialist retailers to see what they have available and may well visit more than one source to judge between different offerings. As customers are likely to consult specialist publications and ask friends who may be camera enthusiasts for their opinions on different cameras, it is important to promote the camera to specialist magazines, perhaps by sending out demonstration samples which can be evaluated by staff. The camera manufacturer would be advised to brief sales staff in retail outlets. This could be achieved by means of briefing notes to sales specialists.

3. Specialty Products

These products are what have come to be called "high-involvement" and "complex" products. While shopping products could be said to be high in involvement, this is qualitatively different in that the perceived risk is high and the product is infrequently purchased. It should be noted that the classification of which products are specialty products is in the hands of the consumer. For some consumers the camera example used above could qualify as a specialty product.

▶ 12.2.3   Understanding of the Product Range

Most organizations offer a range of different products. The product mix is the total sum of all the products and variants of products which are offered by a firm. The product mix for a company such as Procter & Gamble (P&G) might consist of the following lines and items. The product mix may be divided into a number of product lines. A product line is a group of products that are closely related to each other. For example, a clothing company might arrange its mix into shirts, coats and jeans to reflect the particular production requirements and problems for each line. On the other hand, a company might organize the product mix according to market requirements or a mixture of production and market requirements. For example, Michelin has a tripartite product organization into tyres, maps and restaurant rating services. While only a limited number of the actual lines offered by P&G is shown in Figure 12.1, this example helps to illustrate concepts such as the product, mix-width, length, depth and consistency.

The product mix-width refers to how many different product lines the company carries. In the simple example shown above, the width of the mix is four (although other lines such as household cleaning products, disposable nappies, etc., could be added).

A product line consists of a number of product items. These are the individual products or brands, each with its own features and price.

Product line length refers to the number of items within the product line. According to Figure 12.1, Crest has a length of one item. Product line depth refers to the number of variants of each item within the product line. A deep product may have many different variants. For example, if Crest came in three sizes and two formulations (regular and mint) then Crest would have a depth of six items.

The consistency of the product mix refers to how closely related various product lines are according to the criteria devised by management. For example, P&G's lines are consistent to the extent that they go through the same distribution channels to the final consumer. The lines are not so consistent when their end use is considered.

Detergents	Toothpaste	Bar soap	Hair care	
Dreft	Crest	Ivory	Head & Shoulders	Product line
Bold		Camay	Vidal Sasson	
Ariel		Oil of Olay	Pantene Pro-V	
Daz				

Length product mix width

Figure 12.1   The Product Mix, Procter & Gamble

The definitions of product mix-width, depth, and consistency create a common vocabulary with reference to a particular set of products which allows the marketer to analyze the mix and to take strategic actions such as to build, maintain, harvest or divest product items or lines. The product line manager needs to know the percentage of sales and profits contributed by each item in the line so that she can decide whether or not to maintain this item. Another task for the product line manager is in deciding whether or not to lengthen a product line by adding products or to deepen existing products by offering more variants.

12.3 Pricing

12.3.1 Introduction

The price of a product or service will determine how consumers perceive it, reflect on its brand positioning, influence the choice of marketing channel, affect how it is promoted and have an impact on the level of customer service expected by target customers. The price ingredient of the marketing mix will also affect the viability of the supplying organization. The concept of pricing is complex and of fundamental importance to the successful implementation of a marketing strategy.

Pricing is one of the most important elements of the marketing mix, as it affects profit, volume and share of the market and consumer perceptions. Just as pricing plays a crucial role in determining brand image, increasingly companies are being judged on the transparency and equity with which they treat price as a marketing variable.

Generally, it is acknowledged that pricing decisions are the most difficult to make because of the complexity of the interaction between three groups involved in the marketing process: consumers, the trade, and competitors. In addition, pricing decisions often have to be made quickly and with limited, or even no, test marketing. They almost invariably have a direct effect on profit.

Among consumers, price is the principal determinant of choice. Its significance is further emphasized by price being the only element among the four marketing mix components that generates revenue—the others produce costs.

Pricing decisions run the risk of emerging largely as a result of habit rather than of detailed strategic thinking. The haphazard approach to pricing is compounded by the ways in which responsibility for setting prices is allocated within many firms. It is standard practice for pricing decisions to be made by senior management rather than sales and marketing staff who are likely to be closer to the end consumer.

12.3.2 Pricing Objectives

Prices should relate to the objectives of the firm. The price needs to be weighed against the impact on the firm's other products, the need for short-term profits against longer-term market position, and "skimming" as opposed to "penetration" objectives. For example, in launching a new product, a company may decide that, as it is the first to market, there will be little competition and so it will be able to "skim" the market by charging a relatively high price. Alternatively, it may decide to enter the market at a relatively low price so as to gain a high market share before competitors enter. This, in turn, will allow the firm to benefit from experience curve effects. Each decision rests on different sets of assumptions made by planners. On the other hand, pricing may be geared towards earning a particular rate of return on funds invested or, indeed, on making a profit on the product range as a whole. In the latter case a strategy involving "loss leaders" may be used whereby products are sold below their cost of production to encourage purchases of other more profitable products.

As with objectives in any area of management, pricing objectives must be clearly defined, time-specific and consistent with each other. The four types of objectives that pricing decisions can help achieve are:

- income-related. How much money can be made?
- volume-related. How many units can be sold?
- competition-related. What share of the available business is wanted?
- societal. What are the responsibilities to customers and society as a whole?

12.3.3　Setting a Price

The various pricing approaches that are available to the marketer include: cost-based pricing; target return on investment pricing; demand-based pricing; competition-oriented pricing.

1. Cost-based Pricing

In setting a price it is advisable to cover all relevant costs. Costs for this purpose may be divided into two categories, fixed and variable costs. Taken together with price, these may be used to calculate the break-even quantity (fixed costs divided by price less variable cost per unit).

Cost-oriented pricing is the most elementary pricing method. It involves the calculation of all the costs that can be attributed to a product, whether variable or fixed, and then adding to this figure a desirable mark-up, as determined by management.

The simplicity of this method is that it requires no other effort beyond consulting the accounting or financial records of the firm. There is no necessity to study market demand, consider competition, or look into other factors that may have a bearing on price. Cost is considered the most important determinant in the firm's pricing effort, which is then directed towards covering these costs and realizing the desired profitability.

Cost-plus pricing is popular among many retailers and wholesalers. For example, in the case of retailers, the purchase price of the product is added to the product's share of the operating expenses and a desirable margin, determined by the type of product under consideration, is then added to determine the selling price.

2. Target Return on Investment Pricing

This is similar to cost-plus pricing as it assumes that costs can be known or estimated with enough accuracy to feature in the calculation of price. Target pricing, which looks for long-run average rates of return, is one method of cost pricing, used especially when fixed costs at launch are high. Among those who have used this in the past have been the privatized utilities and, in the US, General Electric and General Motors. The calculation is straightforward:

$$\frac{\text{Price to meet}}{\text{return on investment (ROI)}} = \text{Unit cost} + \frac{\text{Target percentage return} \times \text{Capital invested target}}{\text{Unit sales}}$$

This approach to pricing is prone to the same difficulties as any cost-based approach, but it has the advantage of forcing consideration of whether a proposed price is feasible from a purely commercial point of view.

3. Demand-based Pricing

Demand-based pricing looks outwards from the production line and focuses on customers and their responsiveness to different price levels. Even this approach may be insufficient on its own, but when it is linked with competition-based pricing, it provides a powerful market-oriented perspective that cost-based methods ignore.

Demand-based pricing allows the price to go up when demand is strong and, vice versa, for the price to go down when demand is weak. Examples of demand-based pricing can be found within the package holiday industry where prices are highest during the school summer holidays and in the travel industry where prices vary according to the level of demand, e.g. highest during the morning rush hour and cheapest during off-peak times.

This method requires decision makers to make volume forecasts for different price levels and calculations of production and marketing costs at different levels to cover overheads. In setting a price information has to be obtained about demand factors, e.g. the price elasticity of demand. This is calculated by estimating the percentage change in quantity demanded over the percentage change in price. By gaining knowledge of demand factors the marketer helps avoid the potentially disastrous mistake of focusing too much on costs. Typically, this involves estimating likely demand at different prices; estimating what happens to cost as demand rises; estimating the likely effects of raising or lowering price.

4. Competition Oriented Pricing

This method involves setting prices on the basis of what competitors are charging. Once the firm identifies its competitors, it conducts a competitive evaluation of its product. Competitive factors that must be considered include:

- The "market price" charged by the market leader.
- Price sensitivity.
- Market position.
- Product differentiation.
- The type of competition, i.e. whether this is monopoly or oligopoly.

In assuming how a competitor might react to a price move, several factors need to be considered. These include：

- The competitor's cost structure.
- Past price behaviour.
- Market demand.
- The relationship of the product to others in the competitor's line.
- Plant utilization.

12.4　Promotion

12.4.1　The Marketing Communications Process

The aim of this section is to relate this to the context of marketing communications.

1. Organization Source

In marketing communications the organizational source is much more complex than the simple hypodermic model implies. Only a minority of organizations deals with all their marketing communications in-house and even then often these functions are found scattered in various parts of the organization. Marketing communications bring together a range of marketing functions, including marketing strategists, category and brand management, market analysts and researchers, information managers, media relations specialists, media buyers and creatives. In practice, many of these roles are contracted out, with people in the organization acting as clients for those agencies who provide the service. It is common to contract out marketing research, advertising, public relations and direct marketing services, as these are expensive services to build and maintain in-house and as there is a fiercely competitive market place for them. The organizational source is composed of a complex web of relations between a number of parties.

2. Marketing Channels

(1) Above and Below-the-line Communications

Marketing channels represent the range of media available to move the message from source to addressee. It is difficult to measure the volume of many of these channels, e.g. production of "Guinness" T-shirts will be known only to Guinness and to the company which manufactures them. Similarly, promotional literature including brochures, handbooks, leaflets and "give-aways" must be regarded as being "below the line" in that there is no public record or measurement of the cost of the medium.

Detailed records are maintained of all television, press, cinema, and poster advertising, which is known as "above the line" communication because it is measurable.

In general, national and regional newspapers and consumer and business magazines have experienced a relative decline in the UK during the 1990s and into the 2000s. By contrast television increased its share of the total expenditure and outdoor advertising and radio advertising also increased from a low initial base. In the 2000s the relative share of television advertising has declined as advertisers have looked to most cost-effective promotional expenditure.

(2) Fragmentation of the Media

One factor which is of major concern to marketers is the continuing fragmentation of broadcast media, usually related to radio and television. There has been a substantial increase in the number of channels offered as the result of satellite, cable and digital technology. For example, in the UK, consumers up to the late 1990s had access to five main television channels, which with digital television are estimated to rise to several hundred channels. According to some commentators this means that the audience is much more widely dispersed, which makes life trickier for advertisers. However, if "broadcast media" is taken to mean the entire range of media, it is almost impossible to find anything which is not a medium, e.g. T-shirts, cars, billboards, carpets and walls are all used as media. In sporting activities marketing communications are found not only on the conventional advertising hoardings but on the products (footballs, tennis rackets), the players and their apparel, the fans and even on the pitch.

12.4.2　Planning Marketing Communications Campaigns

In this section an overview is provided of the marketing communications planning process, sketching out how an integrated communications campaign might be pieced together.

1. Constructing the Message

Before preparing a specific message the marketing communicator should be aware of the communications platform which forms the basis for the campaign. The communications platform is vitally important, as it is through this that the message, a "tone of voice" to the consumer, is created. If a brand is involved then the communications platform is the means by which brand values are related to customer values. Brand values are not static but must move with the times.

2. Choice of Contact Mix

Contact refers to the manner in which the addressees are to be approached and the kind of message which will be used to appeal to them. Often contact is referred to as a sort of menu including advertising, direct marketing, personal selling, sales promotions, publicity and sponsorship. In many ways this is a mistake, as it reinforces the view that communications planning is mechanistic and formulaic and does not involve the creative intelligence of the planner. Nothing could be further from the truth. Here are some thumbnail descriptions of the various methods, some of which are developed in more detail later.

(1) Advertising

Advertising refers to a paid form of non-personal communication about an organization and its products that is transmitted to a target population through a mass medium. Traditional mass media include television, newspapers, radio, posters, transport and outdoor displays. In the UK precise estimates of expenditure on advertising by brand are calculated by Media Expenditure Analysis (MEAL). The creation of a media plan is central to managing contact in advertising.

(2) Direct Marketing

Direct marketing has evolved out of the direct mail industry and incorporates telephone selling and email. Often direct marketing is used as a pre-sell technique prior to a sales call, to qualify prospects for a sales call, to generate orders and to follow up a sale. Direct marketing requires good database management techniques, as errors can create much bad feeling, e.g. the misspelling of a name or the inclusion of the name of someone who is deceased. In the UK, direct marketing is still used as a crude weapon to engineer sales by double-glazing companies, financial institutions and charities. Sales promotion. Sales promotion offers some form of incentive to purchase a product. Marketers devise sales promotions to produce immediate sales increases, e.g. by means of "two for one" offers and competitions. Supermarkets have used loyalty cards to award extra points to products which they are promoting.

(3) Personal Selling

Personal selling is the process of informing customers and persuading them to purchase products through personal communication. Millions of people are involved in a wide variety of selling roles in retailing, trade, technical support and field operations among others. The cost of training and maintaining a sales force depends on the type of sales operation. However, it is far from inexpensive. Personal selling is considered to be more appropriate to B-to-B marketing, where there are fewer customers and there is a higher volume of transactions than in consumer markets.

(4) Sponsorship

Sponsorship is an indirect form of communication as it involves financing or supporting an activity which usually is unrelated to the business environment, such as sports or the arts, which are regarded as worthy by the target group. For some, such as cigarette companies, sponsorship has provided a convenient means for working around the UK ban on television advertising. The benefits accrue by means of association. For example, if one pairs images of cigarettes with images of various sporting events, a link may be created between cigarettes and sport. Sponsorship has gone beyond its traditional boundaries; well-known television programmes and even educational institutions are sponsored.

(5) Publicity

Publicity refers to the link between marketing and public relations. Where marketing and public relations are integrated within a company then public relations personnel will ensure that journalists are briefed and may even be invited to the launch of a new car. For products such as cars, personal computers and digital cameras the opinions of panels of "experts" in specialist magazines are of great importance and so a large amount of effort is expended in seeking to ensure that they pass a favourable verdict on the product. Many people describe publicity as if it were free. It is not free to the extent that people must be employed to create the publicity. Furthermore, publicity can be a double-edged sword, which can work in favour of or against the product.

12.5   Place

12.5.1   Introduction

Products and services have to reach the customers to be consumed. In the early stages of trade, it is possible for producers and their customers to meet face-to-face to exchange goods and services as in the situation where the farmer takes the produce to the local market. However, when trade becomes more sophisticated, the services of various intermediaries along the supply chain may need to be used to ensure that the goods or services reach the consumer in the right manner at the right place, time and price. It is the process of moving goods and services through these intermediaries to reach the end user that will be discussed in this module.

The channels of distribution used within the market place have evolved to match the needs of the users of these services and they continue to be adapted to meet those needs. The objective is to move the goods or services efficiently, with the lowest possible number of intermediaries between the producer and the end user. Ideally, the producer aims to exchange the products directly with the consumer. However, as the physical distance between the two parties and the volume of goods to be exchanged increases, it becomes necessary for producers to use the help of others to complete the movement of the goods associated with the transaction. These are the intermediaries within the channels of distribution, or alternatively coined the "value chain". This is particularly the situation for producers supplying the consumer mass market, where it becomes impracticable to exchange products directly between the producer and the consumer.

▶ 12.5.2　The Structure of Channels of Distribution

The channels of distribution used to move products to the consumer vary according to the nature of customers, products and manufacturers of the products or services concerned. They are influenced by the characteristics of the environment in which the marketing is taking place. Furthermore, different channel routes may be used by the same organization to target different markets or market segments. An outline of the types of channels and the intermediaries that are available is shown in Figure 12.2.

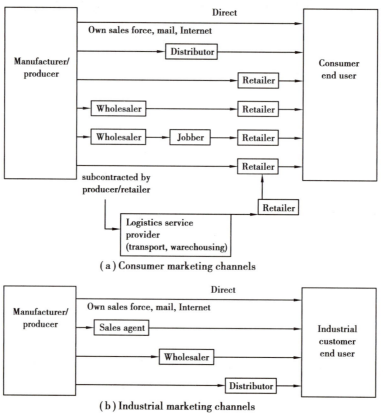

(a) Consumer marketing channels

(b) Industrial marketing channels

Figure 12.2　Consumer and Industrial Channels of Distribution

Within consumer markets, manufacturers distribute their products directly to the customer using their own sales forces, sales agents, direct mail/mail order, or even the Internet, to communicate with the consumer.

▶ 12.5.3　Intermediaries Within Channels of Distribution

As discussed above, the main types of intermediaries used within the channels of distribution are: sales agents; distributors; wholesalers; retailers; franchising.

1. Sales Agents

These are intermediaries who are paid by commission on the sales they achieve. Sales agents do not receive regular employee salaries and associated benefits and, consequently, their commission rates are usually higher, typically between 3% and 10% of sales, than commissions given to sales forces. Sales agents do not hold stock. They do not take ownership of the stock prior to its being delivered to the customer. Sales agents may operate for a number of clients and usually will cover complementary product ranges rather than competing products or services. However, manufacturers can have problems controlling the sales efforts of sales agents, who may have conflicting loyalties.

2. Distributors

These are sales intermediaries who share willingness to hold stock. Usually, distributors are linked to a single supplier for each line carried. For example, in the car industry, Ford has a network of distributors (or dealers) that provide showrooms (and salesmen) as well as car servicing dedicated to the Ford range of cars. The manufacturer contributes to the costs associated with the running of the dealership. However, such distributor agreements are becoming less rigorously maintained, so that some distributors are beginning to carry cars for more than one car manufacturer, which inevitably leads to conflicts of interests for all concerned.

3. Wholesalers

Traditionally wholesalers have been used to service the mass markets, taking manufacturers' production and breaking it down into smaller volumes ("break-bulk") to service retailers who, in turn, supplied individual consumers. Wholesalers carried large volumes of stock and supplied smaller volumes to retailers. Usually wholesalers concent-rated on providing a range of competing brands of similar types of products, e.g. foodstuffs, fashion clothing and building materials. Normally wholesalers did not deal with the end customer.

However, in the UK and elsewhere, since the 1980s, the role of wholesalers has changed. Wholesalers have faced increasing pressures, especially from the major retailers that have taken over wholesaler services within their own traditional services. Wholesalers, like the other intermediaries, have had to adapt their services to the changing market circumstances. Some wholesalers providing consumer goods and food-related products have become cash-and-carry organizations servicing the higher sales volume customer, e.g. Makro, the Dutch world leader, with over 130 stores operating across Europe, South America and the Far East. Usually, in such cases, the stores are large warehouses, one-storey buildings with extensive car parks; customers are mainly owners of small businesses such as restaurants and independent shops.

4. Retailers

Retailers undertake the final link within the channel of distribution. They effect the sale of the goods, or services, to the customer. The other intermediaries between the producer and consumer work towards supporting the retailer so that goods are available in the right place and at the right time to match consumer demand.

5. Franchising

Franchising has been defined as being "an arrangement whereby a supplier, or franchisor, grants a dealer, or franchisee, the right to sell products in exchange for some type of consideration, e.g. percentage of total sales in exchange for furnishing equipment, buildings management know-how, marketing assistance and branding to the franchisee". The intermediary agrees to follow certain procedures and not to buy from others, or to sell competing products or services.

Within the retail sector, franchising arrangements have become an increasingly important source of growth. In the US, franchising accounts for at least one-third of all retail sales. In 1995 the UK had over 750 companies involved in franchise operations which in themselves had 24 percent of UK retail sales volume.

Key Terms

convenience products 便利品	Refer to those types of consumer products and services that consumers buy more frequently with minimum buying efforts and comparisons. These types of purchases are also known as low involvement purchases. 指那些消费者花费最少的努力和比较就经常购买的产品和服务。这些类型的购买也被称为低介入度购买。
shopping products 选购品	Represent something of a risk to the purchaser and so the consumer is likely to be more active in searching out information and evaluating them. 对购买者来说代表了某种风险,因此消费者可能会更积极地搜索信息并对其进行评估。
specialty products 特殊品	What have come to be called "high-involvement" and "complex" products. "高介入"和"复杂"产品。
product mix 产品组合	The total sum of all the products and variants of products which are offered by a firm. 一个公司提供的所有产品和各种产品的总和。
product line 产品线	A group of products that are closely related to each other. 一组彼此紧密相关的产品。
pricing 定价	The act or an instance of setting a price for a product or service. 为产品或服务定价的行为或实例。

Continued

cost-based pricing 成本计价法	A process of setting the price as a result of adding a profit margin to the cost of the product/service. This pricing method guarantees that certain profit is obtained above total cost. 为产品/服务的成本增加利润而确定价格的过程。这种定价方法保证了一定的利润高于总成本。
fixed costs 固定成本	Those which do not vary with output in the short term. 那些短期内不会随产出变化的成本。
variable costs 可变成本	Those which vary according to the quantity produced. 随着产品生产数量而变化的成本。
total cost 总成本	All the cost incurred by an organization in manufacturing, marketing, administering and delivering the product to the customer. 一个组织在制造、营销、管理和向客户交付产品时所产生的全部成本。
target return on investment pricing 目标投资回报定价法	A method wherein the firm determines the price on the basis of a target rate of return on the investment i.e. what the firm expects from the investments made in the venture. 公司根据投资的目标回报率确定价格的一种方法，即公司对投资的期望。
demand-based pricing 需求定价法	A pricing method based on the customer's demand and the perceived value of the product. In this method the customer's responsiveness to purchase the product at different prices is compared and then an acceptable price is set. 一种基于顾客需求和产品感知价值的定价方法。在这种方法中，顾客对不同价格购买产品的响应性被比较，然后确定一个可接受的价格。
competition-oriented pricing 竞争导向定价法	A pricing strategy that the company sets its price based on the price of the competitors. A company decides upon it prices based on the pricing of its present competitors. 公司根据竞争对手的价格来定价的定价策略。公司根据现有竞争对手的价格来决定商品价格。
promotion 促销	The publicization of a product, organization, or venture so as to increase sales or public awareness. 对产品、组织或企业的宣传，以增加销售量或提高公众意识。
advertising 广告业	The business of trying to persuade people to buy products or services. 说服人们购买产品或服务的业务。
direct marketing 直销	The business of selling products or services directly to the public, e.g. by mail order or telephone selling, rather than through retailers. 直接向公众销售产品或服务的业务，例如通过邮购或电话销售，而不是通过零售商。
personal selling 人员直销	The process of informing customers and persuading them to purchase products through personal communication. 通过个人沟通告知顾客并说服他们购买产品的过程。

Continued

sponsorship 赞助	An indirect form of communication as it involves financing or supporting an activity which usually is unrelated to the business environment, such as sports or the arts, which are regarded as worthy by the target group. 是一间接的沟通方式,因为它涉及资助或支持一项通常与商业环境无关的活动,例如被目标群体认为有价值的体育或艺术。
publicity 宣传	The giving out of information about a product, person, or company for advertising or promotional purposes. 为了广告或促销目的而披露有关产品、个人或公司的信息。
channels of distribution 分销渠道	The most efficient and effective manner in which a product is placed into the hands of the customer. The channel is composed of different institutions that facilitate the transaction and the physical exchange. 将产品送到顾客手中的最有效的方式。这一渠道由促进交易的不同机构和实物交易所组成。
sales agent 销售代理商	One who is authorized or appointed by a manufacturer to sell or distribute his products within a given territory but who is self-employed, takes title to the goods, and does not act as agent for a principal. 被制造商授权或指定在指定区域内销售或经销其产品的个体经营者,拥有商品所有权,不作为委托人的代理。
distributor 经销商	An agent who supplies goods to stores and other businesses that sell to consumers. 向商店和其他向消费者销售商品的企业供应商品的代理人。
wholesaler 批发商	A merchant middleman who sells chiefly to retailers, other merchants, or industrial, institutional, and commercial users mainly for resale or business use. 主要向零售商、其他商人或工业、机构和商业用户转售或商业使用的商人中间商。
retailer 零售商	A person or business that sells goods to the public in relatively small quantities for use or consumption rather than for resale. 向公众出售少量商品供使用或消费而不是转售的人或企业。
franchising 特许经营	Arrangement where one party (the franchiser) grants another party (the franchisee) the right to use its trademark or trade-name as well as certain business systems and processes, to produce and market a good or service according to certain specifications. 一方(特许人)授予另一方(被特许人)使用其商标或商号以及某些业务系统和流程的权利,以按照特定规格生产和销售某种商品或服务的安排。

Review & Critical Thinking Questions

1. Identify the product mix of an MNC and analyze its product line as well as its product mix-width.

2. What are the advantages and disadvantage of price penetration?

3. What are the potential risks in franchising?

4. What are the flaws of the theory of 4Ps marketing mix?

5. What are the relationships between pricing and the marketing mix?

6. What do you think will be the best pricing strategy for a newly-invented product such as the auto-driven car to enter the market?

Discussion questions

1. What is cost-plus pricing? Consider the advantages and disadvantages of the system.

2. Discuss the benefits of association with celebrity endorsements for clothing companies.

3. How are the channels of distribution used for consumer goods likely to differ from those used for industrial products?

4. Would you like to use franchise arrangements to expand the market if you are a manufacturer in the electric car industry? Why or why not?

Case Study

Car Price War Looms in China as Shanghai Volkswagen Cuts Prices

Volkswagen (VW) operates two joint ventures, FAW and Shanghai, in China. It is market leader, but with increasing competition from a growing number of MNCs, VW's market share in China fell from about 50% in 2003 to 15.7% in the first seven months of 2005. Indeed, in the first half of 2005 VW made an operating loss of € 23m (US $28.4m) compared with a profit of € 251m in 2004. For the full year of 2005 losses were expected. The joint ventures with FAW and Shanghai sales fell 31% and 49% respectively, according to *Automotive Resources Asia* .

In response to this situation, VW's strategy was to improve efficiency by merging the retail operation of the two joint venture partners, cutting costs and changing sourcing strategies. The Chinese expansion plans were postponed during the restructuring.

In what could be the beginning of a new price war, and as an attempt to maintain its position as the brand leader in China, in August 2005 Shanghai VW's made substantial price cuts of between 6% and 14% on its best-selling models such as the Santana and the Gol. This move could have encouraged other car makers to follow suit and reduce prices, given VW's important position in the market, although some price cutting had already been undertaken. Certainly, the price cuts emphasized the slump in margins that car makers were facing in China.

General Motors' joint venture also saw sales slip. The main gainers have been foreign rivals such as Hyundai and Honda and domestic car makers, including Dongfeng and Chery. Zhu Junyi, analyst at the Shanghai Information Centre, a government-backed consultancy, felt the move by VW was inevitable, as, compared with cars of the same category, VW's prices were fairly high because its labour costs were high. But another industry consultant in China considered VW needed to do something more radical than price cutting. It did not have enough new models. Its two joint ventures did not always work well together and they did not have a competitive cost structure.

It remains to be seen how and whether VW will be able to maintain its leadership in the potentially enormous Chinese market. Clearly, a change in its pricing strategy to cut prices sent mixed messages to customers as well as other competitors in the market for the market leader. Great care to assimilate the other elements of the marketing mix will have to be taken if the leader is not going to lose face in the apparent price downgrade.

Questions

1. Why did VW, a brand leader in China, decide to cut prices?
2. Besides price cutting, what other suggestions can you give to VW to maintain its leadership in China? Why?

中文概述

管理营销组合是营销专业人员的中心任务。**营销组合**是一套营销工具——通常被总结为"四个P":产品、价格、促销和地点——企业用来在目标市场实现其目标的手段。其核心假设是,如果营销专业人员对产品的特性、价格、推广和分销方式做出并实施了正确的决策,那么企业就会成功。根据价值管理的新理念,我们将市场营销的目标定义为开发和实施实现股东价值最大化的市场营销组合。

产品是由许多重叠层组成的复杂实体。产品的基本结构可以表示为四个层次,分别代表核心产品、有形产品、增强产品和潜在产品。按照消费者行为的不同,可将产品分为便利品、选购品、特殊品。**便利品**指那些消费者花费最少的努力和比较就经常购买的产品和服务。这些类型的购买也被称为低介入购买。**选购品**对购买者来说代表了某种风险,因此消费者可能会更积极地搜索信息并对其进行评估。**特殊品**指"高介入"和"复杂"产品。大多数组织提供一系列不同的产品。**产品组合**是公司提供的所有产品和各种产品的总和。**产品线**是指一组彼此紧密相关的产品。

定价指为产品或服务定价的行为或实例。一个产品或服务的价格将决定消费者对它的看法,反映它的品牌定位,影响营销渠道的选择,影响它的推广方式,并对目标客户期望的客户服务水平产生影响。营销组合中的价格成分也会影响供应组织的生存能力。在过去的二十年里,定价已经成为营销组合中一个越来越重要的因素,因为消费者对价格有了更高的敏感度。价格应与公司的目标相关联,如收入、销量、竞争(市场份额)和社会责任等。

市场营销人员可以使用的各种定价方法包括:成本计价法;目标投资回报定价法;竞争导向定价;目标投资回报定价。**成本计价法**是指为产品/服务的成本增加利润而确定价格的过程。这种定价方法保证了一定的利润高于总成本。常见的成本包括4大类:**固定成本**(那些短期内不会随产出变化的成本)、**可变成本**(随着产品生产数量而变化的成本)、**边际成本**(包括如果在生产总额中增加一个单位,对总成本产生的变化)、**总成本**(一个组织在制造、营销、管理和向客户交付产品时所产生的全部成本)。**目标投资回报定价法**是指公司根据投资的目标回报率确定价格的一种方法,即公司对投资的期望。**需求定价法**是指一种基于顾客需求和产品感知价值的定价方法。在这种方法中,顾客对不同价格购买产品的响应性被比较,然后确定一个可接受的价格。**竞争导向定价法**是公司根据竞争对手的价格来定价的定价策略。公司根据现有竞争对手的价格来决定商品价格。

促销是一种营销传播方式,是对产品、组织或企业的宣传,以增加销售量或提高公众意识。营销传播的范围是巨大的,包括所有广告、促销、人员销售、网络营销和媒体关系。任何形式的付费传播都可以被视为营销传播。营销传播的要素包括组织来源、营销渠道和听众。营销传播的流程包括构建信息和选择联络组合。常见的联络组合方式包括:广告、直销、人员销售、赞助和宣传。**广告**是指说服人们购买产品或服务的业务。**直销**是直接向公众销售产品或服务的业务,例如通过邮购或电话销售,而不是通过零售商。**人员销售**是通过个人沟通告知顾客并说服他们购买产品的过程。**赞助**是一种间接的沟通方式,因为它涉及资助或支持一项通常与商业环境无关的活动,例如被目标群体认为有价值的体育或艺术。**宣传**是为了广告或促销目的而传递有关产品、个人或公司的信息。

产品和服务必须到达顾客那里才能被消费。地点是指**分销渠道**,是指将产品送到顾客手中的最有效的方式,这一渠道由促进交易的不同机构和实物交易所组成,其目标是在生产者和最终用户之间以尽可能少的中间商有效地运输货物或服务。分销渠道因顾客、产品和有关产品或服务的制造商的性质而异。他们受到市场营销环境特征的影响。此外,同一组织可能会使用不同的渠道路线来针对不同的市场或细分市场。分销渠道内的中间商有以下几类:(1)**销售代理商**是指被制造商授权或指定在指定区域内销售或经销其产品的个体经营者,拥有商品所有权,不作为委托人的代理。(2)**经销商**是指向商店和其他向消费者销售商品的企业供应商品的代理人。(3)**批发商**是指主要向零售商、其他商人或工业、机构和商业用户转售或商业使用的商人中间商。(4)**零售商**是指向公众出售少量商品供使用或消费而不是转售的人或企业。(5)**特许经营**是指一方(特许人)授予另一方(被特许人)使用其商标或商号以及某些业务系统和流程的权利,以按照特定规格生产和销售某种商品或服务。

UNIT 13 · Internet Marketing and Social Media

Learning Objectives

1. Understand the meaning of Internet Marketing and its evolution with internet technology development.
2. Describe the worldwide social media landscape.
3. Identify the functions of social media in the marketing research process.
4. Understand the different factors affecting the use of social media.
5. Explain the preference on social media in different areas.
6. Discuss the emerging live streaming broadcasts in social networking marketing.

13.1 Internet Revolution and "Internet Plus" Action Plan

The Internet is the most significant invention for human beings to profoundly change the lifestyle on this planet as great evolution and revolution, especially in the context of globalization after the outbreak of COVID-19.

The Internet refers to the physical network that links computers and/or mobile devices across the globe since 1971. It consists of the infrastructure of network servers and wide-area communication links between them that are used to hold and transmit the vast amount of information through this information technology. World Wide Web (WWW) as the milestone of the Internet, was inspired by Tim Berners-Lee (a British scientist working at CERN in Switzerland) and applied commercially since 1993. WWW is an interlinked publishing medium for displaying graphic and text information which changed the Internet from a difficult-to-use tool for academics and technicians to an easy-to-use tool for finding information for businesses and consumers on various web pages; this was called "Web 1.0"; The term "Web 2.0" was popularized by Tim O'Reilly and Media Live International in 2004 as websites which emphasized user-generated content, ease of use, participatory culture and interoperability (i.e. compatible with other products, systems, and devices) for end users, also known as Participative (or Participatory) and Social Web. The internet evolution makes the possibility of digitization of human society and integrated with the social and economic advancement in the digital age. With the upgrades of new technologies such as 5G, the lifestyle and commercial activities are more relying on the Internet, especially after the novel coronavirus pandemic; meanwhile, the Internet has been forming brand new business ecosystems to change the traditional business modes and consumer behaviors as well, such as Virtual Economy, Wireless Business and Contactless Payment or Transaction.

1G—2G	3G—4G	5G and beyond
1980s—2000s Millions of voice users	—2020s Billions of Mobile Broadband users	—2040s Trillions of connected objects & intelligence

Figure 13.1　Wireless Connectivity Drives Major Societal Changes

Since 2015, China carries on an "Internet Plus" action plan aims to further promote the innovation between the Information and Communication Technology (ICT) industry and other traditional industries, by the integration of mobile internet, cloud computing, big data, and the Internet of Things (IOT) with modern manufacturing industry sectors; this attempts aim to greatly foster a healthy integrated ecosystem of E-commerce, industrial internet and mobile internet and incubate leading business from China to explore the global market in the long term. Respectively, China holds the most vast and diverse E-commerce in the world and witnesses many emerging trends in this market. With the wireless and instantaneous connectivity between the vast countryside and multitudinous consumers, many remote agricultural producers transferred to E-commerce have been benefiting to alleviate poverty for the impoverished villagers in 2020.

As the most populous country in the world, China's E-commerce is increasingly promising. The number of internet users in China, released by the China Internet Network Information Center (CNNIC), has reached 989 million (nearly 1 billion) at the end of 2020 with an increase of 85.4 million from March 2020. The Internet penetration rate has reached 70.4%, an increase of 5.9 percentage points from March 2020, significantly affected by the pandemic and formed the world's largest virtual market and digital community to create new business models. Sectors like online shopping live streaming broadcasts, food delivery, and online car-hailing maintained rapid growth. As of December 2020, the number of online shopping users in China reached 782 million, and the number of online food delivery users reached 419 million.

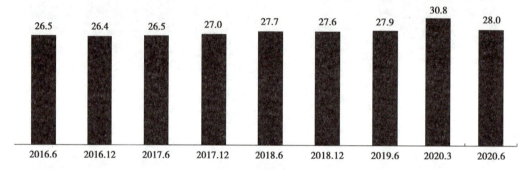

Figure 13.2   Chinese Netizen Per Capita Weekly Online Duration of Internet Users

13.2   Internet Marketing: Marketing Moves Online

Internet marketing or Internet-based marketing can be defined as the use of the Internet and related digital technologies to achieve marketing objectives and support the modern marketing concept and become the most important approach to Electronic commerce (E-commerce) which simply refers to buying and selling by using the Internet. An alternative term is E-marketing or electronic marketing, which plays important roles in the overall marketing process. These technologies include Internet media and other digital media such as wireless mobile media, cable and satellite, smart phone and tablet.

In practice, Internet marketing will include the use of a company web site in conjunction with online promotional techniques such as search engines, banner advertising, direct E-mail and links or services from other web sites to acquire new customers and provide services to existing customers that with closer relationship.

Internet marketing differs from conventional marketing communications because of the digital medium which used for communications. The Internet and other digital media such as digital television, satellite and mobile phones create new forms and models for information exchange. A useful summary of the differences between these new media and traditional media has been developed by McDonald and Wilson (1999) as the "Six-Is of the E-marketing mix". Note that these can be used as a strategic analysis tool since they highlight factors that apply to practical aspects of Internet marketing such as personalization, direct response and marketing research, but also strategic issues of industrial restructuring and integrated channel communications. By considering each of these facets of the new media, marketers can develop marketing plans that accommodate the characteristics of the new media. This presentation of the "six-I's", is an interpretation of these factors using new examples and diagrams to illustrate these concepts.

Table 13.1　6I's of the E-Marketing Mix

I's	Notion	Characteristics Description	Benefits
I_1	Interactivity	Customer initiates contact; The customer is seeking information (pull); It is a high intensity medium-the marketer will have 100 percent of the individual's attention when he or she is viewing a web site; a company can gather and store the response of the individual; Individual needs of the customer can be addressed and taken into account in future dialogues.	Customer initiated contact. Dialogue not monologue.
I_2	Intelligence	A relatively low cost method of collecting marketing research, particularly about customer perceptions of products and services; create a two-way feedback which does not usually occur in other media; Customer's log files could be analyzed as big data.	Ability to collect low-cost marketing research.
I_3	Individualization	Interactive marketing communications can be tailored to the individual unlike traditional media where the same message tends to be broadcast to everyone.	Personalization of communications.
I_4	Integration	The Internet can be used as a direct response tool enabling customers to respond to offers and promotions publicized in other media; Website can have a direct response or call-back facility built into it; The Internet can be used to support the buying decision even if the purchase does not occur via the website, especially in the context of mixed-mode buying referred to customer changes between online and offline channels during the buying process; "360 degree view of the customer" Customer information delivered on the website must be integrated with other databases of customer and order information such as those accessed via staff in the call-centre; Enhance customer service, especially frequently asked questions (FAQ).	Allows further scope for integrated marketing communications (IMC).
I_5	Industry restructuring	Disintermediation: The removal of intermediaries such as distributors or brokers that formerly linked a company to its customers; Reintermediation: The creation of new intermediaries between customers and suppliers providing services such as supplier search and product evaluation.	Remove the effects on communication with intermediaries.

Continued

I's	Notion	Characteristics Description	Benefits
I_6	Independence of location	Create business-to-business(B2B) opportunities to the worldwide by one-to-one or many-to-many communication model; Individualized marketing or mass customization; Pull model for web marketing.	Increasing reach of communications to global market.

Internet and Digital technologies have provided businesses new opportunities to reach their customers directly. The models assess efficiency of online and offline communications with drawing the prospect through different stages of the buying decision. The main measures defined in the model are:

- Awareness efficiency: Target web-users/all web-users.
- Locatability/attractability efficiency: Number of individual visits/number of seekers.
- Contact efficiency: Number of active visitors/Number of visits.
- Conversion efficiency: Number of purchases/number of active visits.
- Retention efficiency: Number of repurchases/number of purchases.

Marketers today have to think of very innovative and eye-catching strategies to entice wary viewers. Viral marketing is an extreme example of internet marketing, which involves the exponential spread of a marketing message by online word of mouth (sometimes referred to a "word of mouse", OWOM) with a major component of viral communication as the meme that spreads virally and embeds itself in the collective consciousness. Viral marketing is mainly and/or closely tied to social media, since social media platforms and their sharing functionality are the main way that a message is able to "go viral" online. However, what needs to be kept in mind is that viral marketing does not make a holistic online marketing campaign and should be just one of many tools used to create awareness and encourage interaction.

Despite all the exciting new strategies, email and website marketing remain among the most useful and effective techniques. These strategies do, of course, use new tools and tactics (like advanced tracking, integration with social networks and customer-generated content), but their essence stays the same.

13.3 Social media: Opportunities and Challenges in the Social Networks

Social media is generally defined as "Internet-based, distributed, and persistent channels of mass personal communication facilitating perceptions of interactions among

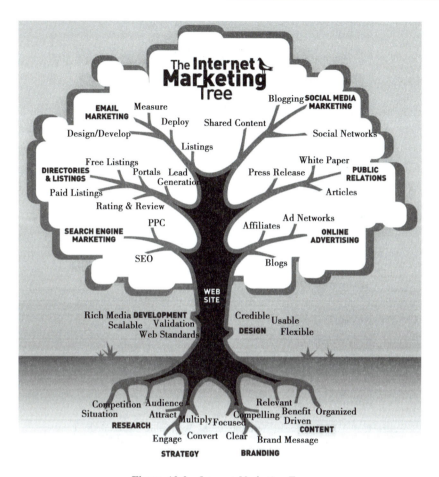

Figure 13.3 Internet Marketing Tree

users, deriving value primarily from user-generated content".

Social media emerged and evolved greatly by the advancement of digital portal devices such as smart phones and tablets; it becomes the most popular and familiar application for people's daily communication in the networks. However, social media is varied around the world due to the local elements, such as regulations, cultures, customs, and preferences.

Marketers could easily justify the target customer's demographic information and their preference to adjust their marketing strategies, which better caters for their needs; meanwhile, the instant feedback of products or services from customers could directly be collected by the producers or managers to make the information circle run smoothly. Social media platforms are much more tailored and effective in internet marketing, especially in the context of big data age. In the future, businesses can actively target to social media initiatives by the segment that best fits with their strategies. For example, for the creators, companies could create possibilities for them to create product-related content that would ultimately promote the company's brand, which could be called the segmentation strategies in social media marketing. In addition, companies could identify micro-segments based on social media use that they could target more effectively.

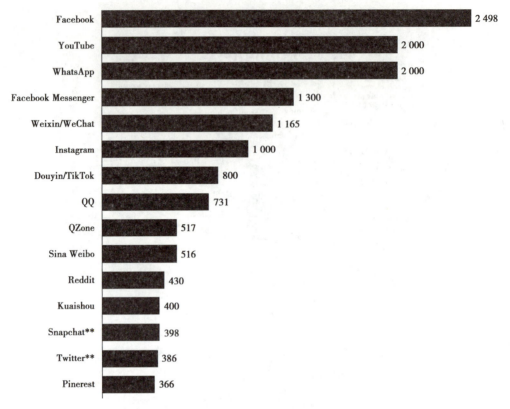

Figure 13.4　Leading Social Networks in the Worldwide Social Media Landscape
(in millions, as of April 2020)

Different regions prefer various social media which formed the worldwide social media landscape. Compared to the website, social media attracts users to post their own contents with the authorization of their privacy identities, such as gender, real name, telephone number, real time location and so forth. The risk is that customers could be the targeted victims if their real information is leaked or illegally acquired by others.

As social media platforms are internet-based applications focused on broadcasting user-generated content, users could easily get online addiction when primarily web-based contents and services are increasingly available on mobile platforms. Communities and individuals share information, photos, music, and videos, providing commentary and ratings/reviews, and more. In essence, social media is about sharing information, consuming information, and repurposing content while social media technologies are centered on social networking services, media sharing, blogging and microblogging to build on prior uses of the internet for social and communicative purposes.

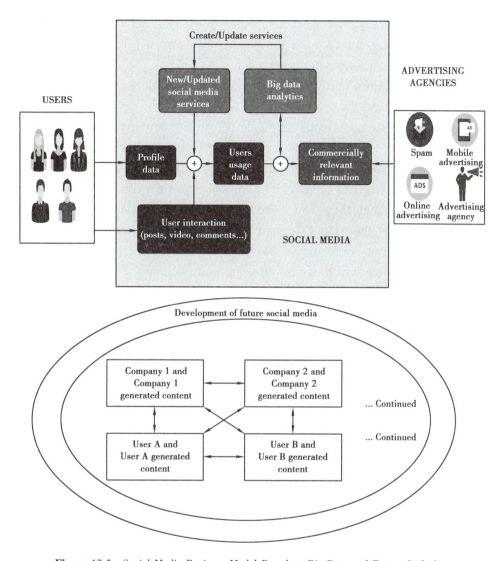

Figure 13.5　Social Media Business Model Based on Big Data and Future Outlook

13.4　Live Streaming Broadcasts: The Future of Internet Marketing?

　　With moving online businesses and the outbreak of COVID-19, Live Streaming Broadcasts integrated the interactive broadcast technology with social media and influencer marketing in online activities or events are ballooning and greatly boosting businesses around China by the **"You watch, You like, You engage and You buy"** mode.

　　Influencer marketing is a form of social media marketing involving endorsements and product placement from influencers, people and organizations which have a supposed expert level of knowledge or social influence in their field. In China, anyone who could persuade the audience to buy the products could be an influencer, such as various celebrities, net influencers, salespersons, industry leaders, farmers, workers and even virtual influencers. Before the 15th UN Biodiversity Conference (COP15, the Parties to the Convention on Biological Diversity) was held in Kunming, the capital city in China's Southwest Yunnan province in June of 2021, 15 wandering elephants surprisingly became the net influencers around the world.

Live Streaming Broadcasts could combine all the E-marketing interactive elements in dynamic and present it to the audience simultaneously by the influencer so as to accelerate the decision-making process from the audience as potential customers. This engaging process is greatly enslaved to influencer's Personality and Skills, Atmosphere, Novelty and Authenticity by **What they Say (Product Placement), What they Mean (Brand Endorsement)** or **What they Do (Content Creation)**. This is the reason why the top influencers' sale volumes could occupy the majority; and the total sales follow the Pareto Principle or the 80/20 rule which named after an Italian economist Vilfredo Pareto in 1895, this states that for many phenomena 80% of the result comes from 20% of the effort while 20% of the employees account for 80% of total production, and 20% of the input accounts for 80% of the result in business as well.

The digital natives, especially the generation Z, are growing up with the Internet and fond of social media. As this new E-market is emerging, a large amount of youth are rushing into this Blue Ocean Market. Yiwu, an international trade city in East China's Zhejiang Province with the world's largest petty commodities market, has started the E-commerce influencer training programs in its local vocational colleges. Ruili, a remote city in Southwest China's Yunnan Province bordering Myanmar, is officially licensing the first batch of 731 influencers on Live Streaming Broadcasts of its Gem E-commerce to promote pillar industries from the neighborhood country.

Taking the 6.18 event of 2020 for example, Taobao TMALL and Jingdong harvested an order volume worth 698 billion and 269 billion RMB respectively.

Figure 13.6   Live Streaming Broadcasting 6.18 Events on Social Media Platforms in 2020

13.5   Social Media Marketing and Popular Livestreamers in China

The term social media marketing (SMM) refers to the use of social media and social networks to market a company's products and services. It provides companies with a way to engage with existing customers and reach new ones while allowing them to promote their desired culture, mission, or tone.

Social media marketing has purpose-built data analytics tools that allow marketers to track the success of their efforts.

Social media have changed the communication channels in the society, including the way people connects with one another. The social media platforms began to use their sites to further their interests through social media marketing, which are able to change consumer behavior.

Social media websites allow marketers to employ a broad range of tactics and strategies to promote content and have people engage with it. Many social networks allow users to provide detailed geographical, demographic, and personal information, which enables marketers to tailor their messages for what is most likely to resonate with users. The five key pillars of social media marketing are as follows:

- Strategy: This step involves determining goals, the social media channels to be used, and the type of content that will be shared.
- Planning and publishing: Businesses should draft plans of what their content will look like (i.e. will there be videos? Photos? How much script?) and decide when it will be put out on the platform.
- Listening and engagement: Monitoring what users, customers, and others are saying about the posts, brands, and any other business assets. This may require the adoption of a social media tool.
- Analytics and reporting: Part of being on social media could be known how far posts are going, so reports of engagement and reach are very important.
- Advertising: Purchasing ads. on social media is a great way to promote and further develop a brand.

Because audiences can be better segmented than many traditional marketing channels, companies can ensure they focus their resources on the audience that they want to use social media marketing. Some of the metrics used to measure the success of social media marketing (which is also known as digital marketing and E-marketing) include:

- Website reports, such as Database Analytics.
- Return on investment (ROI).
- Customer response rates or the number of times customers post about a company.
- A campaign's reach and/or virality or how much customers share content.

China is taking the led on this kind of E-marketing with no doubt and legally defines the marketer and/or influencer who is doing online selling as E-commerce livestreamer in May 11 of 2020 after the outbreak and spread of COVID-19.

Taking all the advantages of various social media platforms and their fames, livestreamers could negotiate with both the commodity producers and suppliers for the most favorable price to their audiences and fans which usually makes waves of "seckill" purchase behavior and records new sales consecutively.

With popular and eye-catching events initiated by various E-commerce livestreamers, the advertising revenue on social media marketing is increasing steadily and competitive to the traditional media.

In 2019, the social media advertising made up around 10.1 percent of the total online advertising revenue in China. E-commerce advertising and search engine advertising are the largest segments in China's online advertisements. market.

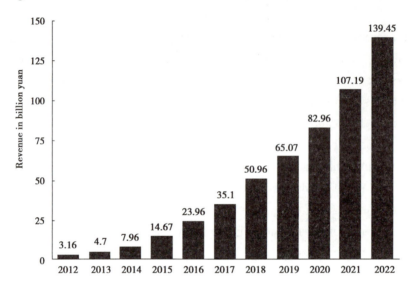

Figure 13.7　Social Media Advertising Revenue in China from 2012 to 2019 with a Forecast Until 2022 (in billion *yuan*)

Key Terms

Internet access 互联网访问	Internet access is the ability of individuals and organizations to connect to the Internet using computer terminals, computers, and other devices; and to access services such as email and WWW. 互联网访问是指两台计算机或多台计算机通过互联网链接到对方计算机或传输数据到对方的计算机，并以第一封跨洋电子邮件发送和接收成功为标志。
World Wide Web （WWW） 万维网	An information system where documents and other web resources are identified by Uniform Resource Locators (URLs, such as https://example.com/), which may be interlinked by hypertext, and are accessible over the Internet. The resources of the Web are transferred via the Hypertext Transfer Protocol (HTTP). WWW 是通过互联网访问，由许多互相链接的超文本组成的系统，由英国科学家蒂姆·伯纳斯·李于 1989 年发明，并于 1991 年 8 月在互联网上向公众开放。WWW 是信息时代发展的核心，也是数十亿人在互联网上进行交互的主要工具。

Continued

"Internet Plus" action plan "互联网+"行动计划	"Internet Plus" action plan initiated by PM Li Keqiang in 2015 aims to further promote the innovation between information and communications technology（ICT）industry and other traditional industries, by integration of mobile Internet, cloud computing, big data, and Internet of things with modern manufacturing industry sectors, which targets to greatly foster a healthy integrated ecosystem of E-commerce, industrial Internet and mobile Internet and incubate leading business in China. "互联网+"是在 2015 年被国务院总理李克强率先提出创新 2.0 下中国互联网发展新形态、新业态，是知识社会创新 2.0 推动下的互联网形态演进；基于互联网的移动与泛在，与传统行业的融合及应用，引领了创新驱动发展的"新常态"。
Internet marketing 网络营销	Online Marketing or E-marketing, the use of the Internet and related digital technologies to achieve marketing objectives and support the modern marketing concept and become the most important approach to E-commerce which simply referred to buying and selling by using the Internet. 网络营销，网上营销或者电子营销，是指以现代营销理论为基础，借助网络、通信和数字媒体技术等实现营销目标的商务活动。
6I's of the E-marketing mix 网络整合营销 6I 原则	Rules of Internet marketing by the digital medium used for better communication and promotion, including interactivity, intelligence, individualization, integration, industry restructuring, and independence of location. 互联网整合营销是通过网络等相关技术和手段帮助企业维护、建立和传播品牌，增强企业与客户之间的关系，对企业的品牌进行计划、实施和监督的一系列营销工作，主要体现为 6 原则：互动原则、智能原则、个性原则、融合原则、重建原则和独立原则。
online word of mouth （OWOM） 网络口碑	People passing along messages about a company or product（or anything else）through digital forums. 消费者通过电子媒介自动传播公司、产品，以及服务。
meme 模因	An idea, behavior, or style that becomes a fad and spreads by means of imitation from person to person within a culture and often carried symbolic meaning representing a particular phenomenon or theme. 文化传递的基本单位，通过非遗传的方式，特别是模仿而得到传递，在类似语言、观念、信仰、行为方式等在文明中的传播更替过程中的地位与基因在生物繁衍更替及进化的过程中相类似。
social media 社交媒体	Interactive digitally-mediated technologies that facilitate the creation or sharing/exchange of information, ideas, career interests, and other forms of expression via virtual communities and networks. 互联网上基于用户关系的内容生产与交换平台用来分享意见、见解、经验和观点，其传播的信息已成为人们浏览互联网的重要内容，并制造众多热门话题。

Continued

Pareto Principle 帕累托法则	A naturally occurring law which shows that effort and reward are not equally matched, named after an Italian economist Vilfredo Pareto in 1895 (states that for many phenomena 80% of the result comes from 20% of the effort while 20% of the employees account for 80% of total production 20% of the input accounts for 80% of the result in business). 即帕累托定律,又称二八定律、80/20 法则、马特莱法则、最省力法则、不平衡原则、犹太法则,认为原因和结果、投入和产出、努力和报酬之间本来存在着无法解释的不平衡。由意大利经济学家帕累托在 1895 年提出,可以解释很多社会问题(比如一般两成人或组织会创造社区或行业八成的价值)和商业现象(如市场上八成的明星商品由该行业两成的生产商提供)。
Internet influencer 网红	People who create content and amass influence through their relationships with their audience by their creative or professional talents to inform or entertain and leverage their talent to generate revenue streams through Internet facilities or platforms. 网络媒介环境下,网络达人、网络推手、传统媒体以及受众心理需求等利益共同体综合作用下凭借自身某种被网络放大的特质因为某个事件或者某种行为被网民关注讨论或长期持续输出专业知识而走红的人。
live streaming broadcast marketing 直播带货	Live marketing initiated by Internet influencers through streaming or broadcasting to attract numerous viewers watching the same online selling in real time and persuades the customers to order or to buy. 主播或称为网络营销师通过互联网平台,使用直播技术开设直播间向加入网络账号的广大观众和线上顾客对商品进行近距离展示、咨询答复、导购并引导受众下单购买的新型网络营销模式。
Z generation Z 世代	Colloquially known as zoomers, the Net or the Internet generation, spent their entire life with WWW and high-tech gadgets, is the demographic cohort succeeding Millennials and preceding Generation Alpha. Researchers and popular media use the mid-to-late 1990s as starting birth years and the early 2010s as ending birth years. Most members of Generation Z are the children of Generation X, but some are children of millennials. Z 世代(1995—2005)也被称为网络世代、互联网世代、新新人类、95 后至 05 后,统指受到互联网、即时通信、社交媒体、智能手机和平板电脑等科技和网络技术影响较大的一代人;相较上一 Y 世代(1981—1995)和千禧一代的成长过程对消费市场的影响持续加大且加重。

Review & Critical Thinking Questions

1. What is internet communication technology (ICT)?

2. What is E-marketing?.

3. Distinguish word of mouth (WOM) and internet word of mouth (IWOM).

4. Describe as the "Six-Is of the E-marketing mix".

5. Name at least 3 Internet influencers or E-commerce livestreamers in China; discuss the reasons why you are interested in.

Discussion Questions

1. What can you learn from the relationship between internet technology and E-marketing?

2. Do you think live streaming broadcasts could be the future of Internet marketing? Support your ideas with evidence.

3. Justify at least 5 types of marketing on Li Ziqi's video-logging with the description of their functions.

4. Express your own viewpoints on internet influencers or "net celebrity" and discuss if Li Ziqi will be replaced or Dingzhen will be forgotten.

5. Discuss the pros and cons of live streaming broadcast marketing.

Case Study

Internet Influencers or E-commerce Livestreamers in China

China's emerging livestreaming E-commerce industry has witnessed explosive growth amid the COVID-19 pandemic, thus creating new growth opportunities for a wide range of businesses and injecting new impetus into the economy. Compared to other countries in the world, COVID-19 only added fuel to the fire for fast-growing online marketing. Thus, livestreaming has become a key means for brands to gain awareness and boost sales and for smaller operators such as farmers, who have better access to consumers, especially during the pandemic period when many people are still stuck at home. Therefore, livestreaming provides an important channel for them to tap into large demographics living in fourth and fifth-tier cities as well as rural areas.

The most important part of livestreaming is that the instant call-in questions from digital audiences in real time could be answered and solved immediately, which will significantly enhances shopping experiences and attracts more netizens to shop online. And some of the livestreaming E-commerce events, such as celebrity guests or big promotion, could easily attract numerous audios and achieve remarkable sales. All the online activities make China step ahead of the world in E-commerce. The number of people likely to watch livestreaming E-commerce events is set to hit 388 million in 2020, according to a report from the China Internet Network Information Center. The number was 265 million as of March 2020.

The typical livestreaming E-commerce session involves celebrities promoting and selling goods while answering questions for online audiences, with everything taking place in real time via devices such as smartphones. Livestreaming is increasingly gaining popularity as a new online shopping platform among Chinese netizens, creating a huge market worth more than 970 billion yuan ($ 149. 9 billion) in 2020, said the Internet Economy Institute.

E-commerce giant Alibaba's Taobao Live has taken the lion's share of livestreaming, as 68.5 percent of consumers use the service, according to a survey conducted by the China Consumers Association. Douyin and Kuaishou have taken second and third spots, respectively. Other large Chinese internet and E-commerce players like JD.com have also thrown their hats into the ring.

In fact, Taobao Live generated more than 400 billion yuan in gross merchandise volume last year alone, up from over 200 billion yuan GMV in 2019, displaying the huge growth potential of the new frontier of livestreaming commerce that combines social networks and E-commerce.

Today, top Chinese livestream influencers have become major online celebrities. Livestreaming E-commerce will help boost the development of industrial chains, including logistics and manufacturing factories.

Livestreaming E-commerce is a key channel for small brands and farmers to reach consumers, helping a wide range of businesses survive the pandemic. However, with the rapid development of livestreaming E-commerce, new problems are also popping up, such as illegal sales of counterfeit goods.

Authorities recently unveiled a trial guideline, effective from May 25, to regulate livestreaming in the booming E-commerce sector.

The new measures, jointly released on April 23 by the Cyberspace Administration of China and six other government departments, aim to protect the rights and interests of consumers and minors, and tackle problems including false advertisings and sales of counterfeit and substandard goods.

Livestreaming platforms are required to handle complaints from consumers in a timely manner and provide necessary evidence when disputes occur, it said.

"Looking forward, livestreaming platforms need to make active moves to maintain normal market order and contribute to the healthy development of the whole industry," said Fang Yizhi, an assistant analyst at the E-Commerce Research Center at the Internet Economy Institute.

Questions

1. What are the reasons for Li ziqi's phenomenon in social media around the world?
2. Why Dingzhen could easily promote his hometown Litang to the world?
3. Why China could be the Top E-commerce Market in the world?

中文概述

计算机网络是指通过电子设备进行信息传输、接收、共享的虚拟平台,通过它把各个点、面、体的信息联系到一起,从而实现这些资源的共享。计算机网络是人类发展史来最重要的发明,提升了科技和人类社会的发展。网络传播具有全球性、交互性、超文本链接方式三个基本的特点。

互联网是指21世纪之初网络与网络之间所串联成的庞大网络。这些网络以一些标准的网络协议相连,连接全世界几十亿个设备,形成逻辑上的单一巨大国际网络。相较万维网,互联网带有范围广泛的信息资源和服务,点对点网络、文件共享,以及IP电话服务等。

万维网是通过互联网访问,由许多互相链接的超文本组成的系统,由英国科学家蒂姆·伯纳斯·李于1989年发明,并于1991年8月在互联网上向公众开放。WWW是信息时代发展的核心,也是数十亿人在互联网上进行交互的主要工具,但它并不等同于互联网,只是互联网提供的服务之一。

"互联网+"简言之就是"互联网+传统行业",利用信息和互联网平台,使互联网与传统行业进行深度融合,利用互联网具备的优势特点,创造新的发展机会。"互联网+"通过其自身的优势,对传统行业进行优化升级转型,使得传统行业能够适应当下的新发展,从而最终推动社会不断地向前发展。2015年7月4日,国务院印发《国务院关于积极推进"互联网+"行动的指导意见》;2020年5月22日,国务院总理李克强在发布的2020年国务院政府工作报告中提出,全面推进"互联网+",打造数字经济新优势。

网络营销是21世纪最有代表性的一种低成本、高效率的全新商业形式,以互联网为核心平台,以网络用户为中心,以市场需求和认知为导向,利用各种网络应用手段去实现企业营销目的一系列行为。虽然网络营销以互联网为核心平台,但也可以整合其他的资源形成整合营销,比如销售渠道促销、传统媒体广告、地面活动等。互联网拥有比拟其他媒体都不具备的综合营销能力,网络营销可进行从品牌推广到销售、到服务、到市调等一系列的工作,包括电子商务、企业展示、企业公关、品牌推广、产品推广、产品促销、活动推广、挖掘细分市场、项目招商等方面。广义的网络不仅包括互联网(Internet),还应该包括外联网(Extranet)以及内联网(Intranet),即应用互联网技术和标准建立的企业内部信息管理和交换平台。

病毒营销(Viral marketing)通过用户的口碑传播网络使得信息像病毒一样传播和扩散,利用快速复制的方式向数以千计、百万计的受众传播;即通过提供有价值的产品或服务,"让大家告诉大家",通过别人为你宣传,实现"营销杠杆"的作用。病毒式营销已成为网络营销最为独特的手段,被越来越多的商家和网站成功利用。在传播病毒时,应该选择那些人群集中、互动性强、传播迅速的平台,如 IM、QQ、论坛、邮箱等常用渠道。但恶意的病毒营销不仅适得其反,同时也容易让受众质疑病毒营销的方式和带来的负面影响。

口碑营销是企业在调查市场需求的情况下,为消费者提供他们所需要的产品和服务,同时制定一定口碑推广计划,让消费者自动传播公司的产品和服务的良好评价,让人们通过口碑了解产品、树立品牌,最终达到企业销售产品和提供服务的目的。菲利普·科特勒将 21 世纪的口碑传播定义为:由生产者以外的个人通过明示或暗示的方法,不经过第三方处理、加工,传递关于某一特定或某一种类的产品、品牌、厂商、销售者,以及能够使人联想到上述对象的任何组织或个人信息,从而导致受众获得信息、改变态度,甚至影响购买行为的一种双向互动传播行为。

网络口碑营销(Internet Word of Mouth Marketing) 简称为 IWOM,网络口碑营销是指消费者或网民通过网络(如论坛、博客、播客、相册和视频分享网站等) 渠道分享的,对品牌、产品或服务的相关讨论以及相关多媒体的信息内容;它是口碑营销与网络营销的有机结合,旨在利用互联网的信息传播技术与平台,通过消费者以文字、电子文本、超链接等表达方式为载体的口碑信息(甚至包括企业与消费者之间的互动信息) 为企业营销开辟营销模式。网络口碑营销(IWOM) 是口碑营销的升级换代,逐步由门户广告营销、搜索广告营销发展而来,是凭借互联网兴起而发展的一种网上商务活动。

社交媒体是基于 WEB 2.0 技术的发展由数量庞大的大批网民自发产出、提取、制造信息资讯并主动传播的基于用户关系的内容生产与交换平台。社交媒体是人们彼此之间用来分享意见、见解、经验和观点的工具和平台,中国的社交媒体现阶段主要包括社交网站、微博、微信、博客、论坛、播客等。社交媒体传播的信息已成为人们浏览互联网的重要内容,不仅制造了人们社交生活中争相讨论的一个又一个热门话题,甚至吸引传统媒体争相跟进。

网络红人或"网红"是指在现实或者网络生活中因为某个事件或者某种行为而被网民关注从而走红的人或长期持续输出专业知识而走红的人,他们可以是通过网络一夜爆红的普通人,也可以是意见领袖、行业精英。原因在于网红自身的某种特质在网络作用下被放大,与网民的审美、审丑、娱乐、刺激、偷窥、臆想、品味以及看客等心理相契合,有意或无意间受到网民的追捧。因此,其产生不一定是自发的,而是网络媒介环境下,网络红人、网络推手、传统媒体以及受众心理需求等利益共同体综合作用下的结果。网红因可直接带来可观的网红经济而备受关注,具备一定的商业价值,但网红要有文明底线,要守住道德底线。

UNIT 14 Global Distribution and Logistics

1. Understand the definition, classification and functions of global distribution.
2. Understand the factors influencing the decision-making of international distribution channels strategy.
3. Master intermediaries involved and their advantages and disadvantages.
4. Understand the classification of international retailers, and challenges they are faced with.
5. Identify the definition and characteristics of international logistics.

14.1   An Overview of Global Distribution Channels

ABC Company sells 120 million pairs of athletic shoes throughout the world annually, which accounts for 31% of the global market share. More than 60% of the sales are from 160 markets outside the United States. It is an incredible achievement considering the complexity of global markets with regard to diversities in language, culture, economies, political environment, government regulations, logistics, consumer demands, etc.

Additionally, ABC Company also engages in design, signs contracts with manufacturers, distributes, and sells sports apparel and equipment. In the picture below (see Figure 14.1) are shoes and apparel (jersey, shorts & socks) made by ABC Company.

Figure 14.1   ABC Company Series Products

It becomes even more complex given the fact that ABC Company designs and manages all products in the United States, but manufactures them in other countries. ABC Company's success mainly lies in management of the supply chain, which includes all things from sourcing materials utilized by outsourced manufacturers to the global distribution of products. ABC Company delivers 120 million pairs of sneakers from Asian manufacturers to consumers in 160 different countries or regions, which requires an amazing competency in global distribution involving transportation, warehousing, currency, financing, and management of unique country requirements for market entry and sales of products. This chapter will introduce the particulars of global distribution channels.

14.1.1　Definition of Global Distribution Channels

Global distribution channels or global marketing channels refer to a sequence of channel members which deliver a product from the producer to the ultimate user, internationally taking profit and effectiveness into consideration. These channel members include manufacturers, wholesalers, retailers, and sales agents, responsible for manufacturing products or providing services ready for customers. Compared with planning of domestic distribution channels, planning of global distribution channels has no difference in terms of goals, structure and procedures of design. However, due to differences in cultural background, belief, etc., different distribution channels should be adopted in different countries. Products can be sold directly to retailers in a small market, while an agent may be involved in distributing products in a large market. An exclusive agent may be used in one area, while in another a number of agents may be necessary. It is possible that for most multinational companies, suitable distribution channels take shape while a company is gradually adapting to the local market.

In brief, distribution is about all the logistics involved in delivering a company's products or services to the right place, at the right time, and with the lowest cost. In order to make these goals come true, a company should attach great importance to designing channels of distribution, because they play a significant role in the process of delivering products or services from producers to consumers. Appropriate channels mean a significant competitive advantage, while unsuitable channels can doom even a superior product or service to failure in the market.

14.1.2　Types of Distribution Channels

Distribution channels can be classified into direct channels and indirect channels. Since there are different tiers of intermediaries between producers and end customers, indirect channels can further be classified into one-level, two-level, and three-level channels.

1. Direct Channel or Zero-level Channels (Manufacturer to Customer)

A direct channel is one of the most conventional types of distribution channels. It does not include any intermediary, which means the manufacturer contacts the customer directly at the point of sale. There are such direct channels as peddling, brand retail stores, company website purchase entry, etc. Some manufacturers adopt direct channels to sell perishable foods such as butter and fruit, while other similar manufacturers whose target consumers are geographically concentrated, including jewelers, etc.do the same.

2. Indirect Channels (Selling Through Intermediaries)

If there is a middleman or intermediary in the distribution channel, who is responsible for selling the product to the ultimate consumer, then this channel is an indirect channel. There are three kinds of indirect channels.

First-level Channels (Manufacturers to Retailers to Customers): The manufacturers sell the product to the retailers who then sell it to the customers. For manufacturers, consumer goods such as clothes, shoes, furniture, toys, etc. are suitable to be distributed through this kind of channel.

Two-Level Channels (Manufacturers to Wholesalers to Retailers to Customers): Manufacturers sell the bulk to the wholesalers who divide it into small packages and sell them to the retailers who finally sell the packages to the ultimate consumers. Two-level channel of distribution works well for durable, standardized and somewhat inexpensive goods, whose target market is not confined to a single area.

Three-Level Channels (Manufacturers to Agents to Wholesalers to Retailers to Customers): Other than the wholesaler and the retailer, if an agent is involved in the distribution channel, then this channel is known as a three-level channel. The agent turns out to be useful in the case that customers place a large order and products need to be delivered in time to them. Agents are responsible for dealing with distribution of a certain kind of products in a specific area or district, and they will get a certain percentage of commission in return. Agents can be divided into super stockists and carrying and forwarding agents. Both of these two types of agents are on behalf of the business. Super stockists buy the goods from producers and sell them to wholesalers and retailers in their area or district. However, carrying and forwarding agents get commission because they provide their warehouses and shipment expertise for order processing and final mile deliveries. Manufacturers choose a three-level distribution channel if the user base is in different areas or districts and large quantities of goods are in demand.

3. Dual Distribution

A manufacturer is encouraged to employ the dual distribution strategy if it uses over two distribution channels simultaneously to reach the ultimate customers. For example, they may use two ways to sell products at the same time — one is selling products through showrooms, and the other is to trade online. Smart phones are a perfect choice for selling through dual distribution.

4. Distribution Channels for Services

Different from physical products, services cannot be put in a storehouse. However, it does not mean that services can never be transferred through indirect channels. Thanks to the Internet, online stores, the aggregator business model, and the on-demand business model, even services use intermediaries to reach ultimate consumers.

5. The Internet as a Distribution Channel

With the advent of the Internet, how manufacturers deliver goods has been completely changed. The conventional direct and indirect channels are no longer the only two ways to transmit goods and services; now emerging ways include using online platforms and other intermediaries, for example, aggregators (DIDI, Instacart). Through the Internet, some unnecessary middlemen for goods like software can be removed, because software can reach the end customers directly online.

14.1.3 Functions of Distribution Channels

As stated above, a distribution channel serves to move goods from producers to consumers, which is completed by diverse channel members including manufacturers, service providers, wholesalers, retailers, marketing specialists, and consumers. Distribution channels provide time, place, and ownership utility. They make the product available when, where, and in which quantities the customer wants. However, except for the above mentioned **transactional functions**, marketing channels also bear the responsibility to perform the following functions:

Logistics and Physical Distribution: Marketing channels assemble, store, sort and transport goods from producers to ultimate customers.

Facilitation: Distribution channels are also responsible for providing pre-sale and after-sale services including financing, maintenance, information dissemination and channel coordination.

Producing Efficiency: There are two ways of performing this function, namely *bulk breaking* and *creating assortments*. *Bulk breaking* means that wholesalers and retailers purchase large quantities of goods from producers and then break the bulk by selling a few at a time to many other channels or directly to end customers. *Creating assortments* means that wholesalers and retailers sell different kinds of goods at one specific place, which is beneficial to customers because they do not need to go to different retailers to buy different products.

Sharing Risks: Some channel members such as wholesalers buy the goods in advance, they also take the risk with the producers and make an effort to promote sales.

Marketing: Distribution channels are also known as marketing channels as they are in the central place where large quantities of marketing strategies are implemented. They directly connect the ultimate customers and help the producers to communicate brand information, goods advantages and other interests related to the customers.

14.2　Decisions of International Distribution Channels

14.2.1　Factors in Decision-making of International Distribution Channels

The decision-making of international distribution channels not only builds on the type of products and users' purchasing requirements, but is also closely related with the specific market situation. When choosing international distribution channels, enterprises usually take into consideration of the following six factors, cost, capital, control, coverage, character and continuity.

1. Cost

The "cost" here includes the cost of investment to develop channels and the cost of maintenance to sustain the channels. Among the above-mentioned costs, the cost of maintenance occurs most frequently and occupies a great share in the overall cost. Enterprises have to shoulder the direct expenditure of managing the sales team, the commission to the broker, the costs of transportation, warehousing, loading and unloading in logistics, fees for bills and paperwork, maintenance fees for credit, advertising and promotion fees provided for the broker, as well as the costs happening in business negotiation and communication.

The cost of developing and maintaining channels is unavoidable for any enterprises, so decision-makers should strike a balance between cost and efficiency. Generally speaking, if the newly-created efficiency can make up for the corresponding cost, the channel strategy is economically reasonable and adoptable. High costs to develop and maintain channels are the major hindrance enterprises have to encounter when they are exploiting the global market. As a factor indicating whether enterprises can reach their sales targets with the lowest payment, "cost" is also significant in ensuring that other five factors play their roles to the utmost extent within certain budgets.

2. Capital

Capital is another important factor enterprises have to take into account when making the decision of international distribution channels. Just like in any other economic activities, if enterprises plan to develop their own international distribution channels, it is their urgent need to raise capital so as to build and manage their sales teams. There is also another way for enterprises to reduce their investment—working with exclusive brokers. Under the circumstance, enterprises sometimes have to give financial support to brokers.

All these considerations exert influences on making the decision. However, generally speaking, "capital" is not the key factor in designing the distribution channels, unless an enterprise's business is under continuous expansion, or it strives to build international distribution channels with its own investment.

3. Control

The best way for enterprises to gain control of distribution channels is to build their own ones, but it will increase the cost accordingly. If they choose to work with brokers, their control will be weakened and undoubtedly be affected by the extent that brokers prefer to be controlled. In general, the longer and the broader the channel is, the weaker an enterprise's control will be over price, sales and customer service.

The control of the channels is closely associated with the nature of products. Manufacturers have very different control over distribution channels when they produce industrial goods and consumer goods. For the former ones, manufacturers gain more powerful control for the reasons that there are less customers, and distribution channels are shorter and brokers rely on the service for the goods provided by manufacturers. On the contrary, for the latter ones, the control is comparatively weak, as consumer goods have a larger number of customers, are traded on a more dispersed market, and the distribution channels are longer and wider.

4. Coverage

The coverage of channels refers to the market enterprises can touch upon or have influence on through certain distribution channels. Three elements should be taken into consideration when enterprises deal with the coverage of markets. The first is whether every market covered by the channels can obtain the maximum amount of sales. Second, whether the market coverage can bring in reasonable market share. The last one is whether the market coverage can achieve satisfactory market penetration.

Rather than being as wide as possible, the market coverage should be reasonable and effective with economic returns. When designing international distribution channels, enterprises should make the decision based on their characteristics, nature of products, and brokers' ability to cover the market. Thus, many large enterprises choose to penetrate into their core markets, instead of making the expansion geographically.

5. Character

The "character" that should be taken into account for enterprises in designing international distribution channels includes the character of the enterprise, of the products, of the market and of the environment.

(1) The Character of the Enterprise

When it comes to the character of the enterprise, the scale, the financial condition, the product mix, and the marketing policy usually have great importance attached to it.

The larger an enterprise is, the easier it is for it to win the cooperation with brokers, so are the adoptable channel designs.

If an enterprise operates in a very good financial condition, it is able to set up a sales office, or it has no choice but to enter the international market by cooperating with brokers.

When there exist various kinds of product mix, an enterprise has to turn to more brokers, whereas exclusive brokers can satisfy its marketing strategy.

The marketing policy is also an important element that cannot be ignored. If an enterprise insists on fast delivery policy, it will choose the distribution channels which are as short as possible.

(2) The Character of the Products

The character of the products play an important role in designing and deciding international distribution channels, including standardization, perishability and the size of the products, as well as requirements for service.

When selling fresh and perishable products, enterprises should employ short distribution channels.

Comparatively, longer distribution channels are applicable to products with lower unit value and produced through standardized processing.

Direct-selling should be adopted when it comes to selling products with high demand for technology support and after-sale service.

As for raw materials and primary products, it's more convenient for them to be sold directly to the manufacturers of the exporting countries.

Enterprises need to implement specific strategies in deciding distribution channels accordingly in dealing with special products, such as selective distribution or exclusive distribution.

(3) The Character of the Market

The market in different countries has different characteristics, among which the following ones should be considered in designing international distribution channels, including features of the market, the customers and the competition.

Features of the market focus on the geographical intensity or dispersion of the market and the customers. If the market concentrates, enterprises can take short channels or direct channels, otherwise long channels when merchandising with large number of customers in a large-capacity market covering broad areas.

As incomes, consumption habits and purchasing frequency of customers vary from country to country, features of the customers require enterprises to adopt different distribution channels. Customers buy daily necessities from nearby stores or supermarkets, so those products fit for wide distribution channels. For special needs, customers turn to specialized stores, and thus wide distribution channels are not applicable. Enterprises can work with brokers when customers purchase products in high frequency but small amounts, otherwise direct distribution channels should be chosen.

The competition on the international market motivates enterprises to work out two strategies when confronting their competitors. One is to build systems of distribution channels that can compete with their rivals. HITACHI (a Japanese multinational company) owns over 1, 000 franchised dealers and a sales team consisting of several hundred stores. In order to compete with HITACHI, IBM hired over 60 brokers to sell their products. The other one is to adopt different distribution channels to earn the competitive advantage.

(4) The Character of the Environment

The environment here affecting the decision of international distribution channels mainly includes the legal environment and the economic environment. For the legal environment, the country, in which multinational companies operate, may carry out laws and measures that constrain certain sales channels. *Clayton Act* of the United States forbids certain channel arrangements which in essence reduces competition or leads to monopoly. Some developed countries make it clear that certain importing and exporting businesses should be completed by franchised enterprises, while some countries and districts levy taxes on consignment. In terms of the economic environment, when a country's economy undergoes recession, enterprises have to use short distribution channels, in which they sell their products at a low price as soon as possible.

6. Continuity

An efficient system of distribution channels is not only an important external resource for enterprises, but also a foundation for them to win differentiation advantage in the international market. Building and maintaining the international distribution channels demand enterprises to devote great costs and efforts. Therefore, maintaining the continuity of distribution channels is a major task and challenge for enterprises.

The continuity of distribution channels can be influenced by the following three aspects: There are the termination of brokers, fierce market competition, and the fading traditional distribution channels due to the emergence of new modes brought by the advancement of information technology and sales methods. Thus, enterprises should prudently choose their brokers, after which provide them with effective support and attentive service, and nurture their loyalty by setting up the brand reputation. Enterprises should also ensure the continuity of their brokers by building up long-term cooperation with them, or arranging potential substitute brokers in case of any changes in the cooperative relations. In addition, business operators should pay close attention to changes, including their rivals' channel strategies, modern technology, and customers' purchasing habits, so as to make in-time adjustments of their distribution channels.

14.2.2　Distribution Channel Strategies for International Enterprises

Strategies of international distribution channels roll out when enterprises transfer their products from the country to foreign markets. Due to different market environment, complicated distribution channel arrangement and characters of products, various options of distribution channels come into being and can be chosen by enterprises according to market situations in different countries.

1. Long Distribution Channels and Short Distribution Channels

Long distribution channels and short distribution channels are determined by whether there are brokers in the distribution process, how many brokers are chosen and how many links are involved. Simply put, if products flow to the ultimate users directly from the enterprise, then there is only one link and the distribution channel is the shortest. Every time products go through one broker, a layer is formed, followed by a longer distribution channel. The longest distribution channel includes all intermediate links.

Therefore, long distribution channels refer to the operation that international enterprises choose two or more brokers to sell the products, while short distribution channels mean that there is only one link for the enterprises, or the enterprises sell products without cooperating with any brokers. When adopting long distribution channels, enterprises can fully concentrate on development and production of products after entrusting the sales task to brokers. And the brokers can make full use of their advantages in capital, resources and experience to promote the sales and gather information for the enterprises. If short distribution channels are chosen, distribution links can be reduced and the product-to-market period can be shortened. What's more, damages and losses can be cut down as products go through fewer links in the distribution process. As a result, if the distribution cost can be reduced, so are the prices of the products. However, since there is only one broker or even no broker in the process, enterprises have to shoulder the responsibility of producing, promoting and selling the products, dispersing their energy and distributing their resources in developing and producing procedures.

2. Wide Distribution Channels and Narrow Distribution Channels

Wide distribution channels and narrow distribution channels are decided by the number of the same-type brokers in each layer within one distribution channel. Wide distribution channels mean that enterprises choose two or more brokers to sell their products in one district. According to different choices made by enterprises when they cooperate with brokers, a wide or narrow distribution channel strategy covers three situations: comprehensive, selective and exclusive distribution channel strategies.

Literally, the comprehensive distribution channel strategy enables enterprises to use as many brokers as possible in one district. Under the circumstance, international enterprises can set up sales outlets in every corner of the market and take up the market to the largest extent by staging extensive advertising and making their products known to the local residents.

The selective distribution channel strategy undoubtedly refers to the situation where enterprises "selectively" choose some brokers to promote their products in one district. It is a strategy applicable especially to shopping goods, high-end goods and very professional products strategy. Compared with the comprehensive distribution channel strategy, selective one improves the efficiency and cuts down the overall cost.

If the enterprises use the exclusive distribution channel strategy, they only choose one broker in the district to sell their products, which is apparently suitable for high-end goods and very professional products. As is implied by "exclusive", the enterprises and the broker sign an exclusive agreement, in which the enterprises promise not to hire other brokers in the district, and likewise the broker cannot sell the same products of other companies. The strategy makes it easier for the enterprises to control the prices and the market, and further reduce the distribution cost, upgrade quality of service and enhance their reputation in the long run. However, those enterprises may lose some potential customers that would affect their sales volume when they lack sufficient sales teams.

3. Direct Distribution Channels and Indirect Distribution Channels

Direct distribution channels mean that enterprises sell their products directly to the customers without any brokers. There are only two layers under this situation, the enterprises and the customers, thus direct distribution channels are the shortest ones.

Several means are practical for direct distribution channels. Salesmen are sent to the international market to promote the products; enterprises sell products in the foreign country directly; enterprises sign the contracts with foreign customers face to face during international or foreign exhibitions; and products are directly mailed to the customers.

Judging from the above five means of direct distribution channels, there are no intermediate links in the process, making the entire circle simpler and easier. Enterprises choose direct distribution channels to cut down the cost paid to brokers, and find an effective way to upgrade their competitiveness. When products are sold in time, it helps to accelerate the capital turnover of the enterprises. Making the decision of direct distribution channels, enterprises have to consider various factors, which implies that only when the sales amount is very huge, can the enterprises regard it as the optimized choice, as the strategy inevitably has some disadvantages. Direct sales consume comparatively more capital and human resources of the enterprises; it is more difficult for the enterprises to grasp a whole picture about the market situations in other countries; and product delivery becomes difficult when the market is dispersed.

As for indirect distribution channels, enterprises complete the sales task by working with brokers. It helps them to concentratively invest the capital to production, and reduces the enterprises' burden of selling goods, but the price increases as there are more intermediate links and longer distribution time.

4. Other Distribution Channels

When enterprises lay out their distribution channel strategy, there are also some other options. One is using single distribution channels and the other may be multiple distribution channels. The former one means that enterprises sell the products to a specific country or district by only one channel, and the latter one means that they complete the sales by multiple channels. The other option is traditional distribution channels and vertical distribution channels. The traditional distribution channels go through the entire process in the sequence of "enterprise—wholesalers—retailers—customers", each of which is separate, while vertical distribution channels adopt integrated operation to take up the market share and achieve monopoly.

14.3　Intermediaries in a Global Distribution Channel

An effective distribution channel is essential for a company to deliver their products to the end customers. Most companies use channel intermediaries to assist in performing the functions related to transaction, logistics, etc. This part will introduce definition, functions, and pros and cons of channel intermediaries.

14.3.1　Definition of Channel Intermediaries

In what way can a customer buy a product? Is it necessary for them to contact the manufacturer directly? Most consumers purchase products they need through channel intermediaries, whose main mission is to transfer goods from the producers to ultimate consumers. In other words, they are able to price the goods and decide the final way of selling products. In this case, the intermediaries would be known as retailers. For example, in the case of Ninja Corp, before it chose to launch their product line, it was necessary for the company to choose which intermediary in order to successfully deliver goods to the end users:

1. Merchant Wholesalers

Merchant wholesalers refer to organizations which buy products from manufacturers and resell them to other businesses, wholesalers or retailers. In this case, the ownership of the products is transferred to merchant wholesalers who can store the products and sell them one more time. Customers of these wholesalers include small-or medium-sized retailers.

2. Agents and Brokers

There are intermediaries who are not willing to hold the ownership of products which is troublesome for them. Agents and brokers refer to those wholesalers who are responsible for promoting sales. They assist in moving goods from the manufacturer to the end user. They work on a basis of commission depending on the sales volume. For example, a newly founded company who expects to have more effective distribution is prone to utilize agents or brokers. In this case, the company can enter into a large market and make a large number of profits provided that the agents or brokers function well.

▶ 14.3.2　Functions of Channel Intermediaries

Using a middleman in a marketing channel can help manufacturers to expand their reach. A distribution channel might involve several middlemen like agents, wholesalers, distributors and retailers. Intermediaries purchase products from one channel member and resell them to another, which indicates that their duty is to bridge the gap between different channel members. They are also likely to hold stock and perform logistical and distribution functions on behalf of the company.

1. Selling Through Agents

Agents work for manufacturers as an independent representative, who sells products and provides services to other intermediaries such as wholesalers or retailers. Agents may be single people or organizations. Agents sell products or provide services, and then they will get a certain percentage of commission. They play a significant role in a manufacturer's internal sales resources.

2. Reaching More Customers Through Retailers

Retailers belong to intermediaries who sell products to customers. Retailers enable manufacturers to get close to customers in diverse places where manufacturers cannot reach with their own resources. Usually retailers place a large order directly with manufacturers or wholesalers and resell them. Retailers usually purchase products from different suppliers, including competitive offerings of similar products. In this case, to promote sales, manufacturers have to attract retailers through some measures such as incentives and discounts.

3. Simplifying Logistics Through Wholesalers

Wholesalers are also intermediaries who buy a large quantity of products from diverse manufacturers. After that, they stock the products in warehouses before selling them to retailers. Through holding stock, wholesalers help manufacturers to reach customers in a number of areas without paying additional costs in warehousing. Moreover, wholesalers also perform logistical functions on behalf of manufacturers, which spares the expenses for the latter.

4. Cooperative Marketing Through Distributors

Like wholesalers, distributors also offer warehousing and logistical functions for manufacturers, but they have more connections with manufacturers at work. Distributors may have exclusive rights of a certain kind of products from the manufacturers, and they may also attend some selling programs to promote sales.

14.3.3 Advantages & Disadvantages of Channel Intermediaries

A large number of startups and large multinational companies utilize channel intermediaries to assist them in bridging the gaps in the distribution channel. There are a number of advantages of using an intermediary, such as increasing sales, expanding the market and appealing to new customers. Whereas a company should select a middleman cautiously, because it has its own disadvantages. In conclusion, it is essential to assess the potential benefits and risks brought by a channel intermediary.

The advantages include:

1. Industry and Geographic Expertise

One of the most beneficial strengths of appointing intermediaries lies in that businesses can get immediate access to industry, market and geographic expertise. A number of firms outsource their marketing strategies and campaigns to marketing agencies which are professional and have contacts with a number of clients having realized their objectives. Therefore, companies which use intermediaries have access to these clients' skill and expertise without any learning curve at their end.

Likewise, traditional sales distributors have geographic and industry knowledge. Representatives in a specific geographic territory are familiar with the location of significant consumers, and know how to get close to them. Some of them may have built strong relationships with customers, which helps to promote sales.

2. Cost and Time Savings

It is time-consuming to recruit a sales representative for a company. At the beginning, the company has to select candidates from numerous applicants, arrange for an interview before the management team discusses the final decision. It may take several months, but turn out to hire an unqualified sales employee, which pushes the company to arrange for one more round of hiring which is a waste of time and resources.

Through outsourcing sales work, companies can not only save time but also a great number of labour costs. According to the Bureau of Labor Statistics of the United States, an employee's salary accounts for about 70% of the total wage package. The remaining 30% consists of taxes and benefits. Thus hiring intermediaries enables companies to reduce the payroll expenses of that 30%.

In addition, appointing a middleman enables companies to avoid wasted resources. For instance, if a company has to launch two sales programs this month and for the next, they need to pay for those specific services. Whereas should they use a full-time sales staff, they would have to pay for extra expenses although there is no promoting activities in other months.

3. Customer Convenience and Relationships

One more benefit of appointing intermediaries is to assist in promoting sales. Sales representatives of intermediaries may have close contact with key customers in their territories. It would be time-consuming for startups to build up close relationships with customers.

Using intermediaries can also bring convenience for customers. Intermediaries offer customers diverse products at a single place, which avoids wasting time, energy and money of the customers.

It is proven to be beneficial for companies to appoint middlemen because the latter has frequent contact with the public as well as media, which may increase coverage of the company.

The disadvantages include:

1. Reputation Risks of a Middleman

Despite the numerous advantages of utilizing intermediaries, there are some disadvantages which should be taken into consideration. One of them lies in that intermediaries may influence the company's image. Although companies trust intermediaries, it is not one hundred percent that the latter follows the stipulated terms and does as what they have been required.

Middlemen may also provide inferior products or services on behalf of businesses which lead to ruin of the business' image in the customers' mind, thus the customers never buy any products from the company henceforth. As a result, intermediaries bring numerous troubles to both the relevant customers and companies.

In conclusion, businesses should be cautious about choosing qualified intermediaries. It is necessary to examine the candidate middleman's previous performance, visit his/her former clients or even customers who are familiar with them. Businesses are suggested to list all qualifications that a middleman should possess before interviewing them.

2. Lack of Attention

It is known to all that intermediaries usually provide services for several companies simultaneously. This brings a large number of commissions for intermediaries, but this may also mean limited attention to businesses. Tight schedules force middlemen to focus on some projects which offer them commission, but divert attention from others. As a result, they may not be able to provide timely services and delay looming deadlines, which will incur losses for businesses.

3. Loss of Communication Control

Businesses invest a considerable amount of time and capital in producing brand communications, striving to make customers impressed by their products and services and training their employees to master the unique features of their own products and services. Whereas compared with full-time employees, outsourced middlemen may not be so familiar with the products, as a result the issue of information losses may arise.

Moreover, intermediaries who are confused about the core values of businesses may deliver wrong messages to customers, which affects sales of products and services. Additionally, due to failure to approach intermediaries all the time, businesses may lose control over their communication. Compared with middlemen, in-house employees can be reached any time in the office to participate in discussing solutions.

14.4   International Retailing

14.4.1   Definition of International Retailing

When looking up the definition of "retailing" in the Merriam-Webster's Dictionary, you will find the following meaning, "the activities involved in the selling of goods to ultimate consumers for personal or household consumption". Some characteristics of retailing can be concluded as follows: Products are directly sold to consumers in small amounts and high frequency for consumption. Therefore, the definition of international retailing can be simulated as, "the activities involved in the selling of goods to ultimate consumers for personal or household consumption in the international market".

Thanks to globalization, the advent of information age, rapid urbanization and economic freedom enjoyed by more and more people, international retailing undergoes unprecedented development in modern times without being restrained by geographical boundaries. More and more enterprises expand their businesses outside their countries, bringing in a major portion of their revenue from the international market.

14.4.2   International Retailer Classification

Wal-Mart, Carrefour, Ralph Lauren and Chanel, the brands mentioned before, are all international retailers. However, it is easy to figure out that there are obvious differences between the four international retailers. Wal-Mart and Carrefour are international chained supermarkets selling various kinds of products, including food, clothing, makeup and so on. Compared with them, Ralph Lauren and Chanel sell a more limited range of products, mainly in the fashion industry. Thus, international retailers can be broadly classified into two categories: One is the international grocery retailers (Wal-Mart and Carrefour), and the other is international fashion retailers (Ralph Lauren and Chanel).

1. International Grocery Retailers

The most well-known international grocery retailers are Wal-Mart, Carrefour, Tesco, Costco, etc., which are multinational companies and have stores in many countries. Generally speaking, these international grocery retailers sell a large variety of products, including food (meat, vegetables, fruits, sweets, drinks, and so on), clothing, makeup, daily necessities, electric appliances, etc. In addition to their products for sale, another similarity among them is that a large portion of their total revenue is made from the international market.

2. International Fashion Retailers

When it comes to international fashion retailers, those world-famous luxury as well as affordable fashion brands pop into our minds, like Chanel, Gucci, Ralph Lauren, and also Zara, Uniqlo etc.. Those brands originally operate in their own countries, while with the development of economic globalization and the prevailing pursuit of fashion by people outside the home countries, people promote their brands internationally and also expand their product mix. Chanel, starting from custom-made clothes, also paves its way for jewelry, makeup, skin care products, perfumes, and even watches.

▶ 14.4.3 Challenges Faced by International Retail Companies

Although international retail companies operate globally with a large number of revenue and high brand value, they constantly confront different cultures of different countries, changeable purchasing habits of different people and unexpected local business environment. During the process of going internationalized, those companies face the following inherent challenges, including localizing their products and service, upgrading the product mix and adapting to the local prices.

Whichever category an international retail company belongs to, an international grocery retailer or an international fashion retailer has to work out an efficient plan to occupy the local market featuring different kinds of consumer behavior, tastes and fashion trends. The most direct challenge that it encounters is how to localize its products and service, so as to adapt to the local market in the shortest time. Those international chained grocery retailers, like Wal-Mart and Carrefour, localize their products by selling almost the same items with their counterparts outside the home country, and perhaps slightly differentiate themselves by presenting distinctive exporting goods on delicate shelves. This is the same case with their services. As "takeaway" or "delivery" service is becoming increasingly popular and prevailing in China, they consider it seriously as one of their main services, which has also become a common thing that they deliver every item of their products or cooperate with Chinese domestic delivery companies.

In addition to the direct challenge international retail companies face in the line of business, the biggest challenge for those companies is how to upgrade the product mix. The products in retailing are fast moving with very short life on the shelf, forcing their sellers to upgrade the product mix so as to attract customers in a time-efficient manner. At present, high-end businesses as luxury brands are, they spare litmited efforts in diversifying the product mix. Hermes, a luxurious French brand starting from making high-quality harnesses and later expanding itself to handbags, Haute Couture, scarves, etc., has entered the beauty industry by introducing Hermes Lipstick.

Pricing is another challenge that international retail companies cannot ignore when they expand to different countries. Influenced by economic development, disposable income and sensitivity of prices, international retail companies should make early plans to set differential pricing strategies. Developing and emerging markets, fueled by comparatively less developed economies and lower GDP per capita, are highly price sensitive, ending up with the fact that pricing cannot follow their tradition back to the home country. Thus, when trying to pave their way for a new market, international retail companies have to make differential pricing strategies by taking into consideration the local economic development level and price sensitivity in accordance with the cost-profit principle.

14.5　International Logistics

14.5.1　Definition of International Logistics

The concept of logistics comes from the United States in the 1950s with its original name as "physical distribution". The Council of Supply Chain Management Professionals (CSCMP) defines logistics as a part of the supply chain, "planning, implementing, and controlling the physical and information flows concerned with materials and final goods from the point of origin to the point of usage". Overall, it is a process including transportation, inventory, packaging, handling, distribution processing and information management. Thus, international logistics happen across the border, at least between two countries.

If logistics was born under the requirement of economic development and integration of domestic market, then international logistics came into being with the advancement of international trade and the specialization of international production, fueled by the gradual integration of the global economy featuring the liberalization of trade and investment.

As a matter of fact, international logistics is not only limited to those logistic activities brought by international trade and international production. Broadly speaking, the flow of various kinds of products and goods across the world all belongs to the scope of international logistics, including the physical move of exporting and importing goods, donations, material assistance, philatelic items, etc. For example, abundant logistic activities are followed by international exhibitions and international aid.

14.5.2　Characteristics of International Logistics

International logistics involves at least two countries, sometimes, more than two, endowing it with very different and distinctive characteristics compared with domestic logistics.

1. As international logistics covers broader geographical areas, and transports goods through long distance with various kinds of transportation tools, it is destined to be more complex in operational environment, transporting process and related certificates.

Complex operational environment, in essence, is determined by the different conditions of countries. When enterprises are engaged in international logistics, they encounter challenges from different economic development, cultures and customs, laws and regulations in logistics, industrial standards, and status quo of the industry. Usually, those challenges are unpredictable and required a long period of time for enterprises to get accustomed to.

International transport inevitably takes advantage of various kinds of transportation tools—air transport, shipping, overland freight and inland water transport. Long-distance transportation, interlocking links, long transportation cycle, complex climate conditions, high demand for maintaining and storing goods in the process all increase the complexity of international logistics.

International logistics requires enterprises to obtain various kinds of logistics documents, including business documents, settlement of exchange documents, shipping documents, transport documents, customs declaration documents, port documents and so on. Every time goods are delivered by another country, documents in the very specific local languages should be presented.

2. As complex as international logistics is in the above-mentioned ways, the smooth operation of it is endorsed by standardized information system, logistics infrastructure and trade agreement.

Standardization of the global information system is the foundation of ensuring high efficiency of international logistics. Unified platforms of information technology and high-quality information transmission and processing help to pass on useful information to relevant logistics nodes in a timely manner. Therefore, integrated operation across the globe is formed, ensuring the interconnection of every link during the whole process, and effectively arranging businesses of each node. Standardized information system saves business time and also shortens the transportation period.

Logistics development levels vary from country to country, but infrastructure can be standardized, such as standard containers, loading and unloading equipment, warehouses and ports. The loading gauge and carrying capacity of means of transport, and standards of railway tracks are different in different countries, leading to constant loading and unloading of goods when crossing the borders, which adds to the workload, resulting in waste and increases logistics cost. Therefore, standardization of infrastructure can effectively reduce the workload, cut down the transportation period and most importantly lower the cost.

Trade agreement, signed by two or more countries, stipulates the most-favored-nation treatment, the value of import and export, the use of currency, preferential tariff, etc.. Applicable and standardized trade agreements can simplify operational steps, reduce the cost and greatly facilitate the transportation. However, in order to protect domestic trade and local economic development, many countries set limited import quotas, and levy very high tariffs on the excessive part for the purpose of restricting imports and bringing about unexpected logistics costs.

3. The entire international logistics period undergoes a long and complicated operational process, enterprises shoulder general risks (such as unforeseen accidents, losses brought by force majeure and so on), as well as higher political, economic and natural risks.

Political risks cannot be ignored nowadays. Some countries and districts around the world are still going through political turmoil that can be wars, riots or just strikes. Those uncertainties interrupt the process, delay the transportation, and damage the goods, bringing immeasurable losses to the enterprises. In a word, the more countries are involved in international logistics, the higher the risks will be.

Economic risks are shown as those in foreign trade, presenting themselves as exchange rate risk and interest rate risk. Due to variable factors like market expectation, macro-economic policies and supplement of currency in different countries, and international balance of payment, exchange rate and interest rate are on the change, bringing more uncertainties to international logistics and potential losses to enterprises.

Natural risks are natural disasters like earthquakes, tsunamis, hurricanes, and so on, which often cannot be prevented from happening, but can give rise to severe losses.

As economic globalization pushes forward at unprecedented speed, international logistics is of great importance to any enterprise, giving them chances to enter the global market, helping to improve the international competitiveness of their products and contributing to the overall development of the enterprises.

Key Terms

distribution/marketing channel 分销渠道	A sequence of channel members which deliver a product from the producer to the ultimate user, taking profit and effectiveness into consideration. 分销渠道指的是本着盈利的目的将产品生产出来，并将其送至消费者手中，该过程涉及的一系列成员。
channel members 渠道成员	Channel members include manufacturers, wholesalers, retailers, and sales agents, responsible for manufacturing products or providing services ready for customers. 分销渠道成员包括生产商、批发商、零售商、销售代理，成员负责生产产品及提供服务，并将其送到顾客手中。
direct distribution channels 直销渠道	Direct channels do not include any intermediary, which means the manufacturer contacts the customer directly at the point of sale. 直销渠道不涉及任何中间人，生产商直接联系并将产品销售给顾客。
indirect distribution channels 间接销售渠道	If there is a middleman or intermediary in the distribution channel, who is responsible for selling the product to the ultimate consumer, then this channel is an indirect channel. 间接销售渠道指的是，分销渠道中存在中间商，中间商负责将商品销售给最终消费者。
bulk breaking 商品松包	Wholesalers and retailers purchase large quantities of goods from producers, and then break the bulk by selling a few at a time to many other channels or customers. 商品松包指批发商或零售商从制造商处大量购入商品，并将其拆分，以销售给其他渠道或消费者。
creating assortments 商品分类	Wholesalers and retailers sell different kinds of goods at one specific place which is beneficial to customers because they do not need to go to different retailers to buy different products. 商品分类指批发商或零售商在特定地点出售分类好的各类商品，免去消费者前往各零售商购买不同商品的麻烦。
capital turnover 资金周转	Cycle of raising capital, making investments, and returning the capital to its source from the profits generated 筹集资金、进行投资、获得利润的周期性资本循环。
channel intermediaries 渠道中间商	Intermediaries, also known as distribution intermediaries, marketing intermediaries, or middlemen, are an extremely crucial element of a company's product distribution channel. 中间商，亦即分销中间商或中间人，是企业产品分销渠道中极为重要的部分。
merchant wholesalers 商业批发商	Organizations which buy products from manufacturers and resell them to other businesses, wholesalers or retailers. 商业批发商指的是从制造商处购买产品，并将其销售给其他商家、批发商或者零售商的组织。

Continued

disposable income 可支配收入	Income remains after deduction of taxes and other mandatory charges, available to be spent or saved as one wishes. 税收及扣除其他费用剩下的可自由支配的收入。
haute couture 高级定制时装	Expensive, fashionable clothes produced by leading fashion houses. 由一线时尚品牌设计制造的昂贵时装。
joint venture 合资企业	A commercial enterprise undertaken jointly by two or more parties which otherwise retain their distinct identities. 由两方或两方以上共同经营的企业,但在其他方面保持各自不同的身份。

Review & Critical Thinking Questions

1. What is a channel of distribution composed of?
2. What are the factors enterprises have to consider when making decisions about international distribution channels?
3. What are the advantages and disadvantages of long distribution channels and short distribution channels respectively?
4. How can firms benefit from good intermediaries?
5. What is international retailing?
6. What categories do Wal-Mart and Carrefour belong to in international retailing?
7. What are the characteristics of international logistics?

Discussion Questions

If a newly-founded company wants to sell daily necessities to foreign countries, what kind of distribution channels should it choose? Explain the answer in detail.

Case Study

Avon's Distribution Channels

Avon, as of 2012, was the world's largest direct seller of beauty products. Headquartered in New York, USA, it reported US $10.7 billion in annual revenues in 2012. Avon's business was based on the traditional marketing model of door-to-door selling, through a network of 6.4 million active sales representatives (reps) who sold the products directly to consumers.

Over the years, Avon expanded its business to other parts of the world, and had a presence in more than 100 countries across the globe. It was highly popular in emerging markets like China and Russia.

The company, with a history of more than 125 years, was a pioneer in direct selling. During the late 1990s, however, the business started to face problems. In 1999, Andrea Jung (Jung) became the CEO and things started looking up for Avon. But business started to decline after 2008, mainly due to problems in the direct selling model in Avon's home market, the US.

The history of Avon can be traced back to 1885 when it was founded by David H. McConnell (McConnell), a traveling book salesman. In 1886, while going from house to house with his books, he found that his customers, especially women, were more interested in the free perfume samples he offered than the books he was selling.

He also recognized that many women had the potential to become good salespeople. He took up the perfume business more seriously and became a perfume entrepreneur. He incorporated California Perfume Company (CPC) and P.F.E Albee (Albee) was the first representative of the company. She travelled by horse, buggy, or even train to sell perfumes door-to-door.

She also appointed other women as representatives. This method of selling directly to the customers went on to become the hallmark of Avon's business model. Albee was called the "Mother of the California Perfume Company". McConnell developed corporate principles which became the guidelines for Avon.

Product Library of Avon

Avon, being an international manufacturer and distributor of beauty, household, and personal care products, had believed in direct selling since its inception. It offered a wide range of beauty products, including skin care products, cosmetics, perfumes, spa treatments, make up, and everyday cosmetics & toiletries like shampoos, deodorants, and body lotions. Its product line included many recognizable names such as Anew, Avon Color, Skin-So-Soft, and Advance Techniques. Avon Color was one of the leading cosmetic brands in the world. The products were mainly targeted at women in the age group of 25 to 50 years old. The products were of high quality, were priced affordably, and positioned as products that provided value.

The Evolution of the Direct Selling Model

Broadly, Avon's distribution channel could be divided into three major categories: Direct Selling, Limited Retailers, and Online. Of these, direct selling was its primary channel while the other two were secondary channels of distribution. The direct selling channel was Avon's core channel, one which the company had relied on since 1886 when its founder himself used to undertake door-to-door selling.

The Distribution Model

The representatives were independent contractors and not employees of Avon. Once a person signed up to become an Avon Rep, the district manager, who was an employee of Avon, called on him to explain the process of selling the products. The new reps were required to remit a sign-up fee of $10. They were given 20 brochures, sample products, sales books, order forms, etc.

Retail

In the early 1980s, retail outlets were gaining a strong hold on the market. Almost 80% of all beauty products were sold through retail stores and this market had become difficult to ignore. However, for Avon, selling its products through retail stores was difficult as it knew the move could alienate its sales representatives. In order to enter into department and specialty stores, Avon entered into a joint venture with Liz Claiborne (designer) and created fragrances and cosmetics line and made these products available in 2,000 stores.

Online

In 1997, Avon became the first cosmetic company to sell its products directly online. There was a dedicated Avon representative website which also informed consumers about new products in the industry. Though it was started in 1997, the electronic commerce strategy was not taken very seriously till 1999.

Channel Conflict

Jung's ventures to establish a retail channel and an online presence made customers and representatives alike feel that Avon was no longer a direct sales company, and that it was turning into a packaged goods company. Jung tried to position some products as premium cosmetics, but that plan did not work out, as the premium products were hard to sell through direct marketers. Similarly, restructuring efforts under her direction also proved unsuccessful.

Discussion Questions

1. What is the distribution channel adopted by Avon? And what are the advantages and disadvantages of direct selling for the company and the customers?

2. Do you think the model is sustainable? Are there any ways in which Avon can improve its distribution model?

中文概述

分销渠道又称为营销渠道,指本着盈利的目的生产产品,并将其送至消费者手中,该过程涉及的一系列成员。**分销渠道成员**包括**生产商、批发商、零售商、销售代理**,成员负责生产产品及提供服务,并将其送到顾客手中。

分销渠道可分为**直接渠道**和**间接渠道**。因制造商与最终消费者之间可存在不同数量的中间商,故间接渠道又可分为**一级、二级、三级间接渠道**。

双重渠道:如制造商同时使用两种及以上的分销渠道,将货物送至最终消费者手中,其使用的渠道则称为**双重渠道**。例如,某商家通过两种方式销售产品,一种是通过展厅销售产品,另一种是通过网络进行产品交易。手机可通过双重渠道进行销售。

服务的分销渠道:不同于实体产品,服务无法储存于仓库中。然而,这并非意味着服务无法通过间接渠道进行传送。如今通过互联网、网上店铺、聚合商业模式,服务可通过中间商传送至顾客手中。

互联网作为分销渠道:随着互联网的出现,制造商传送商品的方式发生很大的改变。传统的直接渠道和间接渠道不再是传送产品和服务的唯二方法,其他新出现的方法包括利用网络输送产品,如滴滴、日用百货之类的网络平台。网络的出现意味着可取消一些产品,如软件的中间商,软件可通过网络直接输送到顾客手中。

影响国际分销渠道策略的因素被称为分销渠道的"6C"原则,在进行渠道决策时,企业需要考虑成本、资金、控制、覆盖、特性和连续性这六个因素。

由于各国市场环境不同、渠道安排错综复杂,企业应根据不同国家的市场状况,采用不同的渠道。主要有以下渠道可供选择:

(1)长渠道和短渠道。长渠道是指国际企业选择两个或两个以上环节的中间商来销售企业的产品。短渠道是指国际企业只采用一个中间环节或自己销售商品。

(2)宽渠道和窄渠道。宽渠道是指企业在同一地区选择两个以上的中间商销售产品。渠道宽度分为三种,广泛性销售渠道、选择性销售渠道、独家销售渠道。

(3)直接渠道和间接渠道。直接渠道是指生产企业在产品的销售中不通过中间商而直接向消费者或用户销售产品。间接渠道是指生产企业利用中间商销售产品。

(4)其他渠道。包括单渠道和多渠道,传统渠道和垂直渠道。传统渠道是指商品流通经过"生产企业—批发商—零售商—最后消费者"这个过程。在垂直渠道中,每个成员采取不同程度的一体化经营或联合经营。

中间商的分类:

批发商:指向制造商购买产品,然后将其销售给其他企业、批发商或零售商的企业。该情况下批发商掌握了商品的所有权,可将其储存或进行二次销售。这类企业的顾客包括中小型零售商。

　　代理商及经纪人：代理商及经纪人指负责推销产品的批发商。他们协助将产品从制造商送至最终消费者手中。根据推销产品的销售额他们可获得一定佣金。

　　国际零售：指的是跨越国界向所有消费者直接销售商品和服务的经济活动。随着经济全球化的发展、信息时代的到来、城市化的不断推进和各国人民经济自由的实现，国际零售业迅猛发展。国际零售实际上与每个人的生活息息相关，比如一二线大城市常见的沃尔玛和家乐福超市，它们是国际零售的典型代表。

　　国际物流是国际供应链活动的一部分，跨国家跨区域专注于物品、服务及相关信息从起源点到消费点的有效流动和储存的企划、执行与控制过程。

　　国际物流涉及多个国家，覆盖地理范围广，跨越海洋和大陆，与国内物流相比具有以下特点：一是复杂性。复杂性主要体现在作业环境的复杂性，国际运输过程的复杂性，国际物流作业单证的复杂性。二是标准化程度要求高。国际物流要求全球信息系统标准化，基础设施建设标准化和贸易协定标准化。三是风险高。国际物流完成周期长、作业流程复杂，面临着各国潜在的政治风险、汇率和利率风险及自然风险。

UNIT 15 / Corporate Social Responsibility and Sustainability

1. Understand the meaning and importance of corporate social responsibility (CSR).
2. Understand the motivations behind CSR.
3. Understand the relation between CSR and sustainability.
4. Understand the meaning of sustainability marketing.
5. Identify and apply sustainability marketing strategies.
6. Identify fraud in sustainability/CSR.

15.1　Introduction to Corporate Social Responsibility (CSR)

15.1.1　Definitions of CSR

As early as 1953, the first modern definition of corporate social responsibility (CSR) was provided by Bowen, saying that "the obligation is to pursue those policies, to make those decisions, or to follow those lines of action which are desirable in terms of the objectives and values of our society."

In 1979, the most popular definition of CSR was created by Carroll: "The social responsibility of business encompasses the economic, legal, ethical, and discretionary expectations that society has of organizations at a given point in time."

The World Business Council for Sustainable Development (2000) publicized the definition of CSR as "Corporate Social Responsibility is the continuing commitment by businesses to behave ethically and contribute to economic development while improving the quality of life of the workforce and their families as well as of the local community and society at large."

The European Commission defined CSR as "A concept whereby companies decide voluntarily to contribute to a better society and a cleaner environment— a concept whereby companies integrate social and environmental concerns in their business operation and in their interaction with their stakeholders on a voluntary basis."

The description of the term Corporate Social Responsibility (CSR) has started to become more explicit in what our society expects and values a business. Other than the positive impact of CSR on economic development, it has been specifically defined as care for the environment and welfare of employees, community and society as a whole.

15.1.2 CSR in Demand

Corporate social responsibility is also called corporate citizenship, corporate conscience and sustainable responsible business. For ages, profits are the only measure of corporations' success; but can profits guarantee that the corporation will still be functioning in the future? As the development of globalization, international trade, global supply chains, human resource management, environmental protection and other health and safety elements are increasingly raising the concerns of CSR. In the information age, communication technology is making it easier to track corporate information that may easily result in crises in business operation when companies do inappropriate activities. Governmental and intergovernmental bodies have developed principles and guidelines to constrain the unethical conduct of businesses. People are aware that corporations are like citizens living in the same place as other flesh-and-blood residents so they should share the responsibility of improving their common home. Many of those factors and influences have led to increasing attention being devoted to CSR. Firms integrate CSR policy into business model because of either external pressures or internal consciousness. In general, there are four types of CSR motives identified as value-driven, strategic-driven, egoistic and stakeholder-driven motives.

Value-driven motive is the belief that CSR is the right thing to do. Companies who hold this value present it as part of their corporate culture and practice it in their business. For example, products like re-sealable goody bag, kitchen fronts made from recycled wood and recycled plastic, water-saving tap and multifunctional sofa are good examples of the application of renewable resources, recycled waste, energy saving and zero waste. The companies who take such product strategy has taken environmental responsibility into account.

Strategic-driven motive is based on the intrinsic demand of a company to increase sales and profit. CSR helps corporations establish positive brand image which is likely to increase favor of consumers and build customer loyalty, thereby resulting in financial returns in a long run. Brands motivated by this strategic intention usually search for authentication of the professional agencies. For example, Little Freddie, a baby food producer, has been certified by both OF & G (an organic certification body) and EU-Agriculture as an organic food manufacturer. The organic authentication is like an admission allowing it to enter the green food market. When parents choose baby food, they would prefer organic baby rice as it seems healthier than other non-organic products.

Egotistic-driven motive is to take advantage of the cause and non-profit organization or the like for itself. The most common practice is that corporate entities engage in charity projects by funding those non-profit, educational and health care organizations, social services, and environmental groups; in return, those organizations and groups promise to provide some benefit with bottom line metrics such as awards, free publicity or other conveniences for their businesses in local community.

Stakeholder-driven motive originates from the pressures of stakeholders. Stakeholders are defined as "any group or individual who can affect or is affected by the achievement of the organization's objective", such as shareholders, employees, customers, suppliers, environment, community, NGOs and investors. Companies' CSR practice sometimes is the response to stakeholders' expectations. For example, fair trade is rooted in the objection to exploitation. When farmers do not receive a fair return for what they produce and many workers do not earn enough for what they do, fair trade provides the possibility of protecting vulnerable populations and promoting environmental protection. Transparency in supply chain is due to the distrust in company's words, so making products traceable can gain trust and build strong relationships with stakeholders. Anti-discrimination against any worker is a claim for equal human rights.

15.2 Values in CSR

1. CSR as Value Creation

Although there have always been doubts about the link of CSR to profitability, the values created by CSR could be both implicit and explicit. It is believed that CSR created **shared value** since company success and social welfare are interdependent. A company needs healthy, educated workforce, sustainable resources and proficient government to compete effectively while a society needs competitive and profitable companies to support its development by paying taxes, creating employment, assisting philanthropy and researching and developing technology. Furthermore, incorporating social value into corporate strategy may threaten the short-term financial performance as partial profits flow out to support the development of a society; however, the opportunities for competitive advantage from building a better society will increase.

2. CSR as Risk Management

Every business faces risks of unexpected and harmful incidents such as corruption, scandals, natural disasters which can affect its normal operation significantly or even cause a permanent shutdown. Risk management allows businesses to prepare for unwanted accidents by minimizing threats and costs before they happen. CSR can be a risk management tool to manage threats from finance, reputation, the environment and supply chains. When corporations take social responsibility, it means that they are acting morally, meet the public expectations and requirements, follow the government rules and instructions and focus on sustainability. The positive image formed by CSR efforts can help corporations to avoid brain drain crisis and customer dissatisfaction, to decrease legal liabilities and to provide protection to both companies and the environment from detrimental events.

3. CSR as Corporate Philanthropy

Philanthropy is the donations and aid given to impoverished communities. Many corporations simply donate money or other resources to charitable organizations while some corporations have dedicated departments to managing charity and philanthropy programs. Organizations devoted to philanthropy usually get enhanced brand exposure that is positively perceived by people. Potential consumers can be attracted by companies and brands that support causes, and existing consumers can be more loyal. Corporate philanthropy has been quickly becoming a marketing strategy **cause related marketing** to further brand development, market recognition and customer relationships. Philanthropy creates a distinctive competitive advantage for corporates who support a cause in their business. Table 15.1 makes comparison among values of CSR from the perspectives of purpose and benefit.

Table 15.1   Values in CSR

Value	Purpose	Benefits
CSR as value creation	to develop a sustainable business model	integrates business into society develops human capital enjoys preferential policies creates a stable and thrived environment
CSR as risk management	to control risks	mitigates crisis from external environment mitigates crisis from internal operation
CSR as corporate philanthropy	to implement short-term marketingstrategy	enhances reputation increases market recognition strengthens customer relationships conducts corporate social responsibilities

15.3 Sustainability Basics

15.3.1 The Link Between Sustainability and CSR

Sustainability is an essential part of the CSR concept. According to Danko et al. and Porter & Kramer, CSR consists of four elements. First, moral obligation is described as the responsibility that corporations should take from commonly believed morality. Second, license to operate is the approval from the local government, communities and stakeholders. Third, reputation is the object that firms want to improve and strengthen by taking CSR. Fourth, sustainability is meeting the needs of the present without compromising the needs of future generations. In practice, CSR involves a myriad of business practices such as fair sourcing, carbon footprint tracking, recycling, research, development and use of clean energy, staff-oriented human resource management, technical and educational support to local communities, donations, etc. CSR performances are to maintain a sustainable society and environment thereby generating sustainable economic income.

On September 25th, 2015, 193 countries reached 17 goals as a global sustainable development agenda[①]. The business sector takes an important role to play in delivering global goals. Many companies, especially multinational companies are liable to disclose their sustainable operations. The terms of CSR and sustainability are often used interchangeably. If you check companies' annual reports, you will find some companies use the name of sustainability report while some others use CSR report.

15.3.2 The Dimensions of Sustainability

Sustainability works on the "Triple Bottom Line (TBL)" approach which includes people, the planet, and profit. The TBL posits that sustainability should not only be limited to environment, but also include economic and social issues. If commercial activities can benefit economy, environment and society at the same time, then they reach win-win-win cooperation which enables the corporations to become sustainable. Each part of TBL is measurable by examining values of certain references as what Figure 15.1 shows. For

---

① The seventeen goals include no poverty, zero hunger, good health and well-being, quality education, gender equality, clean water and sanitation, modern energy, good jobs and economic growth, innovation and infrastructure, reduced inequalities, sustainable cities and communities, responsible consumption and production, climate action, life below water, life on land, peace, justice and strong institutions and partnerships for the goals.

example, economic measurement includes sales volume, net profit, return on investment, tax payable, cash flow, number of jobs created, etc. Environmental measurement consists of the quality of air and water, energy consumption, **carbon emission**, etc. Social measurement includes working hours, health and safety, community impact, human rights, etc. Arguably, someone mentioned that culture as the fourth part should be involved in TBL framework because culture notably affects human's behavior and the value of it cannot be overlooked.

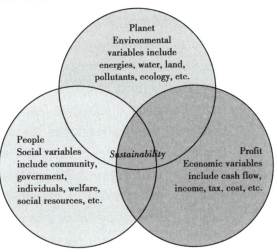

Figure 15.1 Triple Bottom Line

15.4 Sustainability Marketing

15.4.1 The Thin Line Between Sustainability Marketing and Sustainable Marketing

Dam & Apeldoorn defined sustainable marketing as "The marketing within and supportive of sustainable economic development." But Belz & Peattie (2009) argued that the name of sustainability in marketing strategy was sustainability marketing instead of sustainable marketing. From their point of view, sustainable marketing only describes the strategy of maintaining long lasting relationships with customers, whereas sustainability marketing contains more information than that which is maintaining sustainable relationships with people, social and natural environment. Sustainability marketing considers sustainability issues more explicitly. Thus, the following adopts the broader scope—"sustainability marketing" when discussing the marketing strategy of sustainability.

15.4.2　The Concept of Sustainability Marketing

Sustainability marketing is defined as building and maintaining sustainable relationships with customers, the social environment and the natural environment. The concept of sustainability marketing has evolved from social marketing, ecological marketing and green marketing. In the middle of the twentieth century, marketing activities focused on communicating and delivering superior value to customers. Social marketing promotes the well-being of customers and the society through supporting social causes, sponsoring, donating, providing volunteer services, and many other responsible business practices. Ecological marketing deals with ecology and pollution issues. However, it concentrated on the producer's will to improve the environment and did not consider consumer demand. Green marketing replaced the moral obligation in ecological marketing with pressures from stakeholders. Charter et al. defined green marketing as "a holistic and responsible management process that identifies, anticipates, satisfies and fulfills stakeholder requirements, for a reasonable reward, that does not adversely affect human or natural environmental wellbeing". Compared with the above, sustainability marketing provides a more complex concern for the sustainable development of a company. But practically, it is never easy to design such marketing strategies because of the conflict between sustainability principles which require to conserve resources and consume less and marketing principles which need to expand production and promote consumption.

15.4.3　Sustainability Marketing Strategies

1. Positioning

Green market often refers to consumers with a tendency towards sustainability and the corporations provide products and services for those consumers. Consumers have been increasing awareness of sustainability issues. There is an increasing number of them who understand what sustainability is and show interest in environmental issues. The number of consumers who are willing to buy green products is growing, especially when these products are cost saving. Among those consumers, their interest in sustainable products and services is not the same. If the differences are measured from a psychographic point of view, lifestyle can be a simple criterion to differentiate consumers. For some consumers, they have been highly concerned about social and natural environmental issues and support sustainable activities constantly. This reflects on consumer behavior showing as purchasing environmental friendly products, insisting on minimalist lifestyle or any sustainability stance. For some other consumers, they do not change their consumption habits, instead, they seek to recycle or reuse products they bought. Besides, benefits can be another way to segment consumer groups. Some consumers pay attention to functional benefits such as energy saving, durable and long life, health and safety. Some focus on self-expressive benefits, expressing individual personality through consuming green products. Some may be attracted by the experiential benefits that green products bring to them. Successful sustainability positioning is to explore and respond to those customers' psychology and values. The strategy of sustainability positioning can be divided into four aspects: environment, economy, health and safety and humanity.

Environment: The most common sustainability positioning is to develop environmental friendly products or services, like adopting green energy, recyclable and renewable resources, reducing carbon emissions, extending product life cycle, etc. For example, the automobile producer BYD Company Limited defines their products as green. It developed energy storage and solar panels for power plants to ensure the stable output of solar energy. Its popular products are new energy vehicles such as Tang DM and Song Pro DM which adopt electric driven technology. BYD SkyRail and SkyShuttle are another two green solutions as they are powered by electricity without pollutant emissions and the built-in multi-layered network mitigates traffic congestion. It can be seen that its main businesses depend on clean energy, either solar or electricity, specifically targeting the clients who are eager to mitigate pollution problems.

Economy: Another common strategy to position as sustainability is to emphasize the economical characteristics of a product. For example, ENERGY STAR is the symbol backed by the U.S. federal government with the aim of improving and promoting energy efficiency. Products which are certified by ENERGY STAR are promised to save money for their users as well as protecting the environment; therefore, consumers tend to purchase these kinds of products. There are thousands of businesses with cost-effective sustainable positions which choose to register their products in ENERGY STAR. When Haier entered into the North American market, they realized the awareness of being green in the local customers so they sought for the certification of ENERGY STAR to prove their products are qualified as energy saving.

Health/safety: Some products attract consumers by being positioned to be healthy and safe. For example, washing and laundry care products are commonly advertised as fluorescent whitening agents (FWA) free in order to reduce possible skin irritation or allergies caused by FWA. Bis Phenol-A (BPA) free feeding bottle is another example which reduces the worries of parents about the possible harms from chemicals in baby products. Plant-based meat is meat made from plants, but it looks and tastes like conventional meat. The competitive advantage of this veggie-based alternative is just like what it is promoted as being healthier than meat so that it quickly wins the favor of consumers who have weight troubles, suffer from the illness that requires control on meat diet or live on vegetarian diet only.

Humanity: It means that business behaves ethically and does not breach the basic requirements of life. There is an increasing objection to global corporations against their exploitation to impoverished labours such as under payment, overtime, inferior working environments, etc. Thereafter, many multinational corporations began to make a commitment that they followed the rules of fair trade by actively exploring the process of sourcing. For example, Starbucks promises that their coffees are from ethical sourcing by providing technique support such as disease-resistant trees and soil management to coffee-producing countries around the world and practicing farmer loans and forest carbon projects to ensure the enduring supply of high-quality coffees. To make it more conspicuous, some products even have "fair trade" or fair trade related description words on their labels.

2. Product

Product mix is the complete set of products and/or services offered by a firm. A product's impact on the world is throughout its entire life, from design, manufacture, promotion, and use to disposal in the end. In order to make a product mix sustainable, corporations are usually required to take more responsibilities for the life cycle of products. Product stewardship is used to describe the management on the responsibilities of companies for their products. The definition of product stewardship is understanding, controlling, and communicating a product's environment, health, and safety related effects throughout its life cycle, from production (or extraction) to final disposal or reuse. The most influential sustainable product strategy is "cradle to cradle" which is a cyclical process where products manufactured can be recycled and reproduced into new products. The cradle-to-cradle strategy starts from the design stage. The following methods can be applied when designing a sustainable product.

Green raw materials: Products can be designed to use renewable, recyclable raw materials. For example, Circulose® is a new natural material made from cellulose in worn-out clothes. Join Life garments are produced by using ecologically grown cotton, lyocell or other recycled fibers. The clothes made from recyclable raw materials can be recycled again and reused in the manufacturing of new clothes which eliminates wastes and forms a closed circle.

Green package: Packaging not only helps brands to attract consumer attention, but protects and preserves products. It is an inseparable part of products; therefore, the cradle-to-cradle strategy should take the package into account. The package itself is better to be recyclable and it can extend products shelf life and reduce losses across a range of distribution channels, thereby reducing the carbon footprint and waste. For example, Löfbergs, a leading nordic coffee producer collaborated with Amcor to replace the fossil fuel-based PE in their packaging with bio-based PE alternatives which are made from renewable resources including corn, potatoes, rice, soy, sugar cane, wheat, or trees.

Durable in use: Products service life can be extended when they are designed to be durable in use. The way of extending product service life includes improvement in quality and innovation in design. Multifunction is an innovative design to slow down the dynamic process of the life cycle of a product. For example, the Burley bike trailer can be used as bike packing, grocery hauling and pet transport. Also, it can be converted into a jogger, stroller or sled with customized accessories.

Similarly, some products can be re-invented whenever customers feel like doing so. For example, many sofas have extra covers. If customers want, they can just change the cover and get a whole new look; some sofas offer more than that, but also re-arrange the modules to create a new layout. In this way, less bulky waste is generated. The demountable construct of a product makes it easy to be carried, reused, recycled and reproduced.

As part of the product mix, service which either supports the use of products or replaces material products can improve the product's sustainable performance. The first is after sales services which mean maintain, repair and update a product after it was sold. Sales service assists to extend product life so it is a sustainable operation in product strategy. The next is intangible services which mean technology takes place of tangible objects. For example, online banking replaces offline banking which reduces the use of paper, office equipment, consumption of water and electricity, etc., therefore it diminishes waste and consumption of resources. Use services are another eco-efficient services allowing customers to enjoy the benefits of products but without purchasing them. Use services usually include leasing, renting and sharing. A typical example of use service is the service provided with shared products. For example, the apps developed by sharing bike companies help people locate, pay and use sharing bikes. Moreover, result services meet consumers' needs while reducing their demands for material products. For example, public transportation which provides convenient daily transportation service reduces the need for private cars. The above four types of services which are closely relevant to material products or the substitute of physical substances are deemed to be eco-efficient because they help to reduce the consumption of materials and energy, and largely decrease the negative impact of human activities on the ecosystem.

3. Distribution Channels

No one is alone in the process of sustainability marketing. Though each member along the channel tries to maximize its own profit, the relationship between them cannot only be competitive but cooperative. Channel members including producers, distributors and retailers are able to create synergetic value through cooperation:

Upstream channel members: One obstacle in sustainability marketing is that many suppliers lack the ability of producing sustainably because they run small scale businesses and produce simple product varieties, and many of them are in underdeveloped regions. Lack the strong capital support, advanced management consciousness, and research and development ability, they may work inefficiently and unsustainably; therefore, support such as managerial support, knowledge and technique support from purchasing companies are very critical. For example, Apple has a strict supplier code of conduct to make sure its business partners are operating ethically. The supplier code of conduct contains as many as 42 principles and requirements which regulate labor and human rights, health and safety management, environmental protection and work ethics in every aspect of suppliers' businesses. It provides education and training programs to supplier employees. A strict management of suppliers is a way to ensure the sustainable operation of suppliers thereby the sustainable supply of raw materials.

Downstream channel members: The advantage of retailers in supply chain is their close relationship with consumers that decides their multiple roles in creating a sustainable chain. On one hand, they can aid manufacturers in developing sustainable products based on market demand; on the other hand, they can guide and promote sustainable consumption habits through promotion activities, personal selling, educational posters and used products collection. Big retailers help suppliers to be sustainable. For example, Walmart as a large global retailer has big data on consumption. With the information of consumption, it provides assistance for sellers to help meet the demands of customers, thereby ramping up their businesses. The Sustainable Chemistry initiative with suppliers, retailers, and NGOs has been launched by Walmart as a response to the expectation of customers to greener chemistry. Walmart's sustainable chemistry commitment encourages suppliers to disclose full product formulations online and to adopt green chemistry. Retailers can guide consumers to explore the benefits of sustainable products and services. As a matter of fact, many consumers do not know or even are not concerned about sustainability. Under the circumstances, retailers can play the role of promoter to deliver sustainable value and awareness through slogans or banners, product display and oral communication with consumers. For example, many supermarkets have posters at the cash register to remind customers to use fewer disposable shopping bags. The sales assistants introduce the green features of new arrivals to customers, such as the function of energy saving, recycling scheme (old for new service), or free of harmful chemicals. During the presentation, the knowledge and information about sustainability has been instilled in customers. The product display which allows customers to watch, compare or try is helpful to accelerate the broadcasting of sustainable initiatives. Retailers as places collect used products. For example, Kiehl's collects its empty product containers by rewarding samples or travel-sized products for those who return Kiehl's empty products for recycling in their retailer shops or counters. This policy provides convenience for consumers to bring back the used empty bottles so they will be more willing to follow the instructions and form a fixed habit.

Logistics: Distribution consists of warehousing, transportation and channels. The problem in sustainable warehousing lays in the storage of products. Wastes are generated in the storage and energy consumption can be excessive. In the warehouse, the reduction in packaging not only reduces transportation costs but saves energy by moving packed items around the warehouse. Other ways of saving energy are using motion sensors to only illuminate areas in use and applying clean energy by installing solar panels on the warehouse roof. The problem of transportation is the consumption of fossil fuels and exhaust emissions. There are several greener solutions in commercial transport. One solution is changing the package to be lightweight which uses fewer materials and reduces the carbon footprint of product transportation. This is an easier achievable solution. Another solution is to replace fossil fuels with electrification or biofuels. This solution for heavy transport is under research. For example: Maersk ECO Delivery has successfully tested that a biofuel-blend coming from wasted cooking oil can propel vessels, showing promising results in reducing the emissions from the ocean shipping. Too many intermediaries involved in the distribution channels is costly and wasteful. Establishing short channels is a way to optimize the sustainability in distribution. **Disintermediation** is to reduce the number of intermediaries in marketing channels. For example, since E-commerce has been growing rapidly in China, Chinese consumers have an opportunity to buy from manufacturers directly. Those popular E-commerce platforms, such as Taobao, Jingdong, Pinduoduo, are very strong in sales competition due to the removal of middlemen that allows the benefits to be reallocated to both ends of the channel which are consumer and producer. Meanwhile, the costs and wastes in intermediation decrease.

4. Price

When setting the price for a product, people usually consider both internal and external elements which affect the price. Internal elements mainly include costs of sales and operating expenses which contribute to the value of the product directly and indirectly. External elements mainly include market supply and demand, and competitors' pricing. However, there are still some invisible elements commonly excluded from a product's price which are the costs of the economy, society and environment. For example, coal mining damages forests in the process of exploitation, releases carbon emissions into air and discharges waste water into rivers. Then the government and the public have to pay to control deforestation, as well as air and water pollution. Another example is "sweatshops" which underpays employees and ignores their health and safety, leading to poverty and health problems. But society has to deal with the problems of poverty and workers' human rights. Those costs are caused by corporations, but they do not pay for them; society does. Externalized cost refers to the cost generated by producers but carried by the whole society. Paul Shrivastava pointed out "existing economic systems make many polluting and wasteful goods seem alluringly inexpensive because they do not incorporate the full ecological costs of their production or use." Sustainable prices should involve not only the value of a product but the responsibility to the economic, social and environmental costs. In reality, there are many barriers to implementing sustainable pricing.

Competitive barrier: Price is critical in the fierce marketing competition. If one company decided to take its social responsibility and spontaneously added up the externalized costs into the product price, it would lose the price advantage in the competition and that would leave it no room in the market. Most consumers will choose cost-effective commodities. Only a small number of them are willing to pay for the responsible behavior of a company.

Political barrier: Though the government has to afford the damages to ecology and social problems caused by irresponsible corporations, interestingly it does not levy the externalized costs on those businesses. Instead, it seems that the government is rather willing to pay for the mistakes of others. One important reason behind this choice is the concern that too many taxes levied on corporations will impair their profitability. Besides, the consequences of losing market vitality and competitiveness in the international market caused by heavy taxes will eventually decrease the tax income of the government in turn. Yet, the effort of sharing the social responsibilities through taxes has never been stopped. For example, Finland and Sweden were the first two countries to adopt a carbon tax in the early 1990s, then followed by Britain, Ireland and Canada's British Columbia. In 2016, the Chinese government introduced environmental protection taxation law which regulated taxable items like some solid wastes, air and water pollutants and so on.

Cultural barrier: Consumers have various motives for their purchases, such as consumption to meet basic needs, to relax, to keep social communication, to signal social status, to follow trends, to seek meaning and experience, etc. People consume a lot and expect great value from their purchases. However, sustainable prices mean a rise in the sales price of each item. Not everyone is willing to or can afford the extra fees on commodities. If so, consumption will decrease. A paradox has formed because people are aware of the importance of protecting the living environment and sharing social responsibilities to maintain a sustainable society, but they do not want to sacrifice the convenience they experienced in their current lives by lowering consumption standards.

Since the new price strategy may be difficult to be implemented in the short run, companies can apply the existing price strategies to fulfill their social responsibilities.

Cost-based pricing: Cost-based pricing is a process of setting the price as a result of adding a profit margin to the cost of the product/service. The profit margin can be adjusted according to the consumption level in a region. Supposed that the costs are fixed, the profit margin for those products that are sold to rich regions may be raised according to the local market rate; meanwhile, the profit margin for those sold to poor regions may be lowered accordingly. Therefore, people in poor regions are able to afford the same products as those consumed by people in rich regions.

Value-based pricing: Value-based pricing is a strategy of setting prices based on the value perceived by consumers. As an increasing number of people have the sense of social responsibility, it is much more possible for corporations to set prices for green products by using value-based pricing strategy. For those people who expect improvement in their living environment, they do not mind paying premiums for the socially responsible products. Thus, the additional costs imposed on green products can be offset by the demand for green products in the market. Nonetheless, this pricing strategy is suitable for niche markets where customers focus on their specific needs. In the larger market, green products can be widely accepted only when their prices are competitive so it requires technological innovation which can cut the costs below the average.

Market penetration pricing: Market penetration pricing is when you use low prices to facilitate rapid sales. It is generally used on a new product with the goal of increasing exposure and occupying high market share. For example, several years ago, the Chinese government began to subsidize the purchase of new energy vehicles which largely improved the competitive advantage of green cars that led to a large increase in their sales. During that period, several new energy vehicle producers like BYD, GAC, BAIC MOTOR and SGMV gained higher market recognition.

5. Promotion

A corporation's sustainability marketing strategy needs to be well communicated with the public because efficient communication helps to obtain both internal and external understanding and support so as to facilitate the implementation of the sustainability strategy, raise brand awareness and boost a company's reputation. There are plenty of ways to communicate with the public such as advertising, public relations, sales promotion, etc.

Advertising: As the public have come to realize the importance of sustainability, the information about sustainability has become popular in advertisements that corresponds to the public expectation. The sustainability information people usually see in advertisements includes energy saving, clean energy, organic material, no toxic and harmful substances, philanthropy, wildlife protection, etc. The various sustainability information can be sorted by advertising appeals which are strategies of grabbing attention and persuading people to purchase advertised or marketed products or services. The first is rational appeals which emphasize the practical and reasonable desirability of products or services to consumers. They usually focus on whether a product is value for money, such as low energy consumption, great durability, safety and health. For example, P&G strongly lays emphasis on the safety of their products. People who resemble scientists or experts often appear in the brands' advertisements to disclose the process of formulating products in order to convince consumers of the quality of their products. The second is emotional appeals in advertising which is a persuasion method of arousing emotional responses from target audiences. The common practices are likely to cause the feeling of guilt by exposing the life of poor people, the damaged nature and dead wildlife, and arouse the feeling of self-esteem by connecting morality with sustainable behaviours such as reducing the carbon footprint, protecting wildlife, caring for children and juveniles. The Body Shop, a British cosmetic producer, is firmly against animal testing while posting cute pet pictures to arouse the sympathetic feeling of consumers. The third is hybrid appeals which are the combination of emotional and practical desirability in advertising. For example, JUNLEBAO (a dairy brand), on one hand advertised the authentication from both BRC and IFS (food standardizing organizations) for its milk products, on the other hand associated its products with patriotism by building up a Chinese owned impressive milk brand. It advocates that as Chinese people, they have the responsibility to support the domestic produced safe and healthy dairy products.

Public relations: Public relations are applied to create positive image for a company or brand, or deal with negative information against a company or brand through publicity. The sustainability efforts in businesses are often invisible if they are not publicized. Meanwhile, if the efforts are not publicized properly, that will trigger suspicion on authenticity of devotion to sustainability. Effective publicity needs to manage the relationships with media, employees, local communities, government and investors quite well:

(1) Media. Write press releases or newsletters to keep the media and audiences updated on new products, services, issues, or events. For example, Royal Philips, the global health technology company, instantly updated any progresses they made through press releases, newsletters and blogs, such as news on their use of wind farms, lower energy usage of their products, and new technology that improved patient outcomes.

Staging event is another way to draw reporters and the publics' attention. Popular events can show corporate efforts in sustainability which include sponsoring non-governmental organizations' programs, organizing philanthropic campaigns, and attending sustainability related exhibitions. For example, Pepsi has supported the "Water Cellar for Mothers" program organized by the China Women's Development Foundation for more than a decade. Another example is that the Wanda Group held philanthropic children concerts in its plazas, donating the income from those concerts to children charities. That campaign prevailed across China quickly and attracted follow-up reports from the media. Companies may choose to attend sustainability related exhibitions like China International Environmental Protection Exhibition and Conference, IFAT in Germany, Contamination Expo in the UK, Waste Expo in the US, Sustainability Solutions Expo in the Philippine, etc. to display its sustainable products and technologies as well as to swap industry information. Influencer marketing is designed to approach a particular niche market by cooperating with existing influencer to engage his or her followers in social media. For example, Tiffany & Co. collaborated with Jack Morris, a popular Internet celebrity with millions of followers, who shared a kindred value on environment and social good with Tiffany & Co. in causal online captions. Jack's journey of an inside look at Tiffany's responsible sourcing was liked by hundreds of thousands of Millennials. As such, Tiffany & Co. has performed impressively for Millennials.

(2) Employee relations and the local community. Corporations maintain employee relations by providing safe working conditions and treating workers with dignity and respect. Corporations maintain community relations by creating a foundation for the local community to maintain a clean and natural environment, provide training and education opportunities, help vulnerable groups, etc., in general, enhancing the quality of life of people in the community. Volunteerism can be an effective method to give back to the communities as well as unite corporate staff. For example, GE Appliances, a Haier company, encourages employees to participate in community service voluntarily. In 2015, over 1,600 GE Appliances employees participated in 183 volunteer projects in several communities logging 14,000+ volunteer hours. The generosity given by employees won the fame and respect of communities where GE Appliances is located, so did the company as a whole.

(3) Government and investors. In order to maintain investor relations and to meet government requirements, some businesses choose to issue sustainability reports or citizenship reports along with financial reports, the information of which is accessible on their official websites. Sustainability report commonly discloses the information about the sustainable operations on a company's value chain, from the environmental product design, the renewable and recyclable material used, responsible souring, renewable energy used in transportation to waste disposal. Other than that, citizenship reports include more, such as community impact and human rights.

Sales promotion: It is not easy to persuade consumers to buy an unfamiliar new product which is especially true when selling sustainable products. Many consumers have the concern about the quality of sustainable products worrying about whether those products may sacrifice the quality to large economic expenses on sustainability. After all, sustainable operations like dropping cheap fossil fuels, insisting on fair trade, and purchasing pollutant processing equipment will increase the operating cost. However, those green products cannot be set a very high price to recover the extra costs spent on sustainability, otherwise the competitive advantage will disappear. Therefore, it is critical to remove consumers' concern on the quality of sustainable products. One efficient and effective way to reassure consumers about the quality of sustainable products is to invite them to try those products. Surrendering part of profits through discounts, coupons, sampling, or "buy one get one free" is useful in attracting customers to try green commodities. For example, P&G takes use of its official website to encourage consumers to scan receipts and answer questions to earn points online. After consumers accumulated a certain number of points, they can redeem the points to P&G products again. Coupons are distributed through its website as well to stimulate consumption.

15.5　Fraud in Sustainability/CSR

"Sustainability reporting is the practice of measuring, disclosing, and being accountable to internal and external stakeholders for organizational performance toward the goal of sustainable development." Many companies choose to issue sustainability reports though it is still largely voluntary. However, are those pictures, numbers, schemes and stories disclosed in the report definitely authentic? Actually, fraud is an increasing topic in sustainability. Unlike financial reports, sustainability reports are not well regulated efficiently and are not legally verified by an independent third party but the sustainability disclosures may directly impact revenues, reputation and investor activities so fraud or anything inappropriate could be expected in the report. One example of fraud in environmental issues is that a manager switched samples of groundwater so the laboratory received cleaner versions. Then a cleaner analysis report was generated to convince regulators that the company polluted water less severe than expected so the high costs of an appropriate remediation were saved. Another example is that CSR programs are not implemented effectively or even not carried out at all. There is a high dependence on the third party to execute CSR programs, however, some companies are not doing due diligence to review and check the past record of implementation partners that leads to a mushrooming of rubber-stamp charitable organizations and shell NGOs. Meanwhile, some companies were hiring charitable trusts for a commission, to channel mandatory CSR spends into promoters' accounts.

Moreover, a deceptive and manipulative sustainable misconduct is greenwashing which is defined as the act of misleading consumers regarding the environmental practices of a company or the environmental benefits of a product or service. TerraChoice, a North American environmental marketing consultancy classified seven sins of greenwashing in 2009. These sins are as follows:

Sin of hidden trade-off: committed when the marketer depicts only a limited range of qualities to divert the attention of consumers from other significantly negative environmental impacts.

Sin of no proof: committed when the marketer makes claims which cannot be verified through conveniently available information.

Sin of vagueness: committed by the marketer when he uses broad misleading words like "pure", "natural", "organic", "eco-friendly", etc.

Sin of irrelevance: committed when the marketer makes a green claim which is either insignificant or made under regulatory pressure.

Sin of lesser of two evils: committed by the marketer when he makes a true claim in a particular group but has an overall hazardous impact on the environment.

Sin of fibbing: committed by the marketer when making an untrue green claim.

Sin of worshipping false labels: committed by the marketer when he demonstrates the environmental friendliness of the product through fake labels and certificates.

Customers have an increasing demand for transparency and reporting the information of sustainability conducts and CSR implementation. Institutions and investors carefully review corporations' sustainability /CSR report and prudently make decisions using that information. New pressures and risks are developing around sustainability and CSR.

Key Terms

fair trade 公平交易	Trade between companies in developed countries and producers in developing countries in which fair prices are paid to the producers. 发达国家公司与发展中国家制造商之间价格合理的交易。
shared value 共享价值	Creating shared value is the practice of creating economic value in a way that also creates value for society by addressing its needs and challenges. 创造共享价值是创造经济价值的同时还解决了社会需求和挑战,为社会创造价值的实践。
cause related marketing 事业关联营销	Cause-related marketing（CRM）is a mutually beneficial collaboration between a corporation and a nonprofit designed to promote the former's sales and the latter's cause. 事业关联营销是公司和非盈利组织间的互惠合作,一方面促进了前者销售,另一方面帮助后者的公益活动。
carbon footprint 碳足迹	The amount of carbon dioxide and other carbon compounds emitted due to the consumption of fossil fuels by a particular person, group, etc. 个人或者某个群体因为燃烧化石燃料排放出的二氧化碳和其他碳化合物的排放量。
clean energy 清洁能源	Energy derived from renewable, zero-emissions sources（renewables）, as well as energy saved through energy efficiency（"EE"）measures. 可再生的零排放的资源中获取的能量,以及通过能效标准节约下来的能源。
carbon emissions 碳排放	Carbon emissions specifically focus on carbon dioxide, or CO_2. 碳排放专指二氧化碳 CO_2 排放。
recyclable resources 可循环资源	A recyclable resource is one that can be used over and over, but must first go through a process to prepare it for re-use. The process can be human-driven or naturally occurring. 可循环资源是一种可以被再利用的资源。但是这种资源必须先经过处理使得它能够被再次使用。这个处理过程可以是人为的也可以是自然发生的。

Continued

renewable resources 可再生资源	A renewable resource is one that naturally restores or replenishes itself. It is constantly available without human or other outside influences. 可再生资源是可进行自我修复和再生的资源。它持续存在不受人类或其他外界因素影响。
new energy vehicles 新能源车	New energy vehicles（NEVs）encompass various automotive four wheelers and two wheelers which make use of alternative fuel source as opposed to the conventional oil and gas. 新能源车包含应用替代传统汽油和天然气的燃料发动的各式四轮两轮车子。
product stewardship 产品管理	Product stewardship is the act of minimizing the health, safety, environmental and social impacts of a product and its packaging throughout all lifecycle stages, while also maximizing economic benefits. 产品管理是最小化产品及其包装在全生命周期内对健康、安全、环境、社会的影响的行为。
fossil fuel 化石燃料	A natural fuel such as coal or gas, formed in the geological past from the remains of living organisms. 一种天然燃料，比如煤炭或天然气，源于生物体残余，形成于过去的地质时期。
biofuels 生物燃料	Biofuel, any fuel that is derived from biomass —that is, plant or algae material or animal waste. 生物燃料，任何一种源于生物质的燃料——可以是植物藻类物质或是动物排泄物。
disintermediation 非中介化	Reduction in the use of intermediaries between producers and consumers. 减少采用在生产商和消费者之间的中介。
externalized cost 外部成本	Externalized costs are negative impacts associated with economic transactions which concern people outside of those transactions, meaning that neither the buyer nor the seller bears the brunt of the costs. 外部成本对资金交易呈负效应，涉及交易以外的人，既不是买方也不是卖方承担的大量费用。
influencer marketing 影响者营销	Influencer marketing is simply the action of promoting and selling products or services through people（influencers）who have the capacity to have an effect on the character of a brand. 影响者营销是一种通过能够影响一个品牌特征的人（即有影响力的人）推销产品或服务的方式。
due diligence 尽职调查	It is the investigation or exercise of care that a reasonable business or person is normally expected to take before entering into an agreement or contract with another party or an act with a certain standard of care. 尽职调查是一个合理的企业或个人在与另一方签订协议或合同或采取某种谨慎标准的行为之前通常需要进行的调查或谨慎行为。
greenwashing 漂绿	Greenwashing is the process of conveying a false impression or providing misleading information about how a company's products are more environm-entally sound. 漂绿是向消费者传达一个公司产品比它实际上更环保的错误印象或误导性信息的过程。

Review & Critical Thinking Questions

1. What are the social responsibilities corporates should take?
2. Can you provide an example that a company is doing CSR because CSR is its culture? Please explain your opinion.
3. Can you provide an example that a company is doing CSR because of economic benefits? Please explain your opinion.
4. What is fair trade? Have you ever been concerned about this topic? Can you provide more examples of fair trade?
5. How do you think CSR can help corporations control risks?
6. How do companies integrate businesses into society by doing CSR?
7. What are the benefits of doing CSR?
8. What is the relation between CSR and sustainability?
9. Can you apply TBL approach to explain Starbucks' sustainability marketing strategies?
10. What stops sustainability from being promoted? Why?
11. What is/are the key element(s) for corporations to succeed in sustainability marketing?
12. How do you explain that a group of consumers only choose those skin care products which claim that they never test on animals, such as The Body Shop?
13. What is the role of education in sustainability marketing?
14. Please go online and look for a company's CSR report/Sustainability Report/ Citizenship Report, and illustrate the common content involved in such a report.
15. What is the information in the above report that is highly suspected? Why?

Discussion Questions

1. What is your opinion on corporations making profits from taking social responsibilities? Please specify your opinion.
2. Do you believe people, the planet and profit can reach a balance, and eventually we all will live sustainably? Please explain your opinion.
3. It is inevitable that many environmentally friendly products do not have competitive advantages because of high prices and unstable quality. Many sustainability schemes count on the government. Since the survival of sustainability business is so difficult, why do corporations still insist on a sustainability plan?
4. Should cultures be involved in sustainability or not? Please explain your opinion.
5. What are your suggestions for consumers, marketers, companies and regulatory bodies

to deal with the menace of greenwashing?

6. According to your observation, do Chinese companies have a competitive advantage on sustainability in the international market? Why or why not?

Case Study

When mentioning the real estate industry, people usually associate it with dusty and noisy construction sites, high-rises, inflated property prices, safety accidents, service disputes, and sometimes bribery. Though the real estate industry increases the local government tax income, its image is barely positive in the local communities.

There is one real estate enterprise—Garden Town which has been changing the unsatisfactory industry image by making and implementing a sustainable development strategy. This strategy includes six areas—corporate governance, product responsibility, operational responsibility, environmental responsibility, talent development and public welfare investment.

In terms of internal control, it set up the Internal Committee for Environment, Social and Governance which provides guidelines for strategic research and planning for sustainable development, makes sustainable development policies and discloses sustainable information of the company. It also established the Production Safety Committee as the lead agency for production safety to implement risk warning, regulatory enforcement and safety culture.

Garden Town is committed to operational and product responsibilities by signing liability letters requiring all parties to strictly abide by construction and production safety laws and regulations. Many safety themed programs were launched to promote production safety. The safety and quality inspection tours were organized from the start of construction to the delivery process. The "Quality Assurance" APP was developed and launched to manage the construction site intelligently and prevent construction safety risks. Technological innovations were applied to improve project quality and efficiency. For example, a number of "green technologies" were used in construction including pre-fabricated interior decoration which can reduce the construction period by 60% and light pipe-based daylighting system which can save electricity up to 5.3 kwh/m^2 per year. The commitment to building a fair, transparent and sustainable supply chain covers the mechanisms of resource management, assessment system and penalty, constantly evaluating and assessing suppliers' equipment and operation capabilities. The local sourcing provides the priority to local suppliers so as to achieve win-win results for both the company and local communities. Garden Town held a lot of customer care activities to enhance the interaction and communication between the company and its customers so as to ensure customer satisfaction. For example, the Construction Site Open Day allows homeowners to inspect the constructing projects through live streaming; the Furniture Sale Festival enables homeowners to buy furniture at discount prices and enjoy the move-in service.

For internal employees, Garden Town upholds people-oriented values by supporting employee's life and work. It is strictly conducted by the requirements of the Labor Law of the PRC and guarantees labour rights and benefits. It also provides employees with extensive training and development opportunities such as tutor-based training for freshmen, leadership development programs for elites, "E-learning" online school for all employees to help them update knowledge and skills. Meanwhile, employees are encouraged to become a teacher by being certified as a trainer when they are deemed to be qualified. Garden Town improves the welfare of employees by providing them a safer and more comfortable workplace, improving salary and benefit mechanism, offering them free access to company's gyms and swimming pools. It encourages employees' hobbies. Last year, it held the Chinese Chess Contest and enhanced a happy work environment. It has company owned schools for employees' children.

In public welfare investment, Garden Town actively fulfills its social responsibilities and supports community development. It makes an arduous effort for poverty alleviation and the beautiful countryside building. In Y village, Garden Town built family style hotels using local workers, machineries and construction materials. It hired old craftsmen to build houses in a traditional way that respects local construction culture and techniques. The newly built traditional architectures promote rural tourism and increase employment. Garden Town supports rural poor students to complete education. The group provides skills training for rural labourers, such as aluminum film training, gardening training and entrepreneurship training.

Green construction includes land conservation, material conservation, energy conservation, sewage treatment, waste treatment, dust reduction and notice reduction. In Garden Town's most recent project, Forest Town, known as the largest sustainable, green and smart residential project, has been applied with multiple green techniques to ensure its green construction. It built portable project offices instead of mortar and brick offices; used concrete residue to build small subsidiary structures. Energy-saving LED lamps were installed at the construction site. One of the highlights of this project is the sewage water treatment system which can collect and purify sewage water, and reuse the processed water for gardening, cleaning and any other public uses. The other highlight is ecological residential buildings which require less energy for cooling and heating compared with the average building stock. The buildings consist of windows and exterior walls, roofs and floors with good thermal insulation and air tightness that can keep heat during the cold season in the house while keeping it out during the hot season. The energy sources inside the buildings can be from the human body, exhaust air, or solar heat, making heat much easier so that energy consumption can be reduced. Though Garden Town has made a lot of efforts in the sustainable development of the Forest Town project, the presales are not satisfactory. The advantages of the project are obvious, for example, the sales price of each apartment is affordable, the green technologies can create a more comfortable and healthier living environment and living costs may decrease as less energy and water consumed, however customers choose to wait and observe how others behave. Unlike the sustainable living environment, location, medical and educational sources are still the main concerns of customers.

Questions

1. How does the sustainable development strategy create values for Garden Town?
2. If you were in charge of the sales promotion of the Forest Town project, what would you do to promote this project and gain the favor of customers?

中文概述

企业社会责任的定义最早出现在 1953 年。当时认为,企业有义务根据社会价值观和社会整体目标进行决策和建立行为准则。企业社会责任的定义几经修改,如今被赋予了更多详细的内容,明确了社会对企业的期望,既包含了创造经济财富,更提出促进环境和社会的和谐发展。

企业承担社会责任的动机分为:**价值驱动型**,将社会责任视为一种企业文化,将社会责任意识融入生产经营中;**策略驱动型**,从经营策略考虑,将履行社会责任与建立正面积极的品牌形象和牢固的消费者关系相联系,由此增加销售的策略;**利益驱动型**,完全从自身利益出发,通过赞助、捐赠社会公益,扩大知名度、获得社会团体支持等;**利益相关者驱动型**,企业履行社会责任是迫于来自利益相关者的压力。

社会责任的履行确实能为企业带来实际的好处。企业社会责任创造**共享价值**,取得企业、社会、环境三赢的局面。同时,企业社会责任有利于**风险管理**。通过平时树立的良好社会形象,拯救一时不当操作引起的负面舆论,减轻法律责任;或者平时积极开发应用可持续技术,避免自然或意外灾害带来的毁灭性打击等。企业通过做**慈善**承担社会责任有利于建立良好的消费者关系,提高消费群体的忠诚度,这个方面已经形成了比较成熟的市场营销理论,即**公益市场营销**。

可持续性是企业社会责任的一个重要部分。企业社会责任描述了企业的道德义务、运营许可、名誉以及可持续性。企业的社会责任中包含了各种各样经营活动,比如公平交易、**碳足迹追踪**、开发使用**清洁能源**等;这些活动的帮助创造可持续的社会和环境,从而让企业收入也变得可持续。

可持续性的维度包含了三个方面：人类、地球、利润（也称为社会、环境、利润）。这种"三赢"的思想被命名为"**三重底线**"。三重底线的每一个方面都是可衡量的。例如，利润的衡量因素是销售量、净利润、投资回报率、应缴税款等；环境的衡量因素是空气和水的质量、能源消耗、**碳排放**等；社会的衡量因素是工作时长、健康安全、社区影响力等。

可持续性市场营销定义为建立和维护企业与消费者、社会环境和自然环境关系的营销。这个概念从社会营销、生态营销、绿色营销的概念演变而来。可持续性市场营销更多地考虑公司本身的可持续发展。但这绝非易事，因为可持续性要求保护资源、减少消费；与之相反的是，营销的原则是扩大生产促进消费。

可持续性市场营销策略探讨了市场定位、产品、渠道、价格、销售推广策略。

可持续/企业社会责任的骗局。在可持续性话题中欺骗行为也成了热门话题。企业发布的可持续性报告，由于缺乏规范和合法的第三方独立审核，使得报告中的信息并不可靠；同时报告中的信息可能直接影响企业收入、名誉和投资者活动，所以报告中出现欺骗和不实信息是意料中事。欺骗行为有：偷换检测所需的抽样；没有**审慎调查**公益执行人的资格，或者直接通过公益基金转移公司财产；**漂绿行为**。漂绿行为定义为通过公司的环保举动和产品或服务的环保效益误导消费者。漂绿的七宗罪：隐藏、无证据、模糊、不相关、两权相害取其轻、撒谎、崇尚假商标。

Glossary

carbon emissions 碳排放

carbon footprint 碳足迹

causal research 因果性研究

cause related marketing 事业关联营销

centrally planned socialism 中央计划社会主义

channel intermediaries 渠道中间商

channel members 渠道成员

channels of distribution 分销渠道

civil law system 大陆法系

clean energy 清洁能源

cloud computing 云计算

common law system 英美法系

company brand 公司品牌

competition-oriented pricing 竞争导向定价法

complex purchasing behavior 复杂型购买行为

confiscation 没收

consumer market 消费者市场

contact medium 接触媒介

convenience products 便利品

copyright 版权

cost-based pricing 成本计价法

creating assortments 商品分类

creeping expropriation 蚕食征用

cultural diversity 文化多样性

cultural environment 文化环境

cultural values 文化价值观

culture 文化

customer contact audit 客户触点审查

customer experience management (CEM) 客户体验管理

customer relationship management (CRM) 客户关系管理

cybersecurity mesh 网络安全网格

D

data mining 数据挖掘

demand-based pricing 需求定价法

demographic dividend 人口红利

demographic environment 人口环境

demographic segmentation 人口细分

demographics 人口统计学

descriptive research 描述性研究

differentiation 差异化

digital revolution 数字革命

DINK family 丁克家庭

direct distribution channels 直销渠道

direct marketing 直销

disintermediation 非中介化

disposable income 可支配收入

distribution/marketing channel 分销渠道

distributor 经销商

domestication 归化

due diligence 尽职调查

economic freedom 经济自由度

E

Economic Law 经济法

economic system 经济体制

eight Ps of services marketing 服务营销的 8Ps

electronic data interchange（EDI）电子数据交换

exploratory research 探索性研究

expropriation 没收财产

externalized cost 外部成本

extraterritoriality 治外法权

F

fair trade 公平交易

fertility rates 生育率

fixed costs 固定成本

focus group research 焦点小组

fossil fuel 化石燃料

four I's of services 服务的 4I 要素

franchising 特许经营

G

G20 20 国集团

geographic distribution of population 人口地理分布

global economy 全球经济

globalization 全球化

greenwashing 漂绿

Gross National Income 国民总收入

Group of Seven (G7) 七国集团

H

habitual purchasing behavior 习惯型购买行为

harmonious purchasing behavior 和谐型购买行为

haute couture 高级定制时装

Hofstede's Cultural Dimension 霍夫斯泰德文化维度

I

income distribution 收入分配

indirect distribution channels 间接销售渠道

individual brand 个人品牌

influencer marketing 影响者营销

information technology 信息技术

infringement 侵权

intellectual property 知识产权

internal marketing 内部营销

international marketing 国际营销

"Internet Plus" Action Plan "互联网+"行动计划

Internet access 互联网访问

Internet influencer 网红

Internet marketing 网络营销

Internet of Things (IoT) 物联网

J

joint venture 合资企业

jurisdiction 管辖权

L

legal awareness 法律意识

legal environment 法律环境

licensing 授权经营

litigation 诉讼

live streaming broadcast marketing 直播带货

M

marginal utility 边际效用

market capitalism 市场资本主义

market entry and expansion 市场进入和扩张

market segmentation 市场细分

market share 市场份额

market socialism 市场社会主义
marketing information system（MIS）营销信息系统
marketing mix 营销组合
marketing research 营销调研
marketing strategy 营销策略
Maslow's Hierarchy of Needs 马斯洛的需求层次理论
mass customization 大规模定制
material culture 物质文化
meme 模因
merchant wholesalers 商业批发商
MNCs 跨国公司
monopoly 垄断

N

nationalization 国有化
new energy vehicles 新能源车
newly industrializing economies（NIEs）新兴工业化国家
non-material culture 非物质文化
nontariff barrier 非关税壁垒
nuclear family 核心家庭

O

observational research 观察法
off-peak pricing 非高峰定价
omnichannel 全渠道
online word of mouth（OWOM）网络口碑
opinion leaders 意见领袖
organizational market 组织市场

P

parent brand 母品牌
Pareto Principle 帕累托法则
patent 专利
personal selling 人员直销
piggyback 猪驮式出口
political risk 政治风险
positioning map 产品定位图分析法
positioning statement 定位陈述
positioning 定位
pricing 定价

primary data 一手数据

private company 私人股份有限公司

problem-identification research 识别问题型

problem-solving research 解决问题型

product life cycle 产品生命周期

product line 产品线

product mix 产品结构

product saturation level 产品饱和度

product stewardship 产品管理

promotion 促销

protectionism 保护主义

publicity 宣传

R

radio frequency identification（RFID）射频识别

recyclable resources 可循环资源

reference group 参照群体

relationship marketing 关系营销

renewable resources 可再生资源

retailer 零售商

return on marketing investment（ROMI）市场投资回报率

robotic process automation（RPA）机器人流程自动化

S

sales agent 销售代理商

sampling plan 抽样方案

science and technology infrastructure 科技基础设施

scientific and technological environment 科技环境

scientific and technological policy 科技政策

secondary data 二手数据

service continuum 服务连续体

services 服务

shared value 共享价值

shopping products 选购品

social class 社会阶层

social media 社交媒体

social organization 社会组织

social targeting 社交定向

sovereignty 主权

specialty products 特殊品
sponsorship 赞助
statute law system 大陆法系
strategic business unit 战略业务单位
survey research 问卷调查法

T

talents environment 人才环境
target market 目标市场
target return on investment pricing 目标投资回报定价法
targeting 目标市场选择
tariff 关税
text mining 文本挖掘
total cost 总成本
trade barrier 贸易壁垒
(trade) credit insurance (贸易)信用保险
trade distortion 贸易扭曲
trademark 商标
turnkey solution 交钥匙解决方案

U

unfair competition 不正当竞争
unique selling proposition 独特销售卖点
urbanization 城市化

V

value proposition 价值主张
variable costs 可变成本
variety-seeking purchasing behavior 多变型购买行为
virtual reality (VR) 虚拟现实

W

web browsing 网页浏览追踪
wholesaler 批发商
World Wide Web (WWW) 万维网

Z

Z generation Z 世代

5G 第五代移动通信系统
6ls of the E-marketing mix 网络整合营销 6I 原则

参考文献

[1] 陈丽燕,刘永丹,龙凤. 市场营销学(双语版)[M]. 北京:清华大学出版社,2019.

[2] 顾明毅. 上海外国语大学当代传媒与文化研究丛书:中国网民社交媒体传播需求研究[M]. 北京:世界图书出版公司,2014.

[3] 郭全中. 直播电商:从消费红利到数智创新[M]. 北京:人民邮电出版社,2020.

[4] 蒋朦. 社交媒体复杂行为分析与建模[D]. 北京:清华大学,2015.

[5] 李志宏,梁东. 市场营销学[M]. 北京:清华大学出版社,2011.

[6] 陆明,陈庆渺,刘静丹. 海外社交媒体营销[M]. 北京:人民邮电出版社,2016.

[7] 吕一林,冯蛟. 现代市场营销学[M]. 5版. 北京:清华大学出版社,2012.

[8] 迈克尔·利文斯. 市场营销:定义、解释及应用[M]. 北京:人民邮电出版社,2016.

[9] 王吉斌,彭盾. 互联网+传统企业的自我颠覆、组织重构、管理进化与互联网转型[M]. 北京:机械工业出版社, 2015.

[10] 湛军. 国际商务管理英语[M]. 上海:上海交通大学出版社,2016.

[11] 周洪波. 物联网:技术、应用、标准和商业模式[M]. 北京:电子工业出版社, 2010.

[12] Agarwal, Raj, et al. International Marketing[M]. India:Vikas Publishing House, 2019.

[13] Andy Schmitz. Legal Aspects of Markets and Sales[M]. Washington DC, USA:Saylor Academy,2012.

[14] Berners-Lee, Tim. Weaving the Web:The Original Design and Ultimate Destiny of the World Wide Web by Its Inventor[M]. New York:HarperCollins Publishers Inc., 2000.

[15] DB. Saranya. International Services Marketing[J]. Journal of Business and Management,2016,3:37-39.

[16] Evans, Dave. Social Media Marketing:the Next Generation of Business Engagement[M]. Indianapolis:Wiley Publishing, Inc., 2010.

[17] Fontaine, Michael. Corporate Social Responsibility and Sustainability:the New Bottom Line? [J]. International Journal of Business and Social Science, 2013,4:110-118.

[18] Hollensen, Svend. Global Marketing[M]. 7th ed. Harlow:Pearson, 2017.

[19] Howell,Llewellyn D. The Handbook of Country and Political Risk Analysis[M]. 2nd ed. New York:Political Risk Services,1998.

[20] Malhotra, Naresh K. Essentials of Marketing Research：A Hands-on Orientation[M]. 1st ed. Essex：Pearson, 2015.

[21] Sheldon, Pavica. Social Media：Principles and Applications[M]. London：Lexington Books, 2015.